The Complete Book of Sewing

The Complete
Book of Sewing

DRESSMAKING AND SEWING
FOR THE HOME MADE EASY

by Constance Talbot

Edited by Isabelle Stevenson

GREYSTONE PRESS

NEW YORK 19, N. Y.

Printed in the United States of America

FOREWORD

THIS IS A BOOK on Sewing made easy—Sewing made fun! It is based on time-saving ideas.

The author, Constance Talbot, was a small girl when she first learned to sew. As she grew older she quickly became impatient with time-wasting Victorian sewing traditions—became too busy to labor long over a costume that required weeks of work when the same effect could be developed in a few hours with the aid of short-cuts.

In her business career with overflowing hours of work she has kept house and sewed successfully because she streamlined her routine to the shortest quickest timing.

The great modern American Dressmakers are among her close friends and from them she has learned much about efficiency in professional sewing. With countless housewives she has, during her nation-wide lecture tours and sewing demonstrations, exchanged tested short cuts.

Many of these time saving ideas and methods are included in this book to help both beginner and expert to discover that it is truly fun to sew.

Whatever your skill, whatever your interest in sewing, you will find the answers to your questions in this book. Use the Ready Reference Guide at the back freely, as you would the index of a cookbook. What is the easiest placket to make? How do you make a bound pocket? How many curtain poles are needed? What yardage is needed for a chair cover? The Ready Reference Guide will quickly point you to the answer.

ACKNOWLEDGEMENTS

GRATITUDE is due to the following organizations who permitted reproduction of certain copyrighted photographs owned by them:

American Bemberg Corporation; American Viscose Corporation, sponsors of Crown Tested Rayon Fabrics; The Makers of Armstrong's Linoleum; John Barr; Bernside Mills; Bigelow-Sanford Carpet Co., Inc.; Bureau of Fashion Trends; Charm Magazine; Congoleum-Nairn, Inc.; Cordurella; Dennison Klothes, Inc.; Andres Feininger, courtesy Life Magazine; Galey & Lord, Inc.; Good Housekeeping Magazine; Hollywood Patterns; LaMode Buttons; New York Times Studio; Old Hickory Furniture; Pacific Factag Fabrics; Paragon Quilts; Quaker Lace Company; Simplicity Pattern Company, Inc.; W. & J. Sloane; The Spool Cotton Company; Tebilized Crush Resistance; Tennessee Eastman Corporation; Waverly Fabrics; Woman's Day Magazine.

The Photographs and sketches on pages 82, 142, 145 and 159 are copyrighted by Conde Nast Publications, Inc. Illustrations of attachments for sewing machines and the jacket illustration are copyrighted by Singer Sewing Machine Company. Special acknowledgement is due Vivian Seminary for her fashion illustrations.

CONTENTS

CHAPTER I

CHOOSING THE RIGHT CLOTHES

The first step in dressing well is choosing wisely. No one woman can wear all the styles developed, and the fashion industries never intended that she should. They offer a broad assortment so that each woman can choose from it the style that best suits her figure and personality. You often see two women together, both expensively dressed; one seems beautifully dressed and the other just misses it. You may be puzzled about what makes the difference, but the answer is simple—one woman has learned the secret of selecting the right clothes and having them properly fitted, the other has not.

A few simple rules will help you to analyze your type and your needs and to choose the clothes in which you will look your best. Ask yourself first these questions: What are my interests? Where do I go and what do I do? Do I feel better in tailored clothes, in soft feminine clothes, or in sophisticated clothes?

Before you go shopping decide not only exactly what you want, but also what you need. Basic garments are the most important items in your wardrobe, and they should be decided upon first of all. "Basic garments" means the dress, coat, suit, or evening wear from which you plan to get the most use.

BASIC STYLES

Those styles which feature good simple lines, a neutral solid color, perfect fit, and adaptability to many types of accessories are the basic styles in a dress. The same general plan applies to a coat or suit. Look for the following:

1. Convertible neckline which can be worn open or closed, high or low, with collars, scarves, and jewelry.

2. Short or three-quarter-length sleeves.

3. Trimming which is easily removed.

These clothes, the center around which you build your wardrobe, should be of the best material and workmanship you can possibly afford. If you can make them yourself, so much the better. You can save money and select just the right color and style. Never make or buy any garment just because it is fashionable. Your first consideration should always be: Is it right for me? And that means:

times demands a special type of girdle, bras-siere, or slip.

A good posture is always the first step toward making you and your clothes look twice as well, regardless of figure, style, and price. Hold your stomach in until it becomes a habit and you no longer have to think about it. Keep your head and chin up—it takes years off your age. Keep your shoulders straight. No matter how tired you are, resist the desire to stoop—it will ruin your most becoming outfit. Regardless of your actual height—walk, sit, and feel tall at all times. If you follow these few simple rules, you will be off to a flying start on the road to being well dressed. Bad posture causes so many figure de-fects that it is an important consideration in selecting clothes.

CHOOSING YOUR COLORS

We read and hear so much about color, yet most of us still buy our clothes in the colors fashionable that season, instead of the ones most becoming to us. Figure problems can be solved with the right colors as often as with the right lines. Remember that light colors, even neutral grays and beiges, tend to make you look stouter. White, though the lightest color, adds the least weight to your appearance. Blue is a perennial favorite, and almost anyone can wear some shade of it. Gray-blues and deep blues are easier to wear than light blues. There is a shade of red for everyone, too. The most popular reds are deep garnet, dark strawberry, and raspberry red. Be careful of reds with purple tones; very few can wear them well. The yellow-greens go well with most eyes, skin, and hair. The blue-greens, turquoise, and peacock blue are hard to wear. Plain bright yellow and orange should seldom be worn. The burnt and old-gold tones are safer.

Neutral colors are black, white, gray, beige, and medium brown. The bright shades suggested for each type should be used for color accent in accessories. Unless you have a large wardrobe and no figure defects, it is not wise to buy gar-ments in these colors. Whatever color you choose, be sure to study the effect with it of various types of co-ordinated make-up. There is the right color in cosmetics to harmonize with everything you wear.

WALK TALL

To make you and each garment you wear look twice as attractive, learn to stand and walk correctly.

1. Does it express my type of person?
2. Are the lines becoming to my figure?
3. Can minor adjustments to answer my figure problem be made without destroying the original lines created by the designer?

If your budget for clothes is limited, plan your clothes for special occasions so that they will serve more than one purpose and harmonize with the rest of your wardrobe. In a dress or suit, consider its relation to your foundation garment and the outer clothing you plan to wear with it. A tightly fitted or low-cut dress some-

TAILORED EVENING DRESS   TAILORED SUIT

Skin Tones: Study the tone of your skin before you select a color. Unless you have unusually dramatic hair and eyes, most colors that flatter your skin will be becoming. If your skin is white with a pink undertone, you can wear almost any color in the softer shades. Harsh colors or colors with a pink cast will make you look florid. If your skin is a clear olive, the bright colors were meant for you; but beware of purple and the hard shades of blue. They make a dark complexion look sallow.

Color of Hair: Matching your colors to the shade of your hair is not usually a good idea. The effect is likely to be monotonous.

Gray Hair: The gray-haired woman has a much larger choice of colors than most people realize. She can wear warm greens, blues and reds, violets, and dark blue-grays. Scarlet lights up dull hair. An all-gray dress, however, makes gray hair look drab.

Blond Hair: Blonds should never choose harsh strong colors, and they should shun yellow and orange. They can wear all shades of blue and the darker shades of purple. Blue violet is better than red violet.

Red Hair: A lovely redhead is less dramatic in copper-color than in a bright contrasting color. Greens, medium blue, soft grays, and rich browns are the best.

Black or White Hair: Any color is good with black or white hair, provided the skin tone is taken into consideration.

Color of Eyes: Eyes have more character when their color is emphasized. If your eyes are blue or green, select the color which most closely matches them and wear it as often as possible. Brown, black, and gray eyes need bright contrasts to emphasize them. Hazel, gray, or brown eyes are especially attractive with yellow-green.

| SOPHISTICATED | FEMININE | FEMININE |
| EVENING DRESS | DAY-TIME DRESS | EVENING DRESS |

CHOOSING CLOTHES ACCORDING TO PERSONALITY

Your personality should be the governing factor in choosing the type of clothes you wear.

Tailored Type: If you feel unhappy in fluffy, frilly garments, you are, like many of the most smartly dressed women, the "tailored type." You can wear tailored clothes for both day and evening clothes. Never let anyone persuade you to "just one" flowery veiled hat or beruffled evening dress. It may be perfect for someone else, but you will be uncomfortable in it. You can wear all versions of shirtwaist dresses.

Feminine Type: If the more elaborate type of dress appeals to you, never forget that too much veiling and too many fancy accessories make you overdressed, not more feminine. Keep the extremely feminine effects and other glamour styles for your evening wear, when such fashions are smart and in good taste for young and old alike. For daytime clothes, choose graceful lines in soft fabrics which feature detail. Wear pastel colors with lace jabots or frilly organdy at neck and wrists.

Sophisticated Dramatic Type: Select striking colors and designs. Wear new and unusual costumes and bold color combinations. Don't be afraid to be daring in your selections. Choose outstanding trimmings and accessories.

CHOOSING YOUR HATS

Be sure to include your hat in the general effect you are striving for. The lines of your hat are most important, and the suggestions for the rest of your wardrobe can be applied to it. Remember that in general the small, close-fitting hat is more successful on the woman with small or regular features. Brims add grace and help to equalize large or irregular features. A turned-up brim accentuates a turned-up nose, and a thin face or neck looks thinner under a high crown.

CHOOSING CLOTHES ACCORDING TO YOUR FIGURE

The lines of your clothes are dictated by the type of figure you have. If you are:

Tall and Slim: Wear as many horizontal lines as possible—contrasting trimming bands, loose full sleeves or sleeves with fullness at shoulders or wrists, dolman types, and broad-shouldered effects. Wide hems, soft flounces, tunics, and large accessories will be most effective. Rich fabrics will add charm and grace to your figure.

Short and Slim: If you are slim but below average height, always use small accessories.

Short and Stout: Avoid all horizontal lines. Suits may be unbecoming. If you do want a suit, choose one in a dark, light-weight fabric in a simple tailored style with a medium-length jacket. Select garments with full-length trimming details, such as set-in panels and button-front coat dresses, slashed-front treatments with contrasting bindings or vestees. Wear only narrow matching belts and no tight-fitting garments of any kind. Any person who is too short should follow these recommendations, whether stout or not. Both types should include only simple or tailored garments in their wardrobes and use bright colors only as contrasts in trimming and accessories.

DETAILED FIGURE PROBLEMS

Here are some suggestions for minimizing common figure problems. Fundamental garment lines and trimming details can be made to solve your particular problem.

Necklines: If your neck is thin, soften the effect with fine finishing details at the neckline. Soft net or ruffled edgings, full collars in rich fabrics, and bright colors are good. In your coat, a long-haired fur collar is the solution. If your neck is too stout, never use any but the simplest finishing details. Wear a V-neck whenever possible and avoid all rich fabrics or long-haired furs against the throat.

SHORT AND STOUT   TALL AND THIN

THIN NECK

STOUT NECK

NARROW SLOPING SHOULDERS

BROAD SHOULDERS

FLAT BUST

FULL BUST

LARGE WAISTLINE

SMALL WAISTLINE

Narrow or Sloping Shoulders: Never wear a raglan or dolman sleeve unless the shoulders of the garment are well padded to make them look square; and you can do this only if you are above average height with a small or medium bust. If you are short and have a large bust, avoid this kind of sleeve entirely. The square padded shoulder line is the most effective disguise for narrow or sloping shoulders. Bright-colored yokes and neckwear, or horizontal trimming lines across the shoulders will help.

Broad or Square Shoulders: Garments with padded square shoulders and tight sleeves should be avoided. Raglan, dolman, and full sleeves will soften the shoulder line. Any contrasting vertical lines in neckwear or other trimming will be attractive.

Flat Chest: A flat-chested figure requires soft front treatments in all garments. Gathers and tucks and horizontal lines above the waist are becoming, and ruffled jabots or long frilly collars are a good choice.

Full Bust: Vertical and diagonal lines minimize a full bust. Vestees, dickies, or narrow plastrons in contrasting color are effective. A full-busted figure should never appear in a tightly fitted skirt or blouse, or in raglan or dolman sleeves. Deep-slashed necklines set off with contrasting piping are a smart solution.

Large Waistline: A large waistline can be minimized by carrying the lines through the full length of the garment. Never break the lines of the dress at the waistline. Narrow matching belts are the only kind that can be successfully worn. Panel fronts, coat dresses, and trimmings which extend the length of the dress are good.

Small Waistline: With a small waistline you can wear many high treatments which will turn this defect into an asset. The full high-waisted dirndl, peplums, broad belts in bright contrasting colors, broad bands of color set in at the waistline, two-tone garments with color division at the waist, any horizonal line or trimming at the waist—all these will be becoming.

Thin or Heavy Arms: In either case, avoid tight sleeves. Any soft treatment is preferable.

EMPHASIZING YOUR GOOD POINTS

Well-shaped arms and throats should be emphasized by trimming details which will set them off. Lace edgings, contrasting bindings, smart jewelry, and tight sleeves will help focus attention. Well-shaped legs should be dramatized by decorative hems or contrasting trimming bands at the edge of the skirt. The petticoat ruffle sewn under tailored skirt hems is designed for this. The older woman should never wear very low necklines, and her skirts should be at least 3 inches below the knee even when shorter skirts are stylish.

WHERE TO LOOK FOR IDEAS

Make notes of all the suggestions given above which apply to your figure and keep them firmly in mind. Soon you will find yourself getting the most for your money with the satisfaction of knowing that everything you select is right. Your clothes should express you at your loveliest if you want to be well dressed.

When you review the new fashions, discard immediately those which are designed for other types. Each new season will present you with a choice of new lines, new colors, new trimmings meant for you. You can become your own fashion reporter if you will watch out for little points often hidden in extravagant styles. Under the extravagant effect you can find trimming details, cuttings, and color combinations which you can adapt to your own purposes. These advance styles from which you can learn so much are available to you in store-window displays, fashion and pattern magazines, newspaper fashion columns, society pages, and advertisements. Even your weekly visit to the movies can supply you with excellent basic ideas, for Hollywood designers are forced to dress the stars in enduring basic fashions so the film will last several years without looking old-fashioned. This means that both young and older women can look to Hollywood for sound angles in basic dressmaking. Notice, too, accessories and how they are used to give a glamorous effect. Cleverly chosen accessories make your costume unusual and serve to highlight the best points of your figure.

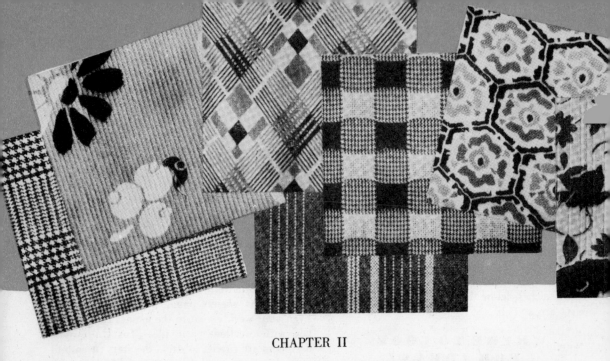

CHAPTER II

HOW TO CHOOSE THE RIGHT FABRICS

Each season textile designers create a broad assortment of new textures and novelty designs. They strive to give you beauty both in everyday wear and in gala costumes; and to that end they plan each fabric for a specific purpose. It is knowing the current fashion in fabrics and understanding how to use them which makes that subtle difference we call "style"; and awareness of style is the active spark of beauty which makes your garment one you are proud to wear.

It costs no more to make a garment in current fashion than an outdated one. As you look over the assortment of fabrics offered in the stores, search for the one best suited to your needs. I always think of an assortment of fabrics as a flower garden. Some flowers belong in the fields and woods; others do well in houses; and others look best in formal gardens. Just so, fabrics belong in their proper setting. As you see them in the store, they are buds with the promise of beauty. Each one expresses texture and color; but its full beauty flowers only when it is made up into the kind of garment for which it was designed, in a pattern keyed to that particular fabric.

This lack of correlation of fabric to style to pattern is the widespread weakness among people who make their own clothes. This chapter is designed to give you information about fabrics and their uses that will enable you to choose the right fabric for the right garment.

Fabrics for Classic Styles: Such classic styles as shirtwaist dresses and tailored sport clothes feature fabrics of subtle weaves and conventional dots and checks. Over and over again you see small conventional designs and tie-silk effects in these fashion cycles. Neutral fabrics in beige and gray, natural or undyed, form an important group; and there are some dyed fabrics that look like neutral fabrics. Like the self-patterned weaves, these fabrics must be made up in patterns that feature construction details.

Printed Fabrics: These fabrics are designed for useful garments, everyday garments, dress-up clothes, and formal evening clothes. They should be made up in very simple patterns.

Novelty Fabrics: The gay novelty fabrics are designed for vacation clothes—such as peasant dresses—which must hold their own on the beaches, for traveling, and in active sports. The colorful weaves or prints in this group are often used for children's clothes; and children love to wear them because they are gay and bright.

Smooth-Surface Fabrics: Flat crepes, satins, plain cottons, and such smooth-surface fabrics show up every detail of cut and construction. They demand a more sophisticated garment of subtle styling.

Luxury Fabrics: Velvet, satin, and the rayon crepes with a rich surface interest suggest festive formality. This group includes metal fabrics and others which introduce glitter. These are often very expensive. Using a little of the rich fabric and balancing it with a plain fabric is a good way to reduce the cost.

Staple Fabrics: These are the tried-and-true weaves which continue season after season. They are offered in woolens as cheviot and flannel; in worsteds as tweeds and men's-suiting effects; in rayons such as crepe and taffeta; and in a long list of cottons, such as chambray, broadcloth, voile, and percale. Staple fabrics are designed for useful everyday garments cut in simple styles; but every once in a while some staple is promoted in a fashion cycle and spotlighted for dress-up wear.

Utility Fabrics: Utility fabrics are for garments which will be given hard wear, day in, day out. Use them when wearability comes first and style second, and aim for a useful beauty which will last. Most work clothes for men and

PRINTED
FABRICS

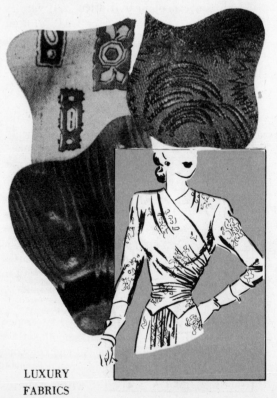

LUXURY
FABRICS

women in factories or homes, or on farms, and most garments in children's wardrobes should be made from utility cottons. Tweeds and other woolens which hold their shape through years of wear are utility fabrics also, and high-tension rayons are rapidly winning a place among these sturdy fabrics.

Pile Fabrics: Velvet, corduroy, velveteen, and other rayon and woolen weaves with a pile are used for cold-weather costumes or as trimmings.

Cold-Weather Fabrics: Besides the pile fabrics mentioned here, satin and many novelty weaves in rayon which look warm are classed as cold-weather fabrics. Prints are taboo in the cool months unless they have a classic allover design which speaks definitely of fall and winter. However, many cottons look like wool and are designed to appear warm. They also wash well.

UTILITY COTTONS

Warm-Weather Fabrics: They should be porous and so allow the heat of the body to evaporate. This does not mean that the fabric must be transparent. Tropical worsteds, for example, are porous So too are cottons, linens, and some rayons.

Fabric Contrasts: Each season the changing cycle of fashion calls for different types of fabric to be combined, blended, or contrasted. This fashion note can be carried out in trimming bands, which should always be related to the garment fabric in texture and color, or be definitely contrasted with it. There are no hard and fast rules for the matching or contrasting of different colors and fabrics. Each season's fashion introduces different fabric contrasts, and the way they are used next year may differ from this year's use. Watch the fashion changes in this respect, for contrast of texture is important in sport clothes, where quick changes and versatile mixing make the garment style-right and the wardrobe seem much larger.

Coat Fabrics: A coat, suit, or jacket costume stands or falls on the fabric. Since coats are the most expensive single item in a family's wardrobe, selecting the right fabric is very important. Will the fabric wear well? Will it show marks easily? Will it pick up lint? Will it rub thin in wear? On the answers to such questions depends whether the fabric is right for the all-purpose town coat.

If the fabric has a tweedlike or camel's-hair effect, it will stamp your coat at once as a classic staple suited to rough wear, bad weather, and country living.

The smooth-surface formal coatings and the rich pile coatings designed for afternoon and informal evening coats will require constant care. If you are planning an all-purpose coat, such fabrics are not a wise investment.

The softer textiles used for such active sport clothes as snow suits and gay summer casual coats are not expected to wear as well as a tweed or all-purpose coat fabric. They are selected for their beauty and novelty appeal at low cost. High novelties, such as plaids and Indian-blanket effects, are produced for the woman with a large coat wardrobe. If you have several coats you can well afford a striking novelty, even though you cannot wear it often.

WORK FABRICS

UNDERWEAR FABRICS

There are four important classes of fabric in the underwear group: (1), bathrobes (2), sleeping garments (3), plain sturdy underwear and (4), luxury underwear.

Bathrobe Fabrics: Fabrics for winter bathrobes must be soft, warm, and blanketlike. Corduroys, quilted rayons and taffetas, are as smart as they are warm. For summer robes, use only spongy cottons and seersuckers which are cool and need no ironing. More formal robes are made of rayon brocade and rayon novelties. For housecoats and negligees, watch the fashion cycles and choose the newest fabric for stay-at-home clothes.

Fabrics for Sleeping Garments: Sleeping garments for every member of the family should be made from fabrics which will stand up under hard wear and look fresh after countless washings. Never waste your time making up bargain fabrics, for, strange as it may seem, your

SUIT FABRICS

sleeping garment gets harder wear than almost anything else you own.

Sturdy Underwear Fabrics: Fabrics for sturdy underwear for every member of the family should be selected from the fine weaves of cotton. These fabrics in mesh constructions or crinkle finishes will save hours of ironing and still be as pretty and dainty as you wish. In selecting fabrics for underwear, by all means plan for beauty, but never buy a fabric which must be ironed, no matter how beautiful.

Luxury Underwear Fabrics: Luxury underwear will of course be ironed, and there is no limit to your choice of dainty cottons or rayon crepes. Before you put time and money into a luxurious embroidered or lace-trimmed fabric, be sure it will wear well. Do not let prejudice blind you to the fact that there are rayons so well made that experts can hardly tell them from silk. There are, of course, cheaper rayons of poorer quality which do not wear so well. In this, as in all buying today, read your labels and be guided by them.

COLD WEATHER
FABRICS

LINING FABRICS

A lining performs a definite and important function. Understanding of that fact makes it possible to appreciate the need for a lining, the best fabric to meet the need, and how wearable the fabric should be to give satisfaction. Linings which are seen must be harmonious with the color and richness of the garment. Linings which are not seen are no less important and should be as carefully selected.

Linings Which Are Seen: These linings are usually facings or collar linings. They can be made from the garment fabric, or from a contrasting or decorative silk or rayon. They can also be made from a light-weight lining fabric such as sateen, percale, or other closely woven cottons. Plan facings and collar linings carefully because they often show.

Linings Which Are Not Seen: Linings such as those which hold the skirt of a two-piece dress may be made of rayon crepe, sateen, or any cotton of firm weave, such as chambray, lawn, or a light cambric.

Coat Linings: Coat linings are made of silk or rayon crepe or satin, or printed rayons or novelties. There are coat linings made of cotton and rayon, or all cotton, especially designed for this purpose. A coat lining should look rich and help make the coat slip off and on easily; and today's fashion, which has stood for the last few years, calls for a matching lining. Useful fashions which perform a definite function seldom change. However, fashions come along which combine warmth, trimming, and novelty all in one, such as the button-in linings usually made in bold or subdued plaids. Remember that a self-color lining which does not soil is the most practical choice.

Give careful consideration to the wearability of the fabric. Do not make the mistake of buying a cheaper fabric when a lining which looks the same but will give twice the wear costs only a little more. Read the labels on lining fabrics; the labels give the results of standard tests. A tested lining may cost more, sometimes as much as $1.50 more for the whole coat; but if it wears longer you save the cost of relining plus the hours of extra work. If you are choosing a lining for an old garment, the cheaper lining is best, of course, unless you expect the garment still to give a great deal of wear.

Coat linings with smooth surfaces are preferable. They soil less and let the coat slip on and off easily. Sport coats are sometimes lined with wool for extra warmth and style effect. Some expensive-looking summer coats are lined with the same wool used for the coat itself, but in a different shade. In a summer fabric which does not wrinkle, this makes a really luxurious garment. Other dress-up coats feature novelty dress or blouse fabrics for linings in rough rayon crepes, printed crepes, or light-weight dress woolens.

INTERLININGS

Interlinings perform two vital functions: (1) They hold an edge in shape so it will not stretch or sag—this is necessary in every coat or jacket. (2) They form a stay to strengthen an edge which must hold the weight of buttons. (3) They strengthen a point which otherwise would rip and ravel. Other interlinings are used to add body or stiffening to some basic construction feature of the garment so it will hold its shape. Still others are for warmth only.

When you want to add more support than unbleached muslin permits, weigh carefully the relative merits of French canvas, French linen. and tailors' canvas, choosing the weight best suited to your needs. Although French canvas and French linen are the same weight, French canvas is cheaper and does not wear as well. Either can be used in suitings. Tailors' canvas is used for the heavier coatings. These are the interlinings used by tailors to insure edges that will not stretch and collars that roll and hold their shape. You can use them to interline handbags in many other accessories.

Interlinings to Hold Edges: In all woolen coats and many rayon ones, an interlining is recommended in the pattern. Sewers who use it carefully produce jackets with firm, straight edges which do not sag or lose their shape. For this simple operation, use unbleached muslin and wash it before you put it in the garment. In interlining double collars that should roll, unbleached muslin must be used if you want to avoid a flat look. Coat collars should always be interlined this way.

Interlinings for Stays: Interlinings for this purpose can be made from the garment fabric, from sateen, or from a light-weight firm cotton such as lawn. Stays are intended to hold a section of the garment in place—for example, under gathers or godets. They also guard against raveling when you slash into fabric in the front of a garment or at a gathered seam. They fortify an edge which holds buttons. Sometimes the band is cut with an extra fold that forms an interlining, or a straight strip of material is added under the buttons.

Interlinings for Warmth: The most popular interlining sold in stores is a loose construction of wool on a cotton warp. Coats are also interlined with flannel or with all-wool interlining. The purpose of the interlining is to add warmth without bulk; and if it looks thin, remember that you can lay one thickness over the other in certain spots of the coat and so gain more warmth without bulk.

STIFFENINGS

Buckram is a stiffener. It is made in several weights. The lighter or thinner types of buckram are pliable, the heavier are stiff. You buy these in millinery supply houses or upholstery shops. You can sometimes use the transparent braids used in millinery to help you in stiffening some piece of work that otherwise presents a problem —for example, in making the stiffened, transparent collars that stand up and frame the face or the ruffle on a hat that you want to flare and look transparent.

Remnants: In shopping for fabrics don't forget remnants. The smaller pieces are priced at less than complete yardage of the same fabric. Often in the better stores you can find remnants for a blouse, collar, or trimming in a truly lovely luxury fabric. This is particularly important in metallic fabrics, as the less expensive are not to be compared in beauty or endurance with those of better quality. Often a child's coat can be lined with two remnants. When one is large enough from which to cut the body of the lining, the other can be used for sleeves, even if it is of darker tone.

To achieve perfection in the finished garment, be sure to co-ordinate the fabric to the pattern.

HOW TO CHOOSE THE RIGHT FABRIC FOR THE PATTERN

Different fabrics behave differently. Each serves best when it is put to proper use. A softly draped skirt demands a different fabric from a crisp full flared skirt, and if you want to make a full pleated skirt you must buy a fabric that will hold pleats. Listed below are many of the facts you need to know to choose the proper fabric for the pattern you have selected.

Has the Pattern Gathers? For scant gathers a medium-weight fabric is appropriate; while for full gathers you *must test the softness* of the fabric. Run a pin in and out at one end and push the fabric together along the pin to see whether it falls softly or sticks out rebelliously.

Has the Pattern Pleats? A certain wiriness in textile construction holds pleats in shape and saves much work in re-pressing. If you are able to make a mark that stays when you crease the fabric firmly with your fingers, you will know the fabric is excellent for pleats. Remember that soft fabrics lose their pleats quickly.

Has the Pattern a Full Circular Cut? The fuller the circular cut, the more firmness is required in the fabric. Transparent fabrics are often firm, and heavy fabrics are often loosely woven and stretch badly, depending on the weave. Hold the fabric up to the light; by looking through it you can quickly see whether it is loosely or firmly woven.

Has the Pattern Straight Lines? Here again firm material is a necessity if your skirt is to hold its shape and hang evenly. The plainer the dress, the more important is the firmness of the fabric.

Has the Pattern a Draped Effect? If so, test your fabric before you buy it. Hold it by one corner and let it fall in draped folds. In this way, you will be sure the fabric has enough weight and not too much stiffness.

Has the Pattern Softness? Patterns which call for gathers, a loose armhole, or a circular bodice require a soft fabric such as crepe, silk or rayon. But remember that transparent fabrics are not successful unless the pattern allows the necessary extra "ease" or fullness.

Has the Pattern Ruffles? For ruffles the fabric must have some crispness; and if you are wise, you will buy organdies, marquisettes, et cetera, for "permanent crispness." Soft chiffons are successful only in extra full ruffles.

Has the Pattern the Cut Especially Suited to Sheer Lace, etc.? Transparent fabrics are not successful unless the pattern allows the necessary extra "ease" or fullness essential to success.

Has the Pattern the Cut Suitable for a Woolen Dress? If so, be sure you are using a light-weight dress wool. It can be soft and loose, or sturdy. Suiting weights, which are heavy, are unsuccessful for dresses.

Has the Pattern a Bolero or Jacket? If so, use a suiting-weight woolen, a cotton, or a rayon with body.

Pile Fabrics: Pile fabrics, either the soft lustrous velvets, the functional corduroys, velveteens, or pile woolens, or spun rayon with a nap, *must be cut* from a pattern which specifies them in its fabric listing. Remember always to cut every piece of your garment running in the same direction. Professionals cut the material with the nap running upward from the hem.

FABRICS

What Is a Fabric?   Spinning and weaving are among the oldest arts known to man, and artists of every generation down through the centuries have added to the beauty of textiles. Those we have today are less expensive and more beautiful than those of the past. More people can afford to have beautiful textiles for their clothing and the decoration of their homes than was possible in former times. Like people, textiles have different characters and are suitable for different uses.

Fiber threads spun into yarn or the continuous filaments of rayon are *knitted* into textiles by hooking the yarn through continuous loops. Jersey is the most popular of the knitted fabrics. Most fabrics are *woven* on a loom. Lengthwise threads strung on the loom are called the warp; and the warp is filled in by threads carried on a shuttle, crossing and recrossing the warp. These cross threads are known as the woof.

Is All Weaving Alike?   No, there are hundreds of different kinds of looms which produce different kinds of woven fabrics. *Firmness* is a quality worth noting in weaving because it is easier to work on a firm fabric. Pulling the fabric is a test for firmness. After you have pulled several, you will realize that some are firm and others stretchy. Firmness has nothing to do with weight. There are heavy fabrics which tend to stretch and many transparent and open-mesh fabrics which are firm.

IMPORTANT FACTORS IN WEARABILITY

There is much misunderstanding regarding the wearability of fabrics. Too many people think of wearability as ONE quality; but the truth is that there are six qualities of wearability in every fabric, and all are of equal importance to insure long, enduring wear. The six qualities are: (1) Fiber quality; (2) Yarn quality; (3) Weave quality; (4) Color Fastness; (5) Shrinkage; and (6) Fabric Finish.

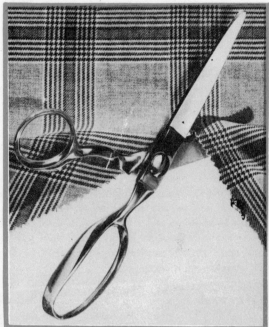

When cutting the material, make certain patterns meet.

To understand better what these qualities mean, check this short list and ask for these qualities when you buy fabrics.

Fibers: There are vegetable fibers, as in cotton and linen; animal fibers, as in silk and wool; and synthetic fibers, as in rayon. Other fibers are made from chemicals such as casein, which is derived from milk. The material of the fiber has nothing to do with the wearability of the fabric. There is a different price for each grade, and there are hundreds of grades. The cheap grades wear badly; the good grades wear well. Ask to have every fabric identified before you purchase; for, though the fiber factor may not influence your buying, it is important for you to know exactly what the fabric is when you begin to take care of the garment. You must know whether you have bought linen, or cotton that looks like linen, wool, or a rayon that looks like wool; for each fabric requires different treatment when you wash it or remove a spot. The different methods for taking care of various fabrics is explained in Chapter XXXI.

Yarns: The natural and animal fibers are spun into yarns for use in weaving and knitting. Rayons and other chemical fibers are also made into yarns. Yarns can be heavy or thin; strong or weak; they can be spun tight and smooth or soft and fuzzy. These elements effect the wearability of the fabric. Wool is resilient; it is brushed smooth for worsteds or spun without brushing for woolens. Its cost is estimated by the resilient quality. Brittle, cheap woolens are low in cost. The tensile strength, so often referred to on labels, is the strength of the yarn of the warp. When this thread breaks from weakness, your fabric is gone. When this thread holds, your fabric endures. In cotton fabrics, rayon, and linens, breakage strength is important. In wool it has no importance at all because wool yarn is resilient and stretches and springs back into shape without breaking. When wool yarn is twisted tight to produce tensile strength, it loses its quality of warmth.

Weaves: Weaves vary, but no matter what the style, they fall into three classes. Those that are close and firm and wear well, even though of mesh construction. Loose, sleazy constructions are cheap because the weaving goes faster and requires less yarn. Such novelties are sold for their eye-catching value and not for wear. In your store examine the fabric carefully. Ask if it roughs up in wear—if it picks up threads and dirt—if it has loose threads that will pull in wear. Look through a fabric to see if it is woven closely or has an open, cheap weave. When you can, as with sheeting, compare the thread count, which is included on many labels.

Color Fastness: There are two important elements in color fastness. The first is the quality of the dye; the second is its use in a particular kind of garment. In other words, garments that will be sun-bleached, such as bathing suits (following repeated wetting), require a stronger dye than outer garments such as coats and play suits that will be worn in the sun while they are dry. Underwear and garments worn under a coat are satisfactory with a lower quality dye, which would be impractical for utility garments exposed to the sun. In a print every color must be fast. In a washable dress the fabric and all the trimming colors must be fast. In your stores look for the important references to color fastness on textile labels. When the label says "washable," you will know the color fastness has been tested.

The label will also tell you if the fabric requires careful hand washing or can be done with the routine family washing at home or in the laundry. When a fabric is described as washable, be sure you know what kind of washing is meant. When color fastness is mentioned, be sure you know the difference between the weaker colors which wash satisfactorily and the stronger colors which can withstand sustained sunlight. Watch these labels carefully.

Shrinkage: The major cause of shrinkage is in fabric finishing, where there is a great temptation to stretch the fabric. Any fabric stretched abnormally and set to dry *must shrink*. Creped weaves and knitted fabrics of cotton, rayon, and linen which have resilience tend to shrink and cannot be preshrunk, as can smooth fabrics such as cotton shirtings. In these fabrics shrinkage is controlled in construction, and the greatest shrinkage is reported in the roughest crepe weaves and the loose, cheap knitting constructions. In your stores the washability labels include a shrinkage test. You will also find sanforizing control specified on textile labels, particularly cotton. When fabrics shrink, you can do as the cleaners do—*stretch them while they are wet.* When the yarn and weaving are strong, this is a satisfactory approach. It is important to stretch the fabrics gently so you will not tear them.

Worsteds that are strong are "LONDON SHRUNK." They are actually soaked in water and then steamed and refinished. Woolens, however, are only steamed, so that their delicate texture will not be marred. Blended fabrics which look like worsteds are shrunk by wrapping them in wet cloths. Spun rayons which look like woolens are preshrunk in the same way. What tailors call "washable woolens" are especially constructed for washability. In buying woolens for dresses or coats, ask the store to preshrink them, or shrink them at home before cutting. Woolens and worsteds should not be washed unlesss they are sold as washable.

Fabric Finish: This is the sizing, or wash, which makes the fabric look attractive and new. In good-quality fabrics this finish is permanent. In cheap fabrics, the finish washes away to reveal poor construction. There are many interesting chemical finishes that render us a service, such as the resin finishes which make fabrics resist crushing. Other resin finishes give fabrics permanent stiffening qualities so that they never need starching, and other chemical finishes make them spot-repellent or germ-repellent. Thin coatings of wax make fabrics showerproof. When a fabric is to be washed frequently, be sure the finish is permanent. When your fabric has a washability label, this is included in the washing test.

Especially in cheap cottons, it is wise to rub the fabric together and look for grains of dust or powder. This denotes a starch filling which will wash away. In buying a fabric finished with a chemical, be sure you understand the difference between the chemical finishes which are permanent and those which are weakened or removed by the first washing or cleaning.

Many of these chemicals will render longer service if a garment is given careful hand washing.

WHEN IS A FABRIC WARM?

Scientists tell us that no fabric is warm; it is the body which is warm. Fabrics either permit body heat to evaporate, or hold the body heat. That is why we call some textiles warm fabrics and others cold fabrics. The tiny cell structures of sheep's wool hold the body heat. Other fibers with hairy surfaces have this element in a minor degree. The warmth of a fabric is increased by a close, even weave, and still more by a nap or brushed surface. Two thicknesses of a warm fabric are warmer than one thickness of a heavier fabric because the space between fabrics forms a warm air cell.

When you buy coatings, blankets, or apparel in worsteds or woolen, you may want intense, medium, or very little warmth. Textiles are made in just those degrees. This applies not only to wool textiles, but to blends of wool and cotton, wool and rayon, or wool and casein fibre. There are also all-cotton fabrics which are warm, for they are closely woven with a thick nap. In our stores, these claims of warmth are often confusing. Claims are made that some textiles such as a spun rayon, which looks and feels like sheer wool, are as warm as wool; or an all-cotton blanket, or a blend of wool and rayon, is claimed to give as much warmth as wool. The tested facts

offered to back up these claims are accurate and dependable, but they do not tell you that there are two thousand grades of wool. Certainly out of this wide assortment there will be wools that may not prove in a test as warm as a blended or cotton fabric at the same price. This does not mean that at an increased price you cannot buy greater warmth in a more costly grade of wool.

Wools which lack warmth are used in tropical worsteds for men's summer suits, and these fabrics give additional coolness by a loose weave that permits the body heat to evaporate.

Blended Fibers: The blended fibers listed on textiles you buy by the yard or in ready-made garments confuse many people who think this is a "new practice." The Mosaic Laws in the Bible give the first account of fiber blending, and in one form or another it has been common through the ages. Wool has always been scarce. For centuries it has been the habit to unravel and respin wool. This is the reused or reprocessed wool you read about on your labels. Reused wool has never been worn and is made from the clippings of garments; while reprocessed wool has been worn and resterilized. It has long been the practice to mix cotton with wool. Sometimes the warp is cotton and the filling wool; sometimes both fibers are spun together into a yarn. It is a recent development to mix wool and rayon, and this blending became fashionable in producing lovely novelties with a rayon thread woven through them. Rayon was also cut into short threads and spun to look like wool, for when 20 per cent of wool is added, the fabric feels like wool; and, of course when it becomes a matter of national necessity to conserve wool, blends of wool and rayon and wool and casein become Victory fabrics.

Camel's-hair, vicuna, and the fibers of other rare animals are classed as wool. In buying them we must consider that there are grades and qualities in these groups and that often camel's-hair is mixed with rayon. You will find this explained on the label.

WHAT CONTROLS SHRINKAGE?

The sanforizing process is mechanical, not chemical. This is an important distinction, because chemicals are often transitory, whereas sanforizing stays with your fabric. When the fabric is finished, it is run through the sanforizing machine, and little fingers in the machine play over the fabric to loosen any extra stretching. All fabrics cannot be treated in this way, but the long list of sanforized textiles include smooth-surface rayons, as well as most cottons.

FABRIC FINISHES

Chemical Fabric Finishes: Many of the new chemicals are permanent. They will last as long as the dyes. Many do not last after the first dry-cleaning, and others do not last after the first four or five careful hand washings. It is important for you to know the difference between various chemical finishes so that you may give each its proper care.

Crease-Resistant: This resin process is permanent. It renders a fabric resistant to creases, not creaseproof. It applies to velvets as well as many types of cotton and rayon.

Permanent Stiffening: This finish is permanent and endures through many washings. You do not starch these textiles. They are sold under many trade names.

Glazed Finishes: Most glazing on fabrics is not permanent. There is, however, a trade process for glazing chintz which makes it permanent and washable.

Stain Resistant Finishes: There are two classes of stain-resistant finishes: those which are permanent and those which are not. These processes protect the fabric from soil and from stains such as ink or tomato. You will be wise to know the difference between the chemical process, which penetrates the fibre, and the wax process, which coats the surface of the fabric.

Sanitary Finishes: These are applied to many textiles and are part of a new chemical development which helps keep fabrics germ-proof.

Shower-Resistants: Most finishes in this class are wax coatings which help make fabrics water-repellent. There is a chemical shower-resistant which penetrates the fabric and offers long wear, for it will last as long as the dye. Cravanetting is another process, in which the fabric is given two alum baths. Most processes require only one finish, and therefore cravanetting is not applied to the less expensive fabrics.

HOW TO SHRINK
OR SPONGE A FABRIC

Cotton and linen which will shrink from ¾ of an inch to over 3 inches a yard should be soaked in water overnight. If the fabric is colored, *only* warm water should be used. Never wring the water from the material. Always squeeze it, hang it on a line to dry, and then press. To shrink wools or worsteds at home, soak two sheets or long strips of muslin in cold water. Spread out the fabric carefully so that it lies smooth and single and lay it flat on one of the soaked sheets. Place the other wet sheet over the material and then roll tightly. Wrap the outside of the roll with paper, dry sheets, or a blanket, so that the moisture has an opportunity to penetrate. After 24 hours, remove the fabric and press it until it is dry. A textile of blended fibers—mixed wool and rayon—should not be pressed until it is completely dried by hanging on a line.

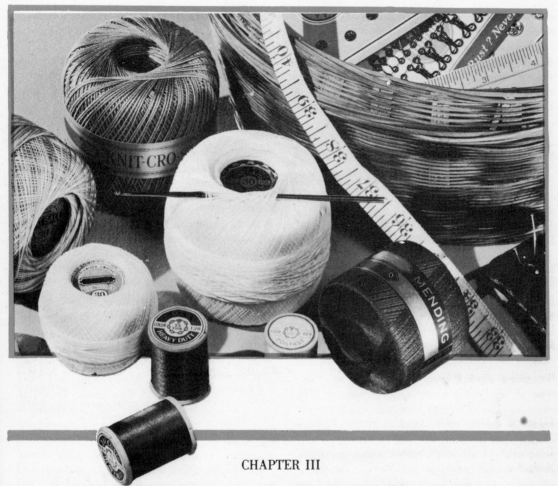

CHAPTER III

SEWING TOOLS AND HOW TO MAKE
THEM WORK FOR YOU

Success in sewing calls for the right tools at the right time. All tools must be in order, and you must know how to use them to save time and produce the best results. Sewing without the right equipment is like trying to cook without the right ingredients.

Some of the things you need, such as scissors, needles and pins, are in the house—others you must buy for the occasion. The "recipe" you follow for sewing a garment is the detailed directions on your pattern. Use it as a shopping list. Check the listing of fabrics and trimmings. Study all the information it gives on linings and interlinings.

Keep your sewing aids in order in one place;

otherwise, you will waste much time in fretful searching. I keep all my sewing aids in a Martha Washington sewing table—others use a large box and store it in a closet. If you have neither use a bureau drawer. Most important of all, you must have the right tools for the right job. You may have scissors in the kitchen for use about the house, and paper scissors in the children's room, but neither of these is efficient for sewing.

Cutting Shears: Your cutting shears should be at least 8 to 9 inches long, and should never be used for anything but your sewing. Professionals use larger shears which they slide along the table in a smooth cutting line. The longer the pair of shears you can afford, the easier will your work be.

You will also need medium-sized scissors (5 to 6 inches) for shaping short work and small pointed scissors (3 to 3½ inches) for cutting threads, ripping, and for cutting buttonholes. A thread should always be cut, never broken. There are professional buttonhole scissors which are easily adjusted with a special screw so that the cut size for each successive buttonhole is the perfection of accuracy.

Pinking shears aid thrift in making underwear or any other "cut to fit" garment, for they finish seams as you cut. You can save time in making garments that may have to have seam adjustments by allowing a little extra material and cutting it away with the pinking shears after the garment is stitched.

Take good care of your scissors; they are noble instruments which will serve you well. Every now and then, be sure to drop a little lubricating oil at the joint to keep them moving freely. Keep them free from dust, dirt, and rust.

Needles and Pins: There is a size and type of needle for every kind of sewing. The chart on page 35 tells you the exact size of needle to use for every kind of fabric. Consult it often. A good needle has a smooth sharp point (except tapestry needles, which are dull) so that it slips easily in and out of the fabric without a catch and has a smoothly finished eye which helps prevent the thread from fraying. Polish your needles occasionally by running them through an emery bag. Never leave your needles sticking in the emery bag, for it attracts moisture and will cause rust.

Most home sewers have an adequate supply of needles in an interesting variety because our notions departments present them in selective packages as well as replacement sizes. But too few sewers consider pins of equal importance with needles. This is a mistake, for only by the generous use of pins can you be sure of accurate work. Add a half-pound box of dressmaker pins to your sewing kit.

Although some sewing cabinets contain a larger size pin, size 5 or 6 fills most necessary functions. They are sharp and thin and will not spoil or leave holes in the fabric. However, in taffeta, satin, or other easily marked fabrics,

needles are used instead of pins. Your dressmaking pins, like the scissors, should not be used around the house. They should be kept clean—you can wash them to clean them—and each size of pin should be kept separately. Do not mix pin sizes in one box.

To save pins for reuse, and to save reaching for pins when you are sewing, wear a small pincushion on your left wrist or tack it on your shoulder. When you have finished sewing, drop your pins into a box, so that they can be covered and kept clean.

Measurers: Never cut without your full assortment of measurers. You need not only the ever-present sixty-inch tape measure—marked on both sides—but in addition a foot rule to use as a gauge in turning edges or measuring hems, tucks, curtains, and ruffles. To help you in measuring such details as hems, braids, and button spacing, keep strips of cardboard with your sewing equipment to cut into gauges. You also need a small flexible composition rule and a yardstick for measuring fabrics, taking skirt lengths, and marking long lines. A tape measure is inaccurate in estimating yardage. An automatic skirt measurer will be a great help when marking a hem.

Thimbles: Supply yourself with plenty of thimbles in assorted sizes, and if you are a sentimentalist who sews in public, cherish a romantic thimble of gold, for during many ages this was the sentimental gift of a man to the woman he loved. Make sure your thimble is chosen with care. The lighter it is, the better. It should be a comfortable fit. Wear it on the middle finger of your right hand, and make sure it has no jagged ridges to snag the thread. Use a nail file to file down any roughness. Choose a thimble finished in chrome, celluloid or silver, since they will not stain your fingers.

Snap Fasteners, Hooks and Eyes: An assortment of sizes suited to different needs and different weights of material should be included in your permanent sewing aids. The cards should be held together with an elastic band, and the loose snaps and hooks stored in glass containers so you can see the size quickly. When you discard old clothes, save the buttons and fasteners to use again.

Thread: Just as a cook keeps her salt, pepper, sugar, and flour on hand, you should always have an adequate supply of staple threads. The chart on page 35 will show you what you should have. Consult it after making a list of your most common sewing duties. You will certainly need large spools of black and white sewing silk, heavy cotton for extra strong work, as well as cotton in the usual sewing sizes, plus spools of heavy linen thread in both black and white. Choose thread a shade darker than the fabric, because the single thread is always lighter than it appears on the spool. The spools of silk or cotton in colors that remain after you have made a dress should be added to the spool box or drawer and laid flat so that you can see the color quickly. When you sew, use the correct length of thread, which is about equal to the distance from your fingers to the elbow. This will help prevent knotting and fraying. To prevent unrolling from the spool, be sure you tuck the loose end of the thread into the notch on the spool after each threading. If the notch has been knocked off, snip another one with a razor blade.

Bindings and Beltings: These are another assortment of useful sewing helps. Single rayon seam bindings in black, navy, and white are continually useful. If you sew much on cotton, you should also have an assortment of the prepared cotton seam bindings and rickrack braids. Hold them together with elastic bands so you can quickly lay your hands on the one you want. Add cordings, weights, chalk, and the many other ribbon threaders, crochet hooks, and small tools that help speed your work.

Tailor's Chalk: This brushes off easily and is used to mark on woolens and velvets changes that must be made in seam lines or construction details. It is very useful in marking through pattern perforations. Keep a piece constantly at hand to mark every change you want to make.

Tracing Wheel: Before removing your pattern, you can use a tracing wheel—firmly but gently enough so that it does not cut fabric threads—to mark through several layers of fabric. Remember to place several thicknesses of newspaper or a board under the fabric before you trace, or you will mark the surface of your table.

Individual sewing aids such as emery, wax, a stilletto, or orange stick for punching eyelets, a darning egg, with or without handle can be added. A tailor's tack-maker will enable you to sew tacks more swiftly than by hand.

The important point to keep in mind is usefulness and accessibility—eliminate everything that is not important to you and the kind of sewing that occupies your time. *There is no must list.* Each sewer develops her own "must list." Take your time, and as you continue to sew, you will gradually become the proud owner of a perfect sewing kit. It is important, however, that you have good light to prevent eye-strain. The light should be to your left, and you should sit near a large window. When you do not work by daylight, use an adjustable light such as the goose neck lamp which you see in many offices.

You will also find great use for French chalk in keeping perspiration under control or to dust lightly on your hands after washing. Keep it on hand, too, in case a spot of machine oil should get on your fabric; you can attend to the blemish immediately. Cover the spot liberally and leave the powder on for 24 hours. Full information on removal of spots is given in Chapter XXXI.

Full-length Mirrors: The long, thin variety which permit you to see the whole figure are a "must" for fitting yourself. They are also a great aid in maintaining a well-groomed look and are not costly (about $2). They are a splendid investment. You will naturally need to see the back of your dress, and for this you need a large hand mirror.

Dress Forms: Some home sewers insure ease in fitting and speed their work with the use of a dress form. Others fit themselves before a mirror or with the aid of a friend. Hereditary dress forms in standard sizes are blurred with old home traditions and memories. The usefulness is still with us, even though the silhouette has changed. You can buy one nearest in size to your own bust measurement, or better still, you should buy it in the size of the smallest adult member of the family so that fitted linings of all the family can succeed one another at will on the form. You make a fitted lining from any lining pattern with a piece of unbleached muslin. You fit it to the figure as tight as a piece of

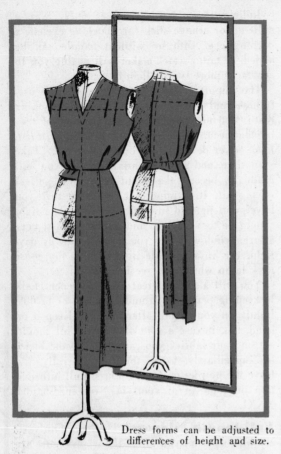

Dress forms can be adjusted to differences of height and size.

plaster so that it becomes an absolute figure-twin and shows any irregularity or individuality. Pay particular attention to the waistline, neckline, and armhole. Then put it on the form and fill it out with cotton batting. There is also a clever mechanical dress form which can be adjusted to differences of height and size.

There are many rubber dress forms which can be inflated, and there are the ultra-modern replica forms which are molded right on your own figure. These silhouette forms duplicate every individual curve, and the women who own them are enthusiastic about the saving of time they represent. Most home sewers fit their clothes on themselves or another member of the family, but for the women who dread a "try on" or those who like to see the dress as an abstract creation, a dress form is indeed an asset.

Sewing Machine: To speed up sewing, a machine is invaluable. You can make the machine work wonders for you, but you must *prac-*

tice. Keep the instruction book in the machine drawer and consult it often. Like the family automobile, a sewing machine must be oiled. For routine family sewing, oil once a month is sufficient. To let the oil penetrate properly, do your oiling at a time when you do not expect to be using the machine for 2 or 3 days. Wipe the machine clean before using, then stitch a few seams on a scrap to absorb the excess oil, and there will be no danger of getting oil on a new dress. After using the machine for a long stretch, while sewing for your local Red Cross Unit perhaps, it will be necessary to clean your machine once a week to remove lint. Oil it after each one of these sessions.

Cutting Board: Your cutting board or table should be large. The dining room table, covered with a pad, is ideal. If your tables are too small so that the pattern pieces will not all fit cut on the floor. In many cases, this is ideal, as with most fabrics the nap of the rug holds the material firmly.

Pressing Equipment: In addition to the ironing board used in the family laundry routine, an extra ironing board for pressing, small, but large enough to cover the average skirt length, should be arranged on the floor of your house where you sew, so that it is instantly available, since for true success in sewing, you must press constantly. This extra board is not an extravagance, but really an economy. Pressing gives the garment its true form and should be done as you work. Even short seams should be pressed right after stitching.

Iron: The iron for pressing as you work can be the household iron, electric or heated on the stove. It should be kept very clean. In addition to your household electric iron, consider one of the newer electric irons which contain water, and steam as you press. This ingenious discovery permits you to press seams open without dampening and to press and shrink fabrics by first running the iron over them to dampen them, then placing a press cloth over the fabric and ironing it dry. This leaves no sheen on the right side of the fabric. Remember that different materials require different pressing treatment. Test your pressing on a scrap of material first, to avoid major errors. Rayons, for instance, like a cool iron. Use a heavy pressing cloth for woolens. Linens and cottons can be ironed directly, provided they are dampened first. If you work on woolens and worsteds or in the heavier cottons that must be tailored, pressing is an important feature of the success of your work. In that case you may want a heavier iron than the one used for average household ironing.

Your pressing equipment is not complete without a bowl of water and a sponge for dampening seams. You should include three clean press cloths free of starch or sizing—usually made from torn sheets—and one of wool.

Tailor's Cushion: You will need a tailor's cushion, which is important when your sewing includes the curving that tailors press into a garment. It is not used in soft dressmaking, and

unless you make a great many coats of masculine type in worsted and tweed you do not really need one. However, to make a tailor's cushion at home, take two ovals of unbleached muslin each about a foot and a half long. There must be no sizing in the material. Sew the ovals together, leaving a space to insert stuffing, and stuff out the material in the shape of a ham. Make a small three-cornered cushion in the same manner for pressing short darts such as you use at the top of a sleeve.

Sleeve Board: For pressing sleeve seams and other small seams you will need a sleeve board. If you do not have one you can easily construct a "make-shift" by rolling newspapers into a tight bundle. Slip the roll into the sleeve and use it as support for your iron.

WHAT SIZE NEEDLE AND THREAD

Sew wool and silk with silk thread. Sew rayons with either silk thread or sewing cotton. Sew cotton with cotton thread. Sew color fast fabrics with colorfast cotton thread.

Fabrics	Cotton Thread	Silk Thread	Hand Sewing Needle	Machine	
				Thread	Needle
1	100	00 & 000	10	100 to 150	9
2	80 90	0	9 8	80 to 100	11
3	70 60	A & B	7	60 to 80	14
4	50	C	6	40 to 60	16
5	20 24	D	6 5	30 to 40	18
6	16	E	5 4	24 to 30	19

(1) Transparent fabrics—chiffon, light-weight rayon, fine dimity, sheer fabrics, also fine lace.
(2) All medium light-weight fabrics—children's clothes, glass curtains.
(3) Light-weight woolens, firm dress silks and cottons, draperies and men's fine shirts.
(4) Heavy suiting, cottons and quilts. For stitching aprons and men's work shirts. For making buttonholes.
(6) Heavy weaves of suiting, ticking, canvas. For wash uniforms and bedding.

Each box should be labeled.

SALVAGE--SAVE AND SEW

A collection of sewing rummage should be part of your sewing equipment. Fabric scraps, buttons, old belts and trimmings should be systematically saved so that you don't waste time searching for them nor money replacing something you have but cannot find.

Over a period of years I have discussed the importance of saving scraps with hundreds of home sewers; and I find that, though most women have some system, it is usually a system that doesn't work. The "box" is too small, or the "trunk" is so hard to get at that it is seldom used, or everything is cleared up in a hurry and dumped in together until it is hopeless to find what you want. I did find a number of homes with a good system, but the prize goes to a woman in Tennessee who showed me in her cellar the following simple system which everyone can use.

Boxes and jars were arranged on shelves with large, clear labels conveniently placed so that the contents of each could be seen at a glance. The secret of the system is plenty of boxes and jars. When one overflows, a larger one is substituted.

The largest box was marked GARMENT SCRAPS. Each fabric was rolled separately, with the trimmings and linings inside the roll. Other fabric boxes were labeled TRIMMING FABRICS and LINING FABRICS. A large box held UNCUT FABRICS. One was marked YARN, another FUR, another RIBBON. There was a box for old BELTS AND ZIPPERS, one for old FELT HATS, one for old LEATHER GLOVES. Glass jars contained buttons—matching buttons strung together—snap fasteners, beads and bead-stringing threads, hooks and eyes. One mystery jar was full of threads. When anything was ripped or remade, the threads were saved for stuffing and shoulder pads.

The family rules were these:

1. Never remove a box or jar from the sewing file. Use a workbox and collect everything needed from the file.

2. When the garment is finished, take the workbox back to the file and put everything back in its proper place.

3. File only clean fabrics.

CHAPTER IV

THE ABC'S OF STITCHES

BASIC INSTRUCTIONS IN SEWING

Chapters IV to IX contain instructions in the fundamentals of sewing. How to stitch and hem, how to make seams and tucks, how to make ruffles and gathers—these and other important skills are simply and easily explained. Beginners will find this section invaluable, and even those who have some experience in sewing will find here valuable hints for saving time, for doing things more easily and accurately. Here you will find the answers to questions which have puzzled you. The fundamentals of sewing are the foundation upon which successful garments are built. With a sound knowledge of these, sewing is easy; and things you have thought too difficult for you will turn out to be fun to make.

First select your needle and thread according to the chart on page 35. A finer needle than usual can often be used for the thread, and will help in making small, close stitches. For general sewing an average-sized needle makes for greater speed. Some people prefer a small-eyed needle, others a long or crewel-eyed one. It is important that each stitch be spaced evenly apart.

For information about a specific stitch, consult the index. Better progress is made by learning only the stitches needed for the garment upon which you are working instead of trying to learn all the stitches before beginning to sew.

Knotting a Thread: Twist the end of the thread twice around the first finger of your hand, and with your thumb roll it off the finger. Pull the thread down between thumb and finger, and at the end will be a small knot. Knotted threads

are used to prevent the stitches from pulling out as you work. In fine sewing, where knots are considered bad form, take two stitches, one over the other, at the beginning of your work to hold the thread.

Use a Thimble: Women who say they sew without a thimble usually do little sewing. Although it may seem awkward until you get used to it, learn to use a thimble when you sew.

Ending a Thread: When you come to the end of a seam, or the thread, it must be secured so it will not pull out as the garment is fitted or worn. Either take three little stitches one over another and break off the thread, or run the needle through the last three or four stitches, then cut the end of the thread. When making gathers, do not secure the thread and cut it;

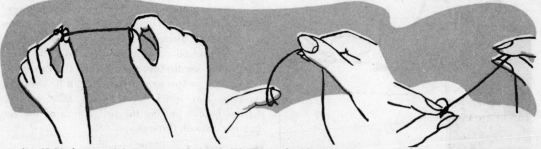

(1) Hold the thread between two fingers. (2) Twist the thread twice around finger. (3) Pull the thread between thumb and forefinger.

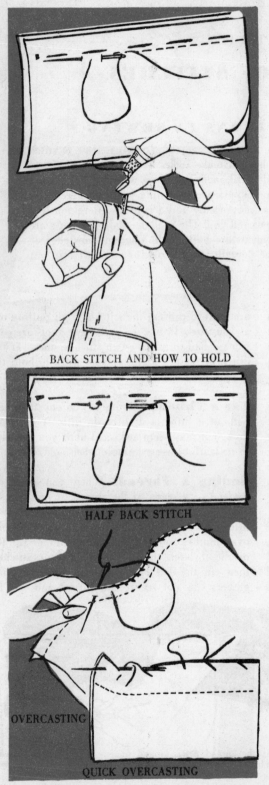

BACK STITCH AND HOW TO HOLD

HALF BACK STITCH

OVERCASTING

QUICK OVERCASTING

instead, put a pin at the end of the gathers and twist the thread around the pin. This will hold your thread until you can draw it and adjust the gathers. Then secure the thread or make a small knot in the end and cut the thread off.

USEFUL STITCHES

Each stitch performs a definite function, and the choice of stitch to use depends upon the purpose for which it is intended. The seams which hold garments together demand *secure* sewing, such as the *back stitch* or *combination stitch*. The hem of a skirt or sleeve is kept in place with *hemming stitches* or *slip stitching*. For quick seaming in light-weight fabrics use *running stitches* or a combination of *running* and *back stitches*. *Running stitch* is also used for gathering. Take tiny stitches or long ones, depending upon the effect desired. *Overcasting stitches* prevent the edges of fabrics from raveling.

Back Stitch: Fasten the thread and take one stitch in the material, *working toward you*. Then pass the needle back in the fabric to the beginning of the last stitch and bring it out a stitch ahead. As you work, you continue to take each stitch backward in order to strengthen the line of sewing.

Half Back Stitch: Make a long stitch and then take a stitch back placing the needle in the material halfway between the beginning and end of the last stitch; bring it out two stitches ahead. Hold the material as shown for a back stitch.

Overcasting: This is an important stitch. There are two kinds of overcasting: the loose quick overcasting used on seam edges, and the closer overcasting used on straight edges. The close overhanding used in piecing is another version of the second type. The stitches are the same in both kinds. Bring the needle up at one end of the work and take a stitch from behind the edge, passing the needle forward through the fabric. A single edge or two or more edges can be overcast together. For quick overcasting, take several stitches before pulling the full length of the remaining thread through.

Hem Stitches: To prepare a hem, turn the material over ½ inch, then turn it again the size of the hem desired. The first folded edge is held to the fabric with hem stitches. First take a stitch through the garment material and then catch the needle through the folded edge of the hem. Pull the thread. This is not the hemming used for skirts (*see below*). It is more suitable for narrow hems on collars and sleeves.

Slip Stitch for Skirt Hems: Turn the hem as directed above. Take a tiny stitch in the garment, as small as possible. Pass the needle through the turned edge (about ¼ inch), then take another tiny stitch in the garment.

Blind Hemming: These stitches are like hemming stitches, except that they are farther apart and the needle is placed on a slant. Take up only one thread of the garment and make a big stitch in the folded edge of the hem.

Running Stitch: Hold the work horizontal between your hands and run the needle in and out of the fabric. These stitches can be very small or large; small for holding a seam or the final stitching of an edge, large for holding a band that will be later caught in a hem.

Strong Stitches: It is often necessary to join a band, a fastening or an end securely to a garment. These stitches must be large enough to take a secure hold around the joining. At each corner make it doubly secure by taking stitches over and over in the same place; then rework the edge for extra security. When a fastening is placed where it will not be covered the same security is necessary, but the stitches must be concealed under the edge of the fabric.

Combination Stitch: This hand stitching replaces machine stitching and strengthens the seam. Begin with two running stitches and then take a back stitch. Repeat this for the length of the seam. The stitches must be close, fine, and even. When the fabric is light-weight more running stitches can be placed between the back-stitches.

Look in the Ready-Reference Guide at the back for exact page numbers of Detailed Instructions

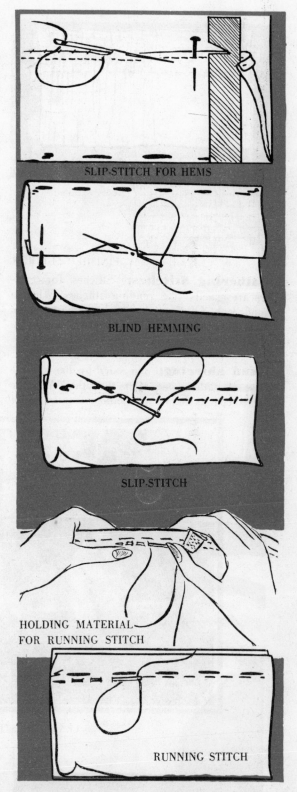

SLIP-STITCH FOR HEMS

BLIND HEMMING

SLIP-STITCH

HOLDING MATERIAL FOR RUNNING STITCH

RUNNING STITCH

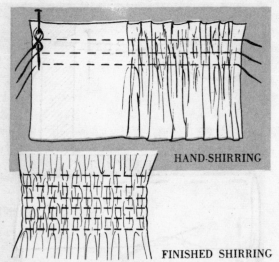

HAND-SHIRRING

FINISHED SHIRRING

Gathering Stitches: Stitches for gathers are exactly like running stitches. When a good deal of fullness has to be gathered close, make the stitches long and even and pull the material along so the stitches are spaced evenly.

Hand Shirring: To shirr by hand place rows of gathers one after the other. When a curved edge is shaped with gathers—at the top of a sleeve, for instance—one row of gathers helps to hold the sleeve in shape as you work. When ruffles are made, at least two rows of gathers are necessary; and when gathers are a trimming feature, you need three or more rows.

LEARNING TO STITCH BY MACHINE

It is easy to learn to make a line of stitching true and straight with a machine. Train yourself to watch the distance between the edge of the fabric and the foot of the machine. When you can keep an even seam line with a gauge without basting the seam allowance, the next step is to learn to do outside (or top) stitching for trimming. In this case let the foot of the machine follow a seam line or a turned edge. When the side of the machine foot parallels a straight seam or edge, your stitching *must* be straight. Any number of rows of stitching can be made the same way. The spacing between these rows can be varied by using the stitching gauge attachment. Practice stitching the outside edges of pockets and collars in a true straight line.. Practice turning sharp uniform corners so they all have the same angle or curve.

LEARN TO STITCH BY MACHINE

CHAPTER V

SEAMS

The dictionary defines a seam as "the fold or line formed by sewing together pieces of cloth." In other words, the seam is the foundation of all sewing, and success in making seams is the backbone of successful sewing. Seams fall into two general classifications: *Inconspicuous* seams, which allow the fabric to drape freely as though there were no seam; and *Decorative* seams, which emphasize the construction and form part of the trimming. Under each of these classifications there are several types of seam, for use with different materials and for different purposes. Each type of seam is described in detail here, but the following hints on successful seams apply to all seams.

SUCCESSFUL SEAMS

In making long seams always work on a table. Lay one piece of fabric out smoothly, then carefully smooth the second piece on top of it so that the edges are even. Never pull the edge. Baste the seam with the fabric *flat on the table*. Do not put your finger under the edge of the material or raise it up from the table; instead, put your left hand flat on top of the material and hold it as you pin or baste. For short seams work in your lap. Seams can be sewed by machine or by hand using back stitches or running stitches. The size of machine stitch should be adjusted to suit the material.

Seam Allowances: Accuracy is an essential of good dressmaking. A single pattern may call for different seam allowances for the various seams. Observe these carefully and follow directions. Or, if you have some reason to allow a wider seam as you cut—for instance, if your material ravels—remember to keep this same width constant as you baste.

Many good sewers baste seams before sewing; others stitch a pinned seam, allowing the foot of the sewing machine to push the material. This method is particularly good in joining two biases in a seam or in stitching velvet or any other napped or heavy fabric.

A seam may be stitched by hand or by machine, but always *the stitching must be strong and even*.

TYPES OF SEAMS

Plain Seam: The type of seam most often used for dresses, coat linings, blouses, and skirts made from fabrics that do not ravel, is the plain seam. The two edges of the fabric are simply pinned or basted together and then stitched.

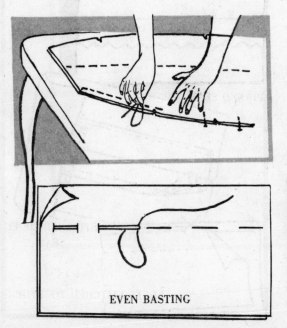

EVEN BASTING

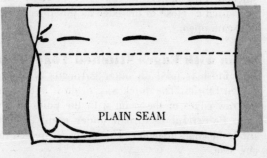

PLAIN SEAM

If the seam is to be pressed open, set the machine for a close stitch; if it is to be pressed all to one side, use a looser stitch. If the seam is sewed by hand, backstitch it or combine running stitch and backstitch. Remove the bastings before pressing.

Pinned Seam: When a seam is pinned for stitching, the pins should be placed close together and set in from the edge so they can be removed as you stitch. This is particularly important when heavy fabric is to be stitched. For complete success remove the seam pins for 2 inches and let the machine push the excess fullness.

Puckered seams are caused by the fabric being strained or stretched. They cannot be pressed out. They must be ripped and the fabric allowed to fall into natural folds and then rejoined. When seams are laid flat on a table and basted strain seldom occurs.

Overcast Seam: To prevent raveling in dress fabrics of rayon, silk, or wool, the seams should be overcast—both edges together or each edge separately as preferred. Take up about ⅛ inch of material and take care not to draw the thread too tight. Only inconspicuous seams in fabrics that tend to ravel require finishing.

Pinked Seam: Pinking is an excellent way to finish seams in taffeta and firmly woven fabrics of wool, silk, rayon, or velvet. For speed, use pinking shears or a pinking machine, otherwise fold the edge and snip it with a small scissors all the way along.

Stitched-Edge Seam: This is a popular finish for silk, rayon, or dress-weight woolens and the heavier cottons. After the plain seam is stitched, turn under the raw edge of each side and stitch as close to the edge as possible. Press the seam open.

Seam with Edges Stitched Together: This finish is used on outer garments of lightweight fabrics. The quick way to do it is to turn the raw edges of the seam with the point of an iron. Be careful to turn it under evenly. Then stitch the edges together. This seam is pressed to one side.

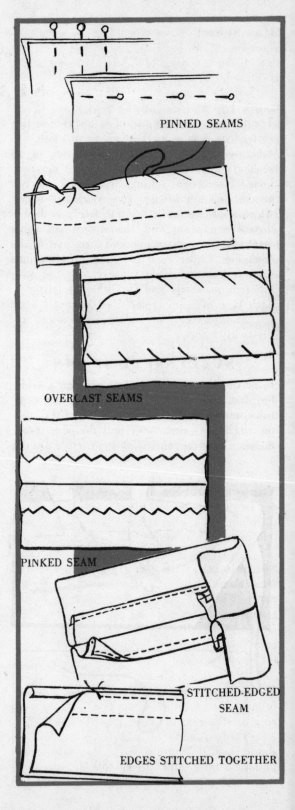

PINNED SEAMS

OVERCAST SEAMS

PINKED SEAM

STITCHED-EDGED
SEAM

EDGES STITCHED TOGETHER

Bias Seam: When the edges joined in a seam are cut on the bias, baste a piece of paper in with the two edges of fabric. After the seam is stitched, tear away the paper.

Seam for Transparent Fabrics: Hemstitching makes a neat finish for seams in dresses, collars, and cuffs made from transparent fabrics. Make a plain seam, then stitch the seam a little inside of the finished line and take it to the hemstitcher. Cut off the raw edge close to the edge of the hemstitching, or cut through the center of it. (This is called *picot*.) If it is a bias seam, baste a piece of paper in with the seam before it is hemstitched. It is important that you do this when working on chiffon, lace, or voile, for it keeps the material from tightening.

Gathers, Darts, or Tucked Edges at Seam: To keep gathers in place and evenly spaced, several rows of gathering should be made, and at least one row must extend below the seam. Darts and tucks must be pressed flat or to one side before the seam is joined. First place the plain edge down flat and the gathered or tucked edge on top. Baste carefully before stitching, and always stitch with the gathers or tucks on top. These seams are always pressed to one side.

Napped Fabrics in Seam: When a napped fabric is joined to a plain fabric, use a loose stitching. This applies also to joining two napped fabrics, as in a velvet dress.

Seam with One Straight Edge and One Bias: Always lay the bias edge on top of the straight edge and be careful not to draw the bias edge out of shape as you work. Pin it at frequent intervals to hold it while you baste, or baste it with paper for stitching. (See illustration for bias seam.)

Eased-in Fullness: Often in fitting a curve, fullness has to be eased in. The fabric of one edge of the seam is longer than the other. The longer edge should be placed on top of the shorter one. Hold the edges together with pins, pushing a little extra fullness into the space between each pin. These seams must be basted.

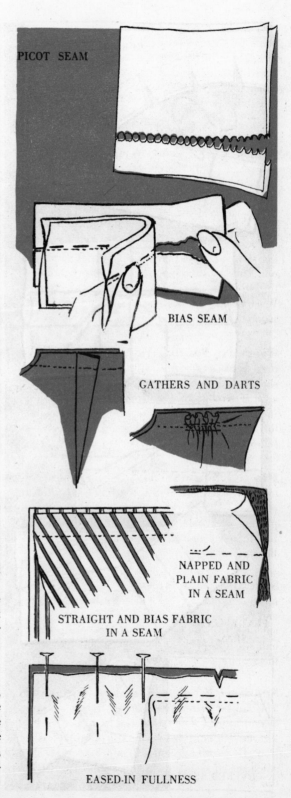

PICOT SEAM

BIAS SEAM

GATHERS AND DARTS

NAPPED AND PLAIN FABRIC IN A SEAM

STRAIGHT AND BIAS FABRIC IN A SEAM

EASED-IN FULLNESS

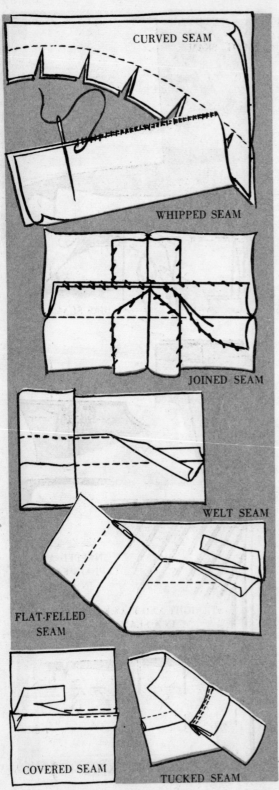

CURVED SEAM

WHIPPED SEAM

JOINED SEAM

WELT SEAM

FLAT-FELLED
SEAM

COVERED SEAM

TUCKED SEAM

Curved Seam: The fabric must be slashed frequently along a curved seam to allow it to curve in or out as desired.

Whipped Seam: Whipped seams are used in piecing, when the fabric is not wide enough to cut the full sweep required by the pattern. For an inconspicuous joining, the grain of the fabric must be just alike at both edges. Turn the edges and overcast them together. The stitches must be close enough to hold the fabric firm and even, but the thread must not be pulled too tightly. The same seam is used to piece together two selvedge edges.

Joined Seam: When two seams cross, the important things are to keep the joining flat and not to add bulk. The seam in each piece should be stitched and pressed open before the two are joined. Clip away the edge of the seam which is to lie under the top seam.

TAILORED SEAMS

Welt Seam: For coats and other sturdy garments stitch a plain seam. Trim ⅛ inch off one edge, put two edges together, and baste flat. Turn the garment right side out and stitch on the outside about ¼ inch from the seam line. For a double welt seam, make two stitchings.

Flat Felled Seam: This is a popular seam in men's shirts, uniforms, and pajamas. First stitch a regular seam, with the raw edges on the *outside of the garment.* Trim off one edge of the seam to within ¼ inch of the seam line. Turn under the raw edge of the other side, ⅛ inch and pull it flat over the short side. Hem by hand or machine to the garment so the seam lies flat.

Covered Seam: The covered seam is excellent for house dresses and children's clothes which are washed regularly. Baste as for a plain seam. Trim off one edge to within ⅛ inch of the basting. Turn the longer edge over the short one —raw edge turned under—and stitch on the basting line.

Tucked Seam: Baste in a plain seam and press the edges to one side. Turn the garment right side out and form a narrow tuck. Stitch the tuck on the seam line.

Outside Stitched Seam: This makes an easy seam finish for heavy cotton or light-weight wool materials. Stitch the seam and press it open. Turn to the wrong side of the garment and finish the edges of the seam by turning the raw edges under and stitch as close to the edge as possible. Then turn again to the right side of the garment and make a row of stitching parallel to the seam. Sometimes two rows are made, one on each side of the seam for trimming. This seam looks like a strengthened seam on the outside of a garment.

Taped Seam: In woolen garments where a bias edge is likely to shrink or stretch, purchase preshunk tailor's cotton tape. Baste the tape to the seam line after the seam is basted, then stitch through the center of the tape.

Bound Seam: In unlined coats or jackets made of wool or heavy cotton, bound seams are important. The binding may be a true bias you cut yourself, or you can buy a bias binding. There is also a straight binding you can buy, but this can be used only when the edges of the seam are straight. Stitch a plain seam and press it open. Bind each edge with the bias binding, stitching as close to the edge as possible in the first stitching.

Strengthened Seam: Stitch a seam and press both edges to one side. Then stitch again, through seam and garment, as close to the seam line as possible. This second stitching will show on the right side of the garment. This is a seam often used in tailored clothes and sturdy cotton garments. It is also very useful in joining a transparent fabric—neck edge, yoke, et cetera—to a non-transparent fabric. Fold both sides of the seam *away from the transparent material* and stitch on the non-transparent fabric. This keeps the seam from showing through.

Slot Seam: The slot seam is a decorative seam for tailored clothes. Cut a straight strip of the fabric twice the seam allowance and the length of the seam. Run a guide basting through the center. Press back the seam allowance of the garment and place it over the fabric strip with the edges meeting. Baste the edges down. When both edges of the seam have been basted to the fabric strip, the pressed edges of the garment should

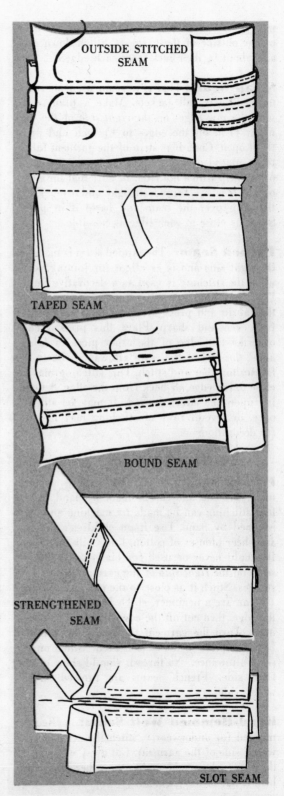

OUTSIDE STITCHED SEAM

TAPED SEAM

BOUND SEAM

STRENGTHENED SEAM

SLOT SEAM

meet at the guide basting. The stitching is done on the outside of the garment. Stitch down each side about ⅛ inch back from each edge.

Strap Seam: This is a seam used on many unlined coats and jackets. Make a plain seam with the raw edges on the *right side* of the garment. Trim off the edges to ¼ inch and press them open. Cut a bias strip of the garment fabric to be placed over the seam, and turn the edges of the strip with a hot iron. Be sure that the edges of the bias are turned straight and true. Place the strip over the seam and baste it in place. Stitch as close to each edge as possible.

Lapped Seam: The lapped seam is made on the right side and is excellent for joining yokes when the stitching is used as a decorative finish. Fold back the seam allowance of one piece of the fabric and press with an iron, making the fold even and sharp. Place this pressed edge over the flat edge of the other piece of fabric along the line of the seam allowance. Baste the fabrics together and stitch. This stitching may be close to the edge, or back from the edge, depending upon the effect desired. It may be stitched once, or several rows of stitching may be used for decoration.

UNDERWEAR SEAMS

French Seam: This dainty seam is used for undergarments and can be made by hand, or the first stitching can be made by machine and then hemmed by hand. Use it on children's dresses, and sheer blouses of cotton, linen, silk, or rayon. It should never be used for bias seams. Baste a seam on the *right side* of the garment with small stitches. Stitch it as close to the edge as possible. (If you are a beginner, stitch back a little from the edge, then cut off the edge close to the stitching.) Turn the garment to the wrong side and baste the seam so the edge is even. Stitch on the seam allowance. No threads should show on the right side. French seams are pressed on the wrong side.

Hand-Hemmed Welt Seam: (Recommended for underwear.) Stitch the seam on the wrong side of the garment. Cut away one side of the seam edge, turn under the other edge, and hem it flat to the garment.

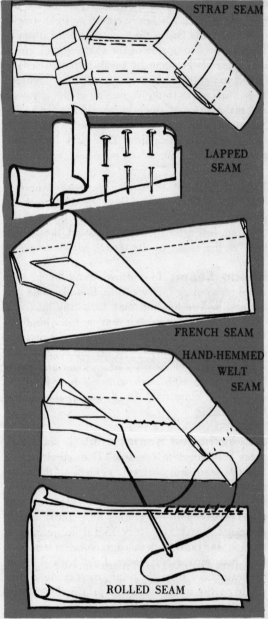

STRAP SEAM

LAPPED SEAM

FRENCH SEAM

HAND-HEMMED WELT SEAM

ROLLED SEAM

Rolled Seam: The rolled seam is used in fine sewing, where bands of embroidery are joined to the garment with *entre deux*, or in joinings where no seam should be visible through transparent fabrics. To make a rolled seam, join the seam with fine running stitches or machine stitches. Cut off half the seam allowance on one edge and roll the other edge between the thumb and first finger. Overcast this rolled edge close to the seam stitching.

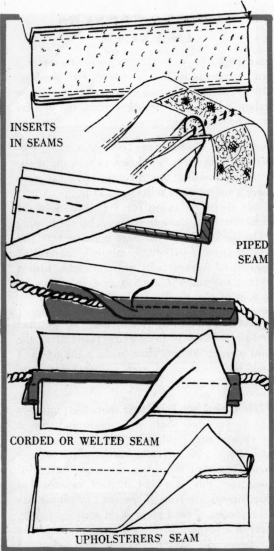

INSERTS
IN SEAMS

PIPED
SEAM

CORDED OR WELTED SEAM

UPHOLSTERERS' SEAM

DECORATIVE SEAMS

Seams for Set-in Inserts: Inserts of lace, embroidery, *entre deux*, or self-fabric trimming bands often have a seaming allowance. Place the trimming wrong side up and lay the edge of it on the garment *at the garment seam allowance.* The two sides of these seams are often very unequal. Baste the edges into a seam close to the trimming edge and stitch. Join the opposite side of the insert in the same way. In the case of *entre deux* and lace inserts, the edge of the seam is cut away and closely overcast; in other inserts the seam is pressed away from the trimming and stitched as close as possible to the seam edge of the trimming.

When the lace or *entre deux* has no seam allowance, baste its finished edge to the garment's seam-line and cut away half the seam allowance from the garment edge, then roll the remaining seam allowance and overcast it, taking the stitches through the lace or trimming.

Inserts: Inserts in a garment are placed on the right side of the fabric and pinned in position. Hem each edge of lace, or insert to the fabric by hand or by machine. Turn to the opposite side and cut through the center of the fabric covered by the insert. Press back the fabric edges and stitch down as described above or roll them by hand.

Piped Seam: A piping is stitched between the seams and serves to introduce a contrasting color or to provide a trimming emphasis in self-color. Prepared bias folds can be purchased, or you can make your own by cutting a true bias an inch wide and any length desired. Fold the bias strip lengthwise and press the fold.

Lay one section of the fabric flat on a table, lay the piping over it, and baste. Then lay the second section of fabric, with seam edges matching, so that the piping is between both fabrics, and baste again. Turn over to the right side and be sure that the piping is straight and the right width. Do not stitch until the basting shows just the effect you want. You can stitch on either the right or the wrong side.

Sometimes two colors are piped into the seam for trimming. To do this, place one binding over the other and proceed as directed above.

Corded Seam: Cut a true bias binding the length desired and baste it over a cable cord. Insert between seam edges as directed for a piped seam. For really satisfactory results, a corded seam must be stitched by machine with a cording foot. The cording foot is not expensive.

Upholsterers' Seam: This seam gives the effect of a corded seam and is often used in slip covers. To make it, follow directions for the French seam, only reverse the process so that the final covered seam is on the outside instead of the inside. The last stitching is made one-fourth inch from the edge, and it is not necessary to enclose the raveled edges on the inside, as in underwear seams.

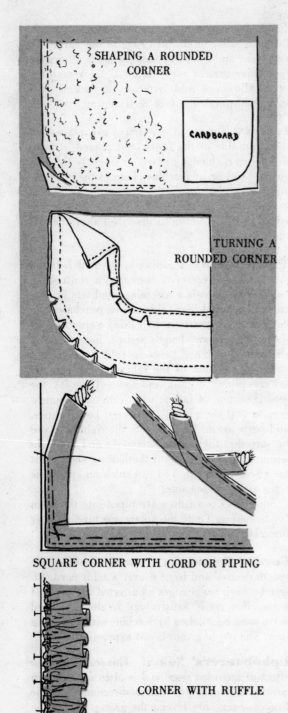

SHAPING A ROUNDED CORNER

CARDBOARD

TURNING A ROUNDED CORNER

SQUARE CORNER WITH CORD OR PIPING

CORNER WITH RUFFLE

TURNING CORNERS IN A SEAM

Sometimes it is necessary to turn corners in a seam, particularly in upholstery. For good results the corners must be as true and even as the straight edges. First decide whether the corners are to be rounded or square.

Rounded Corners: To keep rounded corners uniform, cut a cardboard pattern the shape desired and outline this curve on every flat piece where a corner seam will come. Trim the corners to this shape, allowing for the seam. Join the seam, then snip the curved seam before turning it. On the right side the edge must be true and even. Beginners will baste this edge carefully; experienced workers will press the edge with a hot iron and stitch it, keeping an even seam with the foot of the machine.

Square Corners: These must be watched carefully. Allow a little extra material at the point of each corner. Turn to the right side and check the evenness of each corner before you stitch.

With Cord or Piping: Baste the piping or cord to one edge, shaping it square and true at the corner and holding it with a little cross stitch. Baste with careful attention to true square lines. Then you can place the second piece of fabric over this edge and stitch it, assured that your corners are true. If the cord or piping has to be pieced, always piece it on a straight edge, never in a corner. To piece cord or piping, cross the two ends, keeping as straight a line as possible.

Corners with a Bias: Turning corners with a bias is a simple matter because the material adjusts to curves. Take advantage of this and plan a slightly rounded point at the corner. Baste the material, then turn to the right side and make sure you have not stretched the material so tightly that it draws.

Corners with a Ruffle: Test the effect you want by laying the work flat and pinning the ruffle to the edge of the material so that it lies flat. This will show you how much fullness to add at the corner as you turn. Be careful of the corner as you baste, as you must make a true turn.

CHAPTER VI

DARTS, TUCKS, AND PLEATS

The group included in this chapter—darts, tucks, and pleats—has many uses both in dressmaking and in sewing for the home. Their function is to control fullness and to add to decoration. Darts, which shape the garment, are functional; pleats and tucks are both functional and decorative.

In making pleats and tucks it saves time to work on an ironing board and press the sharp edges before the pleat or tuck is basted. The *second pressing*, which completes the pleat or tuck, should not be done until after it is basted, fitted, and stitched.

Darts are used to curve a straight fabric to the molded lines of the body. They fit out fullness in a smooth line. Because of this, it is usually better to place several short darts one after the other than to fit out the same amount of fullness in one long dart.

A dart is wide at one end and gradually tapers to nothing at the other end. You will find darts indicated with perforations in your pattern. To make a dart, lay the pattern on your fabric, mark the perforations, and fold the fabric so that the two outer perforations lie exactly on top of one another. Crease the fabric from the overlapping point to the perforation that marks the end of the dart. Then make a running stitch by hand or machine from the perforations at the edge to the perforations at the end of the dart.

FITTING DARTS

Plain Darts: The plain darts which shape the underarm or hip line of a garment are marked on each pattern. If you are not using a pattern, pin extra fullness into darts. Two or more short darts close together give better results than one long one. Dart stitching should be shaped to a point in a long, gradual line, so as to leave no awkward bulge at the end. Stitch the darts and press them before joining the seam. In heavy material the dart is cut down the center and pressed open; in light material it is pressed to one side or pressed flat.

Shoulder Darts: A dart longer than the underarm dart can be used at the shoulder, running from the shoulder seam down the front of the waist. Shoulder darts can follow the armhole line, placed 1½ inches from the armhole; or be placed over the fullest point of the bust. Slanted darts are sometimes stitched on the right side of the garment as a decoration.

Neckline Darts: Most women find a neckline more becoming if darts are fitted in the back of the neck. This keeps the collar from standing out or away from the neckline. Two darts are often enough; sometimes four or more are necessary.

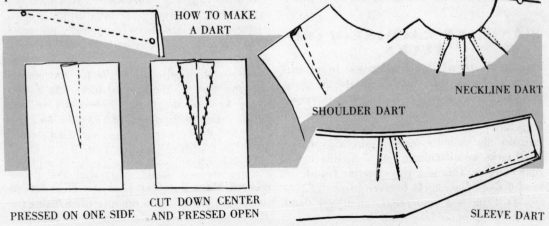

HOW TO MAKE
A DART

PRESSED ON ONE SIDE

CUT DOWN CENTER
AND PRESSED OPEN

SHOULDER DART

NECKLINE DART

SLEEVE DART

Darts for Sleeve Control: At the elbow of long tight sleeves, and at the shoulder of many sleeves, darts are used to curve the fabric. A long fitted sleeve should never be made without darts or fullness to ease the elbow.

Darts for Waistline Control: Darts are often placed above the beltline to hold the waistline fullness. This effect can be used either to create a high-waisted fitting or to control fullness in one spot. In princess lines, or in separate blouses, darts are often used to shape the garment to fit closer to the waistline. To make these body darts fold the fabric on a straight line and mark the widest section of the dart. Shape the dart into points at both ends. For the best effect, darts so used should be long. As in other instances of fullness control, several shallow darts are better than one large one.

Dart Seam Holding Fullness: In this type of dart the material is cut as for a seam. This gives fullness at the armhole or waistline. A straight edge of the fabric overlaps a gathered lower edge, and needs a stay to make it hold firmly. Cut a piece of self-fabric 1 inch longer than the longest edge of the dart and 1½ inches wide for the stay. Lay the stay on the right side of the material. The stitching should outline where the seam of the dart will be—taking care to point the inner edge. When the stay is stitched, cut with sharp scissors between the stitching *into the point.* You must cut to the stitches at the point—if you cut through them, quickly overcast the point. Now turn the stay to the wrong side of the garment, basting the short edge and gathering the long edge. Draw the gathering in and overlap it with the top edge. Stitch the seam.

HAND AND MACHINE-MADE TUCKS

Tucks Controlling Fullness: In soft materials, tucks control fullness and take the place of darts. These are marked in the pattern or must be planned to give fullness where it is needed. A large tuck at the shoulder line is sometimes used to cover the shoulder seam. Again, a group of small tucks, or a continued row of shallow tucks, adds fullness. This is a very popular feature in wash dresses. Long tucks between inserts of lace are used in fine underwear, neckwear, and blouses; they should be made by hand.

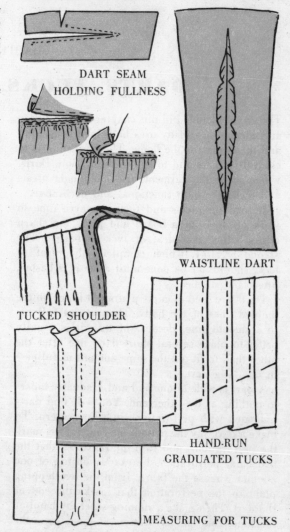

DART SEAM
HOLDING FULLNESS

WAISTLINE DART

TUCKED SHOULDER

HAND-RUN
GRADUATED TUCKS

MEASURING FOR TUCKS

Measuring for Tucks: Every tuck in a group must be exactly the same width, and the space between tucks must be carefully measured.

When tucks are made by hand, use the marking on the pattern or cut a measuring gauge. Take a straight piece of cardboard and notch it (1) the depth of the finished tuck; (2) the distance between the tucks, measured from one stitched line to the next; and (3) the length of the tuck. When the rows are graduated, instead of using this third measure, baste a line on the garment indicating where the tucks should end.

Hand-Run Tucks: Fold the edge for the tuck, then sew it with a running stitch, using fine thread and a fine needle. Measure as you work

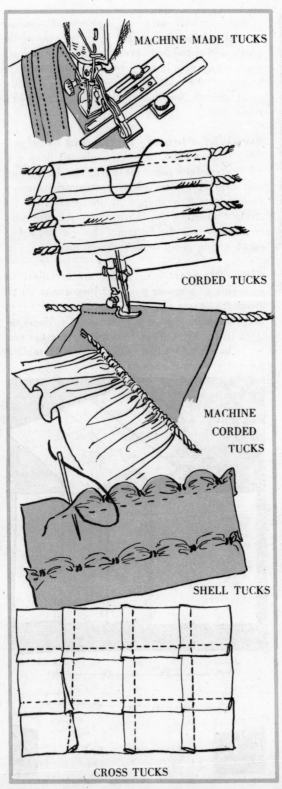

MACHINE MADE TUCKS

CORDED TUCKS

MACHINE CORDED TUCKS

SHELL TUCKS

CROSS TUCKS

Tie your threads securely and cut them close—no knots must show. Never use a draw thread to make a tuck; the tuck would not wear.

Machine-Made Tucks: In making tucks with a machine attachment use the $\frac{1}{4}$ inch or 1 inch cleat provided for the purpose. Set this attachment, and it will space the tucks.

Pin Tucks: These are used as decoration on very sheer fabrics. Run the tuck by hand very close to the folded edge, so close you cannot measure it. Use the measure for spacing and for length of the tuck.

When the tucks vary in length, mark the variations on the material by running a diagonal basting thread where you want the tucks to end.

Corded Tucks—Run by Hand: Mark the edge of each tuck with a basting so it will be straight and even. Encase the cord in the tuck as you run it.

Machine Corded Tucks: Mark the position of the tucks and baste a tuck encasing a cord. Now stitch close to the cord, using the cording foot. If the edges are not covered by a seam, turn the cord to the wrong side and fasten each end down securely. If you unwind the end a little, it will make less bulk. Never cut off the cording flush with the end of the tuck; it would fray. If the side edge is finished before you cord the tuck, first finish the end of the cord by unraveling it a little, turning it back, and overcasting it several times. Then overcast it securely to the side edge before you start to run the tuck. The opposite end of the cord must be finished and overcast firmly in place before the tuck is finished. This makes a beautiful finish on the end of a scarf.

Shell Tuck: First measure for the shells. The gauge should be cut so the shell is about twice as long as the tuck is deep. Mark with a pencil dot. Then make two overcasting stitches across the tuck to hold the shell. Run the tuck to the next dot and make another overcasting stitch.

Crossed Tucks: Crossed tucks are sometimes used for decoration on yokes or allover blouses made of transparent fabrics. Space the tucks as desired. Mark the measures carefully

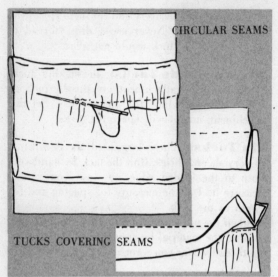

CIRCULAR SEAMS

TUCKS COVERING SEAMS

and make the horizontal tucks all the way across. Press them flat before measuring and tucking the vertical tucks.

Tucks Covering Seams: In skirts and blouses, in curtains and slipcovers, a tuck may be made directly over a seam to hide the joining. Make this tuck the desired width, and stitch the tuck in with the seam stitching.

Circular Tucks: These tucks must be marked carefully *to indicate both edges.* When you join the markings, lay the fullness of the under tuck, spacing it between pins, before basting or running the tuck.

GARMENT PLEATS

Although they are called by different names to describe their particular use, there are really two important types of pleats . . . the *side pleat* and the *box pleat.* When a box pleat is made wrong side out, it is called an *inverted pleat.* When it is short and inserted in the lower edge of a skirt it is called a *kick pleat.* A *knife pleat* is simply the description of a pleat with a very firmly pressed edge. Pleats are spaced across the fabric, or in small groups, and are usually folded to a full depth.

Whatever the type of pleating, first seam the sections of the garment and press the seam open. If you are using a pattern, you will find that the size and spacing of the pleat is marked. Carefully reproduce these marks on the material with tail-

or's tacks, chalk, or a running wheel. If you are not using a pattern, decide upon the size of the pleats and space them evenly. To insure a sharp edge, many people cut a piece of cardboard the length of the pleat and press the edge of the pleat over the cardboard. If you do this, *use a press cloth.*

Straight Pleats: When a skirt or dress is hung from a yoke, or when a pleated flounce is used, a straight piece of fabric can be pressed into straight pleats. (Note particularly whether your pleats are shaped at the waistline.) In straight pleating the fabric is set just the same at the top and the bottom. This can be a box pleat, a side pleat, or an inverted pleat.

Side Pleats: Side pleats are arranged on each side of a center panel, if they are to go all around a skirt. The pleats may be shallow or deep, depending upon the amount of fullness desired in the skirt. They fold away from the center. They can be fitted over the hips by making them deeper at the waistline.

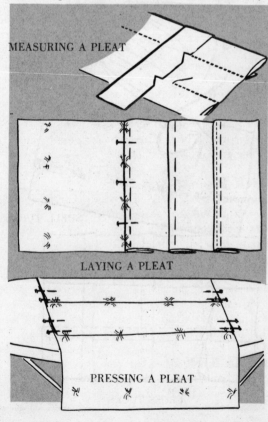

MEASURING A PLEAT

LAYING A PLEAT

PRESSING A PLEAT

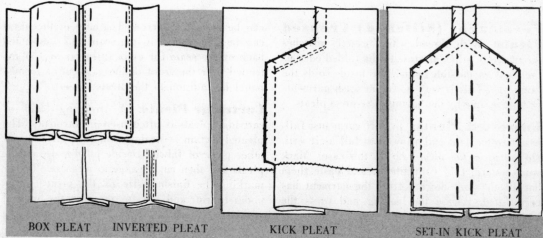

| BOX PLEAT | INVERTED PLEAT | KICK PLEAT | SET-IN KICK PLEAT |

Box Pleats: Box pleats are used in skirts, shirts, and in decorative flounces for bedspreads, slip covers, and so forth. They are used in clusters too; and we often see a box pleat forming a panel. Use the spacing marked on your pattern, or decide on the size and spacing suited to your need and cut a gauge. Mark the folding line with chalk, using a yardstick. Indicate by a basting thread the line to which this folded edge will be stitched. Decide on the top and bottom finish before you fold or press the pleats. A full box pleat is folded under so that the under edges meet: shallow box pleats that save material are made with a shallow fold.

Inverted Pleats: These are simply box pleats turned wrong side out. They are often used in the front and back seams of skirts, and the "action back" featured in sport shirts is made of one or two inverted pleats set below a yoke.

Kick Pleats: Kick pleats are set into skirts below the knee. As a rule they are cut in one piece with the skirt seam. This is a very important construction when pleats are used in transparent material. Stitch the seams and fold the pleat to one side; then stitch across the top of the pleat. This is the only stitch line that shows on the front of the garment and it keeps the pleat from sagging. Turn the hem after the pleat is stitched; cut through the seam above the hem so that the work lies smooth.

Set-In Kick Pleats: Often a feature of pattern construction, these pleats help widen a too-narrow skirt. Fold the seam back and plan

your pleat, fitting a stay (see index for detailed description) in place or cutting a stay to suit your needs. This pleat is made like a box pleat with a pointed top. Stitch the seams, press the pleat, and stitch the point carefully with one or more rows of stitching.

Contrasting Color in Pleats: Novelty pleats are made with striped fabrics pleated so that one color does not show until the pleat opens. This can be done with any pleated skirt pattern *with deep full pleats*. Simply insert stripes of the contrasting color in the exact width of the underfold of your pleats. Unless you have the great patience to insert the many stripes necessary for side pleats, it is better to use this effect in box pleats or inverted pleats.

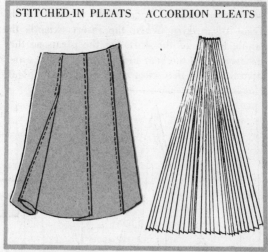

| STITCHED-IN PLEATS | ACCORDION PLEATS |

Look in the Ready-Reference Guide at the back for exact page numbers of Detailed Instructions

Permanent (Stitched) Creased Pleats: With thread which exactly matches the material, stitch as close to the folded edge of the pleat as possible; stitch the inside folds the same way. This is very useful in wash garments or to save time by not having to re-press pleats.

Unpressed Pleats: In soft garments, fullness is often laid and allowed to fall as it will. *Do not press the pleat edge* in this case. Mark your pattern, fold your pleats, and baste them flat all the way down. After the garment has been fitted, release the basting and press the lower edge as if it were gathered.

Accordion Pleats: Accordion pleats are pressed in by steam, and pleating them is a skilled art. You simply finish off the lower edge of the necessary yardage of material and take it to the pleater. To compute the yardage, decide on the finished size, then multiply that figure by three. Many skilled artisans nowadays can offer you sectional group pleating and circular pleating. Ask them for directions on how to prepare your material.

Pleated Circular Skirts: Circular skirts with pleats are usually cut in many gores, often twelve, one for each pleat. Seams must be placed at the edge of an under pleat. The outside pleats are pressed sharply on an edge, like a man's trousers. *They are not folded flat.*

Pleated Circular Inserts: These can be set into a seam or spaced like a panel in the front of a skirt. When the insert extends the whole length of the skirt, lay the pleats so they are broader at the hem and narrower at the waist. Space them so they meet at the center. The pleats can be broad or narrow. The edge of the insert can be (1) joined in the seam; (2) extended back of the seam for extra fullness; or (3) extended over the front of the garment to form a panel in addition to the pleated insert.

Cartridge Pleats: A trimming band of cartridge pleats is often used in garments. The pleated section is straight and is applied to another piece of fabric. Decide on the size of the pleats and then cut a gauge to measure (1) for marking the finished size of the pleat on the under fabric; and (2) for marking the finished spacing of the pleat on the top fabric. Lay the fabrics together with the line of markings matching so the pleats stand out. Then you can stitch all the way down between each pleat, or only part way down so that the end of the pleat falls clear. Do not press cartridge pleats.

GODETS

Godets are circular inserts set into a slash or a seam. They can extend the full length of the skirt or curtain, or they can be shortened to any desired length. Some godets are shallow, others are very broad, at the lower edge. When the godet is a feature of fashion, your pattern will indicate the size and fullness. When you use it in remaking something or in home decoration, you must decide for yourself how much fullness you need. The top of the godet can be rounded or pointed.

To set a godet in a slash or seam, work from the lower edge to the point and shape the point carefully. There should be no wrinkle on the right side. After the seam is stitched, finish the hem.

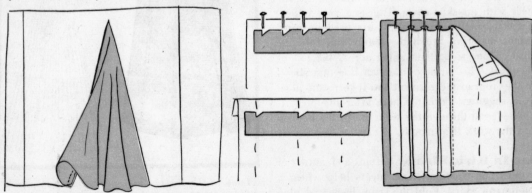

SET-IN GODET   CARTRIDGE PLEATS

CHAPTER VII

GATHERS, RUFFLES, AND HEADINGS

Gathers are used to give fullness to garments or to shape an edge to a curve. Ruffles add gaiety to dresses and accessories, and ruffled curtains adorn many homes. Anyone who sews must learn how to draw fabric together in soft fullness, in gathers and shirrings, and how to make ruffles of every type.

Ruffles are gathered strips used as a trimming and are best made of soft fabrics or crisp, stiff ones. The amount of fullness is important; soft fabrics can be gathered more closely, giving greater fullness; but when the gathers are spaced, it will sometimes prove wiser to take out a little fullness by shortening the length of the ruffle. Fullness in heavy or wiry fabrics is best laid in pleats or darts. If a ruffle wilts, don't add extra fullness, but try binding the edge with ribbon or a double bias of self-fabric. Ruffles can be of any desired width, but the use for which the ruffle is intended will determine whether you (1) gather a single edge—to bind or set into a seam; (2) turn the edge to hem down; or (3) turn the edge to form a heading.

GATHERING

Hand Gathers: Use the coarsest thread a fine needle will hold and always knot the thread. Use a running stitch, and be sure that the stitching is straight. Sometimes it is necessary to use a close stitch for fine gathers in light-weight fabric. A longer stitch is suitable for heavier material. *Successive rows of gathers should always be done with the same stitch spacing.* Many people like to mark the rows for gathering to insure accuracy. Pull the fabric back on the thread as you work. The gathers can be closely or widely spaced depending upon the fullness desired. As each row of gathers is finished, fasten the end of the thread around a pin.

Hand Shirring: Shirring is several rows of gathers in a soft fabric evenly spaced. Shirred effects sometimes form deep yokes, and again are used in allover fullness construction.

Gathers that Shape an Edge: To shape an edge use one row of gathers.

Gathers to Control Fullness: Use two rows of gathers at the top of sleeves, in shoulder lines and other seam construction.

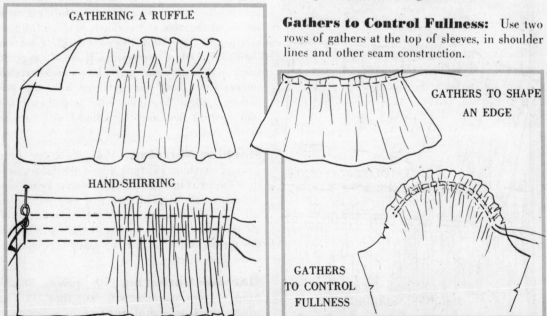

GATHERING A RUFFLE

HAND-SHIRRING

GATHERS TO SHAPE AN EDGE

GATHERS TO CONTROL FULLNESS

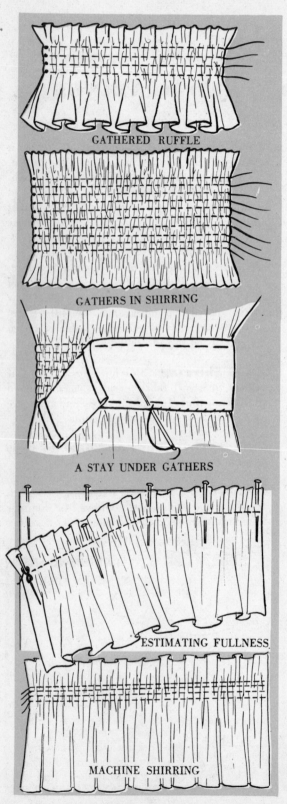

GATHERED RUFFLE

GATHERS IN SHIRRING

A STAY UNDER GATHERS

ESTIMATING FULLNESS

MACHINE SHIRRING

Gathers in Ruffles: To draw fullness into a given measure use at least two and preferably four rows of gathers. For experimenting use a double thread and one single row.

Gathers in Shirring: Use fine thread and make row after row of gathers. You will need ten to twelve rows.

Setting Gathers: After the stitching has been completed, the gathers must be spaced to fall smoothly. Our grandmothers stroked the fabric with the point of the needle, but this too often cuts or damages a rayon or a delicate weave. A safer way is to twist the thread around the needle and pull the material into place.

A Stay Under Gathers: When many rows of shirring are used at the neckline or waistline of a garment, or in the heading of a curtain or flounce, a stay is placed under the gathers to hold the shirring in place, to prevent the threads from breaking, and to prevent the shirring from stretching in wear. The stay is generally a piece of thin fabric cut on the straight of the goods. (If you are working with transparent material use a piece of self-fabric.) Turn the ends in and hem it under the gathers.

Estimating Fullness: In flounces or ruffles where the gathered edge is very long, it will save time to space the fabric before you gather it. Between two pins space the fabric fullness on a section of the edge and decide how much fullness you would like. Mark this point with a pin on both fabric edges. Professionals cut a gauge or mark a tape measure and place pins at stated intervals on both the gathered and the ungathered edge. When the edge is gathered the pins are matched, and the fullness will then be evenly spaced.

Machine Shirring: Make three or four rows of machine stitching across the fabric, setting the machine for an open stitch. Leave the threads on the ends of each row long enough to get hold of. Take hold of the bobbin thread of all the rows together and pull the material on the thread. Machine shirring saves time and insures even stitches.

Machine Gathering: The ruffling attachment of your machine will save time for you when you plan ruffled curtains or other long

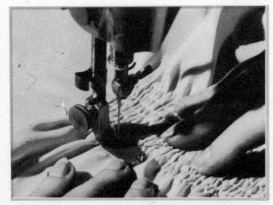

MACHINE GATHERING

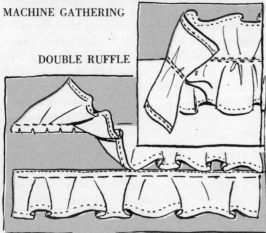

DOUBLE RUFFLE

CIRCULAR RUFFLE

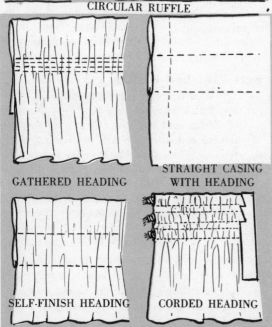

GATHERED HEADING

STRAIGHT CASING
WITH HEADING

SELF-FINISH HEADING

CORDED HEADING

yardages. Always test the fullness of the ruffle on a scrap of material before you begin to work. Finish the edges of the material before ruffling. Your machine also includes a gathering foot which will save you time when you are making ruffles for aprons and so forth.

Double Ruffle: Finish both edges of the ruffle and gather it through the center, using two or four rows of gathers. A band or ribbon can be stitched through the center of this type of ruffle or it can be applied to the material with a stitching down the center.

Circular Ruffle: Many pattern constructions specify circular ruffles. Or you can cut them yourself in either of two ways: (1) a true bias or (2) a shaped circle. It is wise to test the shaped circle in tissue paper before cutting your fabric. In joining circular ruffles to a fabric edge, turn a seam and snip it occasionally so it will not draw. This seam can be stitched under the ruffle, or the ruffle can be basted in place and stitched on top.

HEADINGS

A heading is that part of a ruffle above the gathers, or the fold of the fabric which appears above the casing—as at the top of a curtain.

Gathered Heading: Decide on the width of your heading and turn the edge down far enough to include the heading and the rows of gathers. Run several rows of gathers across this turned fabric by hand or machine.

Straight Heading with Casing: Decide on the width of your heading and casing, and turn the edge as directed above. Run two rows of stitching across this turned edge, far enough apart so the pole or cord can be inserted in the space between.

Self-Finished Heading: Turn the top edge of the ruffle or curtain in a hem before gathering or stitching. If this finish is used on a window curtain, allow enough space for the string or rod between the rows of stitching.

Corded Heading: Turn the edge and stitch it, allowing enough material to cover the cord. If a double or triple cord is desired, turn the

JOINING RUFFLE TO A STRAIGHT
PIECE OF FABRIC

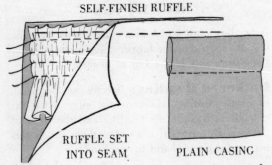

SELF-FINISH RUFFLE

RUFFLE SET
INTO SEAM   PLAIN CASING

edge deep enough to include two or three cords. Stitch on both sides of each successive cord, using a gauge to space them evenly.

JOINING RUFFLES TO A STRAIGHT PIECE OF FABRIC

The top edge of the ruffle can be turned before gathering; after gathering, it is basted on the fabric. This edge can be hemmed by hand or top-stitched by machine.

An unturned edge of the fabric can be gathered. This type of ruffle is joined with an under-stitching.

A ruffle can be turned in a deep hem and the gathering placed at the edge of the turn. When a ruffle is joined at this gathered line, the frill at the top is called a heading.

A ruffle can be gathered without turning the edge and joined with a bias stitched to the fabric with the ruffle.

The edge of the ruffle can be bound before it is joined. Gather the ruffle without turning the edge, then bind the edge. It can then be basted into place.

TYPES OF RUFFLE

Edging Ruffle: Ruffles used for edging collars, sleeves, the bottoms of skirts, and curtains should be carefully spaced, allowing extra fullness in turning corners *so the ruffle will lie flat.* The seam should be pressed away from the ruffled edge, and the seam finish is important. It can be stitched down close to the seam stitching with one or several rows of stitching if a band effect is wanted; or the ruffle can be placed below the joining edge to permit turning the plain edge in a binding. This is called a "French seam turn."

Ruffle Set into a Seam: This may be the seam of a garment, or the contrast band joined to a curtain, or the center front of a blouse with a ruffle down both sides. Finish the outside edge of the ruffle and gather the joining edge without turning—two or more rows of gathers are desirable. Lay the ruffle on the right side of the garment, matching the edges, and baste. Now lay the other edge of the garment over the ruffle, with edges meeting, and stitch the seam.

Self-Finished Ruffle: Place the ruffle over the fabric with edges meeting and space the gathers. Stitch the seam, then trim the ruffle close to the stitches and turn the fabric over the line of stitching and stitch it again, applying the ruffle with bias. Place the ruffle over the fabric with seams matching and space the gathers. Place a binding over the gathers and stitch the three edges in a seam. Turn the binding and hem it to the plain fabric above the ruffle.

CASINGS

Casings through which a pole, cord, ribbon, or elastic is to be run are an important feature in controlling fullness. Stitch the casing securely; be sure it is not too wide nor too tight. Finish ends of fabric before making a casing.

Plain Casing: The plain casing is used at the top of short cotton curtains and also to hold elastic at the bottom of a blouse, et cetera. Turn the edge of the curtain or blouse in a hem deep enough to let the curtain rod or elastic slip through easily. Finish the ends of the casing by turning the edge under and stitching it down. Finally, stitch down the hem of the casing.

Casing with Heading: A heading is a double ruffle above a casing and is used in curtains or garments. Turn a hem deep enough to include both casing and heading and stitch the edge. Next make a second row of stitching that will leave space for a curtain rod or elastic.

Multiple Casing: Plan carefully so you know how deep to make each casing and how much space you want between them. Either turn a wide hem and stitch on the markings, or turn the top edge into the first casing and apply a straight band across the fabric to make the others.

Applied Casing: When the casing does not come at the edge, cut a straight or curved band of fabric in the desired width, allowing for seams. Turn the edges under and stitch the band at both edges.

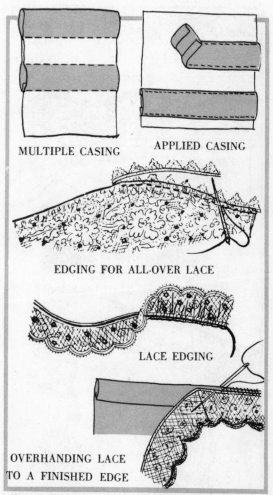

MULTIPLE CASING APPLIED CASING

EDGING FOR ALL-OVER LACE

LACE EDGING

OVERHANDING LACE TO A FINISHED EDGE

LACE EDGINGS AND INSERTS

Edging for Allover Lace: Allover lace, which is cut like a fabric, must be finished with a very narrow lace edge sold especially for this purpose and called a picot edging. Set the picot edging on the right side of the garment, covering the edge. Attach it with tiny running stitches. Turn to the wrong side and hand-roll the raw edge under the picot.

Allover lace can also be bound when you use a narrow insertion or ribbon beading. Crease the beading down the center and bind the edge of the lace, holding the binding in place with tiny running stitches.

When the edge of the lace is joined to chiffon, the seam can be picoted by machine. When the picoting is cut, the joining appears to be seamless.

When a ruffle of chiffon or lace is joined, make the joining as you would for any ruffle; turn the edge and hem it over the stitching, like a French seam. Never make a flat fell in transparent lace or fabric.

Lace Edging: Lace edgings can be wide or narrow; they can be joined to a fabric edge; they can be joined with a beading, (a narrow lace insertion sold by the yard); or they can be joined to a lace insertion. Applying lace should always be considered fine needlework and done by hand. The seams should not show when lace is applied. When the work is done by machine the garment is immediately stamped with the sign of cheap workmanship.

In many of the joinings described here, the lace edging may be applied either straight or gathered. To gather a lace edge, simply pull the thread at the straight edge of the lace until the desired fullness is reached.

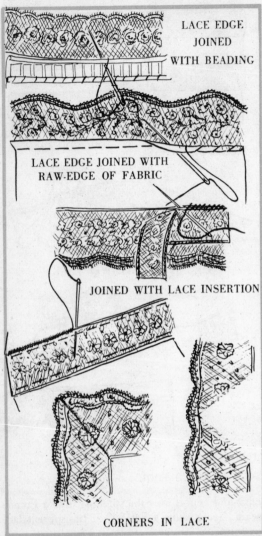

LACE EDGE JOINED WITH BEADING

LACE EDGE JOINED WITH RAW-EDGE OF FABRIC

JOINED WITH LACE INSERTION

CORNERS IN LACE

To Overhand Lace to a Finished Fabric Hem:

Hold the lace toward you and work on the wrong side, use a fine thread, and overcast loosely so that the lace will lie flat.

Lace Edge Joined with Beading:

Turn the edge of the fabric at the side of the beading in a tiny rolled hem and whip the hem, catching the lace in each stitch as you hem the beading.

Lace Edge Joined with Raw Edge of Fabric:

Baste the lace on the right side of the fabric close to the edge. Turn to the wrong side and roll the edge of the fabric, catching the lace with each stitch in the hem.

Lace Edge Joined with Lace Insertion:

With a fine thread overcast the edges together. Do not take too tight a stitch, for a looser stitch more widely spaced will allow the lace to lie flat.

Lace Insertion:

Baste the insertion, or the lace motif to be inserted, onto the right side of the fabric and work a satin stitch to cover the joining. If preferred, the lace can be joined to the fabric with a fine running stitch. Turn to the wrong side and cut away the fabric under the lace, leaving 1/4 inch for a hand-rolled hem. Catch the lace in each stitch of the hem.

Corners in Lace:

You can turn a flat mitered corner in a lace insertion or edging which has a prominent design. Center the design at the corner and cut away the excess material. With a fine thread overcast the lace edges together. The stitches must be so close together that they look like a fine cord.

Invisible Lace Joining:

When a joining is necessary in cutting a garment of allover lace, study the pattern, and whenever possible cut your edge following the pattern of the lace and place it so the pattern looks logical in the lace design. Overcast this edge with fine stitches in a thread that matches. In working with very fine lace it will help to baste the work on paper.

MACHINE EMBROIDERY EDGES AND INSERTS

Machine-embroidered trimmings fall into two groups: white embroidery on batiste, organdy, or lawn; and self-colored embroidery on chiffon, crepe, or velvet. Passementeries and prepared trimmings are part of this group, and are often a feature of current fashion. *Entre deux*, a joining banding, also belongs here.

Embroidered Insertions:

These are often used in vests, blouses, and summer dresses, and are often joined to a plain fabric of the same weave. This joining can be a fine French seam or a lace insert, or *entre deux* can be set into the seam.

Embroidered Edging:

Embroidered edging is used to finish the edge of an embroidered

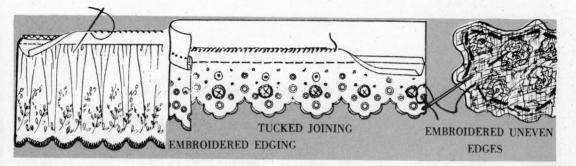

EMBROIDERED EDGING   TUCKED JOINING   EMBROIDERED UNEVEN EDGES

insert or allover embroidery. A narrow edging is generally used for this purpose.

Heavy narrow embroidered edgings are joined in a straight seam; sheer ones are gathered and joined to a straight fabric.

Wide embroidered edgings are usually gathered before joining to a straight fabric.

Tucked Joining: Turn the edge of the embroidery down, then turn it up. Baste this in place. Then turn in the edge of the fabric twice the size of the desired tuck. Place the stitching edge of the tuck over the edge of the embroidery and stitch as if it were a tuck. Place tucks above and below this joining to conceal it. The embroidered edge may be used as a facing. Turn in the raw edges of the fabric and the garment, and apply one over the other in a flat felled seam.

Passementeries and Prepared Trimmings: This type of trimming, sold by the yard or in motif effects, has finished edges. Some of this work is heavy and is hemmed to

fabric to enrich the design; other varieties are fine and sheer and are set into fabric.

Set-in Motifs: Place the design over the fabric and hem the edges with a close stitch. Cut the material away under the motif and overcast the edge.

Embroidered Uneven Edges: These are a feature of most passementeries. It is best to apply them by hand, placing them over the fabric and hemming the edge with fine hand stitches.

Allover Embroidery: Allover embroidery is cut like any fabric with a print that must be watched. The edges must be finished with a narrow embroidered edging, applied in a rolled hem. Only on inexpensive garments is this type fabric finished with cotton binding. Other inexpensive garments join an edging with stitched-down tailored seams or wide, coarse seams that show. It is just as easy to make a dainty finish, and it adds quality to your garment.

CHAPTER VIII

HEMS, FACINGS, BINDINGS

One of the most important techniques in sewing lies in the finishing of edges. It should be remembered that some finishes are purely functional, while others add to the appearance of the finished work. In home sewing, edges are generally straight; but in garments the edges which have to be finished are more likely to be curved or shaped. The first and most widely used finish for an edge is the hem; after that come facings and bindings.

SUCCESSFUL EDGES

It is important that all edges in a garment be considered in their relation to the completed article. There are two important classifications: inconspicuous edges, and decorative edges. Once the style of a finish is decided upon, examine the fabric grain. Be sure to apply straight fabric finishes to straight edges, and bias finishes to curves.

THE IMPORTANCE OF HEMS

Webster says the hem is "the edge of a garment doubled and sewn." Despite this simple definition, hems are far from monotonous; they can be of infinite variety. To make a hem, turn your material to the wrong side and fold over the raw edge about ¼ inch; turn over a second fold to the measure of the finished hem. Hem the fabric to the left side of the garment by hand or machine. A measuring gauge is essential to insure an even hem.

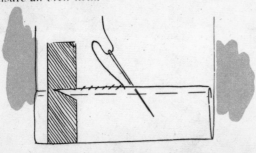

HAND HEM

HAND HEMS

Hand hems are a feature of fine apparel because they hang more gracefully and are less conspicuous than machine hems. The usual stitch used for hemming is called a felling stitch, and is made as follows:

Fasten the end of the material to something firm you can hold across your knees, or on a table (try pinning it to the skirt you are wearing). Sew your hem from right to left and work towards you, taking a tiny stitch in the garment and a tiny stitch in the folded edge of the hem. Train yourself to catch only a thread or two of fabric on the garment side. Some garments require fine, close stitches; but most hems are made with a quicker, slanting stitch.

Blind Hem: Blind hems are used when you wish a hem to be invisible on the right side of the material. Fine matching thread is important. Use a felling stitch. Space the stitches ⅜ inch apart and do not take up more than one thread of the garment fabric with each stitch. On the folded edge of the hem, take a stitch about ⅛ inch deep.

Slip-stitched Hem: This hem is used for facings and for hemming the linings in coats and dresses. It is invisible on both sides. With a thread exactly matching the fabric, take a stitch in the garment, picking up only one thread (in woolens this stitch does not pass entirely through—it only catches the top of the threads). Then pass the needle through the under side of the folded edge and slip it along inside the fold until you are ready to make the next stitch in the garment. The stitches should be about ¼ inch apart, and the thread should not be drawn too tight.

Underwear Hem: They are usually narrow and on luxurious underwear made by hand, even though the first turned edge of the hem is stitched by machine. To do this turn the edge ¼ inch and stitch it. Now measure a hem 1 or

1½ inches wide and hem it by hand. When the edge is short the width of the hem may be very narrow.

Shell Hem: This hem is used in making underwear. Baste a narrow hem (about ½ inch). With matching thread take three overcast stitches across the hem—pull tightly—then hem the edge for ½ inch and take overcasting stitches once more across the edge.

Hand-Rolled Hem: This important feature of fine needlework is adaptable to any soft or sheer fabric and can be used on both bias and straight edges. It is particularly recommended for all scarves and neckwear. Use a fine needle and thread. Roll the edge of the fabric between your first finger and your thumb (moistening the fingers will help). Hem this roll with fine, even felling stitches. To speed your work, pin the fabric and proceed as suggested for hand hemming.

Circular Hem: In hemming flared skirts, first baste the finished edge line of the skirt, then control the extra fullness at the edge. There are two ways of doing this: (1) You can turn the edge ½ inch and gather it, then turn the hem and lay it flat, hemming it flat to the garment. Or (2) gather the edge without turning it, and finish with a bias tape; then fold and secure it to the garment on the wrong side.

Hemming Curved Edges: The safe rule it to make a very narrow hem — ½ inch or less is often enough. Where the decorative effect calls for a larger hem make it the size that looks best and follow the directions for a circular hem. When the skirt edge is very full, circular stitched hems 1 inch wide are effective. Rolled hems are best for transparent fabrics.

Turned Picot Edge: This makes a lovely finish for straight or curved edges in transparent collars and cuffs. Have the edge hemstitched by machine, then cut the hemstitching in half with a sharp pointed scissors. Turn this edge once, as little as you possibly can, and hem it. When a selvage edge is to be hemmed, it can be turned the same way.

Hem in a Pleated Skirt: First rip the bastings that hold the pleats at the lower edge

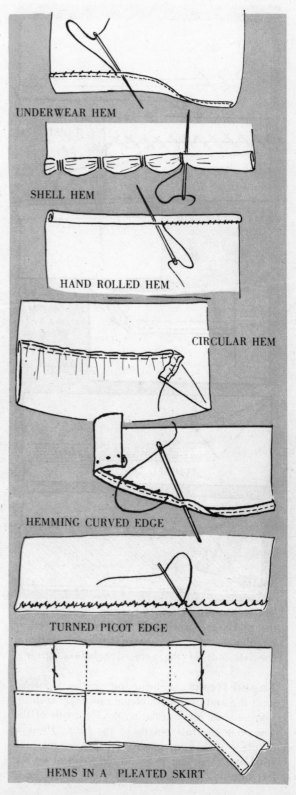

UNDERWEAR HEM

SHELL HEM

HAND ROLLED HEM

CIRCULAR HEM

HEMMING CURVED EDGE

TURNED PICOT EDGE

HEMS IN A PLEATED SKIRT

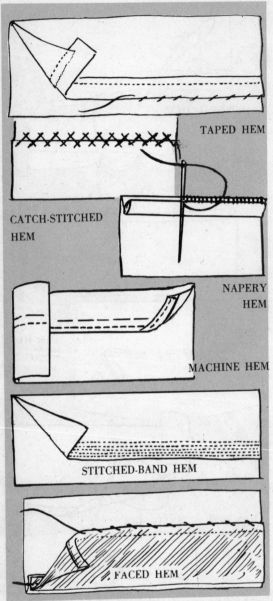

TAPED HEM

CATCH-STITCHED
HEM

NAPERY
HEM

MACHINE HEM

STITCHED-BAND HEM

FACED HEM

Catch-Stitched Hem: In coats and jackets (made of heavy fabric) that are lined, the hem is turned once and the raw edge of the fabric is catch-stitched to the garment. This edge is later covered by the lining.

Napery Hem: On damask linen, first turn the raw edge under about ⅛ inch, then fold the hem—about ¼ inch. Then fold the hem back on the right side of the material so you can hold the edges to be joined as you would for overcasting. Overcast the edge, taking tiny stitches close together across the edge of the work. The thread must be fine, and the stitches should run with the grain. The hem does not show on either side.

MACHINE HEMS

In sturdy cotton garments for men, women, and children, and in most sewing for the home, hems are usually stitched by machine. Prepare the hem as directed for hand hemming and baste it. Run the machine stitching as close to the edge as possible. If your machine is an old-type chain-stitch machine, the hem must be stitched on the right side of the garment.

Stitched-Band Hem: In tailored garments or in wide circular skirts made of opaque fabric, a narrow hem finished with five or six rows of machine stitching *evenly spaced* makes a very attractive finish. Omit the first turn and overcast the raw edges.

Hem for Ruffles: Hems that run into big yardage are finished with amazing speed if you use the adjustable hemmer on your machine. This attachment can be used for many types of narrow hems, especially long hems on straight edges.

Faced Hem: Garment edges which do not permit a hem without becoming too short should be faced. Cut the facing band the desired width of the hem and the necessary length. Stitch a seam holding the right side of the band to the right side of the garment. When you turn a faced hem to the left side, do not fold in the seam; instead, turn ½ inch or more of the garment fabric in the hem so that the facing will not show. Finish as for regular hem.

so the hem can be turned flat and finished before the pleats are pressed. If the skirt is curved or circular, lay the extra material in small darts on the left side of the hem edge before turning.

Taped Hem: In hemming heavier woolens, omit the first turning in of the raw edge. Instead, place a seam binding flat on the right side of the raw edge the full length of the hem. Hold it in place with fine running stitches or machine stitching; then hem it flat to the garment on the left side.

DECORATIVE HEMS

Right-Side-Out Hem: Sometimes decorative hems are made by turning the hem up on the right side of the garment (the seams must, of course, be reversed in the hem section). These hems are often bound in contrasting color or finished with piping or corded. Sometimes they are shaped into scallops, points, or squared outlines. They should be used only in reversible fabrics, such as crepe-backed satin, or in fabrics which are the same on both sides. They are not successful when the fabric is ugly on the wrong side or when the garment is so curved that the fullness must be gathered or laid in darts.

Applied Hem or Double Bindings: These hems are an important decorative feature of bedspreads and curtains; they are also used in peasant-type dresses and sometimes in sport clothes. Girls' dresses of organdy can employ decorative hems, and sometimes they are used on play clothes of chambray, percale, and sturdy cotton. This decorative hem is always *in a contrasting color*. It is cut on a true bias, which is then folded in half. Apply it to the edge of the skirt or bedspread by placing one edge of the binding on the right side of the fabric edge and stitching a seam that leaves one edge of the binding free. Turn to the wrong side of the garment and hem the free edge of the binding on the seam edge.

Stitched Applied Hem Extension: A hem extension may be added to lengthen a woolen garment, especially if the skirt is not too wide. Cut the binding so that it can be applied double as directed above; or cut it in the size of the finished binding and line it with a thinner fabric *also cut on the bias*. Apply it as directed above, then cover it with rows of machine stitching.

FACINGS AND THEIR USE

Facings can be used at the neckline, skirt hem, sleeve edge; at the front of a coat or jacket or open blouse—wherever the edge is too short to turn a hem. They are used in curtains and other home decorations as well as in garments. Stitch the seams by hand or machine, or a combina-

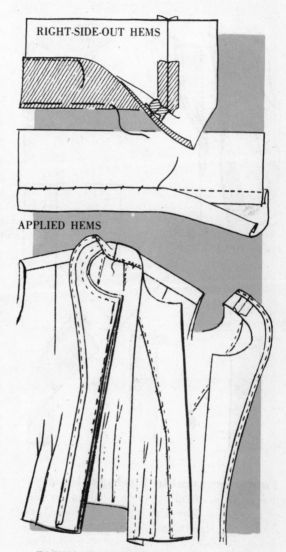

RIGHT-SIDE-OUT HEMS

APPLIED HEMS

FACING ON A COAT CUT SEPARATELY

tion of the two, placing machine stitching where it will not show.

Facings cut in one with garments are turned back; those cut like garment edges are seamed. Facing bands cut without a pattern can be wide or narrow, they can turn back an edge, or extend beyond an edge. Before cutting a facing, decide upon the width, length, and fabric grain you want. Facings should always match the grain of the fabric to be finished; if the edge is straight, the facing should be cut on the straight of the goods, and if the edge is curved, the facing should be either a true bias or an exact duplication of the curve of the edge.

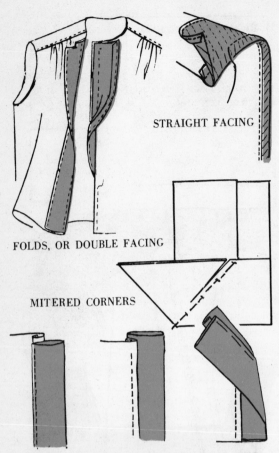

STRAIGHT FACING

FOLDS, OR DOUBLE FACING

MITERED CORNERS

FOLD, OR STRAIGHT EXTENSION FACING

Folds, or Double Facings:

Double facings serve to extend an edge, fill in a neckline, or lengthen a skirt with an added band. Apply the fold under a turned edge, stitching them together; or under a finished edge so the fold can be basted to the garment ½ inch back from the edge; or turn the edges of the fold so they are finished and can be stitched on top of the garment edge.

STRAIGHT FACINGS AND TRIMMING BANDS

Straight Facing: Straight facings are used to turn an edge smoothly when it is not possible to spare fabric for a hem. They can be turned as facings on the wrong side or as trimming bands on the right side. When the facing is to be turned on the wrong side, apply your straight strip of fabric *on the right side of the garment.* Join the edges of the garment and the band in a seam. Then turn the band to the wrong side of the garment, taking care that the seamed edge is basted and the fabric lies flat and smooth. Turn the edge of the band and hem it to the garment or stitch it in place.

To finish a trimming band on the right side of the garment, reverse the instructions given above and stitch the facing band to the wrong side of the garment first.

End Finish for Band Facing: When the end of the band is not included in a seam, it can be finished in any of the following ways: (1) Turn in the end and hem it to the garment; this stitching will show on the right side. (2) Roll the end in a self-hem; this stitching will not show on the right side. (3) When facing and garment edges meet, turn both edges so they face each other and slip-stitch them together. (4) When a band finishes with the edge of the garment and is included in a seam or collar joining, baste the three edges together before stitching the seam.

Applied Trimming Band: When trimming bands are narrow, it saves time to cut a cardboard the width of the band without seam allowance, then put this cardboard over the fabric and press the seam allowance over the cardboard so it makes a sharp, clear edge. Apply the band to the garment and baste the edges for stitching.

Band with Pointed End: When the end of a trimming band is pointed or curved, the cardboard used for pressing the sharp edge can be shaped and the end pressed sharply. Cut away all extra material from this end except the seam allowance before you apply it. When a band is stitched to a garment so the shaped end hangs free, allow a double thickness at the end of the band or else face the point or curve.

When a band, belt, or scarf ends in a point, stitch across the band in a pointed line before turning and cut away the extra material, snipping the corner.

Mitered Corner: When a straight band turns a square corner, fit the edges of the band to the fabric so the corner is square and even. Lay the excess fullness at the corner in a fold and stitch it so the line of stitching extends straight across the corner. Cut away this excess fabric and press the seam open. Turn the band so it lies flat on the fabric, and so the corner is sharp, square, and smooth.

When a band is applied to a deep point, the edges are stitched in an even seam. Lay the fabric flat and pin the mitered corner so the line of pins extends straight through the corner. Cut away the extra material and seam the corner. Snip the seam allowance at the point and turn the band to the right side. This will make the band lie-flat.

Banding a Square Neck:

The band can be turned to the right side or applied as a facing. A straight band is stitched to the neckline with edges of band and garment meeting. Place it carefully so the outside edge lies flat and the excess fullness at the mitered corners is pinned for cutting. Before cutting it away, stitch across this excess material from corner to corner. Cut away the extra material. Press the short seam and turn the outer edge of the binding, then cut into the corner beside this new mitered seam, cutting through the seam allowance. Turn the band and lay it flat, first basting the inside edge.

Fold or Straight Extension Facing:

Cut your fabric twice the width of the facing and the desired length, with seam allowance. Fold it and baste the folded edge. To attach it, place the facing on the right side of the garment and seam the lower edge to the garment edge. Then turn the facing to the wrong side of the garment and hem the other edge on the seam.

Extension facings are often used in waists and plackets to hold buttons or snap fasteners. Make them as directed above, or, for greater strength, cut the facing three times as wide as the finished band. This gives three thicknesses of fabric to hold buttons.

Facing Scallops:

Outline the scallops on the article to be finished, using a cup or other object of desired size. This marking should be done in pencil on the wrong side of the fabric. Cut a bias facing 2 inches wider than the depth of the scallop and the length desired. Lay it right side up on the table and lay the scalloped edge over it with the right side down. Baste the fabric to the facing, following the outline of the scallops, then stitch on this edge. Now cut away excess fabric from the edge, following the scallops,

leaving a 1/4-inch seam. Snip this seam allowance occasionally before you turn the facing over. The edge of the scallops should be carefully basted and pressed. Then the edge of the facing can be hemmed above the scallops—or if preferred the facing can be cut wide enough to extend to the seam above the scallops.

Shaped Facings:

Shaped facings are cut to duplicate exactly the edge of the garment, or are cut in one with the garment and folded back to simulate a facing. Follow pattern instructions for this type of facing.

BIAS FACINGS

A bias facing must always be cut on the true bias. A true bias is the diagonal of a square. If you fold the straight grain of the material parallel to the cross grain, the folded edge is the true bias. Cut across this edge, using a measure. Even though cutting on "a near bias" would save material, it must never be done, because the facing would not lie smoothly.

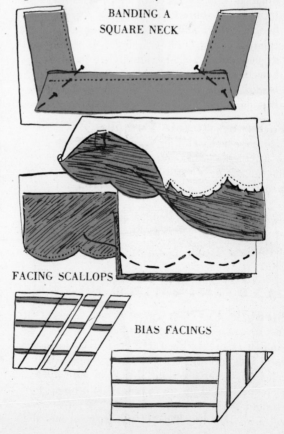

BANDING A SQUARE NECK

FACING SCALLOPS

BIAS FACINGS

Piecing Bias Facing: The ends of the bias facing must be joined with matching grain. The seam is usually diagonal.

Applying Bias Facing: Place the facing on the right side of the garment and join the edges of facing and garment. Stitch the seam, cut away surplus, and turn the facing to the wrong side, taking care that the edge is smooth and even. Smooth the facing flat on the material and hem it to the garment, turning in the edge ½ inch.

Facing Rounded Corners: A bias facing makes a smoother rounded corner than hemming. First shape the corner, then place the facing on the edge and around the corner, stretching it a little at the curved edge. Pin or baste carefully before sewing. It should be flat and smooth.

BINDING EDGES

There is a great difference between prepared bias bindings sold by the yard and the fabric bindings you cut yourself. There is also a great choice between sheer straight seam bindings and the colorful cotton binding or braid or ribbon sold by the yard. Whether bindings are purchased or homemade, always bear in mind that *straight bindings* must be applied only to *straight edges*. Bias bindings are necessary for curved edges.

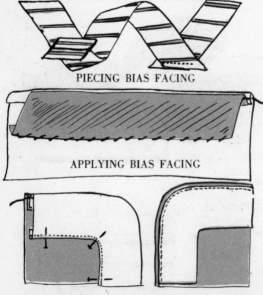

PIECING BIAS FACING

APPLYING BIAS FACING

FACING ROUND CORNERS

Note that binding covers both sides of an edge, as contrasted with facing, which can be seen only on one side.

Applying Straight Binding: Cut a narrow strip of material on the straight or use a purchased binding. To apply it, fold the binding in half the long way and press. Slip the edge of the fabric to be bound between the two halves of the pressed binding and stitch as close to the edge of the binding as possible. This is the simplest way to apply a binding and popular with most home sewers, but it is likely to pull out with frequent washings.

To make the binding more secure, stitch the edge to be bound by machine.

To make a binding secure to withstand constant washing, use the following method: Place the binding on the wrong side of the material, matching the edge to the edge of the fabric. Stitch these edges together ¼ inch back. Then turn the binding to the right side and hem it flat. It can be hemmed on the seam edge to make a true binding, or it can be pulled up as far as possible on the fabric and hemmed there to make a wider trimming. Bias bindings with folded edges, sold by the yard, are applied the same way.

Binding a Square Corner: In the first stitching continue the binding around the corner as you make your seam. Trim the seam close to the stitching at the corner. When you turn the edge and baste it, make the binding form a tiny inverted pleat at the corner so that the edge lies flat and square. This is called a mitered corner.

Braid Binding: There are several widths of flat trimming braid which can be used for binding. The wider widths are creased through the center and basted to the edge so that the binding is deep enough to hold firm when stitched. Narrower braids are applied to simulate binding, as follows: Stitch the braid at the edge and on the wrong side of the fabric, then turn the edge to the right side and hem the braid down.

Bias Binding: On household cottons, aprons, house dresses, children's dresses, and so forth, use a folded bias binding purchased at the store or cut your own. Turn both edges and fold the binding through the center. Apply it to curved edges

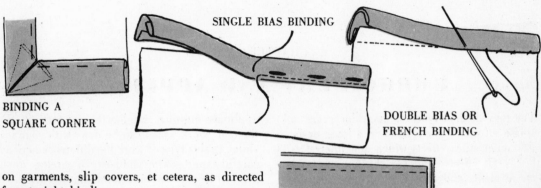

BINDING A
SQUARE CORNER

SINGLE BIAS BINDING

DOUBLE BIAS OR
FRENCH BINDING

BINDING STITCH
IN A SEAM

on garments, slip covers, et cetera, as directed for straight binding.

Single Bias Binding: Rayon crepe dresses or underwear can be bound with self-fabric or contrasting fabric, often from scraps left after cutting the garment. Be sure the binding is a true bias, not a near bias. If you are careful to match the grain, the binding can be pieced any number of times. To apply it, lay it on the right side of the garment with edges matching and stitch by hand or machine. Turn it carefully; first turn the seam of the binding then turn the binding in half and turn the edge under. This is not difficult if you work on an ironing board and turn the edges with the point of an iron. Hand-hem the binding to the seam so that no stitching shows on the right side.

Double Bias or French Binding: This makes a good finish for transparent fabrics, sheer underwear, fine cottons. Cut a true bias ¾ inch wide and the length desired. Fold the bias in half

lengthwise and baste or press the folded edges. Place the binding on the right side of the garment with the unfinished edges paralleling the edge of the garment. Join the edges in a narrow seam run by hand or stitched on the machine, then turn the folded edge of the binding to the wrong side and hem it by hand to the stitched seam. *No stitches should show on the right side.*

Binding Stitched with a Seam: Pin or baste the seam and place the straight or bias binding over the seam, stitching so that the edges of the fabric and one edge of the binding are caught in the seam. Fold the opposite edge of the binding and turn back so that it lies flat on the garment. Hem it down by hand or machine.

CHAPTER IX

EMBROIDERY AND APPLIQUÉ

The four distinct types of embroidery are : (1) splash effects in one spot or in allover designs; (2) quick-stitch effects which add interest; (3) homecraft effects; and (4) the fine embroidery on garments and household linens which gives them an expensive look.

There is a wide choice of embroidery thread, each suitable for a specific type of needlework. Be sure you use the kind of thread suitable to the fabric which you have chosen.

Embroidery in Splash Effects: Many whims in fashion cycles are expressed in great splashes of embroidery which follow the style of the moment. The design can be stamped on the fabric with a transfer pattern that comes off when ironed; it can be drawn with chalk on the garment as the professionals do it; or it can be traced upon tissue paper which is placed over the fabric, then torn away when the embroidery is done.

Running stitch, outline stitch, or chain stitch are used in single or double rows, sometimes combined with satin stitch or appliqué. Current fashion often introduces allover effects in braiding, couching, or quilting, which should be used instead of more old-fashioned routines. Appliqué on a dressy afternoon dress is made of a luxury fabric, and can be sewn down with a metallic or silk thread in a buttonhole stitch which will emphasize the luxury effect. Couching is often held down with metallic thread and thus enriched. It is not so much the stitch as the way you use it which produces a high style trimming effect.

Embroidery in Quick Stitch: On children's clothes, house dresses, peasant-type dresses, and so forth, quick-stitch embroidery is worked in lazy-daisy stitch, outline stitch, and chain stitch. The designs are floral or peasant motifs and the colors gay and bright. When the garment is washable, be sure the embroidery thread is also.

Embroidery in Homecraft: This class of embroidery includes cross stitch, smocking,

appliqué, quilting, candlewicking, tufting, and the craft work which can be done with your machine. In this type of work the difference between careful expert sewing and hasty or careless stitching will be very obvious in the finished article.

Embroidery in Fine Stitches: This last class is further divided into three types: (1) The hand hemstitching, pin tucking, and rolled edge which mark de-luxe neckwear and underwear. It will well repay anyone who spends a few hours putting this fine work into a linen jabot, a collar, and so on. (2) Fine beading and metal embroideries used on luxury garments. (3) The lace inserts, hand-rolled hems, and hand-embroidered monograms which mark fine underwear, blouses, and household linen.

Without going to the extreme of spending many valuable hours on embroidery as was done in former times, we can still keep it up as a graceful art and use it in those places where nothing else will give the same effect. Have in mind the time it will take in relation to the time you can afford to give when you plan a piece of work.

EMBROIDERY STITCHES

For good effects, use heavy embroidery threads.

Outline or Stem Stitch: Knot your thread and bring it through to the right side at one end of the line to be embroidered. Take a stitch ¼ inch away, point the needle back a little way before drawing it through to the right side of the fabric again. Make another stitch the same way, and so on to the end of the line.

Chain Stitch: Bring the needle up through the fabric and hold the thread down with your thumb. Pass the needle back through the fabric at almost the same point and bring it out ⅛ inch forward, or as desired (this regulates the length of the stitch) passing it over the thumb. As you pull the thread, it will form a loop. Put the needle back in the fabric inside of the loop close to the last stitch and bring it forward on the embroidery line so that it passes over the thread and forms another loop.

Running Stitch: With a heavy embroidery thread, run the needle in and out, following the line to be embroidered. The stitches should be ⅛ inch long (or more, depending on weight of the fabric) on the top of the fabric and very short on the underside. The stitch is also known as saddle stitching.

Braiding: Use soutache or rattail braid, or any of the nubbed novelty braids. These can be attached by hand or machine. If you plan to use hand sewing put a row of running stitches through the center of the soutache braid. The thread must match so the stitches do not show. Be sure that the fabric doesn't pucker and spoil your trimming. Hemming one side of the soutache braid to the fabric and letting the other stand up will give a raised effect, if preferred.

Couching: The word couching is used to describe a fine cord in braided effects. The cord may be matching or contrasting in color, and it is simply overcast to the material with evenly spaced stitches. Many interesting effects can be made by using a heavy contrasting color thread for the stitches that hold down the cord. These stitches must, of course, be very carefully spaced, for they are part of the decoration.

Satin Stitch: In fine embroidery, satin stitch is first padded, then the padding is covered with close, even, overcast stitches, outlining the pattern. In the finished work, if you are using a fine floss thread, the stitches are all blended together into a raised satin surface. This stitch used without padding and done in corded silk or cotton makes a very effective combination for embroidery in splash effects.

Lazy-Daisy Stitch: To form a little flower, use a contrasting corded embroidery thread. Stamp the design or draw a line for the embroidery and put a dot at the points where you want a flower. The flowers can be ½ inch in diameter or larger if desired. Be sure to allow enough space. Bring the thread through at the center of the dot. Hold the thread with your left thumb,

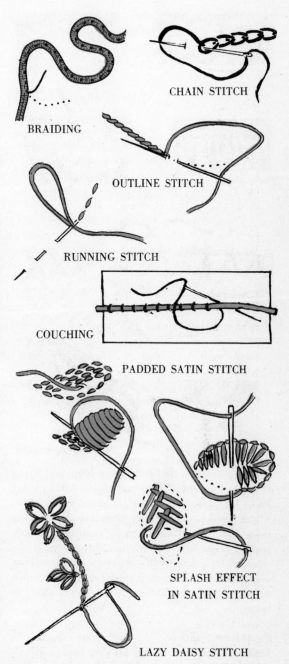

CHAIN STITCH

BRAIDING

OUTLINE STITCH

RUNNING STITCH

COUCHING

PADDED SATIN STITCH

SPLASH EFFECT
IN SATIN STITCH

LAZY DAISY STITCH

then pass the needle back through the fabric at the center, bringing it out on the circumference of an imaginary circle denoting the outer edge of the petals (this makes a ¼-inch stitch). When drawing the needle out, pass it over your left thumb and put the thread under it so it forms a loop when drawn out. To hold the loop in place, pass the needle back close to the last stitch, mak-

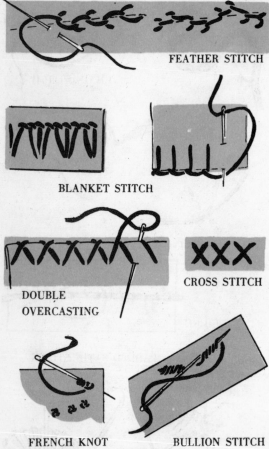

FEATHER STITCH

BLANKET STITCH

DOUBLE OVERCASTING

CROSS STITCH

FRENCH KNOT   BULLION STITCH

stitch on the opposite side of the thread, bringing the needle out at the line. Continue to work first on one side, then on the other until your line is complete. In fine infants' wear, beautifully double and treble feather stitching is a feature of quilts, sacques, petticoats, and everyday dresses.

Blanket Stitch: This important embroidery stitch is used on blankets and infants' clothing and as a quick trimming on house dresses, children's clothes, et cetera. It is also used in neckwear and collars when an extra color is needed. To do this, bind the edge with one color; then work a row of blanket stitch in a contrasting shade and the second row in another color. To make blanket stitch, use a corded embroidery thread and bring it out at one end of the work. Take a stitch ¼ or ½ inch above the edge and bring the needle out at the edge, passing it over the thread. Spread the stitches about ¼ inch apart.

Cross Stitch: This versatile stitch can be developed as a simple background to throw a design into relief. Trace any simple pattern by outlining carefully. Fill the space between the lines with cross stitch. Other uses are for decorative edging, for corner motif, or for banding in simple or classic designs in complex coloring. First stamp a design on the right side of the piece you are going to embroider. Then start stitching with a needle and thread. Make an overhand stitch the length of one side of the stitch to be crossed. Now cross it by making another stitch in the opposite direction, the same length. It is faster to make all the first stitches on one line and then fill out the crosses on the return.

Double Overcasting: With a heavy corded embroidery thread, overcast the turned edge with even, slanting stitches ¼ inch deep. Finish edge, turn fabric, and work a second row, matching the stitches at each end. The wrong side of this edge produces a cross stitch, which you may prefer.

French Knots: Use a tightly twisted thread. Bring the needle up through the fabric and wrap the thread around the needle several times before you pull it back through, at almost the same

ing sure to catch the end of the loop and bring it out in the center. This makes one petal or one leaf. Continue making petals around the circle. These circles are usually finished by joining them with an outline stitch to represent a stem, and an occasional leaf may be introduced if desired. A leaf is generally represented by making one petal if the flower is small and three loops arranged pyramid fashion if the flower motif is large.

Feather Stitch: Outline your design in straight lines, circles, or scrolls, using tailor's chalk. Thread the needle with an embroidery twist and bring it up at one end of the marked line. Hold the thread parallel to the line and take a stitch out from the line about ⅛ inch, bringing the needle out at the line—the needle must pass over the thread. When you pull it through, it will hold the thread as you draw the needle parallel with the line. Take another point in the fabric. Bring the needle out again ⅛ inch away to start the next knot.

Bullion Stitch: The bullion stitch, like the French knot, is made by twisting the thread several times around the needle. When you put the needle back into the fabric, put it farther away so that the twisted threads lie flat instead of making a knot.

Seed Stitch: Thread a needle with twisted thread, either fine or coarse, and fill the space between the outline with tiny running stitches. This stitch is used to finish the centers of flowers when the edge is worked in buttonholing.

Beading: Use a fine thread which matches the fabric. To apply the beads use one of the following methods: (1) Pick up a bead on your needle and pass the needle back into the fabric close to the thread protruding from it. This is fine work and takes a great deal of time. (2) A shorter way is to string the beads on a fine thread which exactly matches the fabric and couch (see index) the string to the fabric with little stitches taken between beads or between groups of two beads or more. (3) Professionals crochet beads in allover designs. For this work the fabric is stretched on a frame, and the worker faces the wrong side of the fabric, so the design must be traced or stamped on the wrong side. The beads are strung on fine thread matching the fabric. With a fine beading needle (crochet hook), draw the thread through to the wrong side. Slip a bead close and draw the thread through again. On the wrong side you form a chain stitch of thread which holds the beads securely.

Eyelets: Use an embroidery puncher and hold your work in an embroidery frame. Punch a hole the size desired. With fine stitches outline the hole, then use a buttonhole stitch or overcast so that the threads are close together. Long eyelets are made the same way except that a slit is cut.

Scallops: In fine embroidery worked with floss, scallops are first padded. In decorative scallops worked with a twisted embroidery thread, they are not padded. Scallops can be worked in buttonhole stitch when the edge is cut; when the scallop is bound or placed above the edge, work it in blanket stitch.

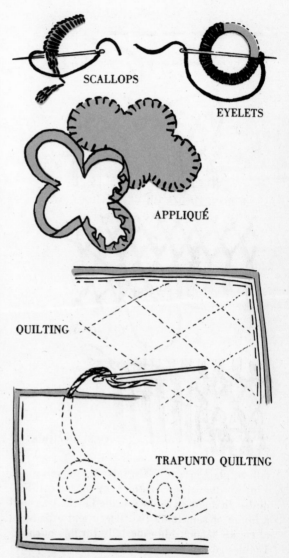

SCALLOPS

EYELETS

APPLIQUÉ

QUILTING

TRAPUNTO QUILTING

Appliqué: Your motif can be a flower, a band, a circle, or part of a large design. Cut the piece of contrasting fabric in the shape of your design, with seam allowance, then cut a piece of cardboard the same shape without seam allowance. Press the edges of the fabric over the cardboard to insure a clean sharp edge. Lay this piece on the material to be appliquéd and join it with a fine hemming stitch or with blanket stitch.

Quilting: In quilting, three surfaces of fabrics are joined with tiny running stitches. Use a very fine needle and a fine sewing thread which matches the color of the fabric. Any fabric can be quilted, but the stitch is particularly good on

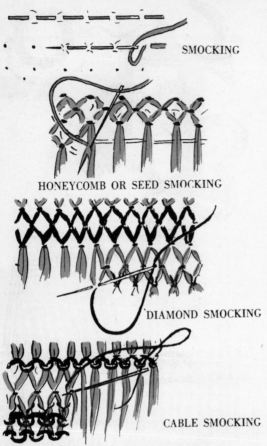

SMOCKING

HONEYCOMB OR SEED SMOCKING

DIAMOND SMOCKING

CABLE SMOCKING

taffeta, plain crepes, plain velvets, and velveteens —or in the classic cottons of historical bed-quilts. In addition to the outside fabric, you need a lining of something like sateen and a padding of cotton flannel sold especially for this purpose. The design can be conventional lines or squares drawn with chalk and a ruler. When a more complex design is used, stamp it on the lining fabric. In quilting large pieces, you will need a quilting frame; for small pieces no frame need be used, but the pieces must be basted around the edges.

Trapunto (Italian) Quilting:
This type of quilting features double lines with a raised design between. No interlining is necessary but the material must be lined. Outline the design in a double line about ¼ inch apart on the right side of the material. Run the outline stitches in matching thread through both the material and lining.

To raise the design thread a needle with a double thread of heavy knitting yarn which is then run between the outside and the lining, following the design. This is done by inserting the needle through the lining and running it as far as you can in the design until stopped by a curve or corner. Then bring the needle out through the lining, making a hole to do so, re-insert, and finish the design. At the end of the design bring the yarn out on the wrong side; turn it back on the outline; overcast it before cutting the yarn thread.

Smocking:
For simple smocking stitches, get an embroidery transfer pattern that stamps on your fabric, and carry out the smocking design planned for this space. For more complex or decorative smocking, professionals first gather the material with row after row of even basting and work the smocking across the bastings, taking care that the lines are even. The smocking stitches include cable stitch done single or double, honeycomb stitch, and diamond stitch.

Honeycomb or Seed Smocking:
Bring the needle through the first dot, or gathered fold, take a stitch through the second dot or fold, and draw the thread together. Take a second stitch across both previous stitches to secure the fullness and emphasize the color of the smocking. Pass the needle under the fabric to the next dot on the line below and draw two dots together just as you did above. Alternate back and forth between the two rows to the end of your marking. Always pass the thread on the wrong side. Then do another two rows the same way.

Diamond Smocking:
This smocking is worked like honeycomb except that the thread is passed on the outside instead of the inside of the fabric. To complete the diamond effect, you work the next row of dots and pass the needle again through the last row of work.

Cable Smocking:
This is an outline stitch worked on one row of dots and can be developed in three ways: (1) Bring the needle up at the first dot and take a little stitch at the next dot with the thread above the needle. Continue in this way all along the row. *The thread is always above the needle, and the line of stitches is straight and even.* To vary this stitch, (2) take the stitches the same way, but in the first stitch pass the thread above the needle, in the next

stitch pass it below the needle, next above it, and so on, alternating all the way across. (3) Double cable stitch is worked on another row of dots placed very close, and the stitches are worked by alternating the thread and placed so they meet the threads of the last row.

Fagoting: This can be worked by hand in bar effect or in a crisscross design. Fagoting can be done by machine, and fine ribbon can be used for it. Fagoting fills the space between two finished edges, and professionals baste their work right side down on heavy wrapping paper. The space between the finished edges can be ¼ or ½ inch, or finer if desired.

Bar Fagoting: Use twisted embroidery thread or buttonhole twist. Take a stitch on one side and secure the thread; then take a stitch directly across the space, catching the opposite edge, and bring your needle back, catching the first edge. This forms the cross thread or foundation bar. Cover it with over-and-over stitches, and make the next fagoting stitch about ⅛ of an inch away.

French Fagoting: This is done like bar fagoting, except that the thread is twisted around the needle several times—enough times to extend across the bar.

Crisscross Fagoting: Use a heavier thread and take a buttonhole stitch in one edge of the fabric; on the opposite edge take another buttonhole stitch, spacing it so the thread slants across the space to be filled. Be sure your buttonhole stitch holds the thread securely so it will not pull in wear.

Ribbon Fagoting: Baste the finished edges to a piece of paper with the wrong side of the fabric up. Pin the ribbon, which should be very narrow, on each edge, crossing it from side to side. Now make a row of stitching through the fabric, catching the folded edges of the ribbon as you stitch.

Machine Fagoting: Purchase machine-made fagoting which is sold by the yard like braid. Baste this fagoting strip to paper and baste the fabric edges over it so that the turned edges of the fabric are face down and the edge covers the

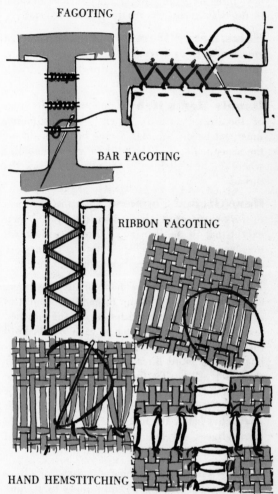

FAGOTING

BAR FAGOTING

RIBBON FAGOTING

HAND HEMSTITCHING

side thread of the fagoted braid. Now stitch close to the fabric edge, catching the braid underneath.

Hand Hemstitching: Hand hemstitching is most successful on linen, basket weave, cotton, or any loosely woven fabric where threads pull easily. Hemstitching can be placed across a fabric or at the top of a hem. First draw the threads in the desired width across the length of the article to be hemstitched. With fine matching sewing thread fasten the end securely and pass the needle behind three or four or more bars of the fabric thread as desired. The sewing thread should pass under the point of the needle. Pull the sewing thread tight so that the bars of the fabric are drawn together. Now take a tiny stitch in the edge of the fabric and pass the needle behind the next three or more bars of the fabric. Continue in this way across the length of the material.

Hemstitched Hems: Hold the hem toward you and work as directed above, except that the little stitch in the fabric between the drawn threads is caught in the hem.

Double Hemstitch: Hemstitch both sides of the drawn threads. When the hemstitching must end before an edge decide on the width of the hemstitching and slash the fabric at the point where the hemstitching is to end. Now draw the threads.

Hemstitched Corners: There are two ways to work corners: (1) Hemstitch in the usual way, except that in the hem more threads are drawn together. (2) In luncheon cloths, collars, et cetera, the corner of the hem can be mitered.

Tassels: Tassels can be made in any size, using embroidery cotton, knitting threads, or wool. Cut a piece of cardboard the length of the finished tassel and cut a small notch at each end to hold the threads. Wind the thread around the cardboard. The more thread you wind, the thicker the tassel will be. Tie the threads securely at one end and cut the opposite end. Now wind another thread around the tassel at a distance of about 1½ inches below the tied end. Decorative tassels for negligees, et cetera, are tied much lower and the top is covered with a crocheted hood.

Pom Poms: Pom poms for hats or dress decoration can be made of embroidery twist, novelty knitting thread, or yarn. They can be large or small. Cut two circles of cardboard the desired size, cut a hole in the center of each, and hold them together. Thread a needle with a long thread and pass it through the holes and around the cardboard until it forms a thick layer around the entire circumference of the circles. The thicker the layer, the fluffier the pom pom. Pass the point of a scissors between the cardboards and cut only the threads around the circumference. Remove the cardboards, holding the threads firmly at their center and tie a thread at that point in a secure fastening. Clip the edges of the thread.

Fringe: Fringe can be bought by the yard, or the edge of a fabric can be raveled. First decide upon the width of the fringe and remove the cross threads to the desired depth. Cover the top of the fringe with a tiny braiding or overcast the fabric above the fringe with a decorative stitch. This will prevent the fabric from raveling. The fringe should then be combed to make it hang straight.

When the fringed ends of a belt are used as a tie they must be knotted where they join the belt.

Knotted Fringe: Fringe can be made from a cord such as twisted embroidery thread or from knitting yarn. Cut the thread twice as long as the desired finished fringe and thread in a long-eyed needle. Pass the needle through the fabric edge and stitch once through this edge to hold the threads. Now tie the threads, using a knot against the fabric, and clip the ends evenly. Repeat this for each thread of the fringe. If you wish cut the threads 1 inch longer than the desired length and knot them twice. You can use two or more threads together to make a heavier fringe.

Rickrack Braid: Rickrack can be used as an edging, or it can be stitched inside of a finished edge as a banding. Turn the edge to the right side and place the braid over the turn so that one edge extends beyond the fabric. Stitch it through the center of the braid. (This should be the edge of the fabric.)

POM-POM

KNOTTED FRINGE

RICKRACK BRAID

FRINGE

CHAPTER X

TIME-SAVING MEASUREMENT ROUTINES

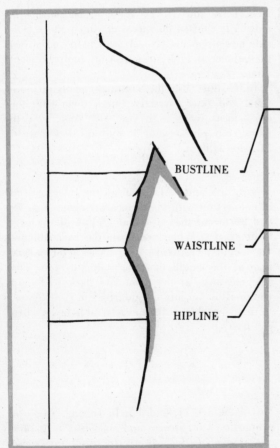

BUSTLINE

WAISTLINE

HIPLINE

Before you buy a pattern, take the measurements of your figure at the bustline, waistline, and hips. To take these measurements accurately, stand straight, with your heels together and your weight on both feet, and measure as follows:

1. Bustline: Pass the tape measure around the figure at the fullest part of the bust and close under the arms. Hold the tape snugly, neither too tight nor too loose. Keep the tape straight across the back; or, if you want to be sure of plenty of ease in the fit of the pattern, slope it up almost an inch in the center back.

2. Waistline: Pass the tape measure around the waistline.

3. Hips: Pass the tape measure around the hips at the fullest part, 6 inches or so below the waist.

When you have taken these measurements, compare them with the measurements printed on the envelope of the pattern, and buy the pattern which most nearly corresponds to your measurements. This pattern size has no relation to the size you buy in ready-made dresses.

Buy dress, waistcoat, and blouse patterns by the bust measure, because the sleeve, armhole, and shoulder are the trickiest parts of any garment to shape or alter. Patterns for separate skirts, shorts, or slacks are bought by the waist measure.

Children's patterns are sold by age groups. Compare the child's measurements with those listed on the pattern envelope and buy a pattern for the age group nearest that size.

To be truly modern you can go a long step forward and learn to cut, baste, and finish a dress to your exact measurements, so that you need waste no time in ripping, fitting, and fussing with alterations. To do this as professionals do it, you must use the long list of professional measurements shown on the following pages.

A MODERN STREAMLINE ROUTINE

To cut baste and finish a garment to your exact measurements it is easier to take measurements from a dress than from your own person. Select a simple dress that fits well. Lay the dress on a smooth surface and study the diagram and chart. The diagram represents the dress—the numbers, the location of the measurements—the arrows are the extremes of each measurement. As you take these measurements, write them on a card and keep it safely. You will find that they save you time. The right hand column of the chart tells you exactly how to use each measurement.

MEASUREMENT CHART

How to Use

How to Take Them

Length Measurements

1. Center front, from neck to waistline
   Center back, from neck to waistline
2. Right side front, from shoulder seam to waistline
   Right side back, from shoulder seam to waistline
   Left side front, from shoulder seam to waistline
   Left side back, from shoulder seam to waistline
3. Center front, from waistline to hipline
   Center back, from waistline to hipline

Nos. 1, 2, and 3: Use these measurements in cutting to shorten the pieces of your pattern. The side measurements (No. 2) will help you adjust the balance if both sides of your figure are not alike.

In basting, use these measurements to join waist and skirt correctly. Check them with the cross measurements so you will know how to mark your placket and how to adjust the waist fullness without a fitting.

4. Center front, from waistline to hem
   Center back, from waistline to hem
5. Right side front, from waistline to hem
   Right side back, from waistline to hem
   Left side front, from waistline to hem
   Left side back, from waistline to hem
6. Underarm, right side, from armhole to waist
   Underarm, left side, from armhole to waist
7. Side seam, right side, from waistline to hem
   Side seam, left side, from waistline to hem

Nos. 4, 5, 6, and 7: These measurements are used in connection with width measurements Nos. 19 and 20 to cut the waist and hipline of the garment exactly. When you baste the garment, use the length measurements to baste a temporary hem at the length most becoming to you. The side measures at the front and back will help you to allow for any irregularities in your figure, so that your skirt will be exactly in balance when you baste it.

Sleeve Measurements

8. Right side shoulder seam to elbow
   Left side shoulder seam to elbow
9. Right side elbow to wrist
   Left side elbow to wrist
10. Underarm seam, right side, armhole to bent elbow·
    Underarm seam, left side, armhole to bent elbow
11. Underarm seam, right side, bend of elbow to wrist
    Underarm seam, left side, bend of elbow to wrist
12. Wrist

Nos. 8, 9, 10, 11, and 12: In cutting, you can proportion your sleeves and make any necessary alterations in the pattern by applying these measurements. The small chart (13) on page 80 shows these measurements actually applied to a sleeve pattern.

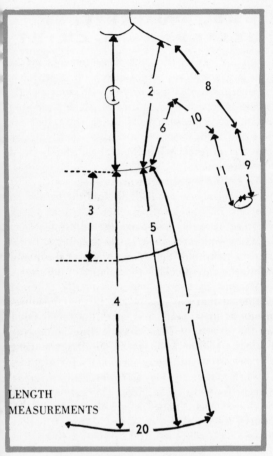

LENGTH
MEASUREMENTS

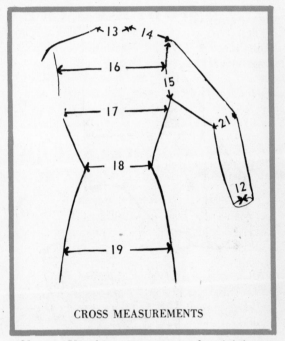

CROSS MEASUREMENTS

Cross Measurements

13. Measure neck in a becoming line
14. Shoulder, from neck to armhole
15. Armhole, from shoulder seam to underarm in front
    Armhole, from shoulder seam to underarm in back
16. Front measure, from armhole to armhole
    Back measure, from armhole to armhole
17. Bust measure, from underarm to underarm
    Back measure, from underarm to underarm
18. Front waist measure, from side seam to side seam.
    Back waist measure. from side seam to side seam.
19. Front hip measure, from side seam to side seam
    Back hip measure, from side seam to side seam
20. Skirt width
21. Width of sleeve

No. 13: Use this measurement when joining a collar, to be sure the neckline of the dress is cut in a becoming line.

Nos. 14, 15, and 16: Used in setting in a sleeve. No. 14 shows your exact shoulder line, and No. 15 shows a comfortable sleeve depth to be used when you set in the sleeve. No. 16 will give you the amount of material you need, front and back, so the sleeves will not tear out.

Nos. 17, 18, and 19: No. 17 separates the bust measure so you know how much width you need in back, compared to the front. Measure your pattern and balance this width as needed. This measure, combined with No. 18, helps you decide how much, if any, fullness should be fitted out at the side seam. No. 18 also makes it possible to fit the top of the skirt to your exact waist measurements. You can measure across the front and back of the garment and baste the placket line without a fitting. Nos. 18 and 19 can be used together to shape the top of the skirt across the hips. Increase or decrease the size of the pattern according to your measurements when you cut; use them to baste the side seams of the skirt.

No. 20 helps you adjust the skirt to a becoming width.

No. 21 helps in fitting the underarm seam of the sleeve if you want a tightly fitted cuff line.

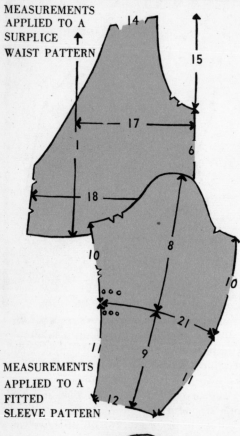

MEASUREMENTS
APPLIED TO A
SURPLICE
WAIST PATTERN

MEASUREMENTS
APPLIED TO A
FITTED
SLEEVE PATTERN

HOW TO USE YOUR MEASUREMENT CHART

Keep the card with your measurements before you as you cut and sew. Check with it often.

Measure the pattern so you will know exactly where to lengthen or shorten it. Make a red ring around any measurements which show that the left and right sides are not alike, then you can cut this difference into the fabric and baste it into the seams.

In cutting a garment with fullness which your measurements do not include, fold the pattern so that the indicated fullness lies flat, then check the measurements and make the adjustments.

When you cut a sleeve, note the dart perforations which mark the elbow. Measure above and below the darts to check the balance of the sleeve.

When a garment is cut in a totally different shape, so that you cannot apply your measurements as they stand, first mark the center front of the garment. Then draw a line across the normal waistline as shown in the diagram. Take the measurements, using these lines for a guide.

When you cut a sheer garment, allow a larger margin for ease of fullness. The garment must be looser than your usual measurements. A pattern designed for a sheer garment is cut looser.

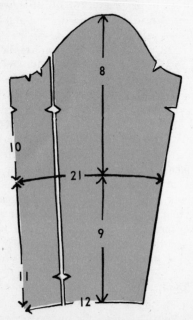

MEASUREMENTS APPLIED TO A
2 PIECE SLEEVE

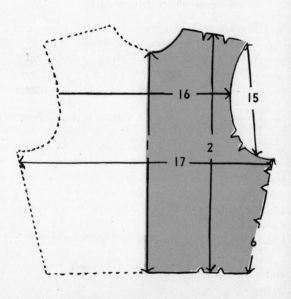

MEASUREMENTS APPLIED TO A
PLAIN WAIST PATTERN

A SIX-STEP-PLAN FOR MAKING CLOTHES

The process of making a garment is an orderly progression from one step to the next, from the choice of pattern and fabric to the finished garment. Professional dressmakers divide the process into logical steps and estimate the time required for each step—cutting, basting, construction, and finishing; and so they know exactly how long it will take to make a given garment.

In many homes, making a dress means a frantic disruption of the home routine because the home sewer has no idea how long it will take her to make the garment she has chosen. Perhaps she has only a day to make a dress, and she chooses a complicated pattern which takes hours and hours to make. These miscalculations can be avoided by learning to plan as you learn to sew.

The steps in making a garment are outlined below, with the processes required in each step listed under it. Make yourself familiar with just what each step involves, then learn to estimate how long each step will take in the pattern you have chosen. In this way you can fit your sewing smoothly into the time you have to give it, and dressmaking will become a pleasant, ordered routine instead of an exhausting scramble.

Practice will make your timing more and more accurate; but while you are learning to plan, here are some pointers:

If you want quick results, choose a pattern with few pieces. An intricate pattern composed of many pieces naturally takes longer to cut and longer to sew.

Styles and patterns which call for tedious handwork require watching because the finishing and trimming details will be time-consuming.

STEP 1—PLANNING

Decide what you need.
Correlate it to your wardrobe.
Decide upon the style.
Choose the pattern.
Choose the fabric.

Keep in mind how much time you have and allow enough time to make a garment you will be proud of. Occasionally arrange to make something special that takes a longer time.

STEP 2—ASSEMBLING EQUIPMENT

Be sure everything you will need for your work is assembled in a large workbox. Never start work without:

1. The right tools
2. All the necessary supplies

STEP 3—CUTTING

Adjust pattern measurements.
Cut out the garment.
Pin the pieces together.

Set aside time to finish this process without interruption. You should preferably be alone while you do it.

STEP 4—BASTING

Baste all curve controls—darts and tucks.
Join the seams of yokes and panels.
Join the long side seams.
Make a temporary hem.

FIRST FITTING — FOR BALANCE AND PROPORTION

You must work near a table.
You will need an iron.

This is social work, the time to ask a friend to join you with her sewing. A friend with a keen eye for line can help you with the first fitting.

STEP 5—CONSTRUCTION

Press as you go.
Make the waist and skirt separately.
Make the neck and collar finish.
Stitch the seams.
Adjust facings.
Make and adjust sleeves.
Make vest, cuffs, et cetera.

Second Fitting—(for final check-up)

Adjust the waistline and hang the skirt.

The making of collars, cuffs, and other small items will go quickly if you plan to pick it up for sewing by the evening lamp.

STEP 6—FINISHING

Finish the waistline joining.
Insert the placket, pockets and buttonholes.
Finish the hem, sleeve edges and trimmings.

Final Fitting—(adjust trimming)

Check all closings.
Give a careful final pressing.

ACHIEVE PERFECTION BY CAREFUL FITTING OF THE PAPER PATTERN

Measure the paper pattern, making all needed adjustments on the pattern, or if necessary on muslin before cutting your fabric. Pin, baste and fit your dress with minute attention to detail. Check your proportions, and make accurate markings to place your trimming. Make a special effort to achieve a professional look in your finishing touches.

CHAPTER XI

HOW TO ALTER A PATTERN

Look in the Ready-Reference Guide at the back for exact page numbers of Detailed Instructions

Most clothes and patterns are designed and sized to fit what is called the "average figure." But a government survey of women in all parts of the country showed that only 50 per cent could wear any version of commercial sizes and appear well fitted! Half the women in the country, then, have to alter their patterns, if they make their clothes, and also their ready-made garments. Learning how to make adjustments in the pattern is essential for many women if they are to be well fitted. Often simple adjustments are all that is necessary, but even those required for the "problem figure" are not too difficult. If you will make adjustments in the pattern before you cut, only minor ones will be necessary later, and much of the ripping out and altering which spoil the fun of sewing will be avoided.

The varied fitting needs of different types of figures are simplified and presented here in two prefitting methods.

Often a simple alteration in the paper pattern saves hours of adjustment after the dress is cut. Many figures need only the adjustment of length; others need to shorten the proportions of a garment. By testing a pattern before you cut, you can adjust width as well as length and so make it wider or narrower across the back, front, or hips. You can also alter one side of the garment only and so make allowances for irregularities in your figure.

Prefitting Method number 1 shows the simple adjustments of length and width that can be tested in a paper pattern.

Prefitting Method number 2 shows how to test in fabric the needed adjustments for irregular figures with broad or low shoulders or a larger hip or bustline. This test is made in unbleached muslin and is described as minor adjustments. Once you definitely know the measures for your adjustment in fabric, you can use them in pre-alterations of all patterns and so save hours of fitting.

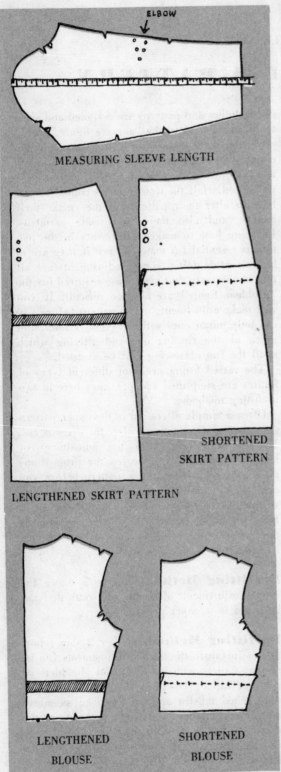

MEASURING SLEEVE LENGTH

SHORTENED
SKIRT PATTERN

LENGTHENED SKIRT PATTERN

LENGTHENED
BLOUSE

SHORTENED
BLOUSE

To Test the Pattern: Pin all the sections of the front and back that will be seamed together. Include yokes, pleats, and inserts. Join the waist and skirt and the shoulders. Do not pin the underarm. Do not pin the sleeve. Stand in front of a mirror and slip the pattern on.

Bear in mind that paper and fabric have different textures. Paper will stand out from your figure where the woven material will hang softly. If the paper bulges at the waistline, don't think you should take out the darts there.

Mark your alterations with tailor's chalk. Pencil will tear the paper.

Prefitting Method No. 1: Have accurate measurements and keep them in an index file. Once a year check them for changes. When you buy a pattern, check your measurements with the pattern measurements printed on the envelope and choose the measurements nearest your size. Buy coat, dress, waist, and blouse patterns by the bust measure; buy skirt patterns by the hip measure.

How to take bust and hip measurements, as well as all other important figure dimensions, is explained and illustrated on page 77. Remember that the pattern should be a trifle longer than your figure because there is a definite allowance for ease in the pattern measurements.

To Make a Pattern Longer: To lengthen a skirt and still keep the line and proportions of the pattern, add the extra length across the pattern just above the knee. Add extra length to the waist 3 inches above the waistline. To do this: (1) estimate the extra length required and divide it by 2; (2) split the pattern and pin tissue paper between the edges of the split, spreading each piece half the length to be added; (3) paste the additional length in place; and (4) verify these alterations with your measurements and if correct repeat for the waist and back of the skirt.

To Lengthen a Circular Skirt: Add the additional length to the lower edge. This increases fullness of the skirt in proportion to the length and makes certain the skirt will hang properly.

To Make a Pattern Shorter: Shortening the pattern at the hem or waistline spoils the proportions of your dress. Instead, pin tucks

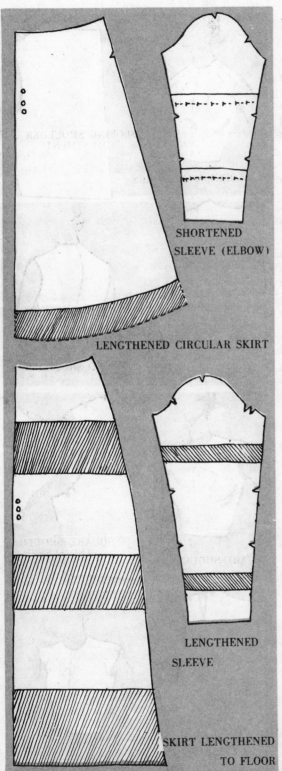

SHORTENED

SLEEVE (ELBOW)

LENGTHENED CIRCULAR SKIRT

LENGTHENED

SLEEVE

SKIRT LENGTHENED

TO FLOOR

across the pattern both in back and in front (1) just above the knee, and (2) 4 inches above the waist. Check these measurements carefully and check the size of the waistline, hipline, and width of shoulder.

To Shorten a Circular Shirt: Take a tuck in the pattern the necessary amount about 9 inches below the waistline. Trim the edge of tuck so it lies flat on the pattern. This makes a new cutting line—shortens the skirt, yet keeps the fullness.

Extending a Skirt to the Floor: Decide on the length required and divide this amount in three. Split across your skirt pattern in two places and separate each part 1/3 of the full additional length. Add the third extension to the lower edge of the pattern. This increases the length without increasing the fullness. If you want to make the skirt fuller, extend the garment more at the lower edge.

Sleeve Adjustments: Adjusting the sleeve pattern is very important, particularly for a long sleeve fitted at the wrist. Have someone measure your sleeve length from the seam at the curve of your shoulder (top of sleeve) to your wrist, with your elbow bent when the measurement is taken. Measure your pattern sleeve. If it needs shortening, do not cut it off at the wrist; instead, check the elbow darts. The sleeves are shaped for elbow action, and therefore these darts must be at the bend of the arm. For a long sleeve, make the adjustment at two places: one halfway between the elbow and the wrist, the other halfway between the shoulder seam and the elbow darts. In each division tuck in half the amount to be shortened or add half the amount to be lengthened. For a short sleeve, take out or add the whole amount in one place, halfway between the shoulder seam and the edge of the sleeve.

Prefitting Method No. 2 Adjust a muslin lining to your figure so all irregularities in your figure are balanced. Once these alterations are tested and cut in muslin following the directions here, you will *know exactly* how much to add to or subtract from your pattern when you cut. You need do this only once if you make a card index of the tested measurements and keep the card before you when you cut. The following paragraphs show how to make each adjustment you may need.

Shoulder Adjustments: When a shoulder is square or slopes, or when you need a broader back or an action back, make sure of the measurements for your particular need and add to the pattern before cutting the dress by prefitting in muslin.

Sloping Shoulders: Raise the shoulder, pin the needed amount, and shorten the underarm. Each shoulder should be adjusted separately, because they may not be alike. When you take up ¼ inch or ½ inch on a shoulder, mark this on your seamline and trace a new line to the neck to form a new shoulder seam. Mark an equal amount at the lower edge of the sleeve and slope it into the sleeve (these marks are your figure cut into the pattern). Be sure you drop the armhole to keep the original size.

Rounded Shoulders: Fullness through the back must be allowed before the garment is cut. Slash the muslin across the back at the shoulder blades or where the shoulders are heaviest and separate the pieces in a dart shape which does not increase the size of the armhole but allows extra width in back. Make a tuck across the chest to reduce the front by the same amount that the back was increased. This type of figure often needs a little extra material in the center back as well.

Wide Shoulders: Wide shoulders often need added material, and the additions should be made at the outside edges of the sleeve, front and back, as well as across the shoulders, tapering to nothing at the neck.

Narrow Shoulders: For figures with narrow shoulders, the shoulder line on all garments should be placed as wide as possible on the shoulders, so that the sleeve does not fall off, but is as near as possible to the edge of the shoulder. To make the shoulders narrower, take a pleat or dart in the shoulder line between the neck and the armhole, taking care not to draw the sleeve too far up on the shoulder.

Square Shoulders: Paste a piece of paper to both shoulders and make a new line to allow

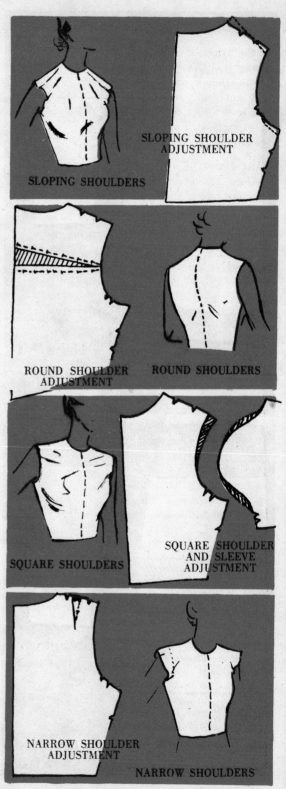

SLOPING SHOULDER ADJUSTMENT

SLOPING SHOULDERS

ROUND SHOULDER ADJUSTMENT

ROUND SHOULDERS

SQUARE SHOULDERS

SQUARE SHOULDER AND SLEEVE ADJUSTMENT

NARROW SHOULDER ADJUSTMENT

NARROW SHOULDERS

for a broad shoulder. When the sleeve is not too tight, you can add the amount at the lower edge of the armhole equal to the amount you added at the shoulder. Your sleeve pattern will then fit the armhole. If the sleeve is too tight, you are both enlarging an armhole and altering for a square shoulder, and the sleeve must be adjusted in proportion. Follow the instructions given in the paragraph on Sloping Shoulder Adjustments.

Flat Bust: To give the effect of fullness at the bust, take in a few small pleats at the waistline and add a fold at the bustline, starting at the side seam and gradually sloping to nothing toward the center. Adjust the sleeve to fit the new line of the armhole.

Yoke: If a sleeve is set in with a yoke, the shoulder adjustment must be made in the yoke section where the seam would normally be placed. To do this draw a line on the yoke across the shoulder. Separate the yoke at this line to fit square shoulders, or take up a tuck to fit sloping shoulders.

Narrow Hips or Small Waistline: It is a mistake to fit out all of the fullness on the side seams. When a skirt has four or more gores, take a little width from each seam except those at the center front and back. Fitted seams are taken gradually into the skirt seam. In a two-piece skirt, take a little out of the side seams and introduce darts into the skirt. Make the darts slender and tapering to take away the additional fullness so smoothly that it does not show.

Large Arm: Cut the sleeve through the center and paste a piece of paper between, spreading the two edges the necessary width. Cut away from the underarm of the armhole half the amount you are adding to the sleeve. To compare your measurement with the measurement of the pattern, measure the fullest part of the arm, about 1 inch below the armhole. For convenient size, the pattern should measure 1½ inches more than the arm.

Small Arm: Pleat the sleeve through the center, taking up the necessary amount. Add to the lower edge of the armhole on both sides pleats to make the armhole small enough to fit the sleeve.

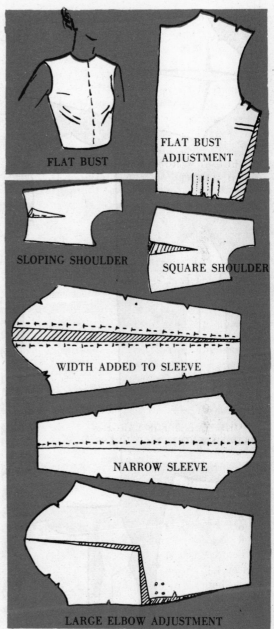

FLAT BUST

FLAT BUST ADJUSTMENT

SLOPING SHOULDER

SQUARE SHOULDER

WIDTH ADDED TO SLEEVE

NARROW SLEEVE

LARGE ELBOW ADJUSTMENT

Large Elbow: Cut and spread the sleeve the necessary amount. In this alteration you do not spread the sleeve at the top, and so no alteration is needed in the armhole. Paste a piece of paper under the sleeve to hold the spread at the elbow and add the necessary fullness in the new cutting line.

Look in the Ready-Reference Guide at the back for exact page numbers of Detailed Instructions

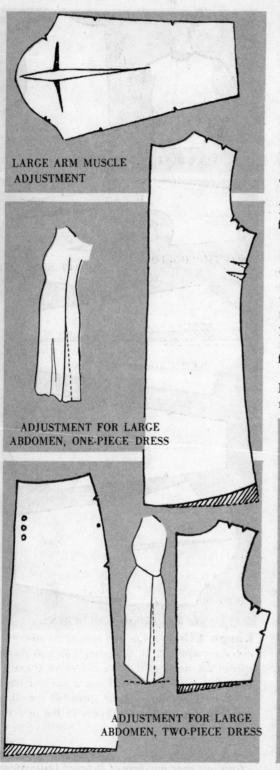

LARGE ARM MUSCLE
ADJUSTMENT

ADJUSTMENT FOR LARGE
ABDOMEN, ONE-PIECE DRESS

ADJUSTMENT FOR LARGE
ABDOMEN, TWO-PIECE DRESS

Large Arm Muscle: To hold the original shape at the top of the sleeve, slit the sleeve through the center and form a dart like the one shown in the illustration. In this way the sleeve is spread, and the extra fullness is laid in the darts without changing the shape of the armhole.

Arms Large at the Top: When a sleeve needs added length in the cap or top, add a strip of paper to separate the sleeve. Half of this width must be cut away from the lower edge of each armhole.

Major Alterations: No matter what the figure defect, balance is the first consideration. Make a test in unbleached muslin. You can slash the muslin and set in pieces wherever they are necessary. It will help to use a contrasting color for the insets, and you will know then what measurements should be set into your pattern every time you cut. Slash the pattern, set in your shaping adjustments, and cut your size into the fabric. Be sure to keep a record of your figure adjustments.

Large Abdomens: If your skirt pulls up, raise the back until the seamline hangs straight.

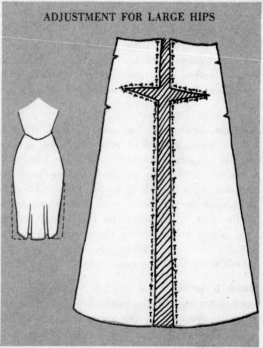

ADJUSTMENT FOR LARGE HIPS

There are two ways of making the necessary alterations: (1) In a one-piece dress, take two darts across the back at the side seam just above the waistline. Take in enough fullness so your side seam swings straight, and add the same amount to the lower edge of the skirt. In a two-piece garment, add half the needed amount at the front waistline and half at the lower edge of the center front of the skirt. This will make your beltline balance. (2) Slit the skirt pattern and drop the hemline of the front to a normal skirt length. In this slit put the necessary extra width to make the pattern balance.

Large Hips: Take measurements so that you know exactly how long you want the skirt to be and how many inches you must add to give a proper fit. Alter the pattern without losing the balance of the skirt. Divide the back gore of the skirt in half, cutting it lengthwise. Cut the back section of this gore across and spread the slit until the skirt length is correct. Paste a piece of paper to hold the two sections together. Be careful to keep the lower edge of the hemline correctly curved. Sometimes skirt balance requires shifting the next gore by adding a little to the lower edge and taking away a little at the hipline.

Sway-Back: This should be corrected by fitting a tuck in the muslin test before the garment is cut. The back line is a little shorter in the center, but the underarm seams are not altered. To do this, pin the fullness at the center back of the waist to test how much you want to take out. Pin this fullness into a tuck at the center back and gradually slope it to nothing under each arm.

Full Bust: If the bust is full, a normal garment will pull up in front and wrinkle under the arms. The easiest way to alter it is to make an extra dart under the arm. Pin up 3/4 inch in the dart. If this is not enough, pin in another dart. Three short darts will bring a garment into balance much better than one long dart. Add to the lower edge of the waist the same amount that you take up in darts under the arm. Every pattern you cut in future garments should have these extra darts and the extra material at the waistline. For an extremely full bust, make a muslin pattern with exactly the piecing you

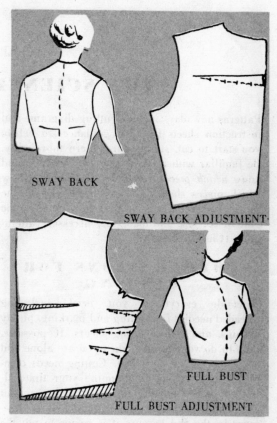

SWAY BACK

SWAY BACK ADJUSTMENT

FULL BUST

FULL BUST ADJUSTMENT

need. Then you can slash any commercial pattern you buy and set in the tested type of piecing. Slash your muslin pattern through the center front and across the bustline and drop it, allowing a piecing to fill in the extra space. Fit this carefully so that the lines are straight and the dress is not too tight.

SHORT-WAISTED FIGURES

A garment can be shortened above the waistline by following the directions for shortening a pattern. But this merely emphasizes a short-waisted figure instead of flattering it. A better plan is to have the beltline below your natural waistline, which gives a more balanced line to the garment as a whole. Use a narrow, inconspicuous belt.

If you have a large figure and are short-waisted only in the back, use a slanted fitting line at the waist, shorter in the back and dipping in the front. This line can be emphasized with embroidery or with a narrow set-in belt. Avoid straight fitted belts and never use a buckle except at the center back.

CHAPTER XII

THE SCIENCE OF CUTTING

Patterns nowadays include cutting diagrams and instruction sheets for your guidance, so before you start to cut, study your pattern thoroughly. Be familiar with the details of construction and know *which pieces are to be cut double.* Know which pieces should be laid lengthwise of the fabric. Naturally, you have already checked the pattern for size and made any necessary alterations (Chapter XI).

PREPARATIONS FOR CUTTING

Assemble everything you need, including threaded needles for basting and marking, plenty of pins, and sharp cutting shears. If possible, plan to do your cutting when you are alone and not likely to be disturbed. Cutting needs complete concentration. In planning your time, allow enough to pin the garment together as you cut. This "work-as-you-go" practice is a time-saver in the end because it is easier to put the garment together while the details of the pattern instructions are fresh in your mind.

Cutting Tables: The table on which you cut should be large. Professionals insist on one which provides plenty of space, a hard surface, and a straight edge for testing the straight of the goods. It won't hurt your dining-room table to be used as a cutting table, provided you use table pads. But if the table is so small that the pattern pieces slide off, cut on the floor instead. In factories all the pieces of the pattern are laid out at once on a large table, and you can do this on the floor. When you are cutting a wriggly fabric, such as chiffon, the nap of the rug holds the material firm, which is a great help.

THE FABRIC

Before you pin the pattern to the fabric for cutting, press out all wrinkles, but leave the center fold. The uncut edge of the fabric must be straight. If the uncut edge is crooked, straighten it.

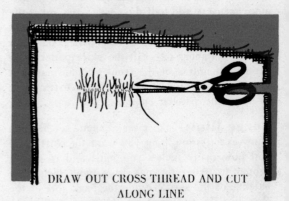

DRAW OUT CROSS THREAD AND CUT ALONG LINE

To Straighten the Edge: Most fabrics can be straightened by drawing out a cross thread and cutting along the line of the thread. In corded and napped fabrics, lay a ruler across the edge and mark a straight line with chalk. In muslins and many cottons, the fabric can be torn for a straight edge.

Holes or Imperfections: If your fabric has any holes or flaws in it, mark them plainly with pins so you can cut around them.

The Right Side: If the fabric has a right and wrong side, be sure to mark the right side with pins so that you can see it easily.

Napped Fabrics: In cutting napped fabrics, be careful to lay out the pattern so that the top section of each piece points in the same direction. The "rough" way as contrasted with the "smooth"—so that the nap will be all one way when the garment is finished. Velveteen, corduroy, and velvet are popular napped fabrics, and many woolens also have a nap. If you are in doubt whether your fabric has one or not, brush your hand up and down it lengthwise. If it has the feel of fur, it is a napped fabric.

Sheen Fabrics: Such sheen fabrics as satin should also be cut with the pattern pieces laid so the top sections all point one way. Otherwise different sections will catch the light differently,

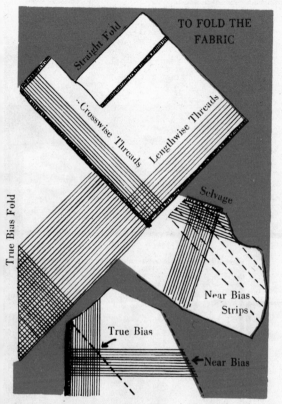

To Fold the Fabric: When you make a fold in the fabric for cutting, the fold must lie exactly on the straight of the goods, or along the lengthwise threads. If the fold is crooked, these lengthwise, or warp, threads—which are the strongest threads in the fabric—will not hang straight, and the garment will never fit. If a sleeve pattern is not placed on the grain of the fabric as marked, the sleeve will always twist.

THE CUTTING ROUTINE

Smooth the fabric on the table, right side up, and straighten the edges. Lay the first piece of the pattern on the fabric as directed in the cutting chart and pin it firmly to the fabric so it will not shift as you cut. Place the other pieces in the same way. The wisest course is to follow the cutting chart with the pattern, because experts have worked out the directions as the most economical way to cut the fabric. There are several such charts with each pattern, according to the width of the fabric, the size and style of and the garment will look as though it was pieced.

the garment. Draw a circle around the chart that applies to your selected version of the pattern; then study the chart carefully to be sure you understand the illustrated instructions.

When you put a pattern piece down on the fabric, smooth out pattern and fabric and pin them together. Insert the pins from the top without slipping your hand underneath the fabric. Put pins closer together along curved edges. If you want wider seams than the pattern allows, or if your material ravels easily, add 1 inch extra on straight seams, such as underarm seams, and 3/4 inch extra on curved seams, such as at the neck. Stitch on original seam line.

To Cut: With long, sharp scissors cut a clean, straight edge. Cut with a long, steady motion to keep the edge of the seam clean, and slide the scissors along so that you do not lift the fabric more than the space necessary for one blade of the scissors underneath. It will help to put one hand on the material opposite the scissors and keep the scissors constantly on the table. Shears are invaluable because of the bow handles into which you can put two fingers; this gives you greater leverage.

The thick blade should be above the material, the pointed blade underneath it. Cut with the middle of the blades, and remember that short snips will make an untidy edge which you will have to even later. Make sure you cut parallel to the edge of the pattern. If your scissors snip inside the edge, you tighten your pattern or narrow your seams. If you run a basting thread down the center front of the waist and skirt, it will help you later in placing yokes, pockets, and belts, and in fitting.

In cutting collars and cuffs and other trimmings, it saves time to cut away the seam allowances if they are to be bound.

Cutting a Sleeve: Because sleeves must be reversed in basting it is important to be careful in cutting them. When the pattern advises that they be cut double, you know that they are reversed. As you remove the pins from the pattern fold one sleeve to one side and pin the seam. Fold the other sleeve the opposite way. When a sleeve is cut single place it on the fabric and cut the first sleeve. To cut the second sleeve, the pattern must be turned and reversed as it is

CUTTING THE GARMENT
The rug holds the fabric firm and makes it easier to work.

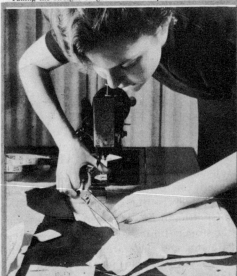

CUTTING A SLEEVE
Taking the straight of goods is a wise precaution.

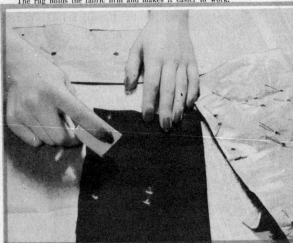

MARKING THE PERFORATIONS
This helps you place a pocket or a pleat.

CLIPPING THE NOTCHES
Notches in seams exactly match another notch in the garment.

placed on the fabric. When the sleeves are cut it is a good plan to lay them side by side and fold them to opposite sides. When you cut a fabric with a right and wrong side be doubly careful. It is easier to be sure of the reverse sleeve if you place one cut sleeve over the fabric and cut the second sleeve with the pattern between them.

MARKINGS ON PATTERN

What They Mean: The edge of each piece of a pattern is marked with notches, which show where each piece is to be joined. Your pattern will be full of sign language which will soon be familiar to you, particularly the perforations which indicate darts, pleats, pockets, and buttonholes.

How to Transfer Them: Notches can be marked on the fabric by taking tiny clips with your scissors. Take care not to cut them too deep, or you may find you can't let out a seam in fitting. For that reason some people prefer to trace these notches onto the fabric and mark them later with a colored thread.

To transfer the perforations, use long double threads of basting cotton and make tailor's tacks.

Take a double stitch with a long loop over each perforation; pass the thread to the next perforation and make another double loop; and so on until you have joined all the perforations with this basting stitch. Then cut the thread and gently separate the fabric from the pattern. If you are cutting the fabric double, you then cut the thread between the two pieces of fabric, thus separating them and leaving little tufts of thread as your guide marks.

Tailors of men's wear mark the perforations with tailor's chalk. You can do this by first chalking the thread and then drawing it through at each perforation. The powdered thread leaves marks on the fabric, and those marks are made larger by liberal use of the chalk right on the fabric. The thread will have to be repowdered with chalk every 7 inches or so of marking.

Some home sewers mark all notches and perforations with pins. If you use this method, you put in the pins, turn the fabric to the wrong side, and mark the position of each pin with a chalk mark. A seaming wheel is sometimes used, but it is likely to leave a permanent trace in many fabrics, although on others it leaves no trace. Try the wheel on a piece of scrap before you use it.

CUTTING PLAIDS AND FIGURED MATERIALS

The cutting measurements in your pattern and the cutting diagram in your pattern, as well as your pattern's fabric measurements, are designed and tested for plain fabrics or those with a small or medium print.

A fabric with a stripe, a plaid, a large spaced print, or a print with a distinct up-and-down pattern, requires special treatment in laying out and cutting. Not only does it require more material to cut these fabrics—you must expect to waste a little fabric when you want to match plaids, stripes, or prints exactly—but also it requires a more careful choice of pattern. When a pattern envelope illustrates a plaid or a matched stripe, you will find instructions in the pattern for carrying out this idea; but patterns that do not illustrate the matched stripe which you want to develop should be analyzed very carefully.

Cutting Plaids: Textiles are printed and woven in classic and decorative plaids which fall

TAILOR'S TACK

MARKING PERFORATIONS WITH A TRACING WHEEL

Cut notches *in* for heavy fabric — *out* for sheer.

into three main categories: (1) a small plaid repeated often; (2) a medium plaid repeated every ¼ yard; (3) a large plaid repeated every ½ yard. The repetition of a printed design does not refer to a single line of plaid; for often several lines in several colors make one complete pattern, which is then repeated over and over again. To estimate the extra yardage, remember that ¼ yard of additional material is required for a design which repeats often, and that when a long space occurs between each repeat, you must allow extra material equivalent to two or three repeats. When you first begin to work with plaids, you will be wise to select a simple pattern with only a few pieces. It can have a two- or four-gore skirt, or it can have pleats. Lay all the material out so you can plot the matching of the plaid in the most becoming manner.

First, place the pattern pieces on the fabric, all running in one direction, and then decide where you want the design of the material to fall

CUTTING PLAIDS

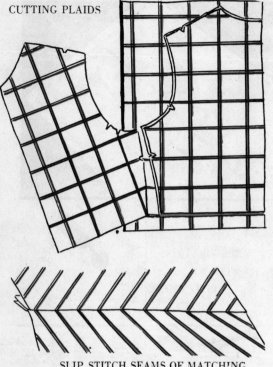

SLIP STITCH SEAMS OF MATCHING
PIECES ON THE RIGHT SIDE

on the garment. It is advisable to center the plaid between the shoulders and extend a straight line of plaids down to the hemline on the skirt. You must carefully adjust the pieces of pattern on the fabric so that the notches are each placed on exactly the same position in the repeated design so that when joined they will show a smooth continuation of the design. It is particularly important that the plaids should match on the crosswise pieces which meet at the armhole and where the seams are to be formed on the skirt.

Pay particular attention to the sleeves. The plaid must match the rest of the garment if a satisfactory effect is to be achieved. Note the notches on the sleeve pattern and place the plaid so that the same line of the design meets these notches exactly as the plaid meets the notches in the armholes. Cut the front and back gores of the skirt first, and take just as much care in cutting the side gores, so, that the pattern matches at the seams. It helps to place an arrow on the notches and put these arrows directly opposite the spot in the design you want placed at that point. This will bring the plaid into harmony at all seam joinings.

Pleated Plaid Skirts: Whenever a pleat is made in a plaid, *it must be spaced* for the plaid, not the pattern. In other words, you must space the pleat to the plaid so the same line of design comes at the edge of each pleat. If your garment has a few pleats, or a kick-pleat, first try out the pleat in the plaid. When you are satisfied with the effect, baste the pleats into the material and cut the pleated section by the pattern as if the pleats were not called for at all. Do this first before you cut the rest of the garment.

Large Checks: When the check in the design is larger than $1/2$ inch, it must be cut so the checks match at the seams. You require only $1/8$ yard more material to do this because the design repeats frequently. Make an arrow opposite the notches which must be matched and place corresponding notches on exactly the same line of the check design.

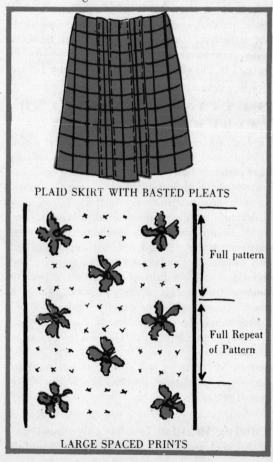

PLAID SKIRT WITH BASTED PLEATS

Full pattern

Full Repeat
of Pattern

LARGE SPACED PRINTS

Large-Spaced Prints: These prints must be cut carefully (1) so the center of the design is in the center front and center back of the garment; (2) so the design is placed in a flattering position where it is not cut off suddenly, thus emphasizing a figure defect. To see where the prints fall in the most becoming way, stand in front of a mirror with the fabric loosely draped around you. Avoid having a large motif centered over the bust or stomach or at the neck. To save using a great deal of extra material, choose a very simple fabric construction and fit the pattern carefully before cutting. Study the repeat of the print, and you will see that when a design is repeated often, you need allow only one or two extra repeats of the print. When a design is spaced wide apart you will require more material—the equivalent of three repeats of the print. In cutting fabrics with large-spaced prints, it is not as important to match the print on the side seam as it is to center it in a flattering position in relation to the garment construction.

Up-and-Down Prints: Prints which cannot be turned upside down must be cut so that all the pieces of the pattern point in the same direction. When the design is small no extra material is required; but when it has a wide-spaced repeat that must be centered in the garment construction, you will require extra yardage—equivalent to two repeats of the design.

Stripes: Stripes which run up and down—especially a wide-striped fabric—must be analyzed carefully. There are simple stripes, all alike and spaced evenly; complex stripes of different widths, spacings, and color (which constitute a design repeat); blended stripes, indefinite and often wide; and simple designs which give a striped effect. If you understand exactly how to go about cutting these lovely materials, you will be proud of the garments you make.

Be sure to select a simple pattern with straight lines. Center the stripe in the front and back of all pieces. In cutting, the stripe should be centered the full length of the sleeve, and any yoke effect should be cut to correspond with the sleeve stripe.

When stripes are cut for decorative trimming bands of self-fabric, you can use any simple house-dress or shirtwaist dress pattern, apron pattern, straight-line dress for girls, tailored shirt type for men, women, boys, or girls. After you have selected your pattern style, make a little diagram (place tissue paper over the picture of the pattern) and mark how you are going to arrange your stripes. Sometimes a dress is cut with stripes running lengthwise; and the pockets, collar, front closing band, and band at the hem are cut crosswise. In other dresses or apron effects, a short sleeve and yoke will be cut crosswise. No matter what effect you desire, it is easy to achieve if you have a little diagram in front of you so that when you lay the pattern on the fabric you know just how to place the trimming touches in relation to the stripe.

Stripes which meet diagonally must be cut with the aid of special pattern directions, and you will be wise to look for a pattern envelope that is illustrated in this way. The skirt should have four gores; the waist should have a seam at the center front and center back. It can be a slip-on or a button-front. For true success, the

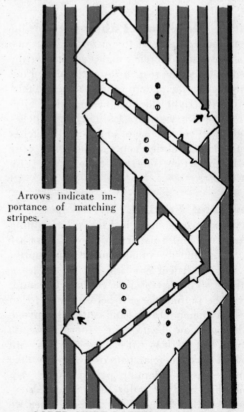

Arrows indicate importance of matching stripes.

GORED SKIRT PATTERN LAID OUT FOR DIAGONAL STRIPES

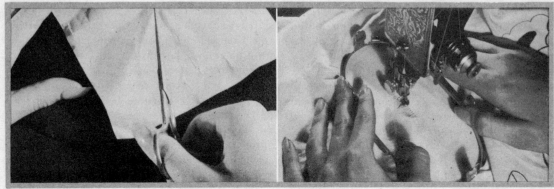

stripe must have a straight line that is definite and can be controlled to run lengthwise on the fabric or across. If you have a four-gored skirt pattern that does not include this cutting information, place it on the stripe as shown in the diagram here. The notches that meet must be placed on the exact line in the stripe (1); each skirt gore is cut twice (2). In the second cutting you must turn it to face in exactly the opposite direction.

Basting Matching Fabrics: Join the seam on the right side of the material. Turn one edge at the seam allowance and place it over the opposite edge so the seam allowances meet. First pin the edge so the pattern exactly matches, then baste on the right side of the material. Slip-stitch the edges together, taking long stitches through the folded edge and small stitches through the flat fabric. You can then turn your work to the wrong side and lay out the seam for stitching.

Free-Hand Cutting: In every period of history some women have had the gift of cutting a garment without a pattern. Most designers use free cutting, and the young woman who aspires to develop her talent as a designer should learn something of the art of free cutting. It would, however, be putting the cart before the horse to suggest an attempt at free-hand cutting to anyone who did not know how to use a pattern correctly. We must first learn to cut a dress that fits with the use of a commercial pattern before we take the next step in adapting patterns. The step beyond this, used by tailors and a few dress-makers. is called draughting a pattern. When we draught a pattern, we learn to take measures and make a basic pattern that is then adapted to a

style idea. To save time, many designers buy a commercial pattern with a basic line or a style cutting that they can adapt. In this way they incorporate their ideas into a dress without the detailed work necessary in draughting a garment.

Adding Fullness to a Skirt: You must first decide where the fullness will be and how much you want. Drape the fabric on yourself or a form and arrange it in the effect you like (it can be a crude effect). Then measure the fullness at the lower edge, waistline, and so forth, and check it with the pieces of your basic pattern. In this way you will know exactly how much fullness you want to add. Slash the pieces of the pattern and spread them so that the amount of fullness added is divided between different sections so that the fullness will be distributed evenly. You can add pleats or make a fuller dirndl skirt by adding extra width to your pattern. You can make a many-gored skirt by cutting another skirt and adding a little fullness.

Fullness added in this way must be tested in a fitting, and a beginner should use inexpensive fabric so that if the effect is not absolutely correct, she can still be happy with an inexpensive if not perfectly cut dress. When you want to set godets, inserts, flounces, et cetera, in a skirt or waist, cut them in paper and pin them on the garment. Many designers use tissue paper to do this and so gauge proportions before they cut.

Fullness can be added to a waist or to sleeves by slitting the pattern and spreading the pieces. If you want the fullness at the top of the sleeve and the front of the waist, you spread the pattern in this one place. If you spread the pattern on each side of the front, you will add shoulder fullness to the design. Experiment with your own ideas and learn as you go.

CUTTING DIAGRAMS

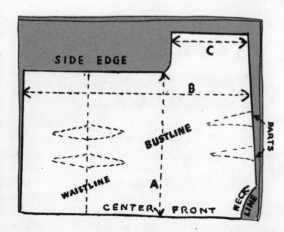

PLAIN SLIP-ON BLOUSE

To cut a simple blouse, draw on a piece of paper the pattern illustrated. Take your measurements as described in Chapter X.

A. is ¼ the width of your bust measure.

B. is the measure from top of shoulder to the point below the waistline where the blouse is to end.

C. is ½ the measurement around the top of your arm.

Shape the sleeveline 3 inches out from the side edge and slope the shoulder line a little.

Place the pattern on folded material with the center front following the folded edge which should be on the straight grain of the fabric. Pin pattern to material and cut, allowing for seams. Now cut the back of the blouse in the same manner without allowing curve at neckline.

Baste darts at shoulder where indicated. Pin side and shoulder seams. Try on, and cut out neck a little at a time until it is becoming. Pin darts at waistline. Bind neck and armholes.

PANTIES

Make a pattern as indicated. Measure waistline, divide in ½ for line A. Measure hipline loosely. Place ½ this measurement on line C, add 2 inches for ease. Panties should be 14 inches deep for size 14; and 2 inches deeper for each size larger.

Shape pattern. Measure down 2 inches at center front, slope waistline from this point to back. Cut across corners at points C until line is 4 inches long. (This is the crotch). At large arrow, measure up 4 inches; shape line from this point. The line must be longer in back.

Pin pattern to doubled fabric; cut, allowing for seams. Make slit at B for plackets. Sew center seams and crotch. Take darts at waistline if desired. Bind waistline and leg edges. Use small flat buttons for plackets.

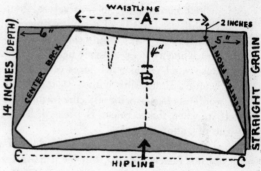

BRA

Cut a pattern like diagram. Place ⅓ of loosely taken bust measurement on line A. Line B should be 6 inches deep, or more if desired. Slope the top and bottom edges to 2 inches at each end. Slope center front.

Pin this pattern to a folded piece of true bias fabric or lace. Cut, allowing for seams. Make darts as illustrated. Join the center seam. Add a band of double elastic or double bias of self-fabric to back ends of bra. Seam to only one back end and fasten the other end with a hook and eye. Bind edges of bra and add straps.

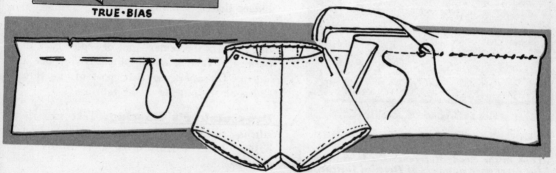

CHAPTER XIII

HOW TO BASTE

Bastings are simply temporary joinings. They hold the pieces of fabric together for fitting, they hold seams together while you stitch. Some bastings merely hold a fabric in place for the time being and are ripped out without stitching. Pleats, for instance, are basted during fitting, but are not permanently stitched.

HOW TO BASTE

To baste you will need an extra-long needle of medium size—or a darning needle—and glazed basting thread instead of ordinary sewing thread. Fabrics which mark easily, such as velvet, should be basted with sewing silk of a contrasting color. Basting stitches in silk should be very small, while firm woolens need stitches nearly an inch long. Loose woolens take two sizes of stitches— a 1-inch stitch alternating with a ½-inch stitch. If the woolen is basted with silk, the basting may be left in when the garment is pressed. This is not true of cotton thread.

When the thread runs out in the middle of a seam, do not fasten the end, but let it hang free and start the new thread back about 2½ inches. Be sure you begin at the top and baste to the end; don't leave the seam ends open.

BASTING SEAMS

Before you begin basting make sure that the pattern notches and the seam lines meet exactly.

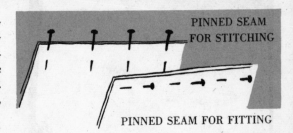

PINNED SEAM FOR STITCHING

PINNED SEAM FOR FITTING

No seams should be joined so that one edge extends beyond the other, or is longer or shorter than its partner. Keep your work flat on the table and take care not to pull or stretch the edges as you put the seams together. Put the pins in at right angles to the seam, pushing them in lightly from the edges. This will make a straight line guide for your basting—an even basting line is a great help when you stitch— and also keeps the pins from pricking your fingers as you sew.

If you are workng on slippery rayon, place the pins closer together. In taffeta use needles instead of pins, for it marks very easily.

To make sure your basting is even, use a gauge until your eye is trained to do it without the aid of a measure.

TYPES OF BASTING

There are several different types of basting stitch, and each has its proper use.

Even Basting: This basting is used to hold seams together. Pass the needle over and under the fabric with equal spacing. The stitches are longer than a running stitch.

Uneven Basting: This is used for a guide line to mark the center front or center back of a garment. Take a small stitch, and space the stitches far apart, so that most of the thread shows on the outside of the fabric.

Dressmaker's Basting: Take two short stitches, followed by one large one. Dressmaker's basting holds a fabric even more firmly than even basting.

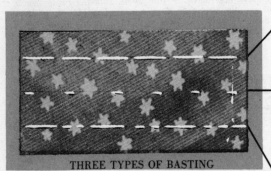

THREE TYPES OF BASTING

Look in the Ready-Reference Guide at the back for exact page numbers of Detailed Instructions

ORDER OF BASTING

When you start to baste your garment, first look to see how your pattern controls the curved lines. This means you first prepare and then carefully pin in the darts, tucks, or gathers, then baste them.

Next, look over your garment construction for small pieces, such as yokes and insets, then note whether it has pleats or straight facings. If there is a yoke, it must be basted on, and the pleats or facings, too.

After the smaller pieces have been disposed of, join the shoulder seams. Begin at the neck end of the seam and work toward the armhole.

Next come the long side seams under the arms. Begin at the armhole and work down to the waist.

After the side seams, baste the long seam in the skirt. Start at the waist and work down to the hem.

If the garment is in two pieces—other than one with a gathered skirt, in which the skirt seams and underarm seams are not meant to match—join it at the waistline before basting the seams under the arms. Place two pins in the center front and center back of the waistline on both waist and skirt. Slip the waist inside the skirt, with both on the wrong side. The fronts and backs should be facing and the waist edges together. Pin the two center backs and center fronts together, then pin the side seams. With the seam thus pinned in the four most important points, space out the fullness evenly as you pin the seam along its entire length. This seam must be strongly basted because it has to hold the weight of the skirt. Use dressmaker's basting.

Finally, turn the dress right side out. Unless one shoulder is higher than the other, only one sleeve need be basted in for the first fitting. Pin and baste any darts or other shapings and put in any gathers at the wrist or the top of the sleeve. To join the sleeve seam, pin the top together and then the wrist. Work from both points toward the middle so that you can lay with tucks or gathers the fullness you need for elbow action. Remember that gathered parts of seams need small, strong stitches.

To baste the sleeve into the armhole, begin at the top of the sleeve and work around to the underarm seam. Here again, it is important to see that the notches are exactly matched. When the notches on the top of the sleeve and the armhole are matched, they will show you exactly where the sleeve seam will come. Smooth out evenly on both sides of the shoulder seam any fullness you find across the top. Shape this fullness to the curve of the armhole.

Collars and cuffs and belts should be basted when cut and stitched when you are stitching the rest. This plan makes the construction of the garment go smoothly and take up less time.

REMOVING BASTINGS

As you stitch the seams, remove the bastings. Professionals stitch just inside the seam line to avoid stitching over the basting line, which makes the basting threads much harder to get out. Train yourself to baste a little closer to the edge of the fabric than your actual stitching will be in the finished seam line. When you fit your garment, notice whether the seams should be stitched a little farther in from the basting to make the garment fit tighter, or a little farther out to make it looser, or just right. When you remove the bastings, never pull a long thread—it may punch little holes in the fabric or stretch a bias. Cut the stitches every 3 inches and pull the short threads gently.

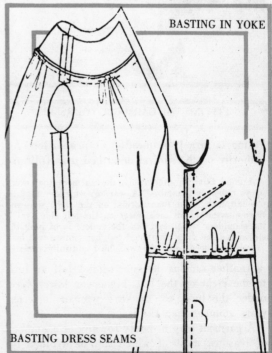

BASTING IN YOKE

BASTING DRESS SEAMS

CHAPTER XIV

HOW TO MAKE FITTING ALTERATIONS

FITTING THE GARMENT YOURSELF

checking your measurements with the pattern and making your alterations in the pattern before you cut (Chapter XI). But even if you do alter the pattern first, you may find a few adjustments to be made at the first fitting, because different fabrics react differently, and a garment fits well only when it hangs well on the figure, without bulkiness caused by too much fullness or wrinkles caused by tightness. Fit your basted dress and examine it minutely, slowly revolving in front of a long mirror. The discussion of professional points in this chapter will help you decide what is wrong, if anything, and how to remedy it.

Look in the Ready-Reference Guide at the back for exact page numbers of Detailed Instructions

HAVING THE GARMENT FITTED

Fitting is largely a question of proportion. An authority on the subject described it as follows:

A good fitter so proportions the garment that every figure defect is minimized. A woman's shoulder may be one-half inch lower than normal on the right side and three-quarters of an inch lower on the left side; yet if the shoulders are altered *and* the underarm of both the sleeve and the dress shortened too, her clothes will look exactly balanced, and she will be beautifully dressed.

Another famous designer said, "Half an inch to the right or the left, higher or lower *here*, under the bust, can make a woman look ten years younger than she is."

A garment may fit badly for any of a number of reasons, most of which can be avoided by

SIDE-SEAM ADJUSTMENTS

Look first at the long lines, the up and down of the figure, on all garments—made, bought, or remodeled. *The side seam must hang straight.* Not just when you straighten yourself or when you tug it into place, but naturally, so that it falls immediately into a straight line after every movement you make.

If the side seam shoots forward instead of hanging straight down, pin a tuck across the back of the garment at the waistline. Make the tuck big enough to make the side seam hang straight. If it shoots backward, make a tuck in the front at the waistline. This tuck can either be placed near a joining so you can rip the seam out and change the line, doing away with the extra fabric in the tuck, or it can be a small dart laid in an inconspicuous place.

Front and Back Lines: Front and back lines must be straight. Unless the style of the garment calls for an exception to the rule, the straight grain of the material must be held in the center front and center back. It does not matter whether the fabric hangs smoothly, is folded in an edge, or is cut in two or more pieces—it will hold its shape only if the length-wise threads of the fabric hang straight. Home sewers often neglect to run the basting threads to mark the straight of the goods when they

FINAL FITTING FOR TRIMMING

cut a garment; but without this marking it is very easy to pull the garment out of shape without realizing it. Always run a basting line down the center of the dress before you cut.

Horizontal Lines: Unless the style demands an exception to the rule, always watch any line which crosses the garment. This includes the hems of skirts, coats, and jackets; the stitched lines which join a garment at the waist or which join a flounce or yoke; and the cross grain of the sleeves. You will save yourself time if you check these lines before you stitch, to make sure they are true. Then look to the shoulder seams, armholes, neckline, and sleeves to be sure they fit and are in balance.

Underarm Seams: When a garment seems loose, bulky, or too full, the most natural adjustment is to pin in a wider seam under the arm. The seams on both sides should be equal. If you

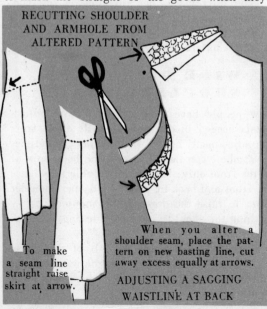

RECUTTING SHOULDER AND ARMHOLE FROM ALTERED PATTERN

To make a seam line straight raise skirt at arrow.

When you alter a shoulder seam, place the pattern on new basting line, cut away excess equally at arrows.

ADJUSTING A SAGGING WAISTLINE AT BACK

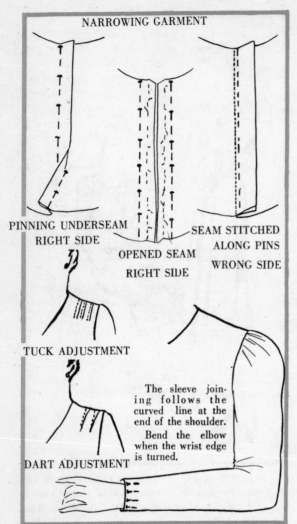

NARROWING GARMENT

PINNING UNDERSEAM
RIGHT SIDE

OPENED SEAM
RIGHT SIDE

SEAM STITCHED
ALONG PINS
WRONG SIDE

TUCK ADJUSTMENT

DART ADJUSTMENT

The sleeve joining follows the curved line at the end of the shoulder.

Bend the elbow when the wrist edge is turned.

take up fullness by making a wider seam on one side only, the garment will be thrown off balance. This underarm adjustment is made on the right side of the material; then take off the garment, loosen the pins, and replace them in one side of the line which you pinned, taking care to put them back exactly where they were each time. Turn the garment to the wrong side and baste the seams on the pin line.

If the garment is tight or seems to draw, you can rip the underarm seam and let out as much material as is possible. If this is not enough to relieve the strain, set in a piece of the same fabric under the arm. This can be a straight strip, the size of the piece depending on the amount of extra room you need, and should extend from the underarm to the waist. If, however, you do not need as much room at the top or at the waist, this piece can taper to nothing at either end.

WAISTLINE AND HIPS

Look to see if the garment is too loose or too tight at any point. If the skirt and waist are too full, take them in at the side seam. To do this, the dress should be on the right side and the seam should be equal on both sides of the figure. First pinch it in at both sides with your hand to gauge the amount, then pin this amount, beginning at the waistline. Pin this seam from the waist over the hips (do not pull the skirt too tightly). When you have extended the line over the hips, look at your skirt and decide which would look best: (1) making the skirt narrower by extending the alteration from the hips to the hem; or (2) making the skirt come gradually to a point at or near the bottom.

When a garment is too tight, open the seam. If you cannot let it out, place a trimming band in the seam.

In making skirt adjustments, remember that too tight a garment makes a woman look uncomfortably larger. Bear in mind, too, that opaque, heavier fabrics are fitted closer than sheer, soft, or transparent fabrics. A semifitted waistline is often important in achieving close-fitting effects because it straightens the figure. When a garment has many up and down seams, a good fitter makes her alteration in full consideration of the garment cutting—sometimes it is best to take in or let out the side seam; again it is best to take a little out of each seam.

WIDE OR NARROW SHOULDER SEAMS

Few people have even shoulders, and adjustments needed in one armhole will differ from the adjustments needed in the other. Sometimes an armhole can be adjusted in the back only or in the front only; but it is preferable to balance the front and back by making a deeper shoulder seam to raise the dress at the shoulder, or by opening the shoulder seam and letting the armhole down.

A good fitter watches the fall of the fabric both at the armhole and across the waist or coat and works for a smooth effect which makes the bustline flatter.

HOW TO FIT SLEEVES

When a figure is rounded, full at the back, in fitting the sleeve take the precaution to take a narrower seam than the usual ½ inch in the top of the sleeve.

When the sleeve draws so that it must be cut away under the arm, clip both the underarm of the sleeve and the underarm of the waist, with short cutting slashes. Continue to do this until the sleeve hangs straight, then rebaste the seam of the sleeve at this lower line. When a sleeve is too short across the top for a very large arm, it forms a diagonal wrinkle from the underarm to the top of the sleeve in both the front and the back. Rip the sleeve from the armhole across the top only. Sometimes letting out a seam will permit the seam to hang straight; sometimes it is necessary to cut away some material at the underarm and make a new seam.

A sleeve which is too long on the top will form wrinkles at the back of the arm. Often this extra length can be fitted out by ripping the armhole and taking up an extra seam on the sleeve edge only.

When sleeve fitting is a problem, it helps to turn the armhole seam and baste it without setting in the sleeve. Pin this seam over the top of the sleeve, inserting the pins from the seam so they can be easily adjusted. Now fit the garment and observe the crosswise line of the fabric. Does the straight grain of the fabric follow a straight line in the sleeve? If not, balance the sleeve at once by taking up a larger seam at the armhole on whichever side of the sleeve the straight line curves away from. You will know how much to take up if you watch the line of the fabric grain take its correct position. It must hang straight. Turn the seam lines toward the sleeve.

If this fitting thus corrects the twisted sleeve, baste it carefully on the wrong side. If the sleeve continues to twist, it may need to be shifted in the armhole. Sometimes a sleeve is shifted to the back, so that the notches do not match. If the sleeve needs turning toward the front of the garment, you make this adjustment in the same way.

After a sleeve has been adjusted, the new seam line must be basted. Before stitching this seam, try the garment on for a test fitting.

Once you have raised or lowered the shoulder seam so that your garment hangs smoothly, you must consider the joining of the sleeve at the armhole. Does it follow the curved line at the end of the shoulder? This is the most becoming angle for sleeves. If you have it placed too far to the back, there will be a bulge at the back of the sleeve top. If it is too far to the front, a similar bulge at the top will appear on the sleeve front. Either way it will be necessary to take out the sleeve and reset it properly.

When the sleeves slip off the shoulder, the sleeve must be moved closer to the neckline or a dart or a few tucks taken across the shoulder. Usually a shoulder seam should be on top of the shoulder from the neck out to the shoulder edge.

Check elbow room and be sure the sleeve is placed so that the fullness adjusts easily when the elbow is bent. Sleeves that tear out at the elbow are often the result of bad fitting, permitting the elbow fullness to be below or above the point where it should be. It may be necessary to shorten the sleeve above or below the elbow. To do this, pin the necessary adjustment in the sleeve and test it, checking the joining of the sleeve in the armhole, the hang of the sleeve, and the correct length of the sleeve.

NECKLINES

There are two important considerations in fitting a neckline. Does it lie smooth? Is it becoming? Careful adjustments must be made to get what professionals consider becoming proportions of the neckline. Is it too high? Is it too low? Will the collar or scarf adjust at the desired angle? Try the effect very carefully. Only when every angle of the neckline has been checked can necessary adjustments be made. When a neckline looks too high and seems to call for adjustment, never cut away on the figure what you think is right. Instead, outline with pins the shape you think would be becoming. Snip your material a little at frequent intervals so you can constantly check as you turn the edge back. Whenever an edge is shaped in this way, lay it on the other edge and make both sides alike. Run an accurate basting, and try on the garment to verify the alteration.

Collars: If you alter your neckline, your collar must be changed. When a neckline is enlarged, add half the extra space on either side of the back so that the shaping is not lost.

CHAPTER XV

BECOMING NECKLINES

The neckline frames the face, and therefore it must be perfect in all the details of fit, style, and shape. More than anything else, the neck finish shows the difference between skilled dressmaking and amateur sewing. Proportion is the secret of a becoming neckline, and each style must be adjusted to the individual. After you have selected the neckline or collar you like, cut it in paper and try it on and decide whether it should be a little lower, or filled in. Should the neck be cut away a little so the collar will be at a more becoming angle? Should the scarf be narrower or wider, the bow larger or smaller?

TYPES OF NECKLINE

Classic Inconspicuous Necklines:
This popular faced neckline is particularly adapted to V necks, bound necks, soft draped necklines, and tailored necklines. To make it, a bias facing of self-fabric or a light-weight lining is stitched to the neckline. It should be cut 2 to 3 inches wide and the length of the neck opening. Place it on the right side of the garment, match the edges, and stitch. Turn the facing to the wrong side, making sure that the edge is smooth and even. Stitch the facing or make an unstitched finish, depending upon the type of garment. In tailored necklines, machine stitching is often a decorative feature of the facing. In soft garments with a draped neckline or a plain neck finish, no stitching should show on the right side of the garment. In tight necklines, used so successfully as a background for costume jewelry, one line of stitching close to the edge is permissible. It forms a tiny corded effect. This is popular also in surplice necklines.

Collarless Necklines: They can be flat and plain, or sometimes they feature gathers or tucks. Gathers are best held with a binding or cord. Square necklines are faced with a *straight* facing, which can be applied on the right side and turned back, or applied on the wrong side and turned to form a decorative band on the right side.

Bound Necklines: The straight or bias binding can bind the neck all the way around, or it can be extended to form a small bow tie. First bind the neck edge, then turn the edges of a tie and overcast them together; or, if buttons are desired, place them on the edges and hold them with hooks.

Corded Necklines: Turn the round neck of a dress over a cable cord and stitch it close by hand. Then draw the fullness of the cord and adjust the neck to the right proportion. Another kind is made by covering the cord with contrasting fabric. Turn the edges of the neck in and gather it, applying the cord. Still another kind is made by hemming a heavy silk cord to the edge of a soft round neckline which has been turned and gathered. Cording can also be hemmed to the edge of a smooth U-shaped neckline.

Square Necklines: A true square neck which is bound or faced depends upon clipping for success. Stitch the band in place, then before you turn it, clip into the seam allowance close to the corner, cutting until you touch the stitching. The corner will lie smoothly when you turn the facing.

Revere Necklines: This is the popular finish for the straight neck of soft dresses. It gives the appearance of no finish at all. It is also the basic construction feature for necklines which roll back softly from a smooth point without a collar, or with a straight collar worn open. Formal dresses with a stitched revere outline use this finish, and it is excellent for the front openings of dress-up costumes with small beaded collars. A short stiff jabot in a slashed opening that seems to have no finish is often fashionable, and the revere neckline is a basic favorite in middy blouses and pointed collar applications.

The secret of the revere neckline is to cut deep into the point *after*, not before, the facing is applied. When the revere is turned to the wrong side, no stitching, wrinkles or dents show. The edge should be straight.

Cut a facing of self-material 2 inches wider than you plan to wear the opening turned back. Lay it on the garment *before you slash the front*. Mark the cutting line and outline it in stitching ½ inch back of the line on each side. The stitching can meet in a point at the end of the cutting

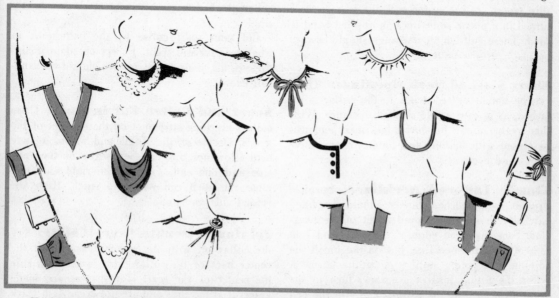

CLASSIC UNOBTRUSIVE NECKLINES   BOUND, SHIRRED OR BANDED COLLARLESS NECKLINES

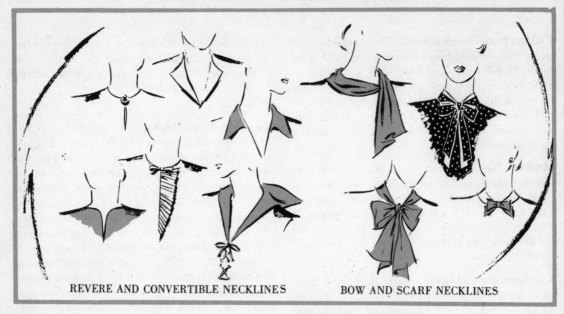

REVERE AND CONVERTIBLE NECKLINES   BOW AND SCARF NECKLINES

line, or square corners can be made. Cut the slash along the marked line between the stitching and down into the stitched point, or out into the stitched corners, so that you almost cut the stitching. Turn the facing to the wrong side of the garment and baste the edge for pressing. In a heavy fabric, overcast the raw edge and slipstitch it to the garment. In a light-weight material, turn the raw edge of the facing under in a narrow hem.

Classic Shirt Fronts: Sometimes classic shirt fronts are cut in one with the garment and turned in a pleat; sometimes an applied band is used. These full-length openings should always be made with a pattern.

Short Slashed Neck Openings: These can be bound or faced before the collar is attached, as in convertible slashed openings. With this treatment the finished edges meet and can be closed with buttons and loops or decorative hooks and eyes.

Classic Tailored Necklines: Surplice dresses with notched lapels should be fitted carefully to give a tailored effect to the neckline. Face the front edge of the waist and join the collar to the neckline, but do not finish the joining and facing until you fit the garment. After the fitting insures accuracy, turn in the seam allowance of the reveres and slip the end

of the collar between. Now stitch across at the top of the revere.

Scarf and Bow Necklines: Scarves and bows are applied to necks of almost any shape. The scarf can be self-fabric or contrasting; it can be cut straight and folded double so the ends can be stitched and turned; it can be straight and hemmed or picoted; it can be cut on the bias; it can be made of ribbon or lace. It can be very narrow, or medium width and cut double up to 2½ inches wide; or very wide and cut single. Collars 4 or 5 inches wide are usually single.

Cut your scarf collar by the pattern or in whatever size you want. Except on plain utility dresses, the hems on all scarves should be hand-rolled.

Scarf and Collar Cut in One: These collars are long strips cut on the straight of the goods. Decide on the length and width, include hem allowance, and cut. Sew seams on the open side and one end. Turn to the right side and close the open end with slip stitch. Baste the folded side and press.

Joining a Double Scarf Collar: Try the collar on with the garment and mark the center back of the collar. This is *not* as a rule the center of the scarf, for scarves are made graceful at the ends and are not even. Also mark the point where the collar joins the center front of your dress; then you know how much space to leave open in the center for the collar joining. You are ready then to fold the scarf in half and seam each end, shaping the ends in points or curves as desired. Turn the scarf, baste the folded side to insure an even line, and press it. Join one edge of the open side to the neckline with the center-back marking in place. Seam this edge to the neckline. Turn the opposite edge of the scarf and hem it to the seam, forming a smooth finish for the neckline.

Single-Fabric Scarves: These scarves are hemmed, bound, or finished with a facing of a contrasting color. They are joined to the neck with a bias binding. Unless the scarf is cut double, it is best to face the neckline, then apply the scarf. Joining the scarf only across the back from shoulder to shoulder often gives a more becoming line. This is particularly true of transparent and lace scarves.

Novelty Scarves: Color contrast in scarves and necklines is often a fashion feature. Ribbon can be used in this way by joining it to the back of the neck and overcasting edge to edge— across the back only. Let one color fall freely and tie the other in a bow.

To introduce color in a broad scarf, decide on the length and width so you can cut one half in a contrasting color. The two pieces can be joined in a lengthwise seam or a short seam at the back of the neck. These scarves can be hemmed and draped as single bows or turned double so that the contrasting color looks like a facing.

In a printed dress, a color of the print can be repeated at the neckline in a double collar and scarf by cutting a 2-inch band of the print long enough to go around the neck, then tying it in a bow with long ends. Finish this scarf and attach it to the neck. Then cut a straight piece of contrasting fabric 2 inches wide and about 8 inches shorter than the first scarf. Fold it lengthwise, seam the ends, and turn it. Overcast the opening and baste the band to the neckline *inside the collar band.* When you wear the dress, let the colored ends cross and hang, and tie the self-fabric scarf.

Applied Bands in a Short Slash: If the short slash is not wide enough, cut a straight facing for the underedge to hold the buttons. Next prepare the outside trimming band which will hold the buttonholes. This must be cut on the straight of the goods 2 inches longer than the front opening and twice the width of the finished band. Cut a pointed edge. Fold the band with the right side of the fabric on top and stitch the pointed end. Clip the point and turn the band. Press the folded edge and the outside edge. Then join the inside edge of the band to the slash in a seam. Stitch or hem the outside edge of the band to the seam. Continue this stitching around the point and up the folded edge. In these neck joinings the point can be stitched flat to the garment or left separate so that it hangs loose.

Placket Neck Finish: Cut a straight facing twice as long as the slashed opening. Seam it around the opening on the right side. Fold it under on the wrong side of the garment, creasing the facing on one edge flush with the seam, and on the other edge to extend beyond the seam. Hem it on the seam line and tack at the lowest point of the opening to insure a smooth fit.

JABOTS

Jabots are straight ruffles finished on the edge and either gathered or pleated into a band; they are either single or double. Nowhere else in your wardrobe are the hand-hemstitched hem, fine hand tucks, hand-rolled hem, and real lace more important. The size and shape of the jabot is a matter of personal taste. Sometimes the jabot forms the finish of a collared neck, and again it is used alone. Sometimes it falls free, other times is inserted in an opening. Sometimes it is stitched to a band—that is, stitched or buttoned to a dress. In another type of jabot the gathered or pleated ruffle is extended around the neck, either lying flat or stiffly starched to make it stand erect. Still other types are small ties or bows.

The jabot's chief function is to add a fresh touch of white to the conservative costume, and we can expect to see it whenever spring arrives. Once in a while fashion sanctions jabots in a color contrasting to the color of the dress. Per-

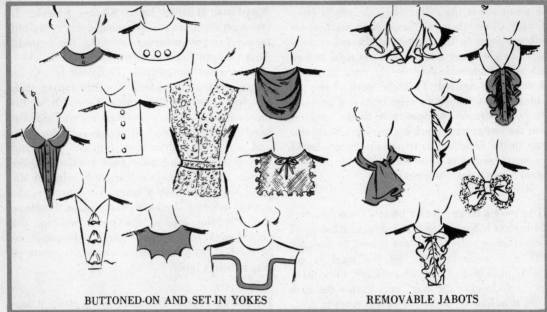

BUTTONED-ON AND SET-IN YOKES   REMOVABLE JABOTS

manent pleating effects are easily produced by tucking the jabot with fine running stitches— the tucks should extend halfway across, leaving the edge free to fall in graceful fullness. The jabot can then be washed continually and always look freshly tucked.

YOKES

Each season sees the recurrence of the yoke in some form. Clothing for women, girls, and boys features the yoke in many constructions. It is a handy detail for readjusting a worn garment.

Yokes can be (1) seamed into the dress construction; (2) overlaid by stitching the garment over the yoke; or (3) detachable and tied or buttoned to the garment. Yokes are often emphasized by an overstitched seam, and they can form the important contrast — for example, a white yoke on a dark garment, or a contrasting color combination. Often a transparent self-color is introduced in a yoke or shiny and dull surfaces of fabrics are contrasted. When a yoke is used in a printed garment, it is wise to consider matching either the background color or the least conspicuous color in the print.

Stitched-in Yokes: The result will be more successful if you finish the closing edge first and attach the collar before inserting a yoke, whenever possible. Then baste the yoke to the dress and try it on before stitching to be

sure there is no strain or pucker, and that the corners are true and square or rounded evenly. Adjustments made before you stitch the garment save time. *Squared corners must be clipped by slashing into the seams on each side of the corner.*

Overlaid Yokes: For overlaid yokes, the seams of the garment must be turned and basted. To insure an even edge, cut a cardboard gauge and press the seams over the cardboard. Finish the neck closing, the yoke, and the neck edge. Then lay the yoke flat on a table and place the finished garment edge on the yoke carefully. *Baste them flat on the table.* Now you are ready to stitch on the outside of the garment. This stitching is often close to the edge, or it can be placed back $\frac{1}{8}$ or $\frac{1}{4}$ of an inch to form a trimming line.

Transparent Yokes: Yokes of net, lace, chiffon, and fine cottons which are transparent will give better results and save time if they are first basted flat on paper. Then either join a seam or place the finished edge of the overlaid yoke on the transparent fabric and baste it in place. *Stitch through the paper.* When a lace yoke has a finished edge, it is applied over the finished edge of the garment and hemmed by hand. When the lace has no finished edge and you want to produce a finished-edge effect, first stitch the garment to the lace and then overcast a lace edge to the seam so it looks as if it were part of the yoke.

Short transparent yokes are not lined, but a long transparent vest is often lined with chiffon. In adding this effect to an old dress, always cut the fabric away under the transparency and be sure your undergarment harmonizes. If not, make a lining for the yoke in self-color chiffon. When a vest effect extends below the beltline, *it must hang free.* Finish it with a narrow picot lace edge and use the same finish on the neck edge.

Decorative Yokes: Transparent yokes can be tucked or shirred, rows of lace can be hemmed to the tucks, rows of beading and embroidery can be arranged between the tucks. The joining itself can be outlined with embroidery or beading in a fancy design. The joining can be a scalloped or scrolled edge. A pretty neckline for a schoolgirl's dress is easily made by filling in the finished neck with a straight piece of net. Seam a straight edge to the yokeline of the dress and gather the opposite edge to fit the neck. Outline this gathered edge with a row of beads to give the effect of a necklace. Close the yoke in the back with one hook and eye at the neck. Hem the edges of the yoke by hand and button the back of the garment. Then outline the edge where the yoke joins the dress with embroidered flowers in lazy-daisy stitch and sew a bead in the center of each flower.

Scalloped or Scrolled Edges: Prepare the yoke as directed for transparent yokes. Then cut cardboard in the exact outline of the yoke without the scroll or scallop. Cut another piece of cardboard showing only the scalloped edge. Turn the garment to the wrong side, lay it on the first cardboard, and run a row of basting to outline the shape of the neck. Then place the scroll-shaped cardboard in place and cut the edge of the fabric, snipping it whenever necessary to make the seam edge fit over the cardboard. Press this edge over the cardboard with an iron. Then you are ready to apply the garment edge to the yoke. First outline with basting the true straight edge of the first piece of cardboard; then place the garment over the yoke with bastings matching. Baste the yoke on this line first. It will then hold in place as you hem the uneven

edge. This beautiful finish is usually hemmed closely by hand, and it can also be arranged at the edge of the sleeve.

Detachable Yokes: Detachable yokes can be tucked inside a finished neckline to form a dicky, or attached to the outside of the garment to form a bib.

Bib Yoke Effects: These are usually short and square like a child's bib, and they can be buttoned in place. Many of these buttoned yokes are shaped. If you have no pattern, cut the shape in wrapping paper and fit it until you see the effect you like, then use this paper for a pattern. Bib yokes are usually lined with a sheer cotton fabric. Buttonholes are made with care both in detail and in spacing.

Plastrons: Yokes worn on the outside of the garment and tied around the waist with a sash, tie, or belt are called plastrons. They are made of pique or linen, or of lace and sheer metallics. To make a plastron, use a dicky pattern and finish the edges with a rolled hem or a narrow trimming edge. Cut the sash 4 inches wide and 12 inches longer then the waistline, or long enough to cross at the back and tie in the front or at the side. Other plastrons are fitted into the center of a belt cut of double fabric in any desired width and buttoned or buckled at the back.

CHAPTER XVI

COLLARS, VESTS, AND DICKIES

All kinds of collars can be made from remnants or odds and ends of fabric left from dresses and curtains—bits of lace ruffling, embroidery organdy, lawn, swiss, and other transparent fabrics. White piqué collars can be augmented by prints and colors.

Dickies are of two types: those that button in front and those that button behind. They can be set into square or rounded necklines, usually they are used with a V slash, either short or cut to the waistline.

DIAGRAMS FOR CUTTING

Diagrams on page 113 show how to cut different kinds of collar, vest, and dickie. Select the type you want, from the illustrations shown here then decide on the fabric and finish.

To use the diagrams: work on a piece of paper ruled off in 1-inch squares. Each square of the diagram represents one square on your paper. The lines which outline the collar can be easily transferred by putting each line in the squares of the diagram in the corresponding ones on your paper. To test the collar or dicky transferred in this way for size, cut the paper along the outline you have transferred from the diagrams and try it on. Make it longer, shorter, wider, or narrower as you like, and shape the paper to a becoming roll.

When your pattern has been tested, decide on the fabric. You will need about 1 yard for a vest, ¾ yard for a dicky, and ¼ yard for a collar.

Dicky A: Use diagram A on page 113. Cut it twice and join the ends marked center back. Fold back on the dotted line, not the one marked center front. This forms the facing, and the edge can be turned back and stitched. If you want a seamless front, slip-stitch this edge so the stitches do not show.

Cut 2 collars by diagram A1 on the fold of the goods. Seam the edges and turn collar. Match the center back of the collar to the center back of the vest; baste one edge of the collar to the neckline of the vest and the other edge to the edge of the facing. Seam and press the seams open. This makes a convertible neckline. Be sure the corners are clipped so the edges lie flat. The front can be finished with buttons and buttonholes, or a button sewed to the garment and a snap fastener under the button.

Vest B: Make it from diagram A. Cut on the crossed line from X to X and make it like dicky A described above.

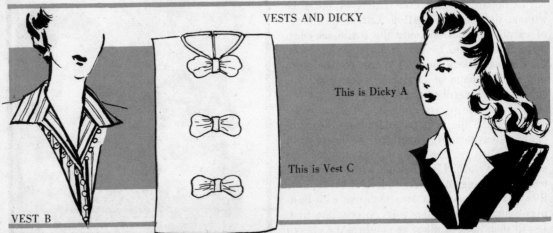

VESTS AND DICKY

This is Dicky A

This is Vest C

VEST B

Vest C: Make a smooth-front vest from diagram A which is cut by folding the pattern on the center-front line and placing this fold on a straight fold of fabric. Finish the neck with a binding or facing and close the center back with hooks and eyes or flat buttons. Hem the edges. Make a row of self-fabric bows for the center front. Using diagram A2, cut each bow double, with the center-front line placed on the straight fabric. Seam the bows and turn them to the right side. Press and fold them through the center. Cut a 1-inch strip of self-fabric 2 to 3 inches long and fold back the edges so it forms a long narrow strip and bind it around the center of each bow. Sew the bows down the center front. If you prefer little tabs, fold the bows in half, a little unevenly, and gather them, then sew them one after the other down the front, as in the illustration. If they are made of organdy, tuck the fabric before cutting and edge the tabs and the neckline with narrow lace. A handmade vest or dicky like this is very costly to buy. You can make it yourself for a fraction of the cost.

Dicky D: Cut from diagram B. Cut it twice, with the center-front line placed on the straight of the goods. Use the collar in diagram B1 or in B2. For a double collar, cut it twice. Stitch the edges and turn the collar to the right side. Hem the edges of the vest and fold it double at the center-front seam. Join the ends at the center back. Join the collar, following directions on page 115. The front edges just meet, so they can be closed with buttons held by loops.

Vest E: Also made from diagram B, this time using the short cutting line marked X to X. Make either a rounded collar or a convertible neckline, as described above for dicky D.

Vest F: Make a collar cut in one. Use cutting diagram C and cut it twice. Join the center back in a French seam. Bind or hem the edges, or finish them with a narrow ruffle or self-fabric or lace. For a tailored collar, cut the pattern four times and make it double so you can turn it and press the edges flat. Fasten it at a becoming neckline with a pin or broach.

Collar G: Cut by diagram D, with the center back laid on a straight fold of the goods. The

YOU CAN CUT THIS GROUP WITHOUT A PATTERN

Two versions of Dicky D

Two versions of Vest E

VEST F

COLLAR G

Look in the Ready-Reference Guide at the back for exact page numbers of Detailed Instructions

COLLARS FOR V NECK LINES

COLLAR H

GILETS

Gilet that can be worn without a jacket.

COLLAR I

edges can be finished with a ruffle or ruching of self-fabric, or with a contrasting color in a binding or in a flat faced band.

Collar H: Cut by diagram E. Cut it double, of a fabric which can be starched stiff. Cut it on a fold on the straight of the goods. Match the edges of the two pieces and seam. Turn and press, then stitch the edge on the outside. If you want a corded effect, the stitching must be close to the edge.

Collar I: Cut from diagram F. Cut it single, of a sheer fabric. Finish the edge with hand crochet or a heavier lace, with motifs not too fine.

Gilets: A gilet is a sleeveless blouse to be worn with suits or sweaters. Cut by diagram I on page 115. First measure your bustline loosely. Center this figure between C-C on the diagram. Then measure your waistline in front to your

waistline in back, passing the tape measure over your shoulder. Center this figure on the dotted line A-B. As you cut, add 4 inches to the length and cut the width to fit your bust measure. Fold the fabric in half and mark the center, M. At this point cut a slash for the neck and pull the gilet over your head. Hold the neckline fullness with pinned tucks; pin the underarm, taking in a wider seam at the back than the front; pin the shoulder and place a row of pins down the center front for the front slash. Cut on this row of pins. Before you take off the gilet, mark the waistline.

Seam the shoulder and underarm, bind the sleeve edge, and make a casing at the waistline through which to run an elastic. To finish the neckline, hem the slashed edge by hand and bind the neck with a straight piece of self-fabric cut 1¼ inches wide. Seam the ends to make a tie. This neckline can be varied to suit your needs.

Plastrons: These colorful vestlike arrangements are made from soft rayon crepes or from satins which are soft enough to gather but not transparent. Measure from shoulder to waist and add 12 inches for the fold below the waistline. Cut the plastron this length and 18 inches wide. Slit the center front in a deep V and hem all the edges. Gather the shoulder lines and shape them to your dress by pinning. This shaping is held by the gathered unit which you cut to fit the neckline. Then slit the lower edge and turn it up into pockets. The top of each turn-up is gathered or plain.

COLLARS CUT BY PATTERN

The collars in most dress patterns, and those you will use in remaking dresses, fall into three classes: small round collars, small straight collars, and collars shaped for a V neck. Directions for making and applying several collars of each type are given below.

The collar can be cut from a single fabric or double. Finish the edge with a rolled hem, a binding, a ruffle, a trimming of tatting or hand crochet, faggoting, or a bias facing in a contrasting color. Transparent collars are often bound with a 12-inch double binding. Plan several dresses that can be worn with a variety of colors.

DIAGRAM FOR CUTTING DICKIES, VESTS AND COLLARS

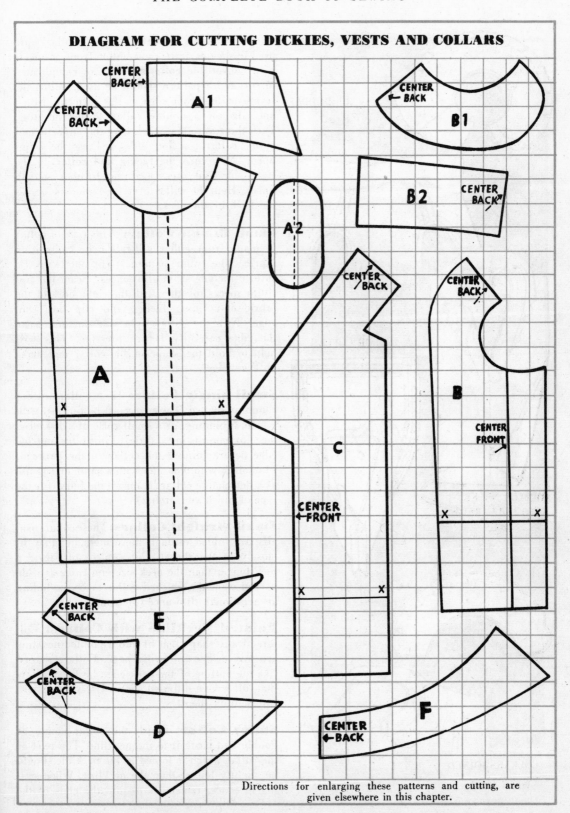

Directions for enlarging these patterns and cutting, are
given elsewhere in this chapter.

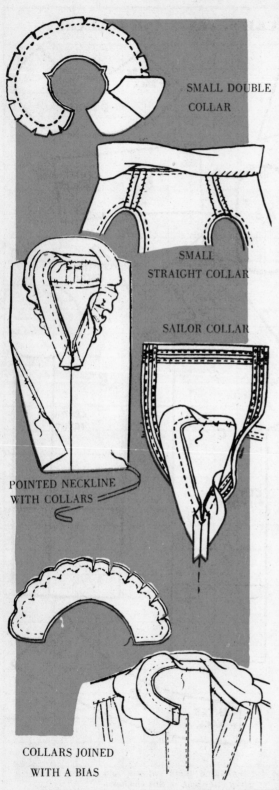

SMALL DOUBLE
COLLAR

SMALL
STRAIGHT COLLAR

SAILOR COLLAR

POINTED NECKLINE
WITH COLLARS

COLLARS JOINED
WITH A BIAS

Collars with Facing: These collars are used in dickies, coats, and button-front garments with convertible collars. They are complicated to cut, and a pattern should be used. Stitch the revere to the front edge of the garment. Stitch one edge of a double collar to the neckline. Turn the revere and stitch it to the opposite end of the collar (on both sides). Press the seams open. Now turn the facing and collar to the right side and press again to form a smooth finish. Hem the collar over the seam line across the back of the neck.

Small Double Collar: This type of collar is made from either self-fabric or contrasting fabric. The collar pattern is cut out twice. Be sure to include seam allowances. Seam the two collar pieces together with the right sides of the fabric and lining facing, and clip the seam edge. Turn the collar right side out and baste the edge carefully before pressing. This will help to hold the shape of the collar and make an even edge.

Small Single Collar: These collars are cut round or shaped. The edge must be finished with a hem, a binding, or a small ruffle of self-fabric, lace, or contrasting fabric. Finish the outside edge before joining the collar to the garment. (1) Join it with bias, (2) with a band, or (3) use as a detachable collar. (Consult the index for the type of finish you prefer.)

Small Straight Collars: These collars usually are folded through the center, and they fit closely to the throat. Cut a piece of fabric 1 inch longer than the neck size and twice as wide as you want the finished collar to be, including an additional allowance for seams.

Pointed Neckline with Collars: Collars of any shape that fit into a pointed neckline are joined. See following page. Collars shaped like the outline of the neck edge lie flat. Collars that roll have a different shape. Use your pattern for shaping them.

Sailor Collar: Finish the collar single or double and baste it to the neckline. The part of the collar which is joined to the neckline should be slightly longer than the neckline. When sewing in place, remember to join the ends of the

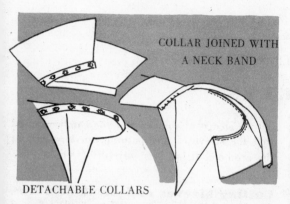

COLLAR JOINED WITH A NECK BAND

DETACHABLE COLLARS

collar at the point of the neckline. To finish, see instructions below for applying collars.

APPLYING COLLARS TO NECKLINES

Collars which are cut double or are lined can be put on like a wide binding. One edge of the collar is stitched to the neckband, and the other edge is turned and hemmed over the joining. They can also be joined with a bias binding or with a band, or they can be covered by a facing or lining.

Collar Joined with a Bias: Place the collar on the right side of the garment and baste it to the neckline with edges matching. Include in the basting a ¾-inch bias and stitch the seam. Turn the seam down and hem the bias to the garment. The ends of the bias must be turned in at the neck, hemmed, and finished neatly.

Collar Joined with a Neckband: The neckband is a straight lined piece cut the size of the neck opening. Its function is to raise the collar higher. Cut a lining the same size as the neckband. Seam the neckband to the collar and place the lining over this joining, with seam edges meeting. Finish the ends of the neckband; bind the neckline with the neckband, using a fine hemming or machine stitching. When a collar is applied to a shirtwaist front finished with a band, the center front of the collar must be spaced to center *at the center of the band—not at the edge of the neck opening.*

Collar Joined to a Pointed Neck: The collar is always cut longer than the neck opening. Baste it to the neck edge with a bias binding. Then cross the pointed ends of the collar at the point of the neckline and baste. Cover this point with a stay and outline it with stitching. Now slash the stay into the point almost cutting the stitching. Turn the stay to the wrong side and hem it.

Detachable Collars: The neck of the dress can be faced, and the neck of the collar bound. Snap fasteners can be sewed to the collar binding and corresponding snaps sewed in the neck facing. Instead of snap fasteners, tiny buttons may be sewed to the dress and button-holes made to correspond in the neck binding. Tape can be bought by the yard with either snap fasteners or buttons and buttonholes attached, designed purposely for removable collars. If you use this tape, overcast it to the turned-in neck and place the opposite side over the binding of the collar. When snap fasteners are not used, this separate finish is completed without them, and the collar is basted to the garment.

Coat Collars: Coat collars of piqué or linen or heavier cottons can be cut double or lined with a sheer cotton. They are finished like small round collars and must be detachable.

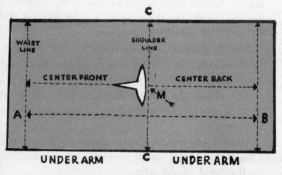

WAIST LINE

C

SHOULDER LINE

CENTER FRONT   CENTER BACK

A   B

M

UNDER ARM   C   UNDER ARM

DIAGRAM FOR CUTTING A GILET

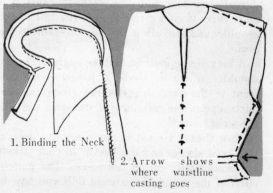

1. Binding the Neck

2. Arrow shows where waistline casting goes

CHAPTER XVII

SLEEVES

Most home sewers quickly master the details of cutting, basting, and fitting; but in the question periods following my lectures, I have found the same questions are asked over and over again—about the principles of construction for sleeves, waistlines, hems, pockets, and trimmings. The details of completing a garment which puzzles one woman are apparently stumbling blocks for most amateur sewers. These finishing details are reviewed here and in the next 5 chapters.

SLEEVES AND ARMHOLES

The line of the sleeve and armhole is the most difficult line to cut in any garment because it must curve to fit a circle around the fall of the shoulder and also allow for the movement of the arm.

A long sleeve must fit at three angles: (1) the shoulder, where the sleeve is joined to the garment in the armhole; (2) the elbow, an important point for movement of the arm; and (3) the wrist or cuff.

Most sleeves are cut in one piece, but decorative band sleeves and the sleeves in coat jackets are occasionally cut in two pieces. The pattern chart of the particular garment tells you how to cut the sleeve, of course; and you can be assured that the sleeve of any pattern you buy will fit the armhole. It has been carefully tested.

Cutting Sleeves and Armholes: Here, for ready reference is a list of "Do's" and "Don't's" in cutting sleeves.

DO note pattern marks for the straight of the goods. Fold the sleeve pattern on this mark and be sure this fold is laid on straight fabric grain.

DON'T lay the sleeve pattern on the fabric carelessly. If the sleeve shifts even a little off grain, it will always twist in wear.

DO prefit the pattern for the sleeve before you alter the pattern length. Prefitting saves hours of work, and often it permits changes that can never be made in finished garments.

DON'T rush your cutting and expect to make changes later in fitting.

DO outline the sleeve pattern carefully no matter how strange it looks. Each type of sleeve has an individual shaping.

DON'T cut off the top of the sleeve. Never straighten an edge because it looks crooked. Never nip off a corner.

DO outline the armhole of the pattern clearly and carefully.

DON'T skimp in cutting an armhole edge. Never let the pattern shift as you cut.

DO fit the sleeve at the shoulder; first, so the sleeve hangs straight when the arm is down; second, so the armhole seam curves around the tip edge of shoulder.

DON'T fit the sleeve up high on the shoulder to eliminate the soft fold of waist at front and back unless you want your sleeve to tear out.

DO check the sleeve darts at the elbow to control arm activity and allow elbow room where it is needed.

DON'T shorten a sleeve above or below the elbow and forget about moving the elbow darts to the bend of the arm.

DO fit the wrist snugly when the arm is bent.

Pin the cuff line and move the arm before deciding on the length of the sleeve.

DON'T fit the sleeve tightly while the arm is hanging straight.

DO make the sleeves fit the curved shape of the armhole. Pin it carefully, then baste it. Fit the sleeves before stitching.

DON'T stitch the sleeves without a fitting.

DO make and insert shoulder pads before fitting the sleeves.

DON'T fit the sleeves and then add the shoulder pads.

DO allow enough length in both the underarm length of the sleeve and the underarm length of the dress to permit raising your arms comfortably to your head.

DON'T fit the underarm of a belted dress so tightly you cannot raise your arm without tearing the sleeve at the underarm.

DO change the sleeve when altering a shoulder line to make the armhole larger or smaller, in order to compensate for the changes (see Chapter XI).

DO recut the armhole (laying the pattern on the armhole and reshaping it) so the sleeve will fit the armhole.

DON'T take up a shoulder seam even a little and think it will not change the sleeve fitting.

DON'T slash the garment under the arm.

TYPES OF SLEEVE

Most garments today are made with a set-in sleeve, which means that the seam at the armhole is curved to the shoulder line and there is no extra fullness at the top. The sleeves can be long, three-quarter length, or short; and the cuff is usually finished with a binding, a bias of self-fabric, a hem, or a band. The top of the sleeve is fitted with little darts or gathers, or, in the case of tailored worsted garments, with "shrunk out" fullness. Most sleeves now have a little padding at the shoulder. Do not be surprised to find sleeves and yoke cut in one. Kimono sleeves are

Look in the Ready-Reference Guide at the back for exact page numbers of Detailed Instructions

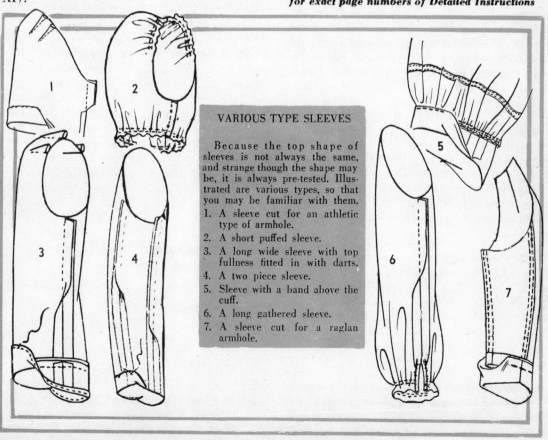

VARIOUS TYPE SLEEVES

Because the top shape of sleeves is not always the same, and strange though the shape may be, it is always pre-tested. Illustrated are various types, so that you may be familiar with them.

1. A sleeve cut for an athletic type of armhole.
2. A short puffed sleeve.
3. A long wide sleeve with top fullness fitted in with darts.
4. A two piece sleeve.
5. Sleeve with a band above the cuff.
6. A long gathered sleeve.
7. A sleeve cut for a raglan armhole.

cut in one. When the fashions introduce a new sleeve cut, you will find it shaped and tested in the patterns you buy.

Puffed Sleeves: Puffed sleeves can be long or short, scanty or very full. They are cut with an extra allowance of fabric, which is gathered across the top in at least two rows of gathers to shape them to the curve of the shoulder. Use two rows of gathers to join the sleeve to the cuff, which can be made of wide or narrow banding *cut straight*. The cuff has no opening; it can be decorated with bands of contrasting material or of lace. Puffed sleeves are usually made of some sheer fabric. When you make your gathers, wind the end of the gathering thread around a pin so that you can increase the thread length as the sleeve is joined to the dress.

Raglan Sleeves: The raglan, from which these sleeves get their name, is a loose overcoat named after an English general. They have a long shaping at the top instead of a curve. Your pattern will give the correct sleeve shape and armhole. Unlike other kinds of sleeve, raglan sleeves are often set into the garment before the underarm seams of the sleeve and blouse are joined. Stitch the seam and press it open. Clip it a little where it curves.

Activity Armholes: Armholes in utility garments are shaped so they will not pull out when the arm is raised. They are cut much longer under the arm, and both sleeve and armhole have a square cut. This workaday sleeve must be cut on the straight of the goods, and the top edge shaped with darts. Set it in the armhole as the pattern directs and take care to match all notches.

Fancy Sleeves: Fancy sleeves are often gathered on the inside seam and on the outside of the sleeve. They are especially cut for this. Banded sleeves are made in two types: (1) the band shaped like the sleeve—the two fabrics are joined and cut by a sleeve pattern, and (2) a short sleeve finished with an extra band, circular or gathered.

Tailored Sleeves: In some coat constructions and in all mannish tailored garments, the sleeves are cut in two pieces. This is the classic tailored sleeve. Instead of being shaped to the

armhole with darts, the fullness is held in with little gathers. In worsteds or woolens, the fullness is shrunk out so that the sleeve fits into the shoulder smoothly without the use of darts or gathers. It is possible to shrink out the fullness in other fabrics, but it is a long, slow process.

How to Shrink Out Fullness: Gather the top of the sleeve on the seam line and gather it again 1/8 inch nearer the edge. Baste the sleeve to the armhole just as you would any sleeve and distribute the gathers evenly. Ease in the fullness for about 2 or 3 inches, with a little more toward the front than the back. Try the sleeve on and make sure it hangs straight. Stitch the sleeve. To shrink out the fullness, press the top of the sleeve with the gathers on the wrong side using a damp cloth. This will lightly steam the fullness. Turn the garment to the right side and hold your pressing mit in the cap of the sleeve. Press it with a damp cloth until it looks as though the fullness has disappeared and you have a smoothly rounded shoulder.

Shirt Sleeves: Sleeve and shoulder are joined before either sleeve or underarm of the garment is seamed. When the shoulder seam and yoke are finished, lay your work flat and join the shoulder seam in a flat fell. Join the seams and stitch so that the seam comes on the right side of the garment. Cut away one side of the seam and turn in the opposite edge; stitch it down. Baste this seam on the right side of the garment as close to the edge as possible. Then you are ready to French-seam the sleeve and underarm.

Bound Armholes: Armholes are not bound except in unlined coats made of very heavy material.

Shoulder Pads: The shoulder pads differ according to the fabric. When the dress is made of cotton or rayon crepe, you can make a little gathered ruffle of taffeta and stitch it into the seam at the top of the sleeve. The edge of the ruffle is pinked. This kind of padding washes easily and keeps its stiffness. The padding for woolen dresses is made out of a square of fabric with layers of cotton held in place. Fold this

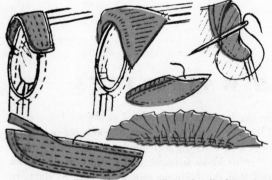

Use large triangles for woolens; Small, long or round shaped for sheer fabrics. Gathered taffeta for washable garments.

SELECT THE PROPER SHOULDER PAD shaping and fit it to the shoulder and sleeve after the sleeve is joined. Raglan sleeves require a pie-shaped padding, with the broad edge wide enough to extend across the shoulder line. Join one point to the shoulder or top of the sleeve, and the other points where the yoke and sleeve meet.

Pressing Sleeve Seams: The seam is usually pressed towards the sleeve and not open.

CUFFS AND SLEEVE EDGES

When you come to finishing the sleeves, there are a number of questions you should take into consideration:

Is it a long sleeve fitted close at the wrist?
Is it a long or short sleeve ending in gathers?
Is it a long sleeve in a tailored garment which requires a cuff?
Is it a long sleeve that requires a mannish cuff?
Is it a short sleeve with a straight edge?
Is it a short sleeve with a shaped edge?
Is it a wide long sleeve that must be faced?

Sleeve Fitted Close at the Wrist: This kind of sleeve can be stitched wide enough to let your hand slip in and out without an opening. Finish the edge with a binding or narrow hem.

If the sleeve edge is to have an opening, decide whether it will be closed with buttons and loops or with snap fasteners. Finish the edge of the opening and the hem of the sleeve with a seam binding. If it is too narrow, apply an extension facing. When snap fasteners are used, the edges of the opening must lap; with buttons and loops, they must meet.

Gathered Sleeve: Gathered sleeves are usually finished with a narrow cuff of straight material. The easiest way to apply it is to seam one edge of the cuff to the gathered sleeve edge, or edge.

Straight Cuff: Both straight and gathered sleeves can be finished with straight cuffs. Cut the cuff the width desired. If it is to be fastened with a button, finish the ends and turn it. Finish the seam opening of the sleeve like a placket and bind the edge of the sleeve with the cuff. Finally, make the buttonhole and attach the button.

Mannish Cuff: Used in shirts, blouses, and shirtwaist dresses. This cuff looks like a double straight cuff when completed. Cut a fold of straight material the desired width (at least 4 inches) and 3 inches wider than your wrist measure. Then proceed as described for straight cuff. Fold back and make marks for 4 small buttonholes through which to slip cuff links. See Chapter XIX for detailed description of various buttonhole finishes.

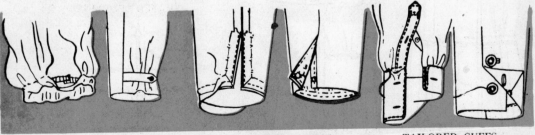

SOFT SLEEVE   CUFFED SLEEVE   TAILORED CUFFS

CHAPTER XVIII

SMOOTH FITTING WAISTLINES

In a typical one-piece dress, skirt and waist are joined with a seam at the waistline. The dress can be worn with a separate belt, or the joining can be beltless and decorated with embroidery or stitching. Other styles feature a set-in belt, which is a band stitched between waist seam and skirt seam. Dresses with waist and skirt cut in one can be fitted smoothly in princess lines, or fitted loosely and drawn in at the waist with a separate belt or a belt run through a casing.

When skirt and waist are separate, the top of the skirt can be finished with a binding, a belt fitted inside so it does not show, a stitched-on fabric belt, or a separate belt.

A smooth waistline depends upon prefitting waistline and properly preparing it before it is joined. Many sewers join the waistline seam before stitching the side seams, but it is much easier if you wait and fit the garment before you join the waistline.

An inner belt is sometimes added to hold the waist firm. One way to join the inner belt is to seam the waist and skirt first, then insert the belt, basting it to seam.

Joined with a Seam: The seam joining at the waistline of a one-piece dress is often complete. It may have fullness, or it may have double seams running into it. First press all the seams. Clip the ends at the top of each seam on the skirt and turn the top-edge seam allowance with an iron. Make sure the end of the waist is fitted and that the fullness laid in gathers or darts is exactly where it is needed to flatter your figure. Decide on the length of waist and amount of fullness before you make the joining permanent.

With Set-In Belt: An extra wide beltline on a dress is often a cleverly set-in band; which is sometimes—in spite of its tight appearance and vivid separating color—edged with cording which makes it look exactly like a separate belt.

When bands in contrasting colors are part of the styling, the pieces must either be cut according to a pattern or joined before the fabric is cut. As many as three colors may be grouped together, or the belting band can be outlined with a separating color. In either case, all the pieces are joined with seams; and those seams must, of course, be extremely accurate. So, unless you are an expert stitcher, be very careful to measure the seam allowance constantly as you baste. Bands of self-fabric, both straight and shaped to a point in the center of the bustline, are a becoming feature often used in gathered circular or gored skirts.

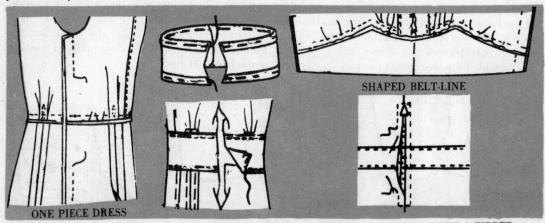

SHAPED BELT-LINE

ONE PIECE DRESS

JOINED WITH A SEAM   SET-IN WIDE BELT   INVISIBLE PLACKET WITH A ZIPPER

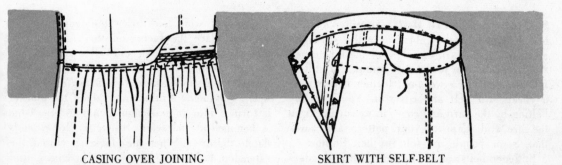

CASING OVER JOINING   SKIRT WITH SELF-BELT

Slenderizing Waistlines: Princess dresses are fitted with waist darts, or the dress is shaped to the waistline by the seams. The more darts you use, the shorter each dart will be and the smoother the fitting line. Princess dresses should not be too tightly fitted.

Never fit a separate beltline so tightly that the flesh bulges around the belt. Women with a large abdomen should not wear a belt buckle except in back. Attractive belts for large women are made of leather and covered part way with self-fabric to break the beltline.

Drawstring Beltlines: When the dress is fitted with scant fullness, a becoming style is to have the belt run through a casing stitched to the dress. This style should not be used on straight-line dresses.

Separate Skirts: Skirts can be finished to wear over a blouse with a separate belt; under a blouse so the belt does not show; or with a self-fabric belt stitched to the top and worn outside.

Inner Belting: If you want your skirt to extend above the normal waistline, you must fit in an inside belt of stiff belting which is sold by the yard at notion counters. Turn in the ends of this inner belt and attach hooks and eyes placed close together. Turn the skirt edge over this belt and hold it in place with catch stitches so

no stitching shows on the outside. Or, if you prefer, turn and press the skirt edge, and stitch it to the belting so that it extends a little above the edge of the belting.

When a skirt is raised 2½ or 3 inches by means of an inner belting, the side seams must be fitted smoothly after the belting is in place. Such skirts are often worn with a narrow leather belt which holds the waist firmly in place.

If a wide belting is not available in your stores, cut a straight strip of buckram and fit it with darts so that it is wide at the top and curves into your natural waistline. Bone it at intervals so it will stay in place and bind the top and bottom with a strip of fabric so the buckram won't cut into you. Fit it snugly and close it with hooks and eyes sewed close together.

SEPARATE BELTS

Soft Fabric Belt: To make a soft fabric belt, cut a straight piece of fabric the desired length and twice the width desired, plus seam allowance. Fold the fabric lengthwise and stitch the edges together with a close-running stitch. Turn the tube of fabric inside out. Most home sewers do not interline fabric belts, but interlining makes a smarter belt. The belt can be 1 inch wide; most are 2 inches. Belts over 3 inches wide are classed as wide belts and must be stiffened.

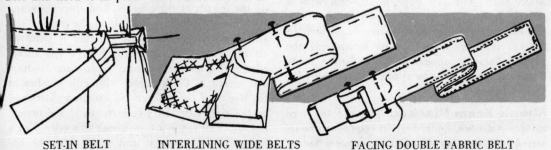

SET-IN BELT   INTERLINING WIDE BELTS   FACING DOUBLE FABRIC BELT

Stiffened Fabric Belt: To stiffen a fabric belt, either turn the fabric over the stiffening and cover it, or turn the edges of the fabric belt and overcast them to the stiff lining. For stiffening you can use a worn-out leather belt or buy a cheap stiff belt and cover it. You can buy belting by the yard and cover it, or cut buckram the size and shape of your pattern and cover that. Some people use felt for belt linings.

Stiffened belts can be finished with both edges straight or pointed or curved; or one end can be shaped and the other straight. They can be exactly the size of your waistline and close with a button, clasp button, or hooks and eyes; or they can be longer and pointed so that one end passes through a buckle or slide. You can make them still longer and tie them or sew on a ribbon tie.

PLACKETS

A placket is a short finished opening. It must be inconspicuous in skirt, dress, and belt. When waist and skirt are joined, the joining must be finished before the placket is inserted. When a belt is attached to the dress, do not join it flush with the placket, but make it long enough to extend beyond the placket and finish it in a point. When the skirt opens at the side and the waist at the front, the inner belt is made to close at the front, and the skirt edge is left free from the front closing to the placket. The free edge of the skirt should be finished with tape and snap fasteners to make a smooth closing.

Invisible Placket: Decide on the length of the placket opening and cut a piece of fabric along the lengthwise threads for the extension facing, 2½ inches wide and the length of the placket. Cut a slit in the skirt for the placket opening and seam the extension in place—it binds only one edge of the placket, the underneath edge. The top edge is finished with a narrow hem about ½ inch wide. Stitch across the lower end of the band extension. When the placket is long, add a snap fastener. If the placket does not appear at the end of a seam, a narrow facing must be applied to the top edge of the placket.

Simple Seam Placket: This placket, used on house dresses, underwear, et cetera, can be inserted in a seam or slit. Cut the placket facing 2½ inches wide and twice the length of the placket. Place the facing on the right side of the garment and stitch one edge around the placket opening. Turn the facing to the wrong side of the garment. *Baste this turned edge at the seam.* The facing on the underside of the placket is formed into an extension facing and the edge is hemmed at the seam. Stitch the lower ends flat to the dress. When the placket is closed, the extension holds the buttons or fasteners, and the two facings should lie smoothly over each other.

Continuous Dress Placket: Cut a facing 2 inches wide and a little longer than twice the length of the placket opening. Place this facing on the right side of the garment and stitch one edge around the opening. Turn to the wrong side of the garment and hem it down on the former seam. Sew the ends of the placket piece and close with the desired fastening.

Placket for Skirt with Belting: Fit the inside belting and finish it with hooks and eyes. Turn the seam allowance at the top of the skirt and attach it to the belting, leaving the end open for the turn of the placket. Cut two pieces of fabric 1 inch more than the length of the placket and 2 inches wide. Apply one piece as an extension facing, to the lower side of placket. After seaming the facing to the upper side of the placket, turn, fold on the seam and make the hem with tiny slip stitches on the left side. This extension will hold the snap fasteners or buttons on one side of the placket. Both facings are stitched firmly close to the edge and extend under the end of the belting. This placket also is good for skirts finished at the waistline with straight bindings.

Tailored Placket: If set in the seam, decide on the length of the placket, and snip the seam. Baste back the right-hand fold of the placket and stitch this edge, continuing the line of stitching all the way down the seam. Finish this inside edge of the placket opening with seam binding, and attach to the garment with slip stitches in the length of the placket. No stitching must show on the right side. To give strength to the fastening, you can stitch a tape under this edge. Cut a facing of self-material and stitch it to the op-

The plackets shown on the right are used for soft dresses, those on the left for tailored.

posite edge. Turn it flat to extend behind the placket and line it with sturdy cotton to hold the fastening.

Placket for Pleated Skirt: When the placket falls in a seam, cut the seam 2 inches wide on both sides and finish it flat so it will not show through the pleats. To do this, turn back the fold on one edge of the seam and place a strip of tape between the fold for extra strength. Stitch it flat, catching the tape in the stitching. Turn the other edge at the seam line and make a double turn. Hold it flat with seam binding stitched to the one edge and hemmed to the garment with small stitches which do not show on the right side. When a slash must be made in the skirt, bind it and try to use a pleat over the placket.

WHEN YOU MAKE A SKIRT

Pleated Skirts: Pleats can be spaced across the front, on each seam, or in all-around effects; they can be deep pleats, shallow pleats, or unpressed pleats.

After you have decided upon the type of skirt, choose the kind of pleat you want—side pleat, box pleat, inverted pleat, and so forth. Begin by marking the center front and center back; next mark the pleats, using a gauge. Decide where the placket will be and cut it. Next hold the pleats into the waistline with a straight belt. Now you are ready to fit.

Turn the hem and decide how far down from the waist you want the pleats held by stitching. When the pleats have been stitched and the hem finished and pressed, press the pleats. Some sewers baste the pleats flat all the way down; but this makes it difficult to fit and adjust the skirt. A better way is to press in the folded crease, then lay and baste the pleats only half-way from the waist. This makes it easier to judge the fullness in turning the hem and deciding the length for the pleat stitching.

Simple dresses can be pleated across the front and the back left straight for variety. Children's dresses, however, should be pleated all around.

Shallow pleats, turning only 1 inch of fabric, should be permanently creased, or they will be difficult to care for. To do this, lay the pleat and stitch it below the hipline. Continue the stitching *on the creased edge only* to the hem. Stitch the creased edge at the back of the pleat. A pleat stitched in this way is easy to press and holds the line of the crease permanently.

When a kick pleat is inserted in the front or back of a dress, first join the piecing for the kick pleat and then join the seam above the pleat. In making a kick pleat without a pattern, it is easier to mark the center of the garment, then lay a box pleat the full length of the skirt. Then decide how deep you want the kick pleat and stitch across the fabric, bringing the stitched line to a point at the center of the pleat. Continue the stitching on both sides of the front, holding the pleat 5 inches below the point. Fasten the threads securely. Cut away the excess material above the stitching and press the pleats. These edges can be permanently creased by making a stitching as close to the edge as possible.

Gathered Skirts: Straight lengths of fabric simply hemmed and gathered like the peasant skirts of Europe are a feature of the popular dirndls. They can be made of soft woolens, rayon prints, or printed cottons.

The width of the skirt must be decided on the basis of the fabric. Only a very soft fabric is effective in a full gathered skirt. Heavier fabrics can be shaped and then gathered. Most women find this kind of skirt more becoming than a straight gathered skirt. For children and growing girls, however, the straight skirt is becoming and easy to make.

Skirts with Yokes: Skirts set on yokes or on a band belt, or featuring a pocket cut in one with the garment, should have the yokeline stitched and pressed before the long seams of the garment are joined. Don't be afraid of fashion details like side pockets cut into the skirt below the waistline. The pocket is adjusted first, seamed to the right side, then turned. Then seam the opposite side of the pocket to the yoke and join the yoke to the skirt panel. At this point you are ready to baste the long seams.

If your hips are full, avoid the straight-backed skirt. The skirt will look straight but give a more flattering line if you add a little fullness.

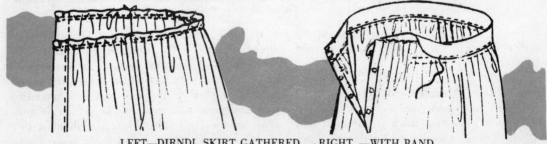

LEFT—DIRNDL SKIRT GATHERED, RIGHT —WITH BAND

HOW TO HANG A SKIRT

When the garment has been fitted and joined at the waist, you are ready to mark and make the correct hem line, which is commonly called "hanging the skirt." Slip on the skirt and look at yourself in a long mirror. Consider the length of the skirt in relation both to current fashion and to your figure proportions. Then have someone measure from the floor with a yardstick and with chalk mark the skirt at the correct height for the turning edge. Be sure you wear the same style of shoe during this fitting that you intend to wear when the garment is finished. A variation in the height of your heels can make a great deal of difference.

How to Even Your Own Hemline: If a helper is not available, you can even your own hemline by standing beside a table and placing a row of pins around the skirt or chalking a line wherever the table touches you as you turn. The table must be low enough so that the mark comes below the hip line. Measure from this mark to the hem of the skirt; and a uniform measurement from your chalkline or pin line to the hem, all the way around, will insure a straight skirt hanging at an even distance from the floor. Another way of using a table as a skirt marker, is to chalk the edge of the table. Then as you gradually turn, the chalk will be transferred to the skirt in a regular line. You must have a straight-edged table to do this; a

rounded edge will give you a chalk line too broad to be accurate.

You can also hang a skirt with an automatic skirt marker. This ingenious device consists of a square base holding an upright piece of wood which has attached to it a sliding container holding powdered chalk. The container can be raised or lowered on the upright to the proper height for the hem line. To the container is fastened a tube and rubber ball. Place the skirt marker on the floor beside you, adjust it to the proper height, and press the bulb. This squirts a little chalk on your garment. Turn around, keeping close to the marker, and continue to press the bulb. On removing the garment, mark the chalk lines with a basting thread. The measure gives best results when the chalk line is above the hem edge of the garment. Then unpin your trial hem and measure from the chalk mark to the edge of the skirt, continuing the same measurements all the way around.

Professionals place a row of pins at the true turning edge of the skirt after hanging. They rip the temporary hem and lay the skirt edge flat; then they baste an outline at the turning edge, and next measure for the width of the hem with a gauge, making the edge even to correspond with either the usual 2½- or 3-inch hem or using the narrowest place in the hem as a universal measure. Before turning the hem, they finish the edge (1) with seam binding, (2) with a stitched turn, or (3) with a turn. Once the edge is finished, the skirt can be turned at the

HOW TO HANG A SKIRT

Placing row of pins at turning edge.

Using edge of straight table as measurer.

Using an automatic skirt marker.

basting. Smooth the edge over the skirt so it lies flat and hold it in place with pins or bastings. You are ready to hem the skirt by hand or machine. Press the hem both before and after stitching to insure perfect smoothness.

Hanging a Circular Skirt: When the style feature of your garment is a full circular skirt, join the seams, make the waist, and join the waist to the skirt before adjusting the hem. The garment should then hang on a clothes hanger for at least two days so the fabric can stretch normally. If the dress is made in a lightweight wool or jersey or a rayon crepe or a cotton, the extra stretch of the fabric will hang out. If your dress is a heavier wool or jersey, it will be helpful to baste a roll of unbleached muslin to the hem to assist in hanging out the extra stretch. Never use weights.

Even the hem of the skirt and mark it carefully. Then measure for the hem turning—1 inch is ample. The top edge of your hem must be turned and held in place with a gathering string so that the extra fullness can be laid flat. In circular skirts of woolen fabrics, a one-stitched hem is sufficient. The top edge is not finished and is not turned. In transparent fabrics the edges of circular skirts are often hemstitched by machine. (Cut the hemstitching in half and turn the edge in a tiny hem.)

ADJUSTING A SKIRT

When you shorten a skirt, take accurate measurements and allow for the edge to be turned and finished. Be careful not to make too deep a hem, as it detracts from the graceful swing of a skirt. Usually 3 inches are allowed in hems. When you lengthen a skirt you may find the edge is so uneven that you cannot turn an even hem, or you haven't enough material to turn any hem. If either is the case, remember that the hemline can be faced with a lining fabric cut on the bias. Stitch the bias facing to the right side of the skirt a little below the line marked for turning. Turn the hem and baste the edge carefully, making sure that the garment fabric turns up a little under the skirt so the facing will not show.

If the center back of the skirt is too long, and sags at the back and behind the knees, remove the skirt at the waistline and lift it, starting at the *center* back and working out toward the side seams until it hangs straight.

If wrinkles form across the middle of the skirt because the center front is too long, it, too, should be lifted and treated the same way in the front.

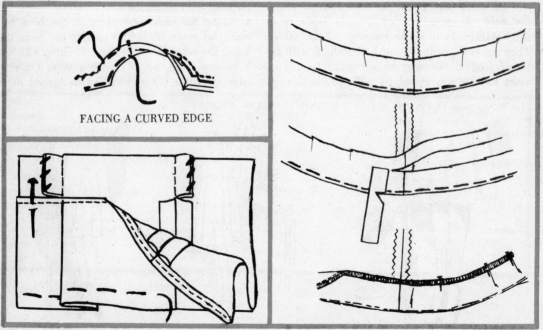

FACING A CURVED EDGE

HEMMING A PLEATED SKIRT   THREE STEPS IN MAKING A CIRCULAR HEM

CHAPTER XIX

FASTENERS — FROM BUTTONS TO ZIPPERS

The closing of a garment may be concealed or emphasized for decoration, depending upon the type of garment and individual taste. In choosing the fasteners it is just as important to understand the uses of the different kinds of fastener as it is to know how to put them on.

TYPES OF GARMENT CLOSING

Concealed: In concealed garment closings the main purpose is to keep the closing flat and smooth. Suitable fasteners are snap fasteners, hooks and eyes, zippers, or flat buttons. Fly closings require buttonholes which must be cut and finished with buttonhole stitch, never bound.

Tailored: Closings such as these are used in shirts and feature tailored buttons or zippers or hooks and eyes. Buttonholes are cut and finished with buttonhole stitch. In cuffs, link buttons can be made to take the place of cuff links, and they are sometimes used as a novelty closing on sport dresses. Be sure buttons used on wash fabrics are washable.

Soft Dress: Dresses often feature closings with edges that meet instead of overlapping. Close them with a zipper or a small self-fabric button held with a loop, a small pearl, a decorative button, or with hooks and eyes. In many cases hooks catch into flat buttonholed loops instead of metal eyes. This is useful in closings at the back of the neck, at sleeve edges, etc. In garments made of lace, embroidered eyelets are used with hooks, and embroidered loops with buttons.

Decorative: Closings which are emphasized for decoration feature decorative buttons of the same or contrasting color and many fascinating novelties are available today. Bound buttonholes or buttonholes worked with buttonhole stitch may be used as preferred. In all cases these decorative notes should be in keeping with the style of trimming of the garment as a whole. In coats and other tailored garments the buttons are large, decorative, tailored, or novelty. Bound buttonholes or cord loops are used to fasten them.

SEWING ON FASTENERS

Fasteners should be sewed securely with a heavy cotton thread (unless used on a delicate fabric).

Look in the Ready-Reference Guide at the back for exact page numbers of Detailed Instructions

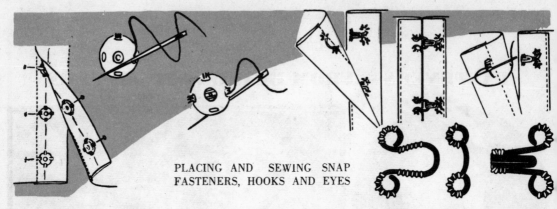

PLACING AND SEWING SNAP
FASTENERS, HOOKS AND EYES

For a large button which will receive hard wear, use linen thread. Never use a rayon or silk thread for buttons, snap fasteners, or hooks and eyes.

An even line and accurate measuring saves much disappointment. Run a straight basting to mark the line where the center of the fastener will be, then mark off with pins where each one will be sewed.

Snap Fasteners: These fasteners are made in matched pairs, and must be put on so they match. Separate them one at a time as you sew them, beginning at one end. Place the fastener at the pin, marking correct position, and center it on the basting line. Sew through the four thread holes with over-and-over stitches, and secure the end of the thread before you break it off. Close the joining and place a pin directly opposite, where you will sew on the other half of the fastener. As you go on to sew a second fastener, watch the spacing. If the closing is puckered when you finish, you have been careless in measuring, and the off-center fasteners will have to be removed and sewed on again.

Hooks and Eyes: Fasten the top of the hook with a loop of thread to the edge of the garment to hold it firmly in place. Then pass the thread to one eyelet and overhand it securely; overhand the second eyelet and then come back to the edge. Be sure the hook is firmly anchored before you fasten and break the thread. Sew the eye on the opposite edge so that when the hook is caught in it, the edges of the garment meet and no fastening shows. When larger eyes are used, they must be sewed on each side of the loop as well as through each eyelet. When the

hook and eye are placed back from the edge, the smaller eye is better and should be sewed on first. Then it will be easy to put the hook into the eye and mark the place where the hook should be.

For greater security, hooks and eyes are often added at the beltline when snap fasteners are used to close a placket. Do not skimp on the snap fasteners or else the placket will bulge.

Inner belts at the waistline, and light-weight separate belts which you can make, must be held very securely with hooks and eyes. These beltings are often stiff, and the edge is turned before the hooks and eyes are sewed on. Use heavy cotton or linen thread and pass the needle back and forth in the fabric. (Do not try to take a stitch over the eyelet of the hook.) Be sure the hook is secure at the edge as well as at the eyelets. This kind of fastening needs the larger eye for security; just enough of the eye protrudes over the edge so that the hook can catch in it. Both sides of the eye must be fastened at the edge as well as through the eyelet. On wide belting the top hook can be reversed, so the eye is on the other side.

Flat Buttons: Use a heavy linen or cotton thread, and never sew a button flat to a garment, or the stitching will not last. Raise it on a "stem" by placing a pin across the top of the button and catching the pin in your stitches as you bring the thread through from the underside and pass it back from the top. Repeat this operation several times, then make the cross threads. When the button is held securely, pull away the pin and wind your thread around the threads holding the button. This stem makes the button easier to manipulate in the buttonhole.

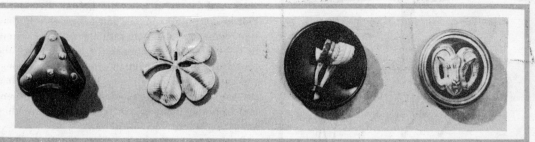

Shank-Stem Buttons: In these buttons the shank takes the place of the stem, and they are sewed flat to the fabric. Round decorative buttons often omit the shank, and it is impossible to use a pin. Allow a leeway in the thread that can be twisted for a stem.

Covered Buttons: Cut a circle of fabric almost twice as wide as the button and gather it near the edge. Place a little cotton over a button mold and secure the fabric in place by drawing the gathering thread. *Be sure it fits tightly.* Secure the end of the thread with many strong stitches. In sewing a covered button to the garment, leave the thread loose and form a stem unless the fabric raises the button enough without it.

Linked Buttons: Some people cut a cardboard to measure the size of the loop between buttons; others work with the thread and gauge the size. Pass buttonhole thread from one button to the other, spacing them the desired distance. Then cover these threads with buttonhole stitch.

Buttons Held with Fabric: In these buttons there must be a large hole. They can be attached for closing or made into linked buttons. Stitch the fabric and turn it; pass it through the button and join it at the back, allowing a little leeway for a stem. Sew this joined stem to the garment. For linked buttons, pass the fabric through two buttons and separate them the desired distance. Turn one end of the fabric and place it over the other end, fastening it neatly and securely. One of the linked buttons should be fastened to the garment on one side so that they won't be lost.

Tailored Buttons: For garments that receive very hard wear, such as overcoats, mackinaws, overalls, or work clothes made of heavy fabrics, tailored buttons are used. To fortify this button, sew a smaller button on the underside of the fabric so the thread passes through both buttons with the fabric between them. Place a pin on top of the big button to make the stem. Twist the thread securely and fasten it before cutting it off.

Decorative Buttons: Often decorative buttons hang like pendants or are attached on one side like clips. Make the buttonholes first and place the buttons in relation to them. Occasionally the buttonholes should be made lengthwise instead of across.

Tiny Buttons: These can be placed directly at the edge or back from it. Round ones should be held with buttonhole loops; for flat ones a slash finished with buttonhole stitch is preferable.

BUTTONHOLES

Lay the buttons on the outside of the garment and space them to give the effect you want. The top button should be close enough to the top edge of the collar to make a finished line; but be sure it does not extend beyond the edge. When you have decided the spacing of the buttons, put a pin under each one and verify the measure so that they are evenly spaced. Then, cut a gauge wide enough to extend from the edge of the garment to the line where you want to put the button; make a notch where each button comes. Run a basting thread on the underside of the closing where the buttons will be to indicate the center line. Put a pin on the center line to indicate the position of each button. Now you are ready to mark your buttonholes.

Lay the garment flat and place the gauge over it with the edge of the gauge at the edge of the garment. Place a pin in each notch to indicate the center of the buttonhole. On a scrap of material, test for the size of the buttonhole by cutting a

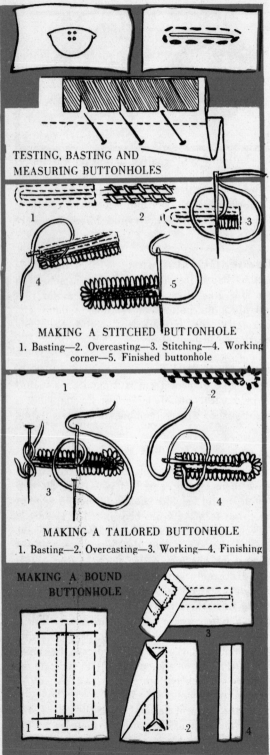

TESTING, BASTING AND
MEASURING BUTTONHOLES

MAKING A STITCHED BUTTONHOLE
1. Basting—2. Overcasting—3. Stitching—4. Working
corner—5. Finished buttonhole

MAKING A TAILORED BUTTONHOLE
1. Basting—2. Overcasting—3. Working—4. Finishing

MAKING A BOUND
BUTTONHOLE

1. Basting—2. Cutting and turning—3. Finishing—
4. Finished buttonhole

slash and trying it over the button. Remember that heavy buttons need a larger buttonhole than thin ones. Cut a gauge with the finished length of the buttonhole and mark the center. Place the center of the gauge over the pins in the garment and baste a line indicating each buttonhole. When the lines have been basted, try on the garment and examine them critically to make sure they are straight and evenly spaced.

Now you are ready to make a buttonhole. It can be finished with buttonhole stitch or bound. In either case, run a basting around each buttonhole to keep the fabric from slipping as you work.

Worked Buttonholes: After your eye is trained you can make the stitches close together and keep them even; but in the beginning it is better to run a basting along each side of the hole to guide you in keeping your stitches the same length. Use a tightly twisted buttonhole thread and work from left to right on the right side of the garment. Cut the buttonhole on the cutting line, beginning at the center and cutting toward each end marking. Finish with buttonhole stitch as follows: Bring the thread up in one corner and take a stitch through the buttonhole and out at your marked line. At the eye of the needle the thread must pass under the point —hold the thread away with your little finger as you do this. When you pull your thread up, it will form a little knot at the edge. Make another stitch close to the last one, and so continue across the buttonhole. Some buttonholes are square at both ends, others round; and still others are square at one end and round at the other.

Tailored Buttonholes: Mark the position before cutting and then punch a hole at one end with a stiletto or the point of a sharp scissors. Overcast this hole fanwise. When you are working through several heavy fabrics, take the precaution of basting the several layers together at the edge before working the buttonhole stitch. In vertical buttonholes it is important to run a stay on each side of the buttonhole before working it.

Bound Buttonholes: Do not cut a bound buttonhole until after the binding is in place. (If the hole is cut first by mistake, only an expert can bind it. If you are not an expert, it is better not to use bound buttonholes, but work them in buttonhole stitch instead.)

Separate bindings can be cut, or a binding of one piece can be placed over a row of buttonholes. The binding piece must match the grain of the fabric; it can be either straight fabric or a true bias. Mark the cutting line and the exact size of the buttonhole on both garment and binding. Put the binding on the right side of the garment over the cutting line. Baste it in place, then outline the buttonhole wth a little box of running stitches, either by hand or on the machine. Be sure the corners are turned sharply and the lines are even. Beginners should use a gauge to insure accurate lines. Cut the buttonholes, beginning at the center and cutting toward each end. Within 1/2 inch of each end, stop and slash into each corner. *Be sure this slash extends to the stitching.* If you cut through the stitches, reinforce them with a few overhand stitches; a beginner would be wise to try making a perfect buttonhole on a discarded scrap of fabric before trying to make it on a garment.

Turn the binding to the wrong side of the garment, through the buttonhole opening, and pull it into shape. Watch the right side while you do this and pull the fabric on the reverse side until you see two even lines on each side of the cut line on the right side. On the wrong side all seams must turn away from the slit. Now bring your needle through from the wrong side at the end of the buttonhole and secure the ends of the binding. Outline the buttonhole on the right side with tiny stitches, taking them in the seam allowance so they do not show. Turn to the wrong side and overcast the edge of the binding.

Bound Buttonholes In a Faced Coat:

When a bound buttonhole is made in a coat, it is worked through the outer garment and the interlining. When the facing is applied, a slit is cut opposite each buttonhole; the edges of the slit are turned back and slip-stitched to the stitching on the buttonhole. This makes the buttonhole look finished both front and back. In unlined garments worn closed, the buttonhole can be left unfinished unless you are an expert at details. Only very skillful work can turn this edge and catch it in place without pulling the buttonhole out of shape or showing telltale amateur marks on the front of the garment.

LOOP AND RING FASTENINGS

Button closings are often loops instead of buttonholes. These loops can be threads covered with (1) buttonhole stitch, (2) self-fabric tubing, (3) soft cord covered with self-fabric, or (4) fancy cord bought by the yard. They can be made singly or in a continuous cord.

Lacing on a garment can be inserted through (1) buttonholed slashes, (2) worked eyelets, or (3) metal rings covered with buttonhole stitch.

Buttonholed Loops: Finish the edge of the garment and sew the buttons in place. Mark the spacing for the loops on the opposite edge. Then, with a buttonhole thread that matches the color of the garment, make a loop of four or six strands and cover it with buttonhole stitch.

Self-Fabric Loops: Make a tubing. The size of the tubing depends (1) upon the weight of the fabric, (2) the width of your seam, and (3) whether it is a bias or straight cut. In cloth, tubing is usually cut on the straight. When a very fine tubing is wanted, cut a true bias and stitch it with a very loose machine stitching.

Fold the tubing lengthwise and stitch it. Clip off the seam at one end so the tubing will not be too thick. Then attach it to a cord or bodkin to turn the tubing right side out.

Applying Loop Fastenings—Joined Loops: Fasten one end of the tubing or cord at the edge of the garment. Use a gauge to measure both the spacing on the edge of the garment and the length of each loop. Where the loop is joined to the edge of the garment, overcast securely (1) both the cord or tubing, and (2) the joining to the garment. When a garment is faced, the loops are applied to the garment and the edge of the facing is turned and applied over the loops. Stitch the edge of the garment through all the edges so that the stitching holds the loops securely.

Single Loops: Cut the tubing or cord in the lengths desired. Either join the tubing or cord in a circle or apply it in a U-shape. Mark the edge of the garment carefully and pin the loops in place. Stitch on the machine, holding the loops and the edges together.

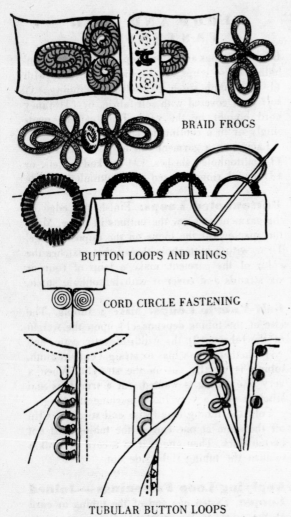

BRAID FROGS

BUTTON LOOPS AND RINGS

CORD CIRCLE FASTENING

TUBULAR BUTTON LOOPS

Corded Tubing Loops: Cut a strip of true bias the length desired and stitch the edges to form a long tube. As you turn this tubing, baste both cord and a thin bodkin to the end of the casing. Push the bodkin through the casing, over the cord. This cord can be applied in continuous loops or cut into single loops and applied as directed for single loops.

Decorative Cord Loops: Decorative loop cord comes in several sizes and is purchased by the yard. It can be applied to an edge in a continuous loop fastening, or it can be cut and attached in single loops. Wind a piece of thread around each end of the cord as you cut it to prevent it from raveling and to give a firm foundation for the stitches.

FROGS AND DECORATIVE CORD FASTENINGS

These fashionable fastenings can be made at home very easily. Women to whom a belted garment is not becoming should learn to make interesting frog closings in striking designs to give variety to the beltline of a coat or dress.

Draw the design for your frog closing on a piece of paper and follow this outline with cord you buy by the yard—or, if you prefer, make it of garment fabric tubing as described previously. As you form your design in the cord, join it securely at each crossing, stitching on both sides. Finish the end at some place in the design where you can sew very securely. Frogs may be single or double. In double frogs, the loop that holds the button goes on only one side.

Cord Motifs: Small or large circles of cord laid close together are easy to make if you cut the size of the circle in crinoline or unbleached muslin. Poke a hole in the center of the fabric circle and push one end of the cord through the hole, fastening it securely on the wrong side. Turn the cord and sew it to the fabric with a slip stitch. The last coil extends beyond the lining. These motifs can be used on each side of a neck closing with a hook and eye beneath them. You can use a row of circles down the center of a garment, or you can put them side by side to decorate a closing. When the circles are made of bias cords of self-fabric, one end can be left free for a tie.

Metal or Bone Rings: Rings—or even a piece of wire twisted into a ring—can be closely covered with blanket stitch, using a coarse embroidery thread. The covered rings can be used on the edge of a garment to hold lacing, or down the front.

ZIPPERS

Zippers are made in different sizes and lengths. They can be inserted in a slash or seam with a closed end, or they can have both ends open, as in a coat or jacket. Many different kinds of slide fasteners are designed for various uses. The ordinary zippers sold at notion counters come in three sizes for three different weights of material. A very convenient style is the zipper slide that locks; this is a zipper that holds instead of sliding open. Heavy zippers are made to resist strain. Special zippers are made for plackets. In buying zippers you must specify the length, size, or weight, and color, as well as other details which explain your needs. The sales person will help you if you tell her what you want it for. In ordering by mail, be sure you specify the use and add the important details.

APPLYING ZIPPERS

Zipper Set into Slash: A zipper set into a slash or seam can be covered so that the edges of the fabric meet above the zipper; or the metal teeth may show if the fabric edge is turned back enough to show the metal but not the tape. Zippers should be applied with machine stitching whenever possible.

Cut the slash the length of the zipper (the metal, not the tape) with a pointed or squared end. For an open-faced application, in which the metal teeth show, place your garment over the zipper and turn back the edges of the slash so the metal shows but not the tape. Baste them in place and stitch close to the edge on the right side of the garment, outlining the zipper. If the teeth are to be covered, (1) cut two strips of self-fabric the length of the zipper, (2) fold each lengthwise, (3) press the edge, (4) baste the folds together so the edges touch and place this fold over the zipper on the right side. Now place the slashed garment over the zipper and fold, and turn under the edges of the garment. This will outline a piped effect on the folds under the edge. Baste carefully and stitch close to the edge, with as fine a stitch as possible. Professionals use a cording foot in the machine.

Zipper Set into Seam: Baste the opening and press the edges open. Place the zipper over the seam on the wrong side of the garment and baste it in place. Work flat on an ironing board or table. Turn the tape ends at the top of the zipper under so they catch in the stitching. Stitch the zipper, with stitching as close as possible to the metal teeth and outlining the zipper. Be sure to turn a sharp corner. Rip the basting at the seam and test the fastener opening.

Zipper Set into Faced Edge: When the garment has a facing, first finish the garment edge. (1) It may be a short slashed closing in a dicky front, or (2) a long slash in a garment

closed at the waistline, or (3) an open jacket. Pin the zipper in place on the garment and baste it, but do not stitch it. If it is a coat, finish the bottom of the garment. Turn the seam edge of the facing and baste it in place on the wrong side of the zipper, a little back from the teeth. Be sure the facing is set smoothly on the garment and basted in place, then stitch through garment, zipper, and facing.

Zipper under a Band or in a Fly Placket: The zipper is set into place after the band of the garment has been basted to left side edge. Do not stitch the band. Pin the garment closed and place the zipper under the center of the band. Open the garment so you can see to adjust edge under the band of the opening, folding it back until it lies flat on the zipper tape. Pin it into place on the under right side. Now close the band over the zipper and pin the opposite tape of the zipper to the band edge so zipper can slide. The zipper and the band are stitched together. Before stitching, test the opening, making sure everything lies flat. Be sure he zipper tape does not show and that the zipper works freely.

Zipper in Jacket Closings: Finish the neck and lower edge of the garment. Fit the closing edges carefully pinning them together on the figure so the garment hangs smooth. Separate the seam, marking it with pins (*see* Chapter XVIII, *underarm seams*). Take off the garment, baste the front edge together with the seam on the wrong side, and press this basted seam open. This gives an exact, well-fitted edge, and the zipper can now be applied. It must be shorter than the garment. Pin one edge of the zipper to one edge of the garment; then pin the opposite edge to the other side. Try on the garment to be sure the edge does not pucker or pull out of shape. Stitch the fabric (1) either close to the edge, (2) or from the edge. A stay is often placed behind the zipper to keep it from catching on clothing.

Tape Fastenings: Tapes can be used if desired in place of any other type of closing. Make the spacing with pins and sew tapes to either side of opening with a firm, tight stitch. If the tape is very decorative you may care to apply it on the right side. Turn the raw edge under and sew securely.

CHAPTER XX
TIME-SAVING DETAILS AND POCKETS

The last touches, when the garment is almost ready to wear, can make all the difference in its smooth finish, smart appearance, and usefulness. This chapter is a list of the final finishing touches worth remembering.

Square Corners: Always nick the corners of a stitched seam which turns a corner. Snip the seam before you turn the fabric to the right side. This will remove surplus fabric, give a sharp edge, and make a smooth corner.

Curved Edges: When a seam curves, or when a facing or binding bunches, slash the seam to let the curve lie flat.

Bulk in a Seam Line: To eliminate bulk in any square seam line. slash into a corner.

Turning a Seam: Slash the seam above a hem or pleat or below a placket, and you can turn the seam any way that fits best and doesn't interfere with the hem.

Smooth Finish: In slashed necklines, pointed V necklines, buttonholes, and pockets, you must slash or cut into the corner until you almost cut the thread if the finished work is to look smooth.

Facings: When a facing covers a hem, joins collar, or if two or more thicknesses of a fabric

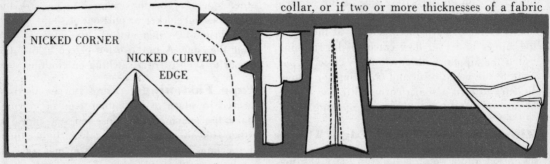

NICKED CORNER

NICKED CURVED EDGE

ELIMINATING BULK IN SEAM LINE   TURNED SEAM   SLASH FOR SMOOTH FINISH

are laid one over the other, the fabric under the end of the facing should be cut away if possible.

Headings for Tucks and Pleats: Gathers joined in seams must lie flat and should be pressed before the joining is made. Cut away any excess bulk.

When a Casing Is Added: Consider the thickness of the fabric, the belt, and the fabric of the casing. You may prefer to make a single belt or use a ribbon and so remove one thickness of fabric. You may want to make the casing of a lighter fabric. In working on heavy fabrics, these suggestions eliminate bulk.

Faced Collars, Joinings: When the collar is double, you may prefer to attach it with a seam and so eliminate added fabric bulk. When the fabric is heavy the facing is often cut of light-weight lining.

To Prepare Collar Facings: It saves time to measure the size and turn the ends and outside edge with an iron before applying. In this way, the collar lies flat without basting as you hem it in place.

Transparent Joining: Press the seam away from the transparent edge and stitch as close to the edge as possible to hold the seam so it will not show. This stitching will barely show and is preferable to a stitched hem at the joining.

Before Joining a Ruffle with a Heading: Press the seam allowance of the fabric in place. It will save time if you turn the end of the fabric as well as the seam with an iron. Then pin the joining and save one basting.

Tie and Scarf Ends: The ends of ties and scarves can be shaped in a point or a slant, a curve or a straight edge. In tubular bands of self-fabric folded and stitched on the wrong side, it is important to shape when you stitch, so that when the band is turned the end of the tubular tie is finished. When a tubular tie is not finished in the first stitching, you can push the fabric up into the tube and overcast the edges together, shaping it into a point, a slant or a straight line.

When the end to be finished is a single fabric,

with a rolled hem or a ribbon finish, the finish of the point is a delicate operation. First turn the end of the point in a seam allowance; then turn it into the shaping for a finished edge, which can be pointed or slanted. Fold the fabric in place and overcast the edge. When an end is to be round, shape it with scissors and finish it by hand.

Attaching Bands and Straps: Straps are sometimes overcast on a straight or pointed edge *at the edge line*. This is very effective in evening dresses or other garments which require little wear. For wearability, the ends of a strap must extend below the edge of a garment and be hemmed or stitched by machine all around each extended end. The extension can be sewed to the right or the wrong side of the garment.

When the trimming band extends on the right side, the end is usually pointed or curved and decorated with a button or a flower. Bands that button to a garment are cut double the finished width, stitched, and turned. The ends are finished carefully. Buttons should be placed far enough above the end so that the trimming effect is balanced.

Look in the Ready-Reference Guide at the back for exact page numbers of Detailed Instructions

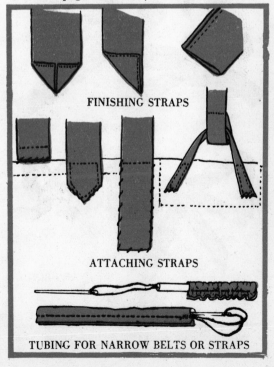

FINISHING STRAPS

ATTACHING STRAPS

TUBING FOR NARROW BELTS OR STRAPS

MAKING BOWS

TUBING BOWS

YARN BOW

Attractive bows can be made from tubing, yarn, lace, ribbons and trimmings.

Making Bows: Cut a piece of material 4 inches wide and 6 inches long—or any size desired for your bow. Cut another piece 3 inches by 3½ inches. Fold both pieces in half and stitch them. Turn these tubes and join the ends of the larger tube; this joining is the center back of the bow. Lay two or three pleats in the center and hold them with a thread. Attach the smaller tubing to the back of the bow and pass it around the center, joining the edge at the back. These little bows can be made of any fabric or ribbon. For extra decoration, make an insert of cotton rickrack braid or gold and silver braid in the center of the bow. The braid must be spaced inside the finished lines. Fold your bow and mark the place for the braid before you stitch it. Lay your fabric out and place the braid before you turn it.

Tying Bows: Bows of self-fabric tubing or ribbon can be joined to the garment edge so that the closing is tied together with little bows. To do this, first decide on the size of the bow by testing it with your tape measure for length and width, then cut your fabric twice this width and 1 inch longer. Stitch the fabric, shaping one end in a point. Turn to the right side—it can be pressed or it can be stitched on both edges— and sew the straight end to the garment edge 1 inch back. When a garment is faced, these stitches will not show. If the garment is not faced, the stitches show; but you can cover them with a beaded or embroidered outline in a leaf shape. Join the opposite ends of the bow and tie them. When a garment has three or more bows, it saves time to join your fabric in a long tube and cut it into the bow sizes after the tubing is turned to the right side.

Tied Bows: Bows you tie and apply can be cut from ribbon, lace, or fabric. Transparent fabric is usually cut single and finished with a hand-rolled hem. Dress-weight rayon crepes are cut double, stitched lengthwise, turned and finished at the end, and then tied. In heavier fabrics, bows are often finished with a binding or a narrow facing of ribbon. This adds to the decorative effect without adding to bulk.

In joining these bows sew them securely on the wrong side so they do not rip or slide out of place, and so they cannot pull off in wear. These over-and-over joining stitches should never show.

Made Bows: These bows are made of two or three pieces of ribbon or double fabric tubing. To make the tubing, cut a strip of fabric, baste it, stitch it, turn it, and cut it in the desired lengths. To make the bow, cut the fabric in two. The first piece should be long enough to form the bow and ends. Cross them but do not tie them. Hold them together in the center with stitches wound around the center or by little folds held with pleats. Now cut a small piece of fabric to fold around the center.

Stiffened Bows: Bows that are stiffened depend on crisp fabrics or a lining. When the fabric is opaque, the bow can be lined with buckram. When it is transparent, use a transparent lining of the type sold in millinery supply houses.

Lingerie Straps: You can make lingerie straps of a crocheted chain stitch, narrow ribbon, or self-fabric. Cut the ribbon or self-fabric tubing 2½ inches long. Sew a snap fastener to each end. Hem one half of the fastener to the shoulder seam of the dress; the other half hangs free and is snapped in place, holding all lingerie straps firmly at the shoulder. When you crochet a lingerie strap, you must sew a snap fastener to one end, and the corresponding end to the dress. In lingerie much strain is relieved by finishing the ends of shoulder straps with a double anchorage. To do this, cut a 3- or 4-inch strip of ribbon or self-fabric casing and sew it securely to the pointed or straight edge of the underwear, forming it so that it makes a little loop. Pass the shoulder strap through this loop and hem it on each edge so that it holds fast.

Ties or Vests and Dickies: Adjust the tape securely, so that the garment may be quickly adjusted without pins. For long dickies,

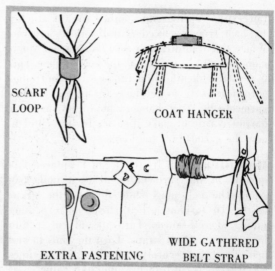

SCARF LOOP

COAT HANGER

EXTRA FASTENING

WIDE GATHERED BELT STRAP

the tape ties around the waist. For short dickies, the tape passes under the arm and joins at the back. When a tied end makes a bump in the dress, the tape can be hooked instead of tied. To prevent the back of a dicky from "flopping out," sew tape to the center back, shaping it in a loop long enough to meet the tape which fastens around the body. Pass the body tape through this loop and it will hold the dicky firmly in place.

Scarf Loop: Scarf loops can be made of self-fabric or of contrasting fabric. Make a casing 3 inches long and 1 or 1½ inches wide. Join the ends with the seam on the right side of the casing. Attach this seam to the garment, sewing it securely at each end and through the center. The tie slips through this fabric loop. Corded necklines finished in long ends are often slipped through a loop of this kind.

Slits for Ribbons: Long eyelets can be cut and buttonholed, or they can be faced like a bound buttonhole. If the fabric is heavy or transparent, binding is not satisfactory; you should buttonhole the eyelet.

Coat Hanger: In men's and boys' garments, in garments for little children, and in utility garments for women and girls, a coat hanger is most important. To make one, cut a strong tape 3 inches long, or cut a piece of lining fabric folded double and turned. This coat hanger is sewed to the seam at the back of the neck. Turn each end of the hanger in and hem it in place.

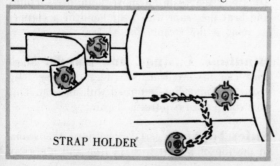

STRAP HOLDER

For extra security, run another row of stitches 1½ inch from each edge and sew it securely. When tiny children go to kindergarten, their names should be written on the coat hanger. This is a useful identification for sweaters and other garments likely to get lost. In little children's garments the coat hanger should be made of narrow elastic to make it easier for the child to take the garment off the hook.

Belt Straps: Belt straps can be placed frequently in the garment or at each underarm seam. The belt must slide through the straps easily. To fashion a belt strap, make a long tubing of self-fabric. Turn it and cut it into lengths for the belt straps. Turn the ends in and hem the straps securely at each end. Sometimes a belt strap is cut 6 inches long and gathered at each side. Shirr this strap into 4 inches and hem the gathered edges to the garment at the waistline. The belt is passed through this gathered tubing. Other belt straps are made of long threads of buttonhole silk covered with blanket stitch. In tailored garments, sew the top of the belt edge to the garment at each underarm seam.

Extra Fastenings: Often when a placket is completed and closed, the outside top corner will be loose. It requires an extra snap fastener set directly in the corner. Sew the corresponding half of the fastener to the garment so the edge of the placket lies smooth. Be sure the closing lies flat, and check whether there are enough fastenings to hold the garment properly closed.

Many home sewers omit buttonholes, and instead sew their buttons on the right side of the garment and fasten the garment with snap fasteners sewed under the buttons.

PRESSING SPEEDS SEWING

Ask any expert dressmaker or tailor how pressing speeds work, and they will say, "Keep the iron nearby and press all seams as you go along. The sewing will be easier, and the finished model will be more professional. After a skirt has been hung, press along the bottom edge of the skirt. This will make hemming much faster." They will undoubtedly add that if you also press the turn-in at the top of the skirt, you will make your work go still faster. See Chapter XXXI for further details on pressing.

Professionals always press as they sew. This is an important time-saving step.

Seams: In lighter-weight fabrics of rayon and in dress-weight cottons, seams can be pressed flat without dampness by running the point of the iron between the seams. When the fabric is made of spun rayon with a wool or linenlike finish, the seam must be dampened slightly, and a press cloth must be used. When the garment is made of dress-weight wool, first dampen the seam and press it open, then place a press cloth over the seam and dampen the press cloth with a sponge soaked in water. If you are making a coat, you will need two press-cloths because in a heavier fabric it is more difficult to insure a flat pressing. The first press cloth should be wool, and over it place a muslin press cloth. Dampen it with a sponge soaked in water and press the seam, bringing the iron down flat. Do not slide or move the iron, but raise it and lay it flat again. Continue in this way all along the seam. Remove both press cloths and beat the seam with your hand or a clapper to remove the steam.

Bindings, Casings, and Bands: Much time can be saved if the edges of these long strips are immediately turned with an iron. This true sharp edge requires no basting.

Skirt Tops: Expert sewers turn the seams at the top of a skirt with an iron and nip away

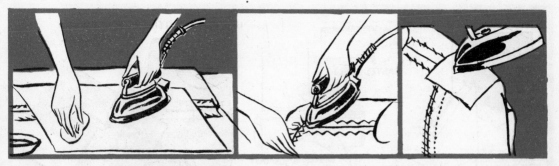

Protect wools and wool blends with a press cloth (left). Press armholes and shoulder seams with care.

the tops of the side seams before joining the skirt to the waist.

Overlaid Seams: When the seam edge is turned for a yoke, a patch pocket, a slot seam, or an overstitched seam, press the edge; your work will be much easier.

POCKETS

Pockets are easy to make once a few simple rules have been mastered. They are useful and decorative and give a professional touch to a garment. Use them in all types of clothes.

Types of Pocket: There are four different kinds of pocket: patch pockets, bound pockets, welt pockets, and pockets with a flap. Each of these fundamental types can be cut in many different styles.

Patch Pocket: The secret of success with patch pockets is to have them absolutely true and even, and the best way to do this is to cut the pocket shape in cardboard, omitting seam allowances. Place this cardboard pattern over each of your pocket pieces and press the seam allowances over the edge of the cardboard. This will insure that all pockets are the same size and every edge is true.

Next finish the top edge. In light-weight fabrics, turn the edge and hem it; in heavier fabrics, cover the raw edge with flat seam binding after you have turned the edge, then hem it. Pin the pocket on the garment and check accuracy of placing.

Decide whether the pocket is to be stitched close to the edge or back from it. Pockets stitched close to the edge are finished at the top with one or more rows of machine stitching. When a pocket is stitched back from the edge, the same

seam line is followed across the top to complete a decorative detail.

Bound Pocket: There are two ways to make bound pockets: (1) In heavier fabrics self-fabric is used for the binding, and the pocket is made of lining fabric. (2) In light-weight fabrics the pocket is used for the binding, which makes for a great saving in time.

Pockets Bound in Self-Fabric: Mark the pocket opening on both garment and binding. The binding is cut 1 inch longer than the finished pocket and 3 inches wide. The grain of the material should match the garment at the cutting line. If the cutting line of the pocket parallels the cross grain of the material, make the binding on the straight of the goods; if the pocket slants across the grain of the goods, it must be bound with a true bias.

Finishing a Bound Pocket: Place the binding on the right side of the garment with the cut lines matching. Pin it in place and baste it carefully.

Stitch a little box around the cutting line by machine or by hand—the size of the box depends upon the length of the cutting line and the effect desired. For a piped effect, stitch $\frac{1}{4}$ inch away from the cutting line on both sides. In a heavy fabric, stitch $\frac{1}{2}$ inch from the cutting line. Turn the corners sharply at each end and make the same number of machine stitches down each side. When working by hand, use a gauge and turn the corners carefully, making them firm with extra stitches.

Cut the slash from the center toward each end, and cut into the corners (see page 140) almost cutting the stitches at the corners. It is far better to cut a stitch accidentally and repair

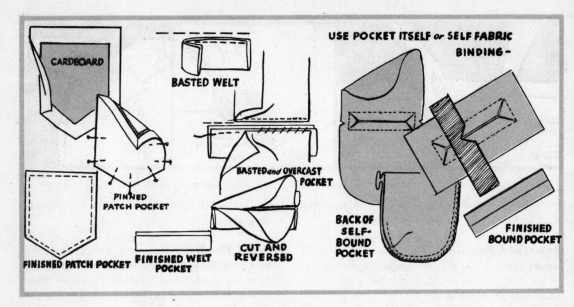

it with overcasting than not to cut deeply enough into the corners.

Draw the binding piece through the slash to the wrong side of the garment and pull it into straight even lines, watching the effect on the right side as you pull. Keep pulling until the binding looks like two perfectly even rows with squared ends. Fasten the material at each end. This stitch holds the edges of the binding together and is caught firmly in the edge of the pocket slit at this point. When both ends have been stitched, outline the buttonhole by making running stitches in the seam edge, catching the back of the binding with these stitches. This makes the seam lay flat away from the edge.

Join the pocket on the wrong side of the garment. First join a pocket piece to each side of the binding, then smooth the two pieces together and baste them. If the edges are not even, it does not matter—you can shape them alike. Stitch, and overcast the seam.

Pocket Used for Binding: Cut the pocket piece any desired size and mark the cutting line on both garment and pocket piece. Place the pocket piece on the right side of the garment and follow the directions for Finishing a Bound Pocket.

Welt Pocket: The welt pocket is very easy to make. To prepare the welt, cut a piece of the garment fabric 2½ inches wide on the straight of the goods. Make it 1 inch longer than the length of the pocket. Fold this piece lengthwise and stitch both ends. Clip the corners before turning, to insure square edges. Press with an iron.

Place the welt below the cutting line of the pocket with the raw edges of the welt piece turned up toward the cutting line. The lower pocket piece is placed over the welt. Stitch across the pocket, paralleling the cutting line about ¼ inch back from it.

Cut the pocket, from the center toward the ends, cutting into each corner to the stitching. Turn the pocket pieces to the wrong side of the garment. The welt piece remains on the right side and is turned up to cover the pocket opening. Slip-stitch each end of the welt to the garment. Turn to the wrong side and join the pocket pieces in a seam. The pocket must lie flat. If the pieces are uneven, they should be reshaped.

Flap Pocket: Pockets with flaps are made like welt pockets. Cut the flap any size and shape desired. When it has been seamed and turned, it should be exactly the length of the finished cutting line of the pocket. Baste the flap to the right side of the garment *above* the cutting line and stitch. Cut and turn it like a welt pocket. When the pocket is turned, the flap falls over the cutting line. Sometimes the ends are finished with tailor's arrows.

CHAPTER XXI

TRIMMINGS

The trimmings described in this chapter do not record current styles; they are designed simply to stimulate your thinking. Trimming details change continually, and you should study trimming types and check them in the fashion news. Watch out for the newest ideas in trimming when you plan your dress. Plan the trimming as an integral part of the garment, not as a last-minute addition. My experience in judging sewing contests has convinced me that few home sewers pay proper attention to trimming details. Yet the use of a dollar's worth of style-right trimming can make the dress a hundredfold more successful.

Trimming Bands: Bands of contrasting fabric or color are an important development in most style cycles. The band is often applied on top of the garment fabric and hemmed or stitched on both edges. Other bands are inserted either in a seam joining or on top of the fabric, which is then cut away under it. These decorative touches of color can be used at necklines, in sleeve trimmings, in cuffs, and to form stripes extending the length of the garment.

Buttons: Buttons often make an effective trimming. They can be the outstanding note of contrast in a costume, particularly when the color of the buttons is echoed in a piping, binding, or belt.

Slenderizing Trimmings: Contrast trimmings can help slenderize the figure if they add height by following the horizontal lines of the garment. Surplice lines and V necks can be emphasized with narrow or wide bands to add interest to the costume and height to the figure. Here are three specific examples:

1. The surplice waistline of a dress is edged with a narrow fold of white. If it ends at the waistline, it has not accomplished its purpose; but if it is extended to the hem of the dress, the trimming helps to make the figure look more slender.

2. The surplice line from shoulder to hem can be trimmed with two or three flat bands in blending colors. Three shades of light blue on a navy blue dress; or brown, tan, and yellow on a brown dress—these give a smart and slenderizing effect.

3. A slenderizing neckline which dresses up a costume can be developed in lace or in a contrasting color. The neck of the dress is cut in a deep V, filled in with a 1½-inch double fold of color or lace. Below this band a large cameo or decorative pin can be placed; and underneath the pin a tab of the same color or lace you used in the double fold. As it hangs down it carries the color down and makes a longer line.

NOVELTY TRIMMINGS

There are three types of novelty trimming: (1) those which add subtle richness or glitter to a simple dress; (2) seasonal color enthusiasms such as the outbursts of red, white, and blue trimmings which greet us every spring; and (3) the garish novelty, bold and strikingly colored.

Trimmings of Subtle Richness: These trimmings introduce beading, braid, and embroidery. The style dictates the design; it may be a banding, an allover effect, or a small spot. Choose the easiest and quickest designs and reproduce them. Most of the embroidery is chain stitch. Often a small piece of appliqué is the trimming of a dress—a white piqué flower on a dark dress; three self-color flowers in a group, or one after another to form a band; three or more circles in different colors arranged in a group—these are only a few of the ideas which can be carried out in appliqué.

Glittering Trimmings: Metallics, rhinestones, spangles, jet, and the shiny-faced textiles

CORD TRIMMING

FIVE EASY-TO-MAKE QUILTED DESIGNS

Even a small amount of quilting used for a trimming will give a luxurious effect. These two jackets give an idea of how well quilting adapts itself to an entire garment.

such as satin and sateen, as well as lacquered textiles, are included in this group. Glitter should be used as current fashion decrees and need not be expensive. You can make outline embroidery with metallic threads or appliqué satin flowers with metallic threads and fill the center with glittering beads. You can outline the edge of a collar with jet or spangles, or buy spangles in bands and apply them. You can paint a piece of soft leather with metallic paint, then cut it into a flower and pin or appliqué it in place.

Garish Novelties: Bold novelty trimmings are often developed by the use of bright colors in braid, bands, rhinestones, and so forth. When glitter is used in too large quantities, it oversteps the bounds of good taste.

Pockets: They are important in trimming all-purpose and simple tailored clothes. The type of pocket and its position is a style feature. Pockets are easy to make and add greatly to the success of a garment. The three types of pocket are: patch pockets, bound pockets, and welt pockets. Once you understand these three simple constructions, you can make a pocket in any garment. First decide whether the pocket is a decorative feature or simply for utility.

Shaped Edges: Edges can be shaped into scallops, squares, or fringed effects, and bound or faced. It is easier to carry out a shaped edge in facing when the design is small. You can do this as soon as you learn to run a machine expertly. The stitching *must outline a perfectly*

BRAIDING

spaced and even design. To do this, draw the desired outline on your facing or stamp the edge with an embroidery pattern. Place the facing on the garment, matching the edges on the right side of the garment, and stitch the outline. Examine the stitched line before cutting it. Then cut and turn it, following the directions for shaped bands on page 67.

Self-Fabric Cords: Festooning an edge with self-fabric cording can be done in two ways:

1. Stitch and turn a narrow piece of fabric to make a tubing. Fold it again and overcast it so it is very narrow. Place this cording on a piece of paper as fully described on page 132. Turn in the edge of the garment and place it over the cording. Stitch the edge of the garment so

SMART USE OF CONTRAST BANDING

that it catches the cording and then tear the paper away.

2. Fringed and corded trimming can be bought by the yard. It is usually finished at the top with an edge which can be placed under or over the garment edge.

Self-cording can be shaped into large or small frogs for closing a jacket or dress. The button used should also be of self-fabric. Self-cord can be twisted into circular designs; and another way is to finish a corded edge by extending the cording beyond the edge and turning it in a loop or leaf outline or inner circle.

Quilting: This makes a simple and decorative trimming. It is often used in small spots or in bands at the edge of wide sleeves or in surplice closings. Quilted belts, tams, muffs and jackets, add richness to a simple costume.

Large women who prefer beltless dresses can add variety to a new costume with two quilted motifs—one at the beltline to emphasize the closing, and the other on the waist. The redingote lines of a dress can be outlined with quilting.

Quilting is used on the collars of dressmaker coats and suits, especially those in soft fabrics. For details on quilting, see Chapter XLV.

BRAIDING

Functional fabrics which lack a texture interest or novelty weave make a perfect background for a trimming touch. To add a touch of distinction, use narrow sutache braid in the simple designs illustrated here. To apply braid in this way, first trace the design on your fabric with chalk. Then apply the braid, stitching it through the center. The stitching can be done by hand or by machine. You can buy braided motifs in the stores and apply them to the garment by hemming them in place.

Before starting your work, consider the line of the garment which you will trim. Place the braiding so that it will emphasize the good lines of the design and your figure. Even a small touch of braiding in the form of a pocket motif adds distinction to a simple jacket blouse.

THAT EXPENSIVE LOOK

The trimming details made from self-fabric and the handwork used in trimming touches are the mark of quality that often makes the difference between the expensive and the inexpensive dress. The home sewer who will note these details and add them to a dress will be abundantly repaid for the additional time. These trimming touches give to dresses what is recognized as "that expensive look." The sketches shown on page 145 show details made in self-fabric that cost so little, add so much, and make the simple dress into an outstanding one.

SCALLOPS are a pretty, feminine finish for yokes, necklines, closings, on soft little crepe dresses. Since they represent quite a bit of labor, they give a dress an expensive, custom-made look.

SADDLE-STITCHING is a very smart, and very simple finish for tailored clothes. It can be done in self-color or in definite contrast, white, for instance, on navy. It is used down the fronts of jackets and on revers, cuffs and yokes of tailored suits, dresses, and coats. Saddle-stitching is done by hand.

RICKRACK is a gay finish for cotton clothes. It is invariably used in contrast, on dresses, pinafores and play clothes of the more feminine variety.

TUCKING when used as an integral part of the design adds interest to a simple dress—and tapers in fullness without any bulk. It is frequently used at waistlines for this purpose. It can also be used purely decoratively.

TOP-STITCHING is the frank use of stitching on the outside of a dress, suit, or coat to emphasize lines that are important in the design. It is often combined, as in the sketch, with *lapped seams*. Top-stitching is done by machine.

GATHERS are used to concentrate drapery and are vitally important in keeping the soft dress slim and svelte. They appear in various positions—at necklines, waistlines, hiplines, even sleeves. Often they are repeated two or three times in the one dress.

PLEATED EDGINGS are best used on simple dresses. They make them charmingly feminine without being fussy. Either self-fabric or contrast can be used. White, on a dark or print dress, is a perennial "white touch" favorite.

CLUSTER SHIRRING is not difficult to do, it just requires a little patience. The result is well worth the trouble as it gives an expensive look to a simple, soft crepe dress. It is used, as gathers are, to concentrate fullness, decoratively, at neckline, waistline, hiplines, or sleeves.

FRINGE can be used on both formal and casual clothes. Narrow wool fringe or self-fabric fringe adds a distinctive touch to casual wool dresses or suits. Lustrous silk or rayon fringe is used on more formal daytime and dinner clothes.

INSERTED BANDING may be shirred self-fabric or it may be contrast, of either color or fabric. It is used to outline simulated yokes, which are often repeated on the skirt—and it is also used instead of cuffs.

BINDING is a functional finish, used to hold the edges of a dress or jacket firm and trim. When it is used purely functionally it is narrow and made of self fabric. But binding often combines a decorative quality with its functional purpose. Then it is in contrast of colour or fabric or both.

DRAWSTRINGS are a pretty way to confine and distribute fullness. They also serve the purpose of fastenings—and thus save on metal.

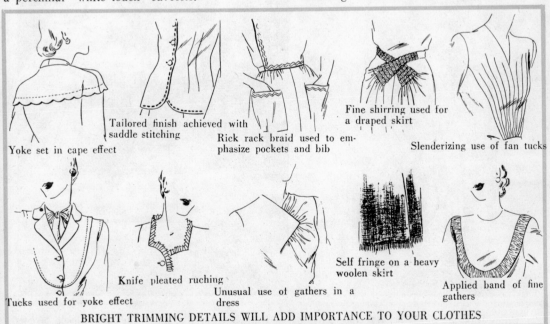

Yoke set in cape effect

Tailored finish achieved with saddle stitching

Rick rack braid used to emphasize pockets and bib

Fine shirring used for a draped skirt

Slenderizing use of fan tucks

Tucks used for yoke effect

Knife pleated ruching

Unusual use of gathers in a dress

Self fringe on a heavy woolen skirt

Applied band of fine gathers

BRIGHT TRIMMING DETAILS WILL ADD IMPORTANCE TO YOUR CLOTHES

CHAPTER XXII

POINTS TO REMEMBER ABOUT UTILITY CLOTHES AND TAILORED CLASSICS

Utility clothes are work clothes as distinguished from everyday clothes in general. They include house dresses and aprons, uniforms, and outdoor coveralls. Whether your needs demand a wrap-around dress, slacks, or coveralls, take care to select a pattern which will be becoming to you—and will permit free action in whatever you have to do, thus freeing you from distracting worry about tearing or soiling your clothes.

Your work clothes should be chosen with three things in mind: good looks, long wear, and economy. To this end, select a textile that will look well, wear well, and clean easily. Most work clothes are made from utility cottons, and the emphasis should be upon *extra tensile strength*. The color must be fast to permit the use of alkali soaps to clean away grease and dirt. A preshrunk fabric is essential.

The Department of Agriculture, through clothing experts and home demonstration agents in every state in the Union, has conducted tests on the wearing quality of garments designed for housework. The tests proved that house dresses made at home from color-fast preshrunk fabrics gave twice as much wear as garments bought at the stores for the same price. The women who made the tests chose a simple pattern and made several house dresses each season, so that they were always supplied.

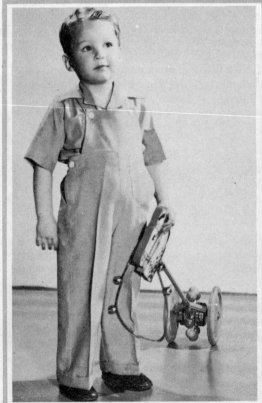

Utility garments should be well constructed and have ample seam allowances. The fabric should be preshrunk and washable. Simple patterns should be chosen.

Women who wear uniforms also report that a really sturdy fabric repays them in longer wear and at the same time makes them "look more capable."

CONSTRUCTING UTILITY GARMENTS

All utility garments are washable garments. hence should be made with seams that will hold through innumerable washings. Consult the index for flat felled seams and covered seams. Big useful patch pockets, bound buttonholes, and bound slits through which to pass a belt are other features in utility garments.

House dresses: For warm weather use seersucker and other sheer cottons which need no ironing. Make them in simple, useful styles with gathered or tucked fullness, and don't forget big pockets. They can be a slip-on model with a drawstring waistline, a wrap-around which ties in place, or a button-front dress, as preferred. For general all-year-round utility, or to wear over sweaters and skirts in the very cold months, the best choice is a wrap-around dress of denim or a heavy cotton suiting which can be run through the mangle. Choose a dress which crosses in front and ties in place, or a single-breasted one which buttons. All house dresses should have short sleeves. See that the waistline is trim and that the neckline fits and is becoming.

Women who cook in a laboratory or large kitchen need a dress which buttons down the front so it can be slipped over another garment. In this kind of dress, remember to plan for a long reach, which demands a garment cut with an action back. Use cotton seersucker in white or a cool light color and make roomy pockets and a self-belt. Crisp starched cottons are attractive, but they have to be washed and ironed often.

Trim Waistline: Choose a pattern with a trim fitted waistline and a gored skirt, or fit a straight-line dress at the waistline with darts. These darts can be stitched in the garment in both waist and skirt. In one-piece garments, darts can be stitched at intervals to take away the baggy look. Even when a string belt is used, these darts improve the appearance of the dress. Many women like a slip-on dress in semifitted lines which requires no placket closing.

Utility house dresses and uniforms should look trim and attractive. They need deep armholes and action backs.

Action Back: House dresses should be cut with back yokes which permit fullness or pleats, or the back should be extra large and wide. The armhole must be large, and is often cut with a square line to permit reaching without tearing out the sleeve. In fitting house dresses, watch for trimness which gives looseness and permits plenty of activity, and allows for wearing a sweater underneath when necessary.

Aprons: Aprons are (1) protective, (2) for utility, or (3) decorative.

Protective Aprons: These aprons are made of denim or cotton drill. They can be coveralls, smocks, or wrap-around aprons with generous bib fronts. Choose the style best suited

Look in the Ready-Reference Guide at the back for exact page numbers of Detailed Instructions

to your need and incorporate pockets which will speed your work. Buttoned pockets will prevent tools from falling out as you work—only one button in the center of the top edge is necessary. Be sure that all ties are securely *stitched* in place.

Utility Aprons: Utility aprons are made of gingham or other housedress fabrics. They can be large or small as desired. Usually they tie or button around the waist and have a bib front joined with a strap. Straps and ties can be made of self-fabric by stitching and turning a tubular band. For a trim appearance, hold the bib with a single band which can be easily slipped over your head.

Decorative Aprons: Many women like a pretty apron with frilled edges and appliqué decorations to wear while serving dinner. They can be made of dainty fabrics in any style your taste dictates. In any home where the men step into the kitchen, decorative aprons should include a man's bar apron in light-weight denim, bound with white tape.

Service Uniforms: Sometimes these are provided; again, the worker must supply her own made to a traditional pattern. If you make your own, it will insure longer wear than uniforms bought for the same price in the stores will give. You have to duplicate the style and the material used in the uniform type, but you can provide yourself with a better-fitting garment and one made of better-wearing material. Buy a pattern of the stated type or rip up an old

uniform and use it for a pattern. Follow the instructions for built-to-measure garments in Chapter X.

Factory Workers' Garments: The kind of garment needed for factory work depends upon which of the many factory jobs you do. Women in nonactive jobs usually wear a coverall apron—not a house dress. Those who work near machinery must wear a coverall, either one- or two-piece. In some jobs button-cuff trousers and long sleeves with tight cuffs are essential for protection. In other work, short sleeves give greater freedom.

Denim or cotton twill is the rule for one- or two-piece coveralls and for slacks. Some jobs require a sweater with slacks, others a plain shirtwaist. Psychological tests prove that a bright color offsets strain. Other tests recommend that pockets be made in open lattice effects (strips of fabric crossed) so that matches and metals can be seen without searching in factory inspections.

Children's Utility Garments: Children of every age need utility garments, and their first requirement is action room. The garment should be very simple so it can be washed easily. Time-saving styles must open at the right length and be easily slipped on and off. Fastenings should be easy to open and close. In cold weather, children of every age wear overalls of heavy cotton —denim, gabardine, or coverts. For warm weather a loosely woven sturdy cotton is more comfortable. For general wear a one-piece coverall or a two-piece slack-and-smock garment is

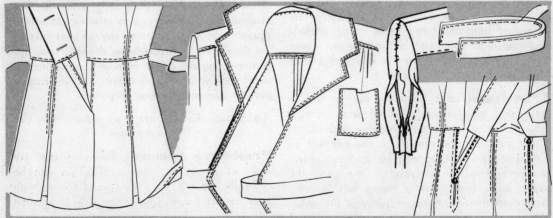

Utility garments are joined and basted like all other garments. The construction details are tailored with sturdy stitching and carefull pressing. Square all corners, turn and stitch the seam edges.

preferable. For summer wear the overall can have a halter top or be cut sleeveless with a V neck. With this type of garment it is wise to make also a jacket or bolero to wear after the sun goes down.

TAILORED CLASSICS

Tailored classics are always correct, and their quality is gauged according to the fine detail. Besides the classic tailored suits and coats—based on men's apparel—this group includes the universally popular shirtwaist dresses based on the man's shirt. Some shirtwaist dresses duplicate exactly the fine tailoring points of a man's formal sport shirt, and the price is set according to the detail of this handwork. Others are based on the casual type of man's sport shirt, and are much quicker and easier to make. Those which really belong in the easy-to-make category skip the details and keep only the general effect of a tailored garment. They do not meet the standards of a classic tailored garment.

Middy blouses are also based on traditional details of line and cut. They are sometimes authentic, and sometimes merely effective simplifications.

Any woman who can make shirtwaist dresses which include all the painstaking details, can also make men's shirts and all kinds of boys' clothes, which have the same tailored effects.

Shirtwaist Dresses: When you select a pattern, choose a skirt that is gored or pleated, a kick pleat front and back, a pleat on each seam, and clusters of pleats. In the waist, watch for bands, yokes, and action pleats in the back. Most of these dresses feature a regulation shirt collar and convertible neck closing. Pockets, trim beltline, and link cuff details are other features to watch for. Many pockets have button flaps set high like the pockets of a man's sport shirt.

An interlined front band, cut in one or separately, is a mark of quality. The quicker-to-make models have the edge folded back without a band, like the man's casual shirt.

Resort shirtwaist dresses are often so beautiful that they are worn for afternoon dresses at formal teas. In this kind of dress, watch all the fine details and use studs instead of pearl buttons.

The choice of material for shirtwaist dresses is wide. For morning wear, or for golf, dresses

in true classic traditions are made of broadcloth in men's shirting patterns, and the striped details are used just as in men's shirts. A striped cotton in trick cutting does not make a classic garment.

SEWING FOR MEN AND BOYS

Men's Shirts: Buy a pattern and follow every detail of the tailor's art. Apply the patch pockets correctly—that is, make it first and pin it in place with a tailor's precision. The stitching should be $3/8$ inch from the edge all the way around, and the same stitching must continue around the edge of the flap. The flap is closed with a button and buttonhole.

Join the yoke lining to the back, then baste the outside of the yoke to the line and stitch them all together, on both inside and outside. Join the front at the shoulder, stitching it first to the inside of the yoke, and basting the outside edge of the yoke over this seam. The sleeve is stitched before the underarm is placed. This seam is a flat fell. Stitch it the first time as you would a regular seam, then clip away half of the edge on the armhole side of the shirt. Turn the other seam edge over and stitch it flat to the garment. Now baste the underarms of shirt and sleeve. Before you make the collars and cuffs, consider whether you want to make an extra set now or to lay away enough material to replace them later. The lower edge of the shirt is hemmed. The collar is interlined with unbleached muslin and the interlining is stitched to the collar. The seam is then clipped away close to the stitching and the collar is turned. Baste the inside edge of collar and lining to the neck and stitch the collar in place. Turn in the opposite edge and hem it over the seam. The collar centers at the center front of the garment, and the edges beyond the collar are turned in and slip-stitched.

The cuffs are finished in a classic line with a band. In casual sport shirts make a single cuff. In this type some men prefer a short sleeve finished with a narrow hem.

Boys' Shirts: Once you learn the simple tricks of constructing a tailored garment, you need not hesitate to make boys' shirts of heavy cotton. It saves time to make several at once, using the same pattern and varying the material.

Boys' garments have double yokes, firm bands, patch pockets and tailored details.

curate turning of edges and corners (use an iron) and straight stitched lines.

Pin the patch pockets in place before you join the garment. Turn the edge of the yoke and pin it in place. Turn the edge of the facing and pin it in place. Put the facing on the sleeve and prepare it for stitching. Now stitch pockets, yoke, facing, and sleeve edge one after the other. Turn all edges for a second stitching except those joined to the garment. Once the shoulders are stitched you can pin the sleeve in place. Turn the facing and pin the collar at the same time. The underarms of sleeves and shirt are stitched in one seam. Do not close this seam until the collar is finished.

Boys' Shorts: Boys' shorts are easy to make if you pin the pieces together as you cut them. The usual difficulty is that the pieces look so much alike it is hard to assemble them if they get separated. Some shorts are finished with a casing and elastic band, others with a fabric belt. When seams are stitched and pressed, hem the edge.

Children's Sailor Suits: Classic middy designs can be made from drill or any heavy white cotton. Once you go to the trouble to make a suit, use the correct braiding so dear to children's hearts. Finish the sleeve ends of the middy blouse and make a bound pocket before the garment is put together. The collar is not only hemmed and braided, but also lined with self-fabric or lawn. When the collar is finished and lined, it is joined to the neck with a bias facing. To insure a clean point, the neck edge is cut shorter than the collar. Baste the collar around the neck, extending it deeper in the center front, and stitch it in place with a binding. Before you turn the bias facing to the wrong side, slash between the collar points. Slip-stitch the facing in place. The shield is usually lined, and the lining can be stitched and the shield joined or the edges can be slip-stitched together.

The shorts can be finished with a self-band. In tiny boys' suits it must be buttoned to the middy.

Use any style suited to your purposes and remember that all this work is machine work and not difficult. Most of the seams are stitched on the outside, and the double yokes and facings are simplified. The most important things are ac-

As you cut the shorts, pin them together. As you cut the facing and belt, pin them in place. Don't hesitate to include pockets in this type of garment. It is not difficult to make slashed pockets. You can buy stars and insignias to complete the decorative effect or omit them, remembering that navy work uniforms are not decorated.

CHAPTER XXIII

POINTS TO REMEMBER ABOUT EVERYDAY AND SPORT CLOTHES

The clothes worn every day—for school, for work, for shopping trips and informal calls—should be simple and made from washable fabrics that wear well. But this does not mean they should be dull and uninteresting. Harmony and variety can be characteristic of everyday clothes as well as more elaborate ones. Make your plain dresses that you wear day in, day out, harmonize with your coat, just as your best street dress does. Introduce variety in them with jumpers and dickies, boleros and jackets. Blouses, too, make everyday dresses versatile.

Button-Front Dresses: One of the most popular styles, because it is becoming to so many figures, is the button-front dress in the redingote style or in the softer lines which introduce pleats or gathers into the redingote cutting. Be sure you work on a table when you face the front opening, whether the facing is cut in one or separately. To be successful, your work must be flat. Press the front edge into a sharp straight line before you join the facing, or to help you turn it if it is cut in one. Facings can be stitched flat to give a tailored effect, or the edges can be turned and slip-stitched so that no stitching shows on the garment. In faced coats or dresses, watch the hemline. The open edge of the facing must end evenly and so must the hem. The end of the facing can be cut short and fitted inside the hem, or it can be extended to the bottom and the hem cut away under it.

If the dress is made of wool or a fabric that looks like wool, the buttonholes can be bound. Bound buttonholes are good in silk or rayon crepes, but they do not show up as prominently, and so are not as important, as the buttonholes of a redingote in wool. The buttonholes can be horizontal or vertical.

Button-front waists are faced and often trimmed with an outside stitching, especially on a plain fabric. They can be closed with buttons or studs.

Look in the Ready-Reference Guide at the back for exact page numbers of Detailed Instructions

BUTTON FRONT DRESSES AND BLOUSES
THAT LOOK LIKE JACKETS, VIE WITH PLAIDS
FOR POPULAR EVERYDAY WEAR.
Boleros are easy to make when you
face the edge with self fabric.

Jumper Styles: Jumper dresses for growing girls should have the added skirt fullness so flattering to youth, but once the girl reaches her teens the skirt should be straighter and more fitted through the waist. This fitting can be a dart construction or a shaped and fitted belt. In misses' and women's jumper dresses, the simple straight line is emphasized by pocket or tucked details.

Whatever the type of jumper dress, it is easy to make. Cut the skirt and fit it; then cut the waist and fit it. When you are ready to finish the edge of the armhole, decide whether you will face it with self-fabric or a sheer lining fabric. If so, the facing is cut on the bias and turned to the *wrong* side of the garment. If you are trimming the jumper on the outside with a trimming bought by the yard, both neck and sleeve edges must be turned to the *right* side of the garment and basted. Snip the turned edge where it curves at armhole and back of neck so it lies flat. Then baste the trimming band to the inside edge so it lies flat and joins at the underarm. Fit the trimming band around the neckline, pulling it a little at the center back in rounding the curve of the neck. Stitch the bands in place.

Jumper dresses can be worn with simple slip-on blouses, sport shirts, sweaters, or gay decorative blouses with jabots and puffed sleeves. Make several blouses to wear with each jumper.

Pockets: Pockets are an important feature in everyday clothes. You can make patch pockets with a straight edge and place them on the bias instead of straight on the garment. You can place a bound pocket straight or on a slant. Be sure the binding matches the grain of the fabric. If the fabric is jersey or sheer woolen, the pocket will wear better if you use a double binding. Cut it the length of the pocket and 1 inch wide. Fold the binding in half lengthwise, with the wrong side together, and *press it.* Then proceed as for any bound pocket. When pockets are made of lining material, one section must be faced with fabric at the top so no lining will show through the pocket opening. It is better to make the pockets of the dress fabric unless it is too heavy.

Dicky-Front Dresses: One type of dicky dress is slashed to the waistline, another is open halfway down. A third type of dicky is worn with a high-necked sweater or dress. A dicky-front dress is made like the jumper dress, with a slender skirtline and a simple blouse. The sleeves can be three-quarter or full length. When the front is finished in a V or a U line, it can be faced. When the front edge is slashed through the center of the waist, it must be reinforced and the slash outlined with stitching before it is cut. This is satisfactory for short openings, but it is not recommended for a slash extending to the waistline. In that case, cut the slash and face it. It will hold its shape better. If you want no stitching to show on the right side, do not stitch the band flat, but turn the edges and stitch them separately, then join them to the garment and make a row of stitching close to the edge, so close it will look like beading. Hold the inside edge in place with catch stitches, holding the thread loose and taking up only one thread of the fabric.

The dickies and vests worn with these dresses can button close to the neck or be cut in V neckline large enough to slip over the head comfortably. A detachable vest must be large enough so that the edge of it doesn't show when you bend over, and it must be firmly hooked in place so that it cannot slip up. In the winter months a bright velvet or velveteen vest of this type adds richness to the dress. In the spring it should be changed to white and several vests made, of satin, organdy, and lace. A print vest is good, too.

Jacket Dresses: Jacket dresses can be a separate jacket with a dress, a two-piece dress that looks like a jacket, or a bolero jacket. These popular styles are becoming to all ages, and they are no more trouble to make than a button-front dress. Cut the jacket or bolero by a pattern and make it as you would a dress, facing back the front edge.

Boleros: Sometimes bolero jackets end above the waistline, sometimes they come down to the waistline and are fitted a little. This is a slenderizing style which looks well on any figure.

Most boleros are made with a dart on each shoulder. Finish the edge with a 2-inch bias facing. Fit the facing carefully all the way around the garment, mitering the corners. These corners must be seamed and pressed open before the band is stitched. After the band is stitched,

the corners must be cut across before the band is turned. Do this work on a table, and turn the edge carefully so it lies flat and smooth. The band can be finished in a hand hem or stitched by machine. The facing band can be a print fabric for variety. This is very pretty if the

Change the effect in grown up Jumper Dresses from softness to tailored trimness with a change of blouse.

Basting an extra peplum to create the effect of a two piece dress.

Add skirt fullness to Jumper Dresses for growing girls.

Join one edge of the collar to the neck and then turn the facing and join the edge to the collar.

bolero is worn with a matching print blouse. Some people bind the bolero with self-fabric and then cover the binding with a bias facing of print. When they get tired of the print, they take it off and the garment is fully finished underneath.

Sewing for Children: Children of pre-school age need a great many plain, simple garments in washable fabrics. Yoke effects and new placements for pockets add interest to the garments and are easy to do. It is fun to work out several variations by the same pattern, using different fabrics and trimmings. Contests prove that every time another garment is made from the same pattern, it goes faster; and when you have a number of garments to make, it will save time to use the same pattern.

Growing girls need gored or gathered fullness in their skirts, and they like the fitted effect of a basque waist. Edges can be bound or faced, and buttons and buttonholes rejoice young hearts.

Pockets always please the youngsters, and they are useful as well as decorative.

The skirt of a daytime dress cut on the straight can be given variety by turning the hem to the right side of the dress and finishing the top with a contrasting binding. Make a collar to match the binding and repeat the color in the buttons.

Plaids are popular in the schoolgirl's wardrobe. Choose a small plaid and buy an extra ¼ yard of material to allow for matching the pattern. Except for precautions in cutting (see Chapter XII), plaid dresses are easy to make and always decorative.

Children's jumper dresses are often made of corduroy. When you use heavy material, be sure the lines of the pattern are straight and slender or cut circular. This kind of fabric cannot be pleated and should not be gathered. All facings are made of a contrasting lining material in a matching color. Velveteen is cotton, but it must be steamed like velvet because of the pile, not pressed. When it is used for children, it is wise to select the natural color tones, because the darker colors mark in wear.

When you sew for girls, encourage them to help you work out band effects and develop individual trimming touches. It will interest them in sewing.

SPORT CLOTHES

Casual sport clothes have a place in the wardrobe of almost every woman, young or old, city- or country-dweller. They include tweeds and tweedlike fabrics in an interchangeable assortment of skirts, jackets, shirts, sweaters, waistcoats, and suits. To this group belong also the casual dresses so different from everyday tailored dresses, as well as the jumper and suspender dresses which make a wardrobe look bigger and more varied than it is.

Fabrics for sport clothes in autumn and winter are wool and wool-like, heavy and really warm. In summer fabrics the wool effect is given to light-weight materials which wear well and do not muss or rumple in damp summer weather.

Wearability in fabric and construction is the keynote of sport clothes. These garments are undated and continue in the wardrobe year after year, with appropriate additions and subtractions.

In making casual jackets, watch for the important differences between those which are easy to make and those tailored ones which require much more work. These differences are explained in Chapter XXVII.

Separate Skirts: Consider your skirts in relation to shirts, jackets, sweaters, and other important accessories. They can be gored, pleated, circular, or gathered.

The 4-piece skirt cut in tweed, serge, or twill is a classic. It should be finished with an interlined self-belt so the blouse can be worn inside or outside. Fit the skirt smoothly through the waist and hips, and be sure the waistband is firm but not too tight. If it is too loose, it will allow the skirt to twist.

A gently flared skirt with a kick pleat in front, or front and back, is easy to make and flattering. In plaid or patterned fabrics, this kind of skirt is easier to match in a novelty fabric than a skirt cut in many gores.

Smooth, fitted hips, smoothly adjusted beltline, and a placket that is invisible and stays closed are the secrets of success in separate skirts. If you plan to wear a leather belt, the top of the skirt can be finished with a bias binding or a straight narrow band of lining fabric; or it can be finished with a self-belt. Some people prefer a high waistline, made by an inner belt

Pockets in sports clothes are set-in before the bias facing is basted around the shaped edges.

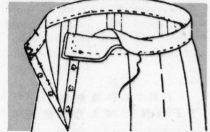

Finish the waistline and place placket. Then turn hem.

2½ or 3 inches wide (see page 121). With this you wear a narrow leather belt at the normal waistline, below the edge of the skirt.

Jumpers and Waistcoats: Jackets and waistcoats, and jumpers in variety, are needed for wear with skirts. Several jumpers made from the same easy-to-make pattern will give variety. For instance have one in white pique, one in black jersey, another in soft pastel wool.

Jumpers: Jumpers can be worn inside or outside the skirt. They can have a close-fitting round neck, a square neck, or a V neck. Select a pattern that suits you, fit it carefully, and keep it for all your jumpers. Buy remnants, a yard or a yard and a half, depending on your size, and width of material. Jumpers are not trimmed. The edges are tailored with a smooth turned band. The high-neck ones are closed on the shoulder with an inconspicuous placket turned toward the back. A jumper can be made in approximately an hour and a half.

Waistcoats: Waistcoats are sleeveless jackets with pockets; or sometimes the man's vest is borrowed and interpreted in flannel. Use a pattern and make the waistcoat of tweed or flannel which is easy to sew. The front edge must be faced. Place a stay of unbleached muslin under the facing and hold it in place with small tailored bastings. Don't hesitate to make bound buttonholes and bound pockets.

Casual Jackets: Casual jackets are usually unlined and often collarless. Cultivate an easy-to-make pattern and fit it to your measurements. The front facing cut in one is a feature which will make the jacket easy to do. Learn to make seams with stitched turned edges so the inside of the jacket will be neat. The sleeves and lower edge can be finished quickly by a hem turned with a seam binding. The lightweight tweeds, wool jerseys, and spun rayons in lovely colors are suitable for jackets and do not reveal a beginner's stitches. You can make gay casual jackets to wear with white skirts and summer tennis dresses—in fact, with all your dresses.

BLOUSES

Blouses correlated to suits, boleros, and jumper-style garments add vitality to the wardrobe. Too many people think of blouses only in terms of the classic tailored variety and ignore their important function in the two-piece costume, tailored or formal, dainty or picturesque. When you choose a blouse pattern, watch out for the time element. A simple-looking blouse can entail long hours, often more than it takes to make a dress. Study the simple, effective constructions, and do not attempt painstaking details unless you can afford the time.

Transparent Blouses: Blouses made of printed or striped chiffon or rayon sheers with full sleeves and classic lines are well worth the time and trouble they cost. They add variety to the wardrobe and can be worn without a coat. Select a pattern especially designed for transparent materials. It may look tailored, but actually it will be cut with soft fullness and full

Little girls love the excitement of quick change made possible by jumper and jacket dresses.

A transparent blouse of sheer rayon introduces softness in the waist and sleeves.

Soft white blouses of voile in white or delicate colors add a frill to frame the face.

Moiré Blouses that stimulate suits are more dressy than the shirtwaist type.

sleeves. Gather the sleeves at both ends to control the fullness, and add three more rows of gathers to insure a smooth stitched line where the sleeve is joined at the armhole or cuff. Cuffs are cut double and buttoned close. Finish the ends of the cuff in the exact size before you turn them.

Festive Blouses: Blouses of taffeta and satin can be made in soft effects with gathered frills. They are worn with or without a jacket. Many beautifully tailored expensive blouses are made in washable satin. There is nothing lovelier than a flesh-colored satin blouse for the woman who excels in creating this type of tailored beauty.

Two-Piece Costume Effects: A blouse with a gay peplum makes a lovely two-piece costume effect. It can be made of taffeta, satin, or moiré.

Evening Blouses: Blouses for evening are usually cut with a square neck and fitted tightly at the waist; or they are made of transparent organdy or rayon marquisette encrusted with wide bands of lace. Black lace on a white blouse is very dramatic with a black taffeta or jersey skirt.

CHILDREN'S SPORT CLOTHES

Until your daughter is teen-age, her skirt and waist should be buttoned together or joined with snap fasteners. Finish the skirt with a self-belt, just as in a grown-up's skirt. Interline the belt so it will hold its shape. Make the blouse as though it were a separate garment, and when it is finished sew a tape at the waistline. Join the two garments with snap fasteners. You can sew them to a tape, or buy tape with snap fasteners already set on it. This latter makes a simple way to join the two garments, for you can sew the corresponding tape to the inside of the skirt belt.

Make your daughter several one-piece dresses in simple casual sport styles with a gored or circular perky skirt and a simple basque waist. Let her plan with you a variety of waistcoats and simple jackets to correlate with the dresses. Small girls can wear shirtwaist effects, and usually they love them; but until they are of school age the garment should be very simple.

CHAPTER XXIV

POINTS TO REMEMBER ABOUT AFTERNOON DRESSES AND FORMALS

The street-length dress in black or a becoming color can be made in simple or deceptively subtle styles. The two look very much alike to the untrained eye, and many home sewers confuse them. When you choose a pattern for an afternoon dress, keep in mind that there are three different kinds: (1) the simple soft dress, easy to make; (2) the soft trimmed dress, easy to make; and (3) the subtle, sophisticated dress which requires knowledge and painstaking detail. Beginners should not attempt the subtle dress, but they can make a simple dress very successfully. As you look over patterns, watch for the placing of the lines. In easy-to-make models, softness is introduced on the shoulders, below yokes in skirt and waist—in either gathers or tucks.

The subtle dress is recognized by its lines. These poems in fabric, so flattering to the figure, must be cut in many pieces; and the wise home sewer will join the pieces of the pattern together and fit it accurately before she begins to cut. Failure to do this is the fundamental reason for failure with this kind of dress. Lines which cross the figure are easier to adjust than those which run up and down. The subtle dress is easier to make successfully in firm rayon crepe or satin. To make one in transparent fabrics, you must have experience in handling such fabrics and in bias cuts.

Dresses which depend upon subtle line and detail must be finished so that no finishing line shows—no outside stitching. This handwork makes these dresses very expensive to buy ready-made. You can duplicate $10 to $65 dresses at about a third of the price if you learn to do this kind of handwork yourself.

CHOOSING THE DRESS

If you add an afternoon dress to your wardrobe each season, be careful not to type yourself by always choosing the same kind. Each season your wardrobe should have the added interest of a totally different kind of afternoon dress—all of them suited to your figure lines, of course. Make a list of your activities to help you choose what to wear to restaurants and the theatre, what to wear to card parties and concerts, both afternoon and evening, what to wear at family gatherings and at holiday festivities.

Girls' and misses' dresses, and those for women, too, which are suitable for restaurants, theatres, dancing, and so forth, depend for success on a wise choice of fabric. The soft black

Look in the Ready-Reference Guide at the back for exact page numbers of Detailed Instructions

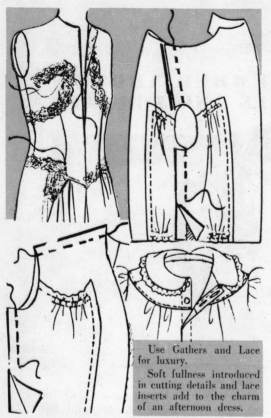

Use Gathers and Lace for luxury.

Soft fullness introduced in cutting details and lace inserts add to the charm of an afternoon dress.

dress which carries over from season to season should be made in a good quality of rayon crepe with both softness and body. If you have several afternoon dresses, you will want one in velvet. For a soft dress with trimming, use a good quality of crepe that will hold decorations and not pull out.

The dress which features contrast in colors is an important means of adding variety to the wardrobe. Choose a pattern which can be made in two tones—a shiny surface and a dull one of the same color—or a harmonious color contrast, or a vivid contrast. Sometimes the contrast is in a two-piece effect which looks like a jacket; sometimes it is introduced in the yoke and sleeves, in a panel front or blouse.

The Basic Dress: The simple basic dress which is becoming to your figure can be in any of several styles. It can be a simple gored skirt with a plain high neck and long sleeves, a surplice line with a little fullness, or a simple button-front dress with soft fullness.

The first step to success is to choose a back-ground dress with no style feature of its own. By developing the right accessories, you change your dress as desired. With one group of accessories you will be simply dressed; with another you will be soft and feminine; with another you can feature the latest fashion (see Chapter XXX).

Children's Afternoon Dresses: In the nursery, dress-up usually takes the form of fine handwork—beautiful smocked voile, eyelet embroidery on batiste, lace and tucked collars and cuffs on fine organdy. School-age children wear the same becoming lines for all occasions, and dress-up is indicated by a plain soft fabric in soft gathered lines; or a plain dress in a lovely color; or a plain dress in a rich fabric such as velvet, velveteen, or moiré.

The teen-age girl revels in the suggestion of a suit. These dress-up suits are usually made of moire or velveteen in a becoming color. They are really a button-front dress with a peplum, very easy to make.

Princess lines are becoming to children of all ages. The fabric can be light-weight wool, spun rayon, velveteen, or corduroy. The dress-up trimming takes the form of a lace collar and cuffs and gay buttons. In summer, girls wear lovely prints in rayon crepe and cotton. Children are sensitive to style—not the grown-up style, but the styles in their own school group. These fads should be watched and taken into account in dress-up as well as in sport clothes.

FORMAL CLOTHES

Most women wear formal clothes less often than any others, and this is the logical place to economize. Formal clothes should be planned to create a big effect for little money; and the way to accomplish this is to have a versatile assortment of garments which can be interchanged to make half a dozen formal outfits instead of one. No matter how old you are, where you live, or how much money you have to spend, let versatility be the keynote of your formal wardrobe.

By working out a basic plan, young girls who go dancing often can have enough changes to look like a debutante, and older women who wear formals only occasionally can do themselves proud without spending a lot of money they would rather use for something else. Even

MAKE THE MOST OF YOUR PATTERN

One pattern made these three dresses. This shows the possibilities of the different cutting lines offered in most patterns. One dress is made of wool, another of plain rayon crepe, and a third of print.

FULL SKIRT WITH THREE WAISTS

Make a full skirt of white or black net. It should be 4 or 5 yards wide and full length. Gather the top with four rows of gathers and finish it with a firm belt. The placket is lost in the fullness of the skirt and need not be finished. Make one waist by shirring a wide piece of net up and down and basting it to the top of a slip to form a camisole top. Make the shoulder straps of rhinestone banding or ribbon, and make a belt to match the straps.

Make the second waist of net shirred on the shoulders and crossing front and back at the waistline. Put a large rose on the shoulder; and when you wear this waist, baste some rose petals to the skirt.

Let the third waist be a close-fitting taffeta one. With this, make little bows of narrow ribbon the same color as the waist and tack them to the skirt.

Long and Short Skirts with One Waist: Make the dress in classic lines that you can wear from season to season, and make it in your most becoming color. The short skirt should be the same color as the waist; the long one can be black or any staple color which harmonizes with the waist. Finish the skirts with fabric belts and snap fasteners so you can wear either one with the same waist. Make some fancy belts and a little hat the color of the dress, and a smart handbag. This is the kind of costume the best-dressed women wear to weddings, restaurants, the theatre, and charity benefits.

Matrons' Formals: The formal dress for the older woman should be made of a rich fabric in slenderizing lines. If you have little need for a formal dress, make a long skirt, carefully fitted to give the slenderest possible lines. Make a halter brassière top, and over it wear a jacket of rich brocade, lace, or velvet in a becoming color. This kind of costume can be laid away and will not go out of style.

Hostess Dresses: A hostess dress has to be comfortable and practical, and yet elaborate enough to match the party clothes of your guests. To be practical, it should be washable; to be enduring, it should be cut in classic lines with a shoulder drapery or a net or lace collar. I have

VARIETY FOR EVENING WEAR

One basic evening dress can be used with different jackets, a tied-on peplum or an over-skirt of net.

women of wealth who need a great many formals plan for versatility nowadays. Their first rule is something simple for restaurants, theatres, and public events in general. Usually this something simple is a long slip of good crepe or satin worn with any number of smart jackets, or a dinner dress with capped or long sleeves. Besides this they have a gala evening dress with a dramatic full skirt. All of these correct formals can be achieved in an interchangeable wardrobe suited to any budget.

used a dress like this for years, made of pink chiffon print with a fichu collar bordered with lovely handwork with inserts of net. It doesn't show spots when I cook, and it has been washed a dozen times. Anyone who entertains at home a good deal will find this kind of dress a blessing. If your budget allows separate formal wardrobes for summer and winter, by all means have a velvet slip or a velvet jacket. If your budget is limited, make your staple slip of crepe and combine it with a colored crepe. Make extra jackets of moiré, heavy faille, and lace. In the summer you can use a jacket of white piqué like a man's white evening jacket. You can also make an organdy ruching or cape to tie on your black slip, or a short ruffled cape of net.

Children's Party Clothes: In children's party clothes there is a distinction between those for informal parties and those for formal ones. At informal parties little girls wear smocked dresses and fresh little dresses of dotted swiss and flowered prints. For special events such as a wedding or a strictly formal family function, the party dresses of even the youngest member reflect the elegance of the occasion. For them make taffeta slips with gay little dresses of net or tulle. Select a pattern with fullness, and add more fullness to the gathered skirt. Make puffed sleeves and trim the dress with bows of ribbon. They can be arranged in rosettes with streamers, or in little bowknots appliquéd to the skirt, with the same ribbon repeated in the child's hair.

For teen-age children's formal parties in spring or fall, lovely flower effects can be created by using a dress of gathered net or chiffon and trimming it with artificial flowers. Pin a bunch of flowers on the shoulder and sew some over the skirt at scattered intervals. In winter the dresses are often made of faille, silk, or velvet.

When parties are more formal, the sophisticated young miss will wear a long formal of taffeta. A wise mother will select a color for this formal which is becoming and can also be used in a daytime dress. Then when it is outgrown as a formal, the dress can be recut to serve again. A short skirt can be made from the old party dress to wear with a new waist of velvet in a matching or contrasting color. If the velvet is made with short sleeves and a square neck, it can be used for afternoons.

THREE DRESSES IN ONE

Several different bodices can be made for one net skirt. Vary the skirt trimming as well.

Look in the Ready-Reference Guide at the back for exact page numbers of Detailed Instructions

CHAPTER XXV

POINTS TO REMEMBER ABOUT COTTON GARMENTS

Cottons are coming into their own in American styles, and the notion that cotton clothes meant cheap clothes is now outworn. Beautiful cottons are available in the stores, and cottons correctly used have a high style value. They have further advantages in that they wear well, are washable, and are easy to sew. There are cotton fabrics for dress-up as well as for utility wear. Afternoon dresses, dinner dresses, and formal evening gowns can be effectively made in cottons, and each season you will find many cotton fabrics for every phase of your summer wardrobe. There are some in wool-like finishes which will serve for fall and winter, too. It will well repay you to explore the possibilities of cotton.

EVERYDAY COTTONS

Cotton fabric will, of course, figure largely in everyday wear for all members of the family.

Wool-like cottons designed for warmth are adaptable for vests and other sport clothes.

Because cotton garments are washable, select patterns which will hold their shape through many washings. This includes patterns with gathered or tucked softness, straight-line skirts gored and not too full, and classic skirts with a kick pleat.

The casual dress with a convertible neckline and gored skirt is a perennial, and excellent for cotton fabrics. It can cross in surplice lines; it can end in a short V at the center front of the waist; it can extend in a long slash to the waistline. The front edge is faced, and the collar is a double fold of straight material with pointed ends which binds the neck. These simple dresses are easy to make and can be varied by trimming and choice of prints. They are particularly good for prints with wide-spaced designs.

Cotton voiles should be made by a pattern which has gathers or tucks, and trimmed with a sheer contrasting fabric—such as organdy collars and cuffs, single bands of organdy joined with hemstitching and hemstitched on the edge, net footing, or velvet ribbon.

Dirndl gathered skirts are suited to every figure if care is taken to select a becoming blouse. Dirndls with contrasting blouses—for instance, a dotted blouse and striped skirt in the same color—offer variety in this popular fashion.

SPORT CLASSICS

Each season offers a new version of the slenderizing button-front straight-line cotton dress, made in piqué, shantung, and shirtings, as well as linen-finish cottons. Yokes are a feature of this dress, either separate or cut in one with the back. The front is usually buttoned, but if buttonholes are a stumbling block to you, stitch the front of the skirt closed in an overlapped seam —stitching back ¼ inch from the edge—and continue the stitching line up the front of the waist. The waist can be closed with snap fasteners to give a tailored classic line. The belt is usually self-fabric, interlined with unbleached muslin thoroughly washed to remove the starch. If preferred, you can wear a leather belt or a novelty belt.

White Summer Classics: These include sleeveless dresses of white piqué or linen-finish cotton, short princess dresses designed especially for tennis, classic golf dresses of men's shirting or seersucker. These garments are easy to make, but always remember that active sport garments should obey the laws of good dress. This means that the patterns should not be selected at random, but chosen from those designed in the tradition of sport clothes.

Casual Suits: The jackets of casual suits are unlined and as easy to make as the waist of a two-piece dress. Choose a pattern with an open front that does not button, or a buttoned front with a facing cut in one. Some jackets have a fitted peplum, which is easy to apply. The seams should be clipped and stitched again in a covered seam; contrasting collars should be double and tailored, even when made of organdy. When a binding is part of the trimming, use a piece of the fabric or a contrasting color. Pockets are a feature of unlined cotton jackets. You can make a welt pocket, matching the welt to the contrasting collar; or a bound pocket, matching the binding to the trimming.

COTTON SUITS

This fashion can be developed in casual suits for the country and vacation; simple suits for city wear, classic suits with that expensive look for cities and resorts. Every woman will want a cotton suit which you can develop into a complete costume. From the wide assortment of patterns and beautiful fabrics, choose the ones suited to your needs and make yourself a costume you will be proud to wear. Be sure your hat is included in your plan, and that the trimming of hat and costume harmonize.

Drapery fabrics make attractive pinafore dresses for Mother and Daughter.

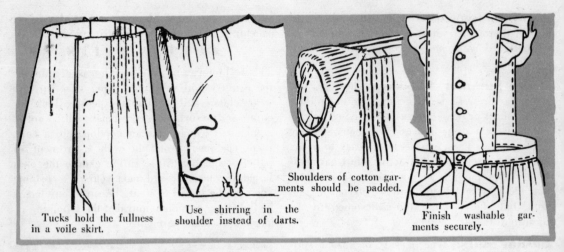

Tucks hold the fullness in a voile skirt.

Use shirring in the shoulder instead of darts.

Shoulders of cotton garments should be padded.

Finish washable garments securely.

A separate cotton jacket of gay print which can be worn with white classic dresses or harmonizing colored dresses is an easily made addition to your summer wardrobe. Choose a box style with a front facing cut in one with the jacket. Long sleeves will make the jacket more effective.

Tailored Classic Suits: Classic cotton suits with that expensive look are a stand-by for the commuter and the business woman. They are made of cotton twill, linen-finish cottons, and piqué in plain colors or prints. Choose a pattern with a semifitted line. It can be cut in a real tailored style or in an easy-to-make style with the facing cut in one with the front. In either case it must have long sleeves.

Simple jackets made in this style can be worn with matching skirt and contrasting shirtwaist, or as a vivid contrast to a single dark dress of navy rayon crepe. The dress can have sleeves or be made with a halter neck like an evening gown; in this case the jacket is not taken off, but it can be worn unbuttoned.

TRANSPARENT DRESSES

In all transparent dresses the slip must be considered an integral part of the dress. Unless fashion specifies a contrasting slip, the slip is always made of a self-colored opaque fabric. Sateen and rayon crepes are the best choice. Be sure the slip is cut on bias lines, and that the top is shaped so that the outline flatters the dress to be worn over it. The shoulder straps can be very narrow self-colored fabric or linen, or they

can be made of net to accentuate the transparent effect.

Tailored net dresses can be made on any pattern with a little fullness, preferably a pattern recommended for lace, chiffon, or voiles. The hem and sleeves can be bound with the slip fabric, or a hem can be turned. The hem must be straight and even and not too wide. A V neck can be finished with a ruching of organdy or lace. If it has a little white collar, it should be a single fold of organdy with a hand-rolled hem.

Dressy afternoon dresses of net or opaque fabrics often have sleeves and a yoke of transparent net or lace. The yoke can be lined with flesh-colored or self-color net. The edge of the neck and sleeves can be bound with dress fabric, using a narrow French binding or narrow ribbon. Never machine-stitch this kind of binding.

VOILE AFTERNOON DRESSES

Printed voiles of the better quality can be made into pretty low-necked dresses with short puffed sleeves or a dropped-shoulder sleeve cut in one. This is the kind of dress to wear with a big hat to summer afternoon parties or to a restaurant on a summer evening. Choose a pattern with tucked or shirred fullness, in the simplest lines. It can have a self-fabric belt, a ribbon belt, or a wide fancy belt. It needs no trimming.

When a dress of this kind is buttoned up the front, use for the facing a material that is both strong and transparent, and the color of the background of your print. The facing will then stay the edge and hold the buttons without spoiling the transparent effect. The edge of the sleeve can be faced with the same material, and the edge must be hemmed by hand so the stitches do not show.

The neck edge can be turned over a cord or faced with a transparent material so that the finish is inconspicuous and the line of the neck clear and even. No machine stitching should show.

Unless you are very skillful, it is not wise to try to make buttonholes in a transparent fabric. Sew the buttons on the outside fold of the dress and put snap fasteners under them.

COTTON EVENING DRESSES

Evening dresses made of cotton can be informal or the formal kind suited to country clubs and summer resorts. The latter are usually made of organdy, cotton net, cotton lace, or lovely open-work embroidery. Often they are made of prints in the heavier cottons as well as the transparent.

Informal evening dresses, made of pique, gingham, dotted swiss, organdy, or voile, can be cut by pattern with full dirndl skirts or gored skirts with more fitted lines. They are usually trimmed with contrasts of organdy or net and are very becoming.

COTTON CLOTHES FOR CHILDREN

Pattern books offer a wide assortment of one-piece dresses suited to every age group and every type of child. Mothers faced with the problem of dressing a child for summer vacation can save a great deal of time by planning all the clothes at once. As far as possible, use only two patterns for a dozen garments, and vary them by selecting different types of fabric and print and using different trimming details. This will make the work go more quickly; and another time-saver is to plan every detail of each garment and make a shopping list. Keep the list in your handbag and pick up an item here and there as you pass by instead of making special trips. Then sort out your purchases and put everything needed for each garment together and tie it into a roll. Put the rolls in a big box with all your sewing accessories. Then when you sew everything will be ready, and no time

Cottons and washable corduroys are both practical and attractive for children's clothes.

will be wasted running to the store or searching the house for something mislaid. If you make sewing fun, your daughters will want to sew.

Pinafores of white lawn, dotted swiss, or a quaint print, plaid, or calico are easy to make, and many little girls like them. This is something your daughter can be encouraged to make, along with simple dresses with puffed sleeves cut in one, or ruffles for sleeves.

CHAPTER XXVI

MATERNITY DRESSES
AND INFANTS' WEAR

Conservative Maternity Dresses:
Conservative women prefer plain dark fabrics or dark prints with very small designs. The dresses are made in simple lines—a surplice, a coat effect, or a one-piece dress with a drawstring at the waist. A fresh white collar or jabot is a feature of these dresses. Select a pattern that fits your neck and shoulders so you have the correct shaping for sleeves and armholes. Then add fullness to the rest of the pattern to fit your measurements, as described in Chapter XI, in the sections on enlarging a pattern. Dresses which cross and tie are particularly good for the summer months. Put large pockets on these dresses, especially low skirt pockets on the side. They help to balance the figure. Some women find a surplice-front dress with a little fullness across the skirt is comfortable when the fullness is held by elastic. Others feel more comfortable in a surplice dress with a little fullness at the shoulders and in the skirt than in the more tailored

models. It depends upon your figure which type you will prefer.

Allow an extra deep hem in the dress so that adjustments can be made from time to time. A half-inch longer in the front is barely perceptible, and it will allow for the "jumping up" which occurs in the later months.

Casual Maternity Dresses: Women who wear decorative color prefer casual maternity clothes. They find that a jumper dress with gay sleeves and vest and plenty of changes relieves the monotony of their wardrobe. Jumper dresses with dirndl skirts—the waistband drawn through a casing—are easy to adjust. The self-fabric bow can be worn for a time, then changed by crossing the tie strings in front and looping them at the center back. Two jumper dresses with several blouses give a wide variety adaptable to climate changes. Other women prefer a jumper or dicky dress of wool supplemented with a plain fabric dress in a dark rayon crepe — semisheer cool crepes are good. Add a summer print for variety, made of a cool cotton or rayon print. Print dresses are often made with an extra tuck or pleat on the hip which can be adjusted. Others are made in jacket, or pleated jumper styles.

Two-piece costumes lend themselves to decorative effects, and women who prefer a garment hung from the shoulder can choose between a jacket type and a loose jumper. The skirt is hung on a lining, and both skirt and lining can be laid in unpressed pleats spaced to be let out one at a time. Over this wear a jacket or jumper so the pleats do not show. In summer wear fresh touches of organdy that make you look and feel cool. Don't limit yourself to a collar; wear a jabot, a scarf tied in a bow with long ends, or face the lapels of your jacket with crisp pique or print.

Decorative Maternity Dresses: Women who understand line and color contribute constructive ideas aimed at distracting the eye from the waistline. Yokes and sleeves of contrast color introduced in wrap-around dresses are good when the color extends to the hem, thus drawing the eye away from the width. The contrasts can be white on dark colors or light and dark shades of one color.

Other decorative costumes combine gathered skirts and contrasting blouses worn with a boyish-cut jacket, loose with low pockets and long enough to fit well over the hips. This breaks the line and helps conceal width at the waist.

One enterprising young artist determined to wear pretty clothes, so she made herself a petticoat with hoops and wore over it gay peasant dresses of striped cotton with full gathered skirts. Her housecoat had a frill up the center from neck to floor. The longer the skirt, the more slender the effect; so wear a full-length skirt whenever you can.

Maternity Dress Made without a Pattern: Another workable idea is a dirndl with a dicky top cut broad in a decorative outline and slipped over the head. Finish the top of the full skirt with a casing deep enough to pass a belt through $1\frac{1}{2}$ inches wide. Finish the ends of the belt with loops and adjust it from time to time, putting a button at the waist-

DIAGRAM FOR YOKE

This maternity jumper is attractive and deceiving when worn with light-colored shirts, and sheer blouses.

line of the dress wherever the belt ends comfortably. A separate blouse is worn with this, so it adjusts easily. This dress can be made with a street-length skirt or a long skirt; it can be carried out in cottons or heavy rayon crepes. Made in rich fabrics and metallics, it is a perfect evening dress.

To make this dress, decide whether you want a cotton suited to country life, a light-weight wool, or a rayon crepe, either plain or printed, or a formal dinner dress. Plan the fabric for the skirt and dicky, and plan two or three blouses to wear with the dress. When the dress is cut in a short length for daytime wear, the blouses can be cotton, in the peasant types, or tailored blouses. When you cut the dress with a long skirt, plan a blouse suited to formal wear. It can be chiffon, georgette, or a sheer metal cloth. No matter what the fabric, the skirt is made of three full widths of material. Cut it in the length desired, allowing a hem. Seam the straight pieces and gather one edge.

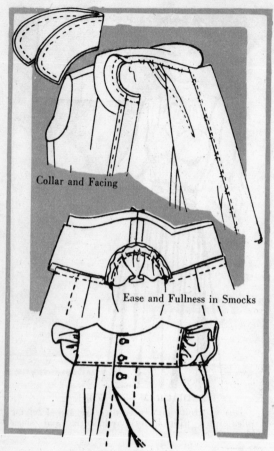

Collar and Facing

Ease and Fullness in Smocks

Yoke Stitched in Smock

Plan a placket opening at one side. Draw the gathering into a 60-inch measure. Stitch a double band to the top of the skirt. It should be 2 inches wide when finished. Make an opening at the center back. Now cut the heart-shaped dicky by diagram. To do this measure your length from shoulder to waist and divide this figure by 3. Two-thirds of this measure will be the length of your dicky. Mark it on the diagram. Now measure the width suited to your proportions and mark it on the diagram. Cut a piece of fabric for the dicky in the measurements you have set on the diagram. Fold this in half; measure down 2 inches from the top in a curved line as in the diagram. Measure in 2 inches from each edge and slope the sides as in the diagram. The dotted lines on the diagram show you how to shape the dicky. You can bind it or edge it with a ruffle. Now make the belt by cutting a piece of self-fabric twice the length of your waist measure

and 4 inches wide. Cut an interlining of un-bleached muslin in this length, making it 1½ or 2 inches wide. Cut the shoulder straps long enough to extend from the dicky to the waistline in back. They cross at the center back. These strips can be in contrast color or self-fabric and should be 3 inches wide. Fold the belt and the shoulder straps lengthwise and stitch the edges in a seam in the belt. It is necessary to stitch the interlining in this seam. Stitch the interlining at the opposite edge of the belt before you turn it. Turn the belt and the shoulder straps. The shoulder straps are joined to the dicky in the front. The opposite ends are finished with hooks and eyes. The belt is turned and run through the casing at the top of the skirt. Finish the ends with hooks and eyes. When this dress is made, the belt will hook in the front. As the figure increases in size, the belt can be spread and hooked to the casing at the most comfortable angle. In this way, you are continually changing the position of the hooks and eyes which hold the belt. Otherwise, the blouse and skirt adjust themselves.

INFANTS' CLOTHING

In selecting a pattern for an infant's clothing, the important things to consider are protection, comfort, room for activity, and room for rapid growth. Requirements for protection differ in different climates, and in this respect you should have your doctor's advice.

Approach the making of a layette with a practical and not a sentimental plan. The kind and number of garments is a matter of personal adjustment, but wise mothers plan for very few infants' clothes. Few of them make the gift-type of garments, and those who do usually regret it when their friends begin to send gifts.

When you select your patterns, keep these three things in mind: the garments must be comfortable; they must be easy to launder; they must be easy to slip on and off. Select garments that tie instead of button. Give preference to those that open and close in front, and to raglan sleeves. Resist tiny collars that crumple up, no matter how cute they are; and resist garments that slip over the head. They are hard to adjust and hard to iron. A christening dress is enough of this type. You can make that as elaborate as your heart desires.

The fabrics must be soft. Fine nainsook, lawn, and batiste, and soft crepes are satisfactory. The soft flannels are made especially for babies. Finish the seams flat or in French seams and hand-roll or bind the edges. Ribbon binding is decorative and can be made into bows, thus serving a double purpose.

CLOTHES FOR THE TODDLER

The baby who is crawling or learning to walk needs special consideration. Plan garments which allow the greatest freedom for reaching, kicking, getting around on hands and knees, and trying out the first steps. Rompers with raglan sleeves and a little fullness set in the shoulder are good. They must be long enough, and the neck opening large enough so the garment can be easily slipped on and off. They should be buttoned at the crotch for easy changing. Babies at the creeping stage need a romper that is longer in the back and shorter in front. At this stage they are difficult to keep clean, and frequent changes are necessary. For this reason the garments should be made with a little fullness and no frills.

Bind the neck and make the garment in pretty colors which can be washed continually. Soft, flexible fabrics with a smooth surface which does not pick up dirt should be used. They should be preshrunk and color-fast. All seams should be narrow, flat, and smooth. All neck edges and arm and leg openings must be smoothly finished and easy to iron. All stitching should be secure—the garment will receive hard wear. Buttons and buttonholes must stay fast and keep their shape. Remember, they will have to stand a great deal of buttoning and unbuttoning.

At this age a coat and bonnet of challis or soft wool is an important part of the wardrobe. They can be lined with washable silk, but a more practical way is to make an unlined challis or flannel coat with a tiny yoke and turned-down collar. Make it with French seams if it is unlined.

Little dress-up garments in white or colored nainsook or batiste are made by hand, and the tiny frill on the collar can be lace or a hand-rolled ruffle of the garment fabric. But dresses are a sentimental addition to the toddler's wardrobe, and the time might better be spent on making a coat and an assortment of rompers in progressive sizes. Boy babies get into rompers earlier than girls, as a rule; but when the baby begins to creep, dresses are hampering and the wise mother will curb her desire to dress the child like a doll until her active offspring is steady on her feet.

CLOTHES FOR THE TOT

Clothes for a child who has learned to walk must have action features—raglan sleeves that permit high reaching, seats with extra length that permit freedom in bending and spread for squatting, shoulder lines with gathers or tucks to add fullness. The garment should fit the child. Little girls' dresses with hems can be adjusted; little boys' suits with trousers buttoned to the waist permit of some adjustment, but they are outgrown more quickly than dresses because of the crotch length.

To encourage self-reliance in the child, fastenings and plackets should be in front within easy reach. Very large or very small buttons, snap fasteners, and hooks and eyes are taboo; they are too difficult for tiny fingers. Tests show that little children can easily learn to use a medium-sized round, flat button. It should have a slight groove to keep fingers from slipping off, and it can have a tape adjustment to give the child something to pull. The garment should have as few fastenings as possible.

Dresses should be slipped over the head and fastened at the neck with one button. Boys' suits can be buttoned together and slipped on and off like a one-piece garment with one or two fastenings. Drop seats controlled by a belt which buttons in front are easy for a child to manage and should be used in boys' suits, underwear, and pajamas. Drop seats are also arranged with an elastic run through a casing, which stretches easily and flies back into shape. An elastic run through a casing is also used on little girls' panties. These can often be made from pieces left from a dress, but they should not be too brief and short.

Children are active and the textiles and workmanship of their clothing should above all be sturdy. Make the armholes extra size, and make sleeves that allow plenty of freedom. In warm weather the child needs no other garments under a denim coverall with a drop seat. This is easily made and easily washed, a utility garment as becoming as it is practical.

CHAPTER XXVII

HOW TO MAKE COATS AND JACKETS

Contrary to what many people think, coats and jackets are not hard to make at home. Their success depends upon a careful choice of pattern. Different styles of coats and jackets look much alike, but with a little attention you can learn to tell the easy-to-make ones from those requiring intricate tailoring and construction; and then you can choose a pattern that accords with your sewing ability. With the help of the following simple rules you can tell the difference, and with their help learn to make new coats for yourself or your children, or remake and reline old coats.

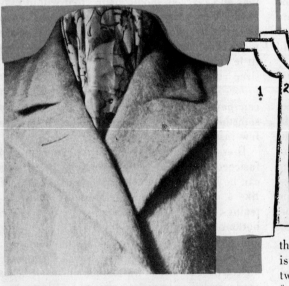

Though these two coats look alike, the one on the right is easy to make. The other, because of its pointed reveres and tailored detail, is more complicated.

RULES FOR IDENTIFYING EASY-TO-MAKE COATS

Train yourself to check the cutting diagram on the back of the pattern, noting particularly the front closing edge of both single and double-breasted coats and jackets. Learn to recognize from the pattern pieces whether the front edge is (1) straight, (2) curved, or (3) has excessively pointed lapels.

Most coats are faced with a shaped piece which is seamed to the front edge, but by asking, the beginner can find the easier straight coat with the facing cut in one with the coat. This edge is creased and turned instead of being joined in two pieces in a seam. Choose a pattern with the fewest possible pieces.

The tailored classic coat is deceiving. Home sewers often select a plain tailored coat or suit as the easiest to make, and immediately they are in trouble because garments in men's-wear fabrics call for fine details perfected through centuries of tailoring. Lapels with points must be reinforced; edges must be taped; fullness must be shrunk out at the tops of the sleeves. As none of these details are necessary in casual and dressmaker garments, home sewers can make innumerable coats without selecting models which require rigid tailoring. So look at the front edge in the pattern. If it has a sharp point extending beyond the collar, you will be faced with tailored construction. Compare the different cutting lines on the preceding page. The first two are used in all coats except those with pointed revers; the third is used for a pointed revere.

For your first coat, choose one that is not lined. You will finish it sooner and more easily. This practice will make your second coat easier to do, and to this one add a lining. The third coat can be more complex, with more pieces in the pattern, and be interlined for warmth. After that, you will be able to make any coat you like, until you will feel competent to master the intricate tailored models.

SELECTING PATTERN AND FABRIC

Pattern: It is not necessary to buy your coat pattern in a larger size than your dress patterns. Commercial patterns are always made up and the garment tried on a figure before they are placed on sale, so you can rest assured that any pattern you buy has been fitted over a dress, and is loose enough for a lining. Always buy your dress size in coat and jacket patterns.

Fabric: Select your material before you buy your pattern, then choose the pattern and examine the cutting detail before you buy the material. Be sure to look at the chart of pattern pieces on the back of the envelope. This cannot be overemphasized. When the fabric is heavy, such as camel's-hair or a heavy napped woolen, avoid patterns which call for pleats or gathers. Softer, light-weight fabrics, designed for lighter coats, can be made into lovely warm garments by putting in a wool interlining, which is easy to do, as explained later in this chapter.

A suiting fabric is lighter than a coat woolen, and better adapted for a light coat or spring suit. Both napped and smooth surface fabrics are used in coats for city wear. Dress coats are made of wools or worsteds with a smooth surface; casual coats of sport fabrics with a nap. A summer coat which does not crease can be made from a soft, spongy wool, or in soft fabrics with a little rayon or rabbit's-hair mixed in. These need no pressing. To make a warm summer coat, you can line it with the same fabric

The raincoat and these four jackets can be cut from the same basic pattern. Variety can be achieved in fabrics and trimming details.

in a lighter tone. Flannel and smooth-surface fabrics are also suitable for summer coats, but they must be pressed.

SUCCESS IN MAKING THE COAT

You will soon find that you can make many different coats with just one pattern. For example, the same straight-line pattern can be used for a raincoat, a warm winter coat, and a spring plaid coat. This will speed up your work because you won't have to study a new pattern routine each time, and yet the coats will look different because of the different materials.

Sewing on heavy coating fabrics is no different, you will soon discover, from sewing on dress materials, except that the machine stitch must be loosened. You can easily make successful coats in very heavy fabrics, in ordinary winter-coat weights, in light-weight coatings warmly interlined, in spring tweeds and sport fabrics—provided you avoid the classic tailored garments. In addition, you can make reversible coats and raincoats in cotton treated to repel water.

Many women find that lining or interlining a coat already made is a good first step to making a new coat. Remaking an old coat is excellent practice too. A coat is usually the largest single item in the budget, so that learning to make your own is a considerable saving. If you can use a discarded garment for the interlining of a reversible coat, if you can line and interline coats that need it, you make an important contribution to your wardrobe and your budget.

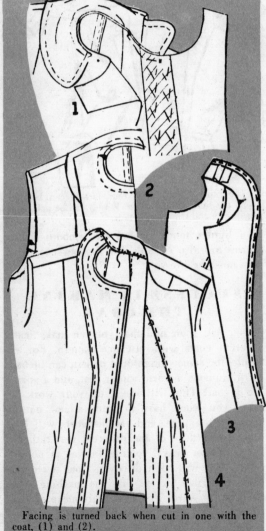

Facing is turned back when cut in one with the coat, (1) and (2).

Facing cut separately is joined and turned (3) and (4).

CASUAL COATS

This includes the important sport coat, the straight-line coat, the raglan-sleeve coat, the open-front summer coat; and it includes jackets in tailored lines, single or double-breasted, jackets with revere collars, and jackets that hang straight without closing. All of them are very easy to make.

Adjusting the Pattern: To save hours of work in fitting, the pattern must be fitted and adjusted to the figure before the coat is cut. Your coat pattern will show you exactly where to lengthen or shorten it.

Making the Coat: Pin before basting. When you have basted the darts in the shoulders and pinned the pieces together—except the sleeves—try on the coat to check the proportions. Make any necessary alterations, then stitch and press the seams. Then you are ready to adjust the interfacing.

Interfacing: Cut it by the pattern and apply it as directed there. Both the *front edge* and the *collar* are interfaced. In casual coats, the best material for interfacing is unbleached muslin, thoroughly washed to remove all starch. For a heavy fabric, use tailor's canvas. The interfacing is held to the coat by slant basting, which is done by using a fine thread which exactly matches the coat fabric and taking tiny stitches through both muslin and coat. The stitches should be spaced an inch apart, and must not show on the right side of the coat.

Facing and Collar: After the interfacing has been basted in, join the facing by stitching it to the edge of the coat (the front edge only). Pin the collar to the coat on the right side. One edge of the collar joins the neck edge of the coat either flush with the front edge or 2 or 3 inches back from the front edge. Join the opposite edge of the collar (in the front only) to the facing and seam it to the top of the facing. Press these seams before you turn the facing to the wrong side of the coat, and check for a smooth collar line. Hem the collar across the back of the neck after the lining is adjusted. Then you are ready to finish the lower edge.

Finishing the Lower Edge: Turn a hem at the lower edge. In coats hems are laid flat and the top edge covered with a seam binding, or catch-stitched flat and covered with the lining. Fit the end of the facing even with the hem edge and clip away the hem under the facing. Be sure to nip away the corners that make bulk so that hem and facing will lie flat in a smooth coat finish.

Sleeves: Coat sleeves are often cut in two pieces. Seam them as you would in any garment and baste them into the armholes. Then make your final fitting, watching the sleeves and the front closing. Mark the places for the buttons, and watch the pockets and mark them accurately. The sleeves are adjusted like the sleeves in any garment, and the shoulder padding can be made from a circle or a square in any size desired. The hem of the sleeve is turned like any garment hem. When the coat is lined, you catch-stitch the sleeve hem; when it is unlined, you cover the edge with seam binding instead of turning it. In unlined coats, the armholes are bound with lining fabric.

Pockets: Pockets are not hard to make, and they add to the success of a casual coat. In sport coats the pockets are either a patch pocket buttoned at the top, a patch pocket with a flap buttoned down, a welt pocket, or a bound pocket. The pockets are placed as current fashion dictates; often they are slanted. (The index gives the page numbers for detailed directions for making pockets.)

Lining: When the pockets have been made, you are ready to line the coat. Complete directions for this are given on page 179.

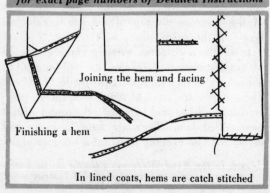

Look in the Ready-Reference Guide at the back for exact page numbers of Detailed Instructions

Joining the hem and facing

Finishing a hem

In lined coats, hems are catch stitched

Dressmaker coats feature rolled collars, soft details and can be made as easily as a dress.

Buttons and Buttonholes: Bound buttonholes and worked buttonholes are easy to make, but they take a little practice. Until you become proficient, you can have a tailor make them for you.

DRESSMAKER COATS

The simple coat with fitted lines, known as the dressmaker coat, features soft rolled collars, princess lines, and body softness. Often these lovely afternoon coats introduce gathers and pleated inserts. You can select the type that meets your need in full confidence that these coats are no more difficult to make than a dress. Follow the routine for making a casual coat.

Collars: White coat collars are made separately of piqué, linen, or heavy cotton. Cut both collar and lining by the coat pattern and seam them together. Clip the corners before you turn to the right side. Bind the inside edge with a tape and baste the collar into your coat.

Inlaid collars of velvet or velveteen can be added as a third facing as described in the next paragraph, except in garments made of very heavy fabric. In this case the velvet or velveteen can be made to look like an inlay by cutting it without seams and then slip-stitching it to the edge. An extra seam allowance should be cut at the front edge of coat and collar when this is done.

Printed Facing: When it is fashionable to face your coat with the print from which your dress is made, the coat is finished with self-facing and an extra facing of dress fabric laid over it. To do this, cut the third facing without seam allowances. Turn the seams and baste them. Place this third facing over the coat facing and slip-stitch it in place, leaving a little border of coat all around so it looks like an inlay.

EVENING COATS

Luxurious evening wraps are really very easy to make. There are five distinct kinds: (1) the full-length formal coat of velvet or velveteen, interlined and warm; (2) the three-quarter-length velvet-lined box coat of tapestry damask or metallic fabric; (3) the capes, full-length or short, of velvet or rich metallic novelties; (4) the short fancy jackets of moiré or taffeta for summer evenings; and (5) short summer capes, lined or unlined, of velvet, velveteen, heavy rayon crepe, or taffeta.

An evening coat need not be expensive, but it must be fashionable, with well-fitted lines. The fabric must be luxurious. If your budget is low, use velveteen, but keep in mind that velveteen will not wear season after season like a more expensive velvet coating. Remember also that, although a dress velvet will do for short wraps or capes, a long velvet coat must be made of a Lyons velvet or rayon velvet with a cotton back and erect pile.

Select your pattern from among the dressmaker coats or the coats designed for casual sports wear, or use a cape pattern especially designed for evening wear. If you want a full-length princess coat and no pattern is available, use a shorter coat pattern with the lines you want and lengthen it. Don't be afraid of a coat with a little cape. If you have enough fur to border the cape, you can lengthen the coat to full length. Three-quarter-length evening coats are box and loose-fitting. Use a sport-coat pattern and follow the routine for casual coats.

The short evening coat of taffeta or moiré which goes so well with full skirts can be made from a jacket or fitted coat pattern, single- or double-breasted. Cut the pattern at the waistline, and add full gathered balloon sleeves. To do this, split the sleeve pattern through the center and spread it 6 or 8 inches. Fit the shaped end of the sleeve to the armhole and gather the extra fullness across the top, spacing it carefully. Gather the lower edge of the sleeve into a band.

Evening Capes: Full-length evening capes are very becoming to larger women; shorter capes are flattering to the slender one. Elbow-length capes are a graceful complement to a narrow-skirted evening dress. When you cut a velvet cape, make sure the grain of the fabric runs the same way in all the pieces, or it will not fall in graceful folds. Match the seams carefully and steam them so they are indiscernible. When you are cutting a large cape from 39-inch material, estimate the piecing and join the fabric and steam the seams before you cut the cape. Piece and seam the lining fabric the same way.

Gathered capes are often in fashion, and they are easier to make than circular capes. Interest and beauty are added to the lining of a cape by making half of it out of metallic fabric and the other half out of the cape fabric or satin the same color. These linings are often appliquéd with large, elaborate designs, made by outlining a small plate on a piece of paper and drawing a conventionalized flower in this space. Put a row of these across the top of the hemline in the lining of the garment.

In southern climates, evening capes are made of such transparent fabrics as tied and dyed chiffon or batik; they are also made of taffeta. These capes are straight lengths of fabric gathered into a band and hemmed all around with a hand-rolled hem. They are easy to make and lovely with an evening dress on a summer night.

Look in the Ready-Reference Guide at the back for exact page numbers of Detailed Instructions

TAILORED CLASSIC COATS

Making the Tailored Coat: Cut, fit, and pin the garment like any other coat. The interfacing must be put in painstakingly. Use tailor's canvas in the pointed lapels — many professionals use it for the whole interfacing. Others make the interfacing of unbleached muslin with a revere stayed with tailor's canvas. This interfacing and revere are placed *inside the seamline* and held in place with slant basting. The basting can be open and wide in the long straight edges, but must be very close and fine in the pointed revere. The collar must be interlined and reinforced with stitches the same way. These tiny padding stitches must not show on the right side of the garment.

Tape all edges. The tape is placed 1/2 inch back from the edge and must continue all the way up the front edge of the coat and around the neckline to the shoulder seam. This tape is mitered at the corners and held in place with catch stitches.

Turn the edges of the collar and the coat over the tape and baste them. Turn the edge of the facing over tape and place the facing over and slip-stitch the coat; match the edges.

Then place the collar on the right side of the garment and join one edge to the neckline. The opposite edge—at the front only—is seamed to the edge of the facing. One seam is over the other seam. Stitch these seams and press them open, fitting the collar and facing smoothly across the shoulder and neckline.

Finish the lower edge. Turn up a hem and catch-stitch it in place. If the coat is not to be lined, finish this hem with a seam binding. Turn the end of the facing in place and fit it over the hem. Before you do this (1) clip the seam above the turning, (2) nip the corner before turning, (3) cut away a little of the seam, and (4) cut away the hem under the facing.

Bound buttonholes are a feature of all tailored garments. In classic tailored suits they are often worked over a cord to give them an extra finish. In other suits a lining facing is placed under the buttonhole on the wrong side of the garment, and a binding of self-fabric on the right side. The buttonhole is then outlined through all these fabrics. Tailors stitch the outline of all bound buttonholes.

Evening wraps and capes can be short or full length. By simple pattern adjustments they can be cut from a casual coat pattern.

Sleeves: In classic tailored garments the sleeves are always cut in two pieces. Stitch them, press the seams open, and turn the lower edge. The top of the sleeve is not notched into little darts. Instead, the fullness is shrunk out of the cloth so that it is round and smooth (see page 118 for directions). After the fullness is shrunk out of the sleeve, it is placed in the armhole and the sleeve padding adjusted.

CHILDREN'S COATS

The easiest patterns to adjust for length are those with straight lines. As the child grows and the hem has to be lengthened, there is no telltale beltline to spoil the effect of an otherwise good garment. Many mothers prefer a double-breasted coat for children. They also save a little fabric to make cuffs when the sleeves shoot up, and one mother tells me she not only adds cuffs, but

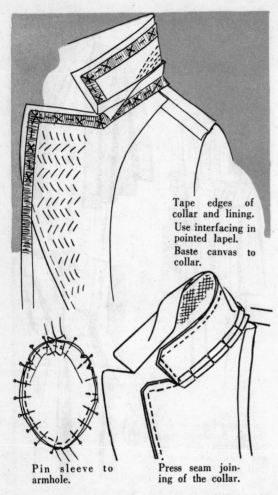

Tape edges of
collar and lining.
Use interfacing in
pointed lapel.
Baste canvas to
collar.

Pin sleeve to   Press seam join-
armhole.   ing of the collar.

has often stitched a band down the center back
and let the garment out in front.

Fabrics: Fabrics for children's coats must be
durable and colorfast. A "bargain" which fades,
shrinks, or wears poorly will not in the end be
as economical as a first-quality woolen which
lasts several years. Plain-colored fabrics and
smooth-surface tweeds wear longer than rough
tweeds and novelties. But children love gaiety,
and every child wants at least one gay plaid
coat.

Don't overlook the possibilities of the soft
woolens made especially for snow suits, some
of which are treated with a water-repellent.
These fabrics, however, do not wear well enough
to be used for all-purpose coats. Raincoats,
lined with wool or unlined, are easy to make; the
heavy cotton in close weave, treated to repel

water, is easy to manage when you use a straight,
simple cutting construction.

The section on Casual Coats at the beginning
of this chapter will give you many pointers on
constructing the most popular types of children's
coats. Don't hesitate to use pockets, inlaid collars, white collars of piqué or lawn (see index
for directions).

Children's Reversible Coats: Select a
boys' or girls' coat pattern in a straight-line
model, either single- or double-breasted. It will
be worn on both sides, and you will work with
two fabrics, wool and cotton. Both fabrics should
be treated with a water-repellent. Fit the pattern
carefully and make the necessary adjustments.
Do not use the facing in the pattern; you simply
cut two full coats, one from each fabric.

Cut the cotton first and pin it together. Fit it
to the child and make any alterations needed.
Use this fitted garment for a pattern to cut the
wool. Remember that if your wool is a plaid,
you must match the pattern of the plaid.

Join the pieces and make two separate coats,
one cotton, the other wool. Seam the underarm
and shoulder and press the seams open. Turn
up the lower edge and hold it with a catch
stitch. Make the pockets and sew in the sleeves.
Do not join the collar or finish the front edge.

The front edge of the woolen coat must be reinforced with an interfacing of unbleached
muslin, adjusted exactly as the pattern directs.
Turn the woolen coat wrong side out and have
the child stand still while you adjust the cotton
one. This must be done on the figure. First, pin
the shoulder seams and neck edges together, then
the underarm seams down to the elbow. Pin the
front edges together and test the closing line of
the coat, marking it for buttons and buttonholes.

Lay the coat on a table and turn the front
edges so they face. Slip-stitch these edges together. Run a machine stitching at the top of the
hemline, through both the woolen and the cotton.
The edges will not be joined below the stitching.
Stitch the edges of the sleeves together, turning
them so they face each other. The edges should
meet exactly and be slip-stitched together.

Join the collar as directed before under Tailored Classic Coats. Make the buttons and buttonholes so they are finished on both sides. If you
are not expert at this, have the tailor do it.

Children's Raincoats: Select any straight-line tailored coat and follow the directions in the pattern. The fabric should be a heavy cotton treated with water repellent. These garments have felled stitched seams, and the facings are stitched to the garment. These rows of stitching are part of the trimming and are repeated at the edge of the collar and pockets. Raincoats often have inlaid collars of velveteen.

Children's Fitted Coats: Coats in princess lines or with definite waistlines require more tailoring than the straight-line casual coat. They are not difficult to make, however, and amply repay the time spent on them. They are usually made of luxurious fabrics of tweed or plain-colored woolens. Often tailored leggings are made from the same fabric to go with the coat.

Cut the garment from a pattern which has been carefully fitted, and make allowances for growth in your cutting. These coats have separate facings which are applied after the interfacing is adjusted. The pattern directions show you clearly how to make the coat. For lining and interling, see pages 179 and 180.

Extra Heavy Fabrics: For boys' mackinaws and boys' and girls' all-purpose coats, extra heavy fabrics are often fashionable. Use whatever fabric is fashionable at the time. The extra weight of the fabric will not complicate your problems. These coats are cut in straight lines, and all you need do is remember that these fabrics have a pile and must be cut with the top of each piece pointing in the same direction, and that you must adjust the needle, thread, and stitch of your machine. You will need a heavier thread, a coarser needle, and a looser stitch.

These coats are not faced. Instead, the front edge is bound with a straight binding of thin woolen, easy to apply. It must be wide enough to hold the buttonholes comfortably. Make the collar to match the binding. These coats are often lined with the same kind of wool used for the binding. Some textiles are double-faced and need no lining. In that case, make flat stitched seams and bind the armholes

Hoods: A hood can be added to any child's coat to protect from rain.

Tailored Jacket

Soft Jacket

These three reversible coats can be made of a rain-proofed cotton and lined with wool.

Adjustments for Growth: When you are making a garment for a growing child, you will want to make some adjustments to allow for growth. Write the child's measurements on a piece of paper — length, sleeve length, bust

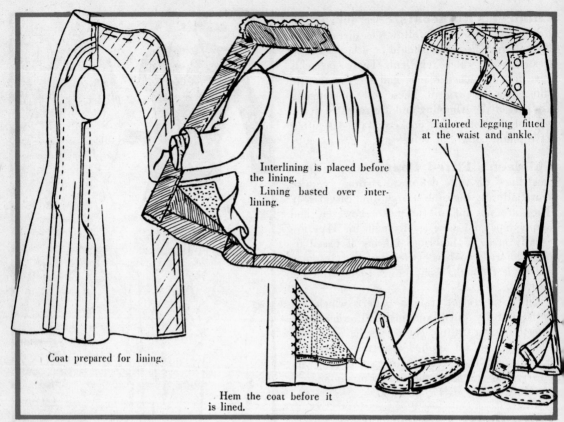

Coat prepared for lining.

Interlining is placed before the lining.

Lining basted over inter-lining.

Tailored legging fitted at the waist and ankle.

Hem the coat before it is lined.

measure. Then decide how much extra you want to turn up in the hem—4 inches is about right. Decide what you will add to the sleeve length—2½ inches is the average. Decide whether you can add any extra to the front edge without spoiling the line of the garment. Write these extra allowances on the paper beside the measurements and keep the paper before you as you cut. Do not try to cut by eye, but measure the additional length with a tape measure and add it to the edge. When the addition is more than 2 inches, it must be added in the center of the pattern as described in Chapter XI.

WORKING IN FUR

For your fur trimmings you can buy new fur, use some from a cast-off coat or muff, buy fur trimming, or buy fur cloth by the yard. Fur is cut, joined, strengthened, taped, and lined; but it is not nearly as difficult as it sounds or as most home sewers think.

Odd bits of fur applied as trimming can be hemmed to the garment without binding or strengthening. Will the fur be simply orna-

mental, or will it get hard wear, as in the collar or banding of a coat, or in a muff?

Fur Collars: Collars of fur can be straight or shaped. Use a pattern. If you are remaking a garment and must cut the pattern yourself, take a piece of paper and shape it into the pattern desired. Try it on to be sure of the size and the effect you want.

Lay the fur face down on the pattern. If none of the fur pieces are large enough, you can piece them, matching the hair on the right side, then turning to the wrong side and overcasting the edges together. Make the overcasting close and fine, and be sure not to catch any hairs in it. The joining must not show on the right side. When the piecing is done, lay the fur on the pattern again and cut.

Lining Fur: To hold the pelt so the edge does not tear, first overhand a tape to the pelt. Hold the fur toward you with the tape against the pelt and be careful not to catch the hair. Then put in a lamb's-wool interlining to make your collar fluffier. Lay it over the pelt and catch-stitch the tape over it, mitering the corners. Then cut a collar lining like the coat lining, of satin, damask, fabric or crepe and turn in the seams. Slip-stitch this to the tape, again watching out for the hair, both in short as well as long-haired fur.

Fur Trimming Bands: Bands of fur cloth or fur must be taped on the edge as directed above for collars. The interlining is an open soft canvas, and if the band is hemmed to the garment on both edges, no other lining is necessary.

Small Fur Details: When bits of fur are applied to a garment or hat, overcast the joining when necessary. If you are making a band of many little scraps, it is better to take it to a furrier. If you are using tiny tails from a muff, paste a tape to the end before you join it to the garment. Furs cannot be sewed like fabric; the edges are delicate and tear away easily.

Fur Cloth: This can be handled like a heavy pile fabric. Turn the edges back and catch-stitch them down without the taping necessary to reinforce fur.

LINING A COAT

Most coats and jackets are lined throughout, but certain types of classic sport coats are lined only to the waist or have a yoke lining. This usually includes a sleeve lining. The purpose of a lining is to permit the coat to slip on and off easily and to add to its appearance; it should resist soil. Select your lining with these things in mind, and remember that it should be a closely woven, smooth fabric which will wear well.

Cutting a Lining: Use the coat pattern, folding the front edge back so that the finished lining will overlap the facing 1/2 inch. When the coat will receive hard wear, some sewers lay a pleat in the fabric before cutting the back, so that a soft fold or pleat extends the length of the center back. This extra fold is not used in jacket linings.

Making a Lining: The lining is stitched like a dress. Stitch the seams, press them open, and turn in the front edge in a narrow seam. The sleeve lining is inserted later; do not join it at this time. Check your coat for these points: (1) Is the hem turned and finished? (2) Is the facing turned and catch-stitched to the coat? (3)

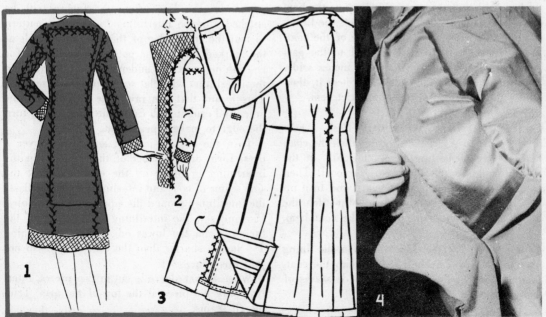

(1) Interlining (without seams) is catch-stitched to the coat. (2) For added warmth place an extra layer. (3) Lining is made separately and added to the coat. (4) Slip-stitch the lining to the coat.

Are the lower edges of the sleeve turned and catch-stitched? (4) Is the coat pressed?

When all these things have been done, turn the coat inside out and have someone else wear it while you insert the lining—or put it inside out on a dress form. Slip the lining over the coat and adjust it so that the shoulder seams of coat and lining match. First pin the neck edges in place. This seam is usually a straight joining. Then catch-stitch the underarm seams of the lining to the seams of the coat with long stitches so the lining will not slip. At the front edge, pin the lining over the edge of the facing, turning the lining edge so this seam can be slip-stitched. The pleat at the back of the lining is catch-stitched for 5 or 6 inches, then the pleat falls loose.

Slip the sleeve linings in place and baste them to the armhole edges, matching the lining to the coat fabric at the top of the sleeves. Turn the top edge of the lining in so it can be slip-stitched into place.

Finishing Hems: The hem of a lined coat can be finished in any of four ways: (1) The lining is hemmed to the garment—this is when the hem is narrow. (2) The lining is hemmed separately and allowed to hang over the hem at the lower edge of the coat—this is when the hem of the coat is wide. (3) In other coats the lining and garment hems meet at the edge of the coat. (4) The coat hem is catch-stitched to the garment. Turn the lining in a hem 2 inches wide. Turn this up in a 1 inch pleat and hem it, then release the pleat, to fall over the skirt hem.

Coat with Narrow Hem: Baste a hem in the lining so it is 1 inch shorter than the coat. Place a row of basting across the coat at the hipline, holding the lining to the coat. Then place the coat on an ironing board and turn up the lining hem so that you can slip-stitch the lining to the coat at the top of the coat hem.

Coat with Wide Hem: Hem the lining separately, 1 or 2 inches shorter than the coat. Join the edge of the lining to the side seams of the coat with a long tack.

Coat Lined with Wool: Extend a lining to the edge of the hem so they can be slip-stitched together at the edge. This is a feature of reversible coats.

Half-Lined and Unlined Coats: In these coats the hems are turned and finished with a seam binding or bias binding of the coat lining. They often feature bound seams to match.

Sleeve Edges: Hem the lining to the top of the hem at the lower edge of the sleeve, covering the catch stitches which hold the sleeve edge in place. Be careful not to pull the sleeve lining down too tight, or it will not wear. Many good sewers turn a deep hem in the lining so it can be let out if they find the lining too tight at any spot.

Neckline: The collar is sometimes hemmed over the lining. In tailored coats the lining is hemmed over the edge of the collar. In other coats the facing of the collar is cut in one with the front facing and the lining slip-stitched over this facing.

INTERLINING A COAT FOR WARMTH

Coat-Style Interlining: Mark your coat pattern at the line where the facing will be stitched. Cut the interlining by the coat pattern so that the front edge of the interlining ends at the marked line on the pattern. Interlinings for warmth never extend under the front facing. Join the interlining with flat seams to minimize bulk. This means that one raw edge is laid over the other and caught with catch stitching. Never turn the edge to make a neat seam.

Turn the coat inside out and slip it over a dress form or a member of the family. Pin the interlining in place on the coat and tack the side seams of coat and interlining together. Baste the interlining around the edges of the armholes. Pin and sew the interlining to the edge of the facing. Trim the lower edge of the interlining 1½ inches shorter than the coat length. Do not join this edge.

When a coat sleeve is cut in two pieces, interline only the piece at the top of the arm. Trim off all seams.

At this point you are ready to line the coat as directed above. At the lower edge, turn the lining hem over the interlining and let them both hang free of the coat. At the top of this double hem, tack the lining and interlining to the coat at each seam with French tacks.

Overlaid Interlining:

In cutting the heavier types of interlining, all seam allowances in the garment pattern are omitted, and the interlining ends at the facing line on the front of the coat. These bulky interlinings are usually ended below the knee; in straight-line coats they can go down to the hem, and this is always true of children's coats.

In joining the seams of the interlining, lay the edges together so they meet, but don't let them overlap. Catch-stitch these edges together. If you have a dressmaker's form, it is easier to adjust these seams after the interlining is pinned to the coat. If you adjust the interlining while someone wears the coat, then join the seams on a flat table.

Turn the coat inside out and place it on the form or figure. Pin the interlining in place, and catch it around the neck and down the front edge. Baste it to the armholes. Put the lining for the sleeve on the garment and catch-stitch it in place. See that it does not extend below the top of the hem at the edge of the sleeve. Catch-stitch it to the top of the sleeves but do not catch it in a seam. These precautions will keep you from adding bulk to your garment.

For Extra Warmth:

An extra layer of the interlining can be placed wherever you want extra warmth. The top of the sleeve and the center back are the usual places. Make them as large as you like, but be sure they are smaller than the first layer of interlining. Only amateurs cut two thicknesses and seam them together.

Children's Coats:

Coats for children are often shortened one year and lengthened the next. Take care when you do this to add as little bulk as possible at the hemline. In this case the rules of good coat-making have to be broken by turning both the facing and the coat, and sometimes even turning up the interlining too. When you do this, catch-stitch the interlining in a hem, then turn the lining of the coat over the interlining and catch-stitch it. Press the lining and join it to the coat with long French tacks placed at the seam.

TAILORING FINISHINGS

Shoulder Padding for Coats:

Cut a piece of lining or unbleached muslin 5 inches wide and 12 inches long. This includes ¼ inch for seam allowance. Fold it in half and cut the ends in a curve; open it out flat and put a piece of cotton batting over one side, extending not quite to the seam allowance at the edge. Turn the seam allowance, fold, and stitch the edges together. If this pad is put in place after the coat is lined, cover it with coat-lining material and tack it in place. If it is placed before the lining is put in, baste it to the shoulder. The padding can be varied as desired—made thicker on the outside edge and thinner on the shoulder; or the padding in one shoulder can be made thicker than in the other if the shoulders are not quite alike.

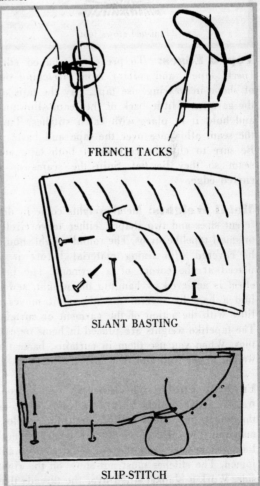

FRENCH TACKS

SLANT BASTING

SLIP-STITCH

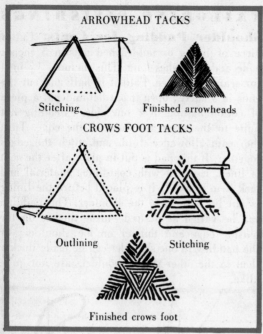

ARROWHEAD TACKS

Stitching · Finished arrowheads

CROWS FOOT TACKS

Outlining · Stitching

Finished crows foot

Taped Edges: To prevent a shaped edge (neck, lapels, and collar) from stretching out of shape in wearing, use tape. Lay the tape on the garment a little back of the seam allowance and hold it in place with catch stitches. Turn the seam allowance over the tape and baste it. Be sure to clip the corners of both tape and seam so they lie flat. Snip the seams on a curved edge.

Metal Weights: Metal weights come in different sizes and two shapes, either large circles or small tapelike strips. The round weight should be covered with lining material before it is placed at the corner of a garment. The best effect is achieved by hanging the weight, sewed into a bag, by several threads, so it moves a little with the action of the garment or curtain. The tapelike weights are placed in hems or casings. When you use them in curtains, baste the weight to the fold and then turn the hem.

French Tack: This stitch is used to control an edge which falls free and looks as though it hung loose. With embroidery floss matching the color of the garment, take several long stitches between the two edges you want joined. The stitches must not show on the right side. Work a blanket stitch over the threads that join the edges, reversing the needle so the eye passes through the stitch first.

Slant Basting: To hold the interlining in a faced lapel or a rolled collar, slant basting is used. On heavy coatings the stitches are wide and open; on worsteds and tweeds used for men's suits they are close and small. Pass the needle through the interlining and let it catch only a few threads on the top of the garment fabric. Leave a space or long thread on the lining and take another small stitch. *These stitches do not show on the right side of the garment.*

Slip Stitch: Slip-stitching is used in many ways: At the hem line of all faced garments where two edges are turned and must be joined; it is used to join the edge of garments that are taped—to do this the facing edge is turned and basted all around, and the edge of the garment is slip-stitched. When a facing is used in a garment which will not be lined, the edge is turned, basted, and slip-stitched when you want no trace of stitching on the outside of the garment. When there is a row of stitching on the outside, this edge is stitched. When a garment is to be lined—with a silk or rayon lining—the edge of the facing and the hem are caught with a catch stitch, and the lining is turned and slip-stitched to cover these edges.

Crow's Foot: At the end of pockets or darts in tailored garments a crow's foot is sometimes used. Mark the shape of the crow's foot with basting, then bring a needle threaded with embroidery twist through the left lower corner up to the top corner taking a small stitch from *right* to *left*. Bring needle down to right lower corner again taking another small stitch (this time from *left* to *right*) and continue on to starting point taking small stitch (*left* to *right*). Continue up to top point again and thus outline the crow's foot with row after row of twist, each row close to the next.

Arrowhead Tacks: Mark the shape of the tack. Use a needle threaded with embroidery twist. Bring the thread through the left lower corner up to the top corner taking a small stitch from *right* to *left*. Pass the needle to the right lower corner and insert it bringing it out close to the starting point. Continue working around so that each thread lies close to the last.

CHAPTER XXVIII

UNDERWEAR FOR ALL THE FAMILY

All underwear and sleeping garments can be made in two types: plain sturdy garments or frail, luxurious ones. The fabrics of both kinds should first of all wear well. The advantage of making underwear at home is that it can be made from the kind of material which gives longer wear than that in garments we buy. Be sure to ask for a textile label on the fabric you buy, because fabrics which look very much alike may have very different wearing qualities. Read what the label says about color fastness, preshrinking, tensil strength, fiber quality, and washing directions. See charts in Chapter XXXI.

In the selection of both fabric and pattern, consider how the garment is to be washed. If you include underwear in the family washing done in your own washing machine or by a laundry, don't select a garment which needs hand care. If you expect to run it through the mangle to save long hours of hand ironing, choose a simple pattern construction. If it is to be ironed by hand, select the kind which irons easily. Making underwear of crinkled crepes, seersucker, canton flannel, and other fabrics which need little or no ironing will save you hours of work.

SLEEPING GARMENTS

Pajamas: Pajamas can be one-piece or two-piece, with full-length trousers or shorter ones. The pattern companies offer a wide assortment of tailored pajamas for every member of the family. Select pattern and fabric to give you a garment which will be comfortable, serviceable, and attractive. Cotton, percale, broadcloth, novelty shirtings, cotton mesh, and seersucker are all used for pajamas. If you choose seersucker, be sure it is fast color and will not shrink. Winter pajamas for cold climates are made of cotton flannel, flannelette, baby flannel, challis, knitted wool or cotton novelties.

Look in the Ready-Reference Guide at the back for exact page numbers of Detailed Instructions

A two-piece garment with a slip-on top will save much work. One-piece pajamas and coat-front pajamas necessitate buttons and button-holes. There are no construction problems in pajamas except those for tots, which must be made with a drop seat.

To save time in making sleeping garments for all the family, adopt the assembly-line technique of the factory. Adjust all the patterns and assemble all the materials. Cut all the garments, pinning each one together as you cut it. As you pin, sort out all the "stitch first" pieces and put them in one pile. In your next sewing period do all this preliminary stitching at once, including front-edge bands and facings, pockets, and cuffs —when they are applied flat. Then prepare for the second stitching. Join the shoulder seams, apply the neck bands, and apply the sleeves to the armhole before you stitch the underarm and sleeve seams. Full-length trousers are easy to do if you pin the seams, stitch them, then turn the hem and stitch it all at one time.

A garment in several pieces is not so easily adapted to the time-saving routine described above. But you can save some time by spreading one fabric over another and cutting two or three garments at once. Work on a very large table or on the floor. Spread each layer of fabric flat and smooth, and use more than the usual number of pins to hold the pattern so the fabric cannot slip as you cut.

Nightgowns: Utility nightgowns made of cotton or cotton flannel are cut from patterns especially designed. These garments are simple, and you should plan to make several at one time and speed the stitching, as described above for pajamas. Speed depends upon planning and assembling the material so that everything is ready to work with. Check your pattern details and decide whether the neck and sleeves will be bound; whether any tape or bias binding is required; whether buttons will be required.

Summer utility night-
gowns and pajamas can
be made from Rayon jer-
sey or cool cotton prints.
For cold winter months,
use flannel or flannelette.

Utility garments need not be drab. Much can be added by selecting a fabric with a tiny dot, stripe, or flower; by using rickrack braid or bias trimming in contrasting colors; by outlining contrasting yokes and hems (stitched bands). The cotton flannel nightgown can be edged with a little ruffle or heavy lace or hand crochet. The buttons can repeat the color of the trimming.

BATHROBES AND LOUNGING ROBES

Every member of the family needs tailored bath-robes, warm ones for winter, and cool, light ones for summer. For all of them, the keynote should be simplicity and usefulness. Choose the patterns with care to give the necessary comfort. In winter a double-breasted bathrobe is an asset; for warmer weather the single-breasted coat type is preferable. Slip-on robes are another possibility, and easier to make.

In winter, flannel or a blanket material assures warmth. Remember that a napped fabric gives warmth. Costly bathrobes made out of wool blankets are lifetime treasures. Warm robes made from cotton blankets with a thick napped pile will wear through continual washings for four or five years. Upholsterers' plush, which is a heavy napped cotton, is used for bathrobes, and so are some of the soft woolen coatings designed for summer coats. When warmth is not the prime consideration, tailored bathrobes can be made from corduroy, velveteen, the heavier rayon novelty ribbed fabrics, and the heavier cottons. Mixtures of cotton and rayon are developed in lovely fabrics especially for bathrobes.

Fabrics which will keep you cool in hot weather are found among the cool cottons—light-weight toweling; cotton crepes, printed or plain; seersuckers; and any opaque dress fabric. Cotton meshes which permit quick evaporation are very cool, and residents of the tropics report that fine linen is cool and does not stick.

Men's and Boys' Bathrobes: First adjust your pattern, shortening or lengthening the sleeve, testing the length and width across the back. The robe should fit loosely. Be sure that the robe is ample through the hips and crosses over to give just the protection the wearer likes. Some people like a large overlap, others a small one. Find out whether your menfolk like a notched collar or a rolled collar in contrasting satin. Men have distinct preferences in sleeves—some like a set-in sleeve and others a raglan. Your pattern will give you a choice of sleeve, and adjusting it for the one which will give the greatest pleasure will save hours of work and fussing.

Baste the seams and insert the interfacing, except in cotton fabrics. In blankets or heavier woolens, this interfacing must be cut from French canvas; in lightweight woolens, it is cut from unbleached muslin. Pin on the pockets and finish and join the collar. When a tailored revere is used, the collar must be carefully interfaced to hold its shape. A rolled collar requires less tailoring, but it must be interlined with unbleached muslin. Join the sleeves to the armhole. Before stitching, fit the robe for proportions, and at this time turn the lower edge and mark the buttons and buttonholes.

If you are experienced in working with heavy fabrics, make the buttonholes yourself. Otherwise, take them to a tailor. Select the buttons and belt with care. The belt can be self-colored or contrasting, fabric or cord. Many men like a plain bone button in a harmonizing color. Be sure to include slides to hold the belt and a hanger at the back of the neck. These finishing touches should be carefully made and sewed on with strong stitches which will hold through hard wear. If your men belong to some organization, it is often possible to buy a shield with its insignia on it. Apply it to the pocket or sleeve of the bathrobe.

Women's and Girls' Bathrobes: Use a pattern designed for women and make the bathrobes as described above for men's robes. Women often prefer utility colors, but it is possible to use pastels and gay designs in the novelty fabrics to make the bathrobe decorative as well as useful. Many are bound with the blanket binding sold in stores. If you prefer, you can cut a bias binding of any trimming fabric and apply it.

Lined Bathrobes: Bathrobes are sometimes lined, but this is not usual. If a lining is used, cut it from the bathrobe pattern and put it in like a coat lining (see page 179).

Cotton Bathrobes: These are quickly and easily made. Finish them wth flat welt seams or

Tailored bathrobes must cross full in front. Use washable flannelette or a warmer fabric.

upholstery seams. All trimmings—buttons, binding, and stitching—must be washable and colorfast.

Housecoats: Select a pattern with becoming fullness. One that slips on over the head is easier to make than one buttoned from neck to hem. Most housecoats have short sleeves, but a dressier effect can be achieved by long sleeves, fitted or full. The design of the fabric and the simplicity of line of the pattern are the secrets of a good-looking housecoat. Use any opaque cotton dress fabric.

Some older women prefer a fuller, more comfortable housecoat, which can be made with a surplice closing and includes a little fullness at the shoulder. Use a short self-fabric belt that buttons or a beltless closing. A flattering finish is a ruffle around the skirt, up the front edge, and around the neck. It is sometimes made of self-fabric and sometimes of contrasting color of net or organdy. Other people trim a simple, plain-colored housecoat with cord or braid.

Blanket Bathrobes: In cutting a bathrobe from a bed blanket, lay the pattern so that all

Luxury Underwear

Hostess gowns can be made from sheer cotton or chiffon.

The costume slip should be carefully fitted and finished with hand details.

Insert lace banding in seams of luxury nightgowns.

the edges touch the binding. When the bottom edge, the sleeves, and the collar are cut this way, the robe is partly finished before you join the seams. These robes are not faced; the front edge can be turned in a hem or bound to match the bottom edge, or you can simply use the blanket selvage for the front edge. The seams in these heavy fabrics are overlaid—one edge laid over the other and basted flat without turning. When you stitch both edges, you have a flat seam; it should overlap at least ½ inch. The armholes should be bound.

LUXURY UNDERWEAR

Fine needlework is the hallmark of luxury underwear. Tailored underwear depends for its beauty upon fine hand finishing, and the most popular types feature edges bound with self-fabric or ribbon. All ruffles should be finished with hand-rolled hems, and lace should be applied with the same kind of hems.

Lace trimmings are important features of luxurious nightgowns, slips, and panties. Women who enjoy handwork can make really beautiful underwear, and it's not hard to apply lace motifs or sections of lace cut from allover patterns. The better quality of machine embroidery is often used in combination with tucks and lace. For directions for applying these finishes, consult the index.

Costume Slips: A slip improves the appearance of the dress worn over it and protects it from soil. Slips should be carefully fitted through the hips and waist. The fabric must be smooth and lovely to look at, and in addition must wear well. National tests of the wearing qualities of slips can give us information on the better-wearing fabrics and points in cutting and construction which add to wearability.

Seam Slippage: The commonest cause for discarding slips is "seam slippage," which must not be confused with a ripped seam. "Seam slippage" means that the fabric tears and frays at the seam. Tests prove that to avoid it you should: (1) buy textiles which have been tested for extra strength and are so labeled, and (2) cover all seams to prevent raveling. Use a flat fell or a French seam; overcast seams do not show good results in these tests.

Holes and Fuzz: If the fabric roughs up in fuzz or wears through in holes, it was unwisely chosen. French crepes tested for wear give twice the value of taffeta or satin in the long run. Viscose rayon and viscose acetate blending are recommended for good wear. Novelty fabrics rough up more quickly.

Twisting: If a bias slip twists, the reason is either scanty cutting, or that the seam does not lie on the *true bias* of the fabric. Even if it entails cutting the slip a little wider, make sure that the seam lies on the true bias. A slip cut with straight-panel front and back does not ride up. This popular four-gore construction has bias sides which ensure a fitted line.

Shoulder Straps: Shoulder straps must be double-stitched. When the strap is turned, both edges must be stitched; when it is joined to the garment, it should extend 3 inches below the top of the garment. This joining is double and triple stitched through all the thicknesses of the fabric. If the top of the slip is lace or a single thickness of fabric, it is often reinforced at the joining with a small patch of fabric or net.

Making a Slip: Whether the fabric is rayon crepe, broadcloth, chambray, sateen, or silk crepe, fine needlework should be employed. Before cutting decide whether the top is to be single or double. Decide upon the length and allow a generous hem. Fit the pattern carefully before you cut, and save a fitted pattern for use again and again.

First join and finish the brassière top. The edge can be bound or finished with a narrow lace edge. When the edge is single, the lace can be applied in a hand-rolled hem. When it is double, the lace is basted on the right side of one section and held in place by hand running stitches, the work is turned to the wrong side and the second section applied so that the seam under the lace is turned down and the edge of the second section is turned in; the turned edges are matched and basted, then stitched on the right side as close as possible to the edge of the lace.

Seam the slip and apply the top. The seam which joins the top to the slip does not receive as much strain as the long seams of the slip; it is pressed down and overstitched close to the

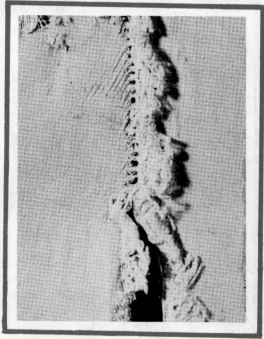

Because the fabric ravels, seam slippage is responsible for most discarded slips. Tests show covered seams prevent this loss.

edge and the edge is then overcast to prevent raveling. The long seams, however, must be covered, by either a French seam or a flat felled seam. Make shoulder straps of ribbon or fabric. Fit them carefully so they will not slip off your shoulder, then fasten them securely.

Nightgowns: Recently nightgowns cut on the bias like some evening dresses have become very popular. There is no reason why the home sewer should not make them herself. Buy an evening dress pattern which has the following characteristics: (1) is sleeveless; (2) has fullness in the shoulder; and (3) is cut in a point which shapes the waist below the bustline— either a belt, or the lower part of the garment extended into a high fitted line. Commercial patterns for nightgowns in this style are also offered. Between the two, there is a wide choice for your nightgown pattern.

The fabrics can be decorative or plain, or encrusted with lace and fine needlework. Cottons in dainty prints and colorful challis in quaint designs lend themselves to the more decorative nightgown. It is not difficult to make these garments, but contrasting bindings should be hand-

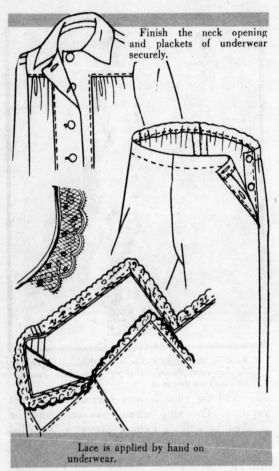

Finish the neck opening and plackets of underwear securely.

Lace is applied by hand on underwear.

finished and ruffled edges finished in hand-rolled hems.

Panties and Brassieres: Choose a pattern which fits smoothly through the hips and at the waist. Bra and panty sets are easy to make and are welcome gifts. Use any cotton—dimity, batiste, cotton shirtlings, et cetera; or use rayon crepes, the plain French crepe, or printed crepes. The edges of the garments are bound with self-fabric or a contrasting color. The button fastening must be very secure.

Negligees and Hostess Dresses: They can be simple and feminine or very glamorous. Especially in sheer fabrics, wide, sweeping gowns are more becoming and luxurious than more scantily cut ones. Washable gowns of dotted Swiss, organdy, or lawn have the advantage of a permanent finish, a feature which keeps the garment lovely through countless

washings—and all too often not to be found in a ready-made one.

Women who wear luxurious negligees of chiffon, velvet, moiré, and taffeta are careful to plan two different kinds of garments for summer and winter wear. There is a great distinction between bedroom negligees and hostess dresses. Both are made of beautiful fabrics, and they may be equally becoming; but the negligee is not worn out of the bedroom. Hostess gowns are really dinner dresses, with long skirts fitted so loosely that a girdle need not be worn. They can be made from evening dress patterns if the pattern is fitted to the figure without a girdle and the necessary alterations are made.

Negligees and hostess gowns need not be costly. They can be made from a washable printed cotton or rayon and worn in the kitchen. They should be made in a becoming color to last for several years. They flatter a woman and permit her to relax in her own home and still be attractively dressed to receive guests. Several wealthy women have told me that they alter their old evening dresses to make hostess gowns.

Men's Lounging Robes: Beautifully lined moiré and faille silk lounging robes make excellent gifts for men. Any woman who can make a simple coat can make a lounging robe. Choose a pattern and follow its directions. Choose a luxury fabric which will not show spots.

Men's Lounging Pajamas: Many men like a lounging suit cut on more fitted lines than ordinary pajamas. Select an opaque fabric which will not muss—a rayon faille or a novelty stripe, a decorative cotton or a moiré. This garment when successful is a comfortable suit for wear in the living room, so take care to select a fabric which will not suggest either beach or bedroom clothes. The coat is unlined, and a slack pattern can be used for the trousers. Many have slip-on tops or smock tops.

Quilted Robes: Quilted robes are usually cut by patterns designed for tailored garments. You can buy a quilted material or do your own quilting before you cut the garment. To do this, stretch three layers of fabric in a curtain stretcher or a quilting frame. See directions on Chapter XLV.

CHAPTER XXIX

TEACHING YOUR DAUGHTER TO SEW

This chapter is dedicated to all girls—those who love to make things, those who have talent and creative ideas, those who want fashion careers, and those who can't afford frills on their budgets.

Sewing should be thought of as an art expression and you should learn to develop beauty and line in textiles. Rid yourself of the fear of drudgery. Have fun as you sew. Learn about careers that are open to girls who know how to sew. Many of the creative workers of America's great fashion industry—designers of dresses and accessories—writers who describe garments for magazines and newspapers—artists who illustrate for the fashion industry—the highly-paid sales-promotion women and editors of magazines—have told me that as girls they sewed with their mothers.

The editor of one of the leading fashion magazines is the daughter of a dressmaker. When she graduated from college, she received a small salary on a newspaper. Advancement to a magazine was open "to a girl who knew how to sew." Her salary at the present time is more than $25,000 a year, and she tells me that no one can properly describe a garment who does not understand how it is made.

The editor of another famous woman's magazine, left a widow with a child, worked first for a pattern company. Her great opportunity arrived when the pattern company was bought by the publisher of a magazine.

A sales promotion job that paid a very high salary was once offered me, and I was chosen from among many applicants because one of the men felt that I could help garment manufacturers understand his product because I knew how to sew.

One of our best-known American designers tells me that as a girl she and her mother sewed together. During a college holiday she decided she must learn professional sewing methods and, because she was interesed only in costly clothes, she went as a finisher into a great dressmaking house. Had this girl not known how to sew, the door to opportunity would not have opened. Later she went to Paris and progressed still further.

Many established designers say the girl who wants to design clothes or develop ideas should *first seek out her talent* before she chooses her schooling. Many vocational directors advise girls to finish their schooling and then choose a specialty course of some kind that will lead them into the fashion world. The girls who learn how to sew at home and really practice fashion co-ordinating and the solving of home problems will be best qualified to advance into the splendid positions offered by industry for this talent.

DEVELOPING TALENTS

Youthful talent is sometimes clearly marked, but often it is deeply hidden; and unless it is given free and natural expression, it cannot develop. Home sewing that is fun, based on a streamlined routine, permits girls of any age to make what

Look in the Ready-Reference Guide at the back for exact page numbers of Detailed Instructions

they like without restraint or tradition and helps bring forth talent. In developing a talent, a girl must not think of sewing. She must think of expressing her ideas. Beginners should not be asked to learn more than to work neatly.

A beginner's first problem is to overcome the false fear that sewing is difficult and to banish the feeling that one cannot sew without learning a long and complex science. The best way to prove that this is wrong is for the girl to make something all alone. It should be a garment she really wants, it should be made in a hurry; and when it is finished, good or bad, she will be proud to wear it.

Girls who make themselves a basic dress, and continually change it with accessories and trimming so that their wardrobe looks five times larger than it really is, are preparing for jobs as fashion co-ordinators — equipping themselves with experience that is needed in all stores in every city—to assist the window trimmers, to arrange interior displays, to develop advertising approaches.

Too many beginners with artistic talent who set out to take courses tend to believe in nothing but art for art's sake, and make their designs around fairytale dresses. They are so seldom needed that it is pitiful to spend time this way. Instead, they should set out to solve actual problems in the home—take their eyes off fanciful dreams and help dress the problem figure. Industry needs women who can do this.

In several states, sewing is a required study for school children. The enrollment in Home Economics classes and trade schools is increasing. In facing your child's future, consult with the teachers. They may advise that home sewing be used as I recommended—to develop a talent followed by special courses; and they may already have recognized your daughter's talent.

HELPING YOUR DAUGHTER TO SEW

I have taught many girls to sew, and I find that too often youth is discouraged by Victorian methods. Our daughters live in a machine age and want streamlined speed. To them, samplers and long-drawn-out routines vanished with the horse and buggy.

Therefore, sewing, like all other sciences, should be presented in modern dress. When a girl between the ages of eight and fourteen wants to sew, expressing the natural urge to make things, meet this wish with an invitation to have "lots of fun." Lay aside pet traditons and let the girl prove *to herself* that she can sew. Let her make something she will be proud to wear. She will surely make mistakes, but you and she can laugh them off together and learn as she goes. Once the fear of "spoiling something" is proved false, both mother and daughter can progress in one of the happiest bonds — making pretty clothes. When a little girl says, "I would like to make a dress," I have but one answer: "By all means; you can make a lovely dress. What kind would you like?" Youthful taste is simple, and if the choice is not wise, can be easily guided to something "prettier" that an adult head knows is easier and youth describes as quicker. If, however, a young sewer's heart is set, whatever her choice, let her make it, explaining only that it will take longer—and so prepare her for unusual patience.

The secret of helping a girl to love sewing, or developing a talent, is to concentrate on speed in making the first garment. It must be finished so quickly that she, you, and all are amazed. It must be cute, so that she is proud of her work. She must do it all by herself.

If you do not sew, join your daughter and make your first dress with her in a merry class for two. Why not make "mother and daughter" dresses and conduct a family contest that the men of the family can cheer? Beginners should choose their own patterns and fabrics. Without any help, they should assemble the trimming and anything else they may need. For success this program must be filled with gaiety. Make no suggestions that she must learn to hem before she makes a dress.

It should be made by hand with no preliminaries and no outside help or assistance. It will be fun for any mother to watch the capable efficiency of her daughter when she examines her first pattern—especially if she has gone to the store alone and bought this pattern. Our commercial patterns do not need to be explained to modern girls. Just say to your daughter that all the directions are there, and she need only open the package and read the directions. She must circle with a pencil the cutting guide for her size and width of material. It is a good idea to check

The pattern should all be laid out before cutting.
Perforations and notches are abbreviations which
show what pieces are joined and where.

the pattern before cutting, as sizes differ from those in dresses we buy in the stores. A suitable time should be set for cutting the garment so that you and your daughter can be quiet. Either cut your own dress on another side of the room or sit quietly and do some mending. Your daughter will pin her fabric to the pattern and cut it with quiet determination. When girls have sewed with me, I always ask that they let me see the pattern when it is all pinned before the actual cutting. In looking back over this long list of earnest young faces, I have no memory of one who did not capably lay her pattern exactly like the diagram.

Immediately the dress is cut, it should be pinned together with speed. Here again the girl must be on her own. The picture diagram in the pattern will help her speed things up. Watch her joy as she tries it on.

The seams are run and backstitched; the hem is turned. Even if this is her first hem, no matter; she can do it. Girls are deeply interested in the

trimming touches and can make facings, casings that hold ribbon, or wool pompoms, or tiny bows to decorate a dress. They usually have good style-right ideas about trimmings and should be encouraged to develop any idea that is not time-consuming or difficult. Your daughter will appreciate your help in hanging the skirt and in fitting, otherwise let her be an independent artist.

I place great emphasis on the fact that the mother is not to help. This is most important in developing confidence and establishing a desire to learn more about sewing.

The secret of success in teaching girls to sew is the simplicity of the first pattern. The making of your daughter's first dress should not require more than a few hours. When a bright-eyed youngster goes to a store and tells the sales-girl she would like to be measured—she came to buy a pattern for her first dress—rest assured she is in the hands of an expert; for the pattern sales-woman knows what is simple and easy. The sales person will gladly show her where to look

Follow the picture instructions in the pattern for step by step directions. Press cotton and rayon on the wrong side. Wool or wool blends need a press cloth.

for the correct yardage if she is buying her fabric in the same store. A printed cotton that is not too thin, chambray, percale, broadcloth, and shantung are the easiest fabrics to work on; but I have seen girls cut wool jersey and trim it with wool pompoms. In a large club of beginners, smocked shirtwaists of white voile were a great success.

Remember the pattern should have as few pieces as possible. This insures speed. It is also wise that the fabric be printed so that unskilled stitches are not emphasized. It is important also that the trimming touch be style-right.

Once a beginner has made her first dress, she should be encouraged to progress only when she wants to. When the first experience has been quick and a lot of fun, she will want to sew again; but her own timing is the best guide to a happy mother-and-daughter sewing relationship.

WHAT IS EASY TO MAKE?

The first garment should be a one-piece dress cut in 2 or 3 pieces (sleeves cut in one or set in). This slip-on type of dress, made of a printed cotton, a rayon crepe, a wool jersey, or a spun rayon that looks like wool, will be easy and quick to make. These fabrics absorb amateur stitches.

The second garment should have a set-in sleeve and a joining at the waistline. It should be made in a textile with a surface interest, such as a novelty rayon crepe, a print, a wool jersey, or a spun rayon fabric that looks like wool. Avoid plain-surface crepes or transparent fabrics, satin, and fabrics that are not firm.

The third garment should be a one-piece dress with a jacket—one with the fewest number of pieces, with the pattern marked "Easy to Make." It can be a simple dress with a jacket, a bolero, or a waistcoat. It can be made from printed crepe rayon, spun rayon, lightweight wool, or the firmer types of cotton.

The fourth garment should be a coat or a coat-style dress or a smock.

When these four types have been made successfully, the sewer is no longer a beginner and she can choose any garment in the pattern books. Beginners often prefer to make a curtain or couch cover for the home. Because this work is straight, it is an easy approach to sewing. Many beginners approach sewing by altering or remodeling garments, which quickly encourages them to venture into the making of a new garment of the simpler kind.

Look in the Ready-Reference Guide at the back for exact page numbers of Detailed Instructions

BEGINNER'S LUCK

The pattern of this soft dress in floral, color-fast cotton was designed for this book so that Mother and Daughter can make their first dress in streamlined speed. An experienced sewer can make the dress in two hours. The speed is possible because there are only three pieces in the pattern. You seam the front and back, make the hem, set in the sleeves, make 5 casings, run in ribbon, tie the bows and step out in a dress you are proud to wear.

Remember to lengthen or shorten the pattern before cutting. How to do this is explained on Page 81. Use combination stitch for the seams and hemming stitch for the hem and the casing edges. Use the Ready Reference Guide for the page numbers of exact instructions on these stitches.

CHAPTER XXX

ACCESSORIES AND GIFTS

Accessories make one dress do the work of three, bring last year's dress up to date, turn a simple dress into an elaborate one, and impart an air of luxury to an expensive dress. They are easy to make and cost practically nothing if you use scraps of material left over from suits and dresses, or keep your eyes open for remnants. They can be quickly added when you dress, and they make an incalculable difference in the smartness of your appearance.

Everything from shoes and hats to collars, belts, and jewelry is included in accessories. Directions for making dickies, gilets, collars, and cuffs are given elsewhere, and in this chapter you will find directions for many others you can make yourself.

THE RIGHT ACCESSORIES FOR THE OCCASION

To test your accessories for any costume, stand in front of a long mirror to finish your dressing. Make sure your shoes and hosiery, your handbag, neckwear, and jewelry are all co-ordinated. Too much jewelry makes you look overdressed, so after you are dressed look at the effect with a critical eye and remove or change your jewelry or flowers to give the most flattering appearance. Hats are always important. With the help of flowers, bows, and veiling, they can completely change the appearance of a costume.

Use what you have in the way of accessories, but use it so that you look fresh, up-to-the-minute, perhaps even ahead of the season. Remember to change accessories from one costume to another, or to change them with the season on the same simple dress. A basic dress is the perfect background for a continual change of accessories.

SEASONAL CHANGES IN ACCESSORIES

The dates for seasonal changes differ in different climates and localities; but the check list which follows is general and can be adapted to your wardrobe and the climate in which you live. The recommendations in the list are by no means definite rulings; they are simply suggestions designed to stimulate thought so that you can make your own plan according to your particular needs.

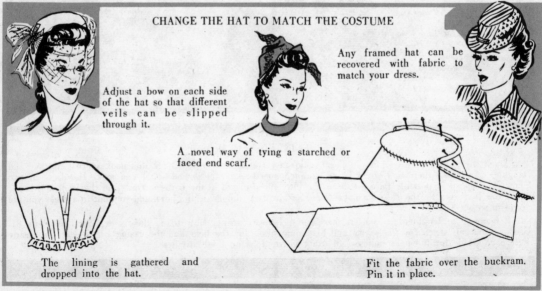

CHANGE THE HAT TO MATCH THE COSTUME

Adjust a bow on each side of the hat so that different veils can be slipped through it.

A novel way of tying a starched or faced end scarf.

Any framed hat can be recovered with fabric to match your dress.

The lining is gathered and dropped into the hat.

Fit the fabric over the buckram. Pin it in place.

JANUARY: To brighten your winter coat, wear a huge flower boutonniere of violets or gay vari-colored felt flowers. Carry a muff-bag and repeat the flowers on the bag. Match your gloves to the flowers.

FEBRUARY: Remove flowers and make a new print turban and dress or blouse with scarf ends. Pull the ends through to show at the opening of your coat. Wear gloves in the predominating color of the print.

MARCH: Begin to look springlike. Add a starched white piqué or linen collar to your coat. Make a pert bow for your hat and sew matching cuffs onto your gloves.

MAY: Bring back your February print blouse and turban to wear with suits. Alternate the blouse with frilly ruffles and jabots worn on the outside of your suit. Wear snow-white gloves and add crisp new veiling to your hat.

APRIL: Bring back your January boutonniere, or make a new smaller one in daisies. Sew matching flowers around the brim of your hat. Repeat the color of the flowers in linen touches on your dress or suit.

JUNE: Wear printed redingotes or suits to introduce a cool look into all your clothes. Face a dark bolero with a bright print and wear a matching print hat, or put new veil in matching color on your old one.

JULY: Wear sheer voile, nets and crepes, tailored or dressy. For special dress-up occasions sew flowers around the neckline of a dress, and for extra flattery repeat the flowers around the crown of your hat.

SEPTEMBER: Wear a suit dress, one that can be worn under a winter coat. Plan your new suits and dresses with an eye to the color of your winter coat. Add a braid or wool loop fringe to a plain jacket and repeat it in the trimming of your hat.

NOVEMBER: Plan a basic dress. Add a detachable collar of black sequins; carry long net sequin-sprinkled gloves. These and a sequin belt can be folded in your purse. At the end of the day, with these additions you are ready for dining and dancing.

AUGUST: For advance style, rip off the white collars and flowers from your dresses and suits. Wear a brilliant, jewel-colored velveteen hat with bag and gloves to match, and a dark sheer crepe or wool crepe dress.

OCTOBER: With a warm suit, carry a tweed bag and line one side of your hat with the matching tweed. Face your boleros in velvet; make velvet collars and cuffs, dickies and belts for your dresses.

DECEMBER: Add a tie-on peplum of rich lamé, or lustrous satin to your basic dress. Make gloves to match and wear them alternately with your net gloves. With such interchangeable accessories, you can always be well dressed with a minimum of expense and time.

Diagram for turban.

A wrap-around turban you make yourself assures you of a becoming line.

Pill-box cut of buckram and covered, is quickly and easily made.

Diagram for pill-box.

HATS

The woman who knows how to change the trimming on a hat or make a new one can always have smart millinery to go with her newest costumes or accessories. From fabric left from a garment she can re-cover an old hat or cover a new shape to make a hat to match.

Covered Fabric Hat: Use a new buckram frame or an old one from which the fabric has been removed. (*See diagram on page* 194.)

1. Cut a circle of new fabric to fit the top of the crown, allowing about ¼ inch for seam or hem. Baste it to the crown with catch stitches.

2. Cut a strip of fabric on the bias, 1 inch wider than the height of the crown and long enough to go around the crown with ¼-inch seam allowance at each end. Turn one edge of this strip over a narrow cord and baste it. Place this edge over the edge of the circle on the crown; fit it smoothly all around and pin it in

place. Then sew it with matching thread just under the cording, using a fine running stitch. Be sure to catch the material on top of the crown with each stitch. Join the ends with a fine slip stitch. If the hat is brimless, turn the remaining cut edge of the fabric in a hem inside the hat edge.

3. To cover a brim, cut a piece of material on the bias long enough to go around the brim and twice as wide as the brim plus 1 inch on each side for the hem. Stretch this bias fabric around the brim so that it lies as smoothly as possible above and below. Pin it firmly. A few tiny gathers will probably be unavoidable when the fabric is joined to the frame. Sew it in place with large strong stitches through the crown, catching both ends of the brim fabric. Then sew the loose end of the crown covering in place with a hemming stitch at the joining of crown and brim.

4. Finish the inside of the hat with a lining. First cut a circle of thin lining fabric about 4 inches in diameter. Put this inside the hat against the top of the crown. Cut a piece of bias fabric wide enough to reach from this circle to the brim edge of the crown, and long enough to fit smoothly around the head size. Allow ¼ inch seam allowance on all sides. Sew the ends of the band together. Then gather one side and sew it to the circle of fabric, distributing the gathers evenly. Drop this lining into the hat, pin it around the brim edge of the crown, and hem it in place about ¼ inch from the edge of the crown.

The hat body is then complete and can be trimmed.

Pillbox: Cut a band and a circle of buckram as shown in the diagram. To get the size, measure the head with a tape measure. Use this measure on line A of the diagram, and cut a strip of paper, shaping it as shown in the diagram. Join the ends of the band and place it over a piece of paper so you can outline on that paper the circle formed by the band. This circle is the top of the crown. When you have fitted the paper band to the head in the effect you like, cut a band and a circle from the buckram with these patterns. Cover them with fabric and join the two pieces with small stitches which do not show. Line the hat with pieces cut by the same patterns and seamed together.

Diagram for Hood Capelin

Diagram for Babushka

Use felt or heavy fabric
with wool embroidery
for this matching set

Diagram
for Beanie

To embroider
this design,
trace it on to tissue paper
and pin it to your fabric.

Wrap-around Turban: Use soft woolen, a wool jersey, or a very firmly woven rayon crepe. A yard of 40-inch material will make two turbans. Cut the turban 36-inches long and half the width of the material. Fold at A and seam the folded end. With a series of gathers, gather this seam into a 2½-inch measure. Place the gathered material at the beginning of your hairline in the center front, mark the turban, as shown at B. Split the unfinished end through the center of the fabric up to the mark on the material, so that the ends can cross and wrap around the head. Tie the turban and make sure you have split it so it ties at the most becoming angle. When the effect is just what you want, hem the unfinished edges. *See diagram page* 196.

CHILDREN'S HOODS

Hood Capeline: This protecting hood, made from a triangle of fabric, is popular with children and easy to make. Measure the child's head from forehead to back of neck. Add the amount you want for the cape effect—for a child it would be from 4 to 2 inches. On the center of your triangle of cloth measure up this distance from the base (A to B on the diagram). Fold along this center line and cut straight across the fabric at B. These cut edges are then seamed together and form the front of the hood. From this point measure down the number of inches in the head measurement (B to C) and run a basting at this neckline. It is easier to fit the hood if the neck is finished first. Use a self-fabric casing, or run a twisted cord of contrasting wool in and out through the fabric with a large needle to make a drawstring. When the hood is drawn in to the neck, turn it on the wrong side and fit it across the top of the head. Make a seam and cut away the excess fabric. Finish the edge around the face with a narrow hem. If you want to draw the hood close around the child's face, use this hem as a casing for a drawstring. Hem the edge of the cape or finish it with knotted fringe.

Babushka Hood and Mittens: To shape the hood, follow the diagram. Measure the child's head and place this measure in the center line of the diagram between the arrows. Measure around the child's face and put this measure at the edge of the diagram marked "center front." Measure

Sun-bonnet Diagram

Sun-bonnets cut from stiffened fabric need no interlining.

Trace this kitten's face to embroider children's mittens, pockets and slippers.

Cut mitten in any size.

Make a muff to match your coat.

Diagram for Peplum

around the neck and divide the result by three. Put one third of the measure at each end of the front, and the third at the center back. Cut a piece of paper the shape of the diagram, following the measurements you have inserted. Pin the dotted edges at the sides together for side seams and fit the paper to the child's head. When it is snugly fitted, you are ready to cut your material.

Seam the sides and hem the front edge. Cut a self-fabric tie long enough to go around the neck and make any size of bow you want. It should be 1½ inches wide. Seam this strip at each end, leaving the center open far enough to bind the lower edge of the hood. When this binding is complete, make embroidery in gay colored yarn by tracing the flowers in the diagram on to tissue paper. Pin the tissue paper flowers to both hood and mittens and embroider through the paper with a loose running stitch. Tear away the paper when the embroidery is finished.

Make the mittens as directed for Kitten Mittens on opposite page.

Beanie and Bag: To shape the beanie, take a tape measure and pin it into a band which fits the child's head closely. This band must be placed so that it is as small as possible and still stay on the head. Measure across the head from front to back and from side to side. Adjust the tape-measure band until the cross measure is the same on front and back. When the measure is set, divide it in half. Place this measure on the dotted line in the diagram. Divide the measure around the head into six equal parts and place the measure of each sixth on the wide edge of the diagram. Then cut a piece of fabric like the diagram, using your measure to enlarge it to actual size. Allow ¼-inch seam allowance on all sides.

Cut six sections like this and seam them into a little round cap. Face the front edge with a bias strip folded back. Stitch the front edge by machine, on the outside as close to the edge as possible. Make two rows of outline stitch in gay colored wool around the outside of the beanie. Place flowers from the diagram on page 197 on the beanie. Make the bag to match.

Look in the Ready-Reference Guide at the back for exact page numbers of Detailed Instructions

Sunbonnet: A sunbonnet can be made from any firm cotton fabric in a gay print. Shape it as in the diagram; and to adjust it to the head size, cut a piece of paper in a rough outline of the hood so you will know how much shade you want beyond the face. It may be 3 or 4 inches. Set this measure at line A on the diagram. Measure the head from the center of the forehead where the hood ends, across the head to the end of the hairline at the back of the neck. Set this measure on line B of the diagram. Then measure line C, which is from chin bone to chin bone, across the top of the head. When this figure has been set in the diagram, you will have the size for cutting a pattern. Cut the pattern first in paper, and when it is shaped as desired, use it for cutting the fabric.

Cut a piece of lightweight buckram the size of the pattern, then two pieces of fabric the same size plus seam allowance. Cover the buckram with one piece of fabric so that it is smoothly fitted. Turn in the seams of the second piece of fabric and baste them. Put this piece over the covered buckram with all edges meeting. Stitch the edges all around. *Diagram on page* 198.

KITTEN MITTENS

Make mittens to match the children's coats, or buy remnants of fuzzy fabrics and make a scarf with mittens to match. Mittens of any size can be made easily by shaping them as shown in the diagram. Have the child lay his hand flat on a piece of paper and draw the outline of the hand, with the thumb sticking out and the four fingers together. Measure the length of the hand in the tracing and place this measure on the diagram at A. Measure the width of the hand and put this on the diagram at B. Cut a piece of fabric by these measurements and round the front edge in the shape of the fingers. The thumb must be outlined from your tracing of the hand. Allow ½-inch seams all the way around. Unless it is made of very heavy fabric, the mitten should be double. *Diagram on page* 198.

Seam the edges of the outside mitten and turn it right side out. Seam the lining and slip it over the hand. Pull the outside over the lining so that the tips of the fingers meet. Join the seams of the two with slip-stitching and slip-stitch the wrist edges together. If you like, finish the wrist edge with a casing and gather it on a cord.

Trace the kitten's face on tissue paper and baste it over your mitten. Outline it with embroidery stitches and tear the paper away.

FABRIC MUFF

You can buy a muff foundation with a purse pocket, or make one of unbleached muslin filled with feathers, down, or cotton batting. First cut a paper, shaping it to the exact size you want for a muff. Join the ends of this paper and dart the edges. Cut another paper the length of the muff and half as wide. Join it—it must make a circle large enough to join to the edge shaped with darts. This is the center of the muff, through which your hands pass.

Cut both pieces of paper in muslin and seam the small piece to the darted edges. Fill this muff bed with stuffing and overcast the seam.

To cover the muff, use coat fabric or a contrasting material. Cover the muff foundation smoothly with the fabric. The edges can be corded, or you can seam them and cover them with bands of fur or fur trimming.

PEPLUM

To cut a peplum without a pattern, use the diagram on page 198. Measure your waistline. Set this measurement on line A of the diagram. Then estimate the depth of the peplum in the back, setting a figure which you consider becoming. Try 6 inches. Then cut a paper pattern shaped like the diagram and made to these measurements. Try on the pattern and shape it to the effect you prefer. You can make it longer, wider, shorter, or deeper. You can change the curve of the line as you please. When your pattern gives the desired effect, cut the fabric, allowing for seams.

Cut a self-fabric waistband 4 inches wide and long enough to tie around your waist and make whatever bow you want. The bow can have long or short ends. Seam the fabric together in a long strip, then fold it lengthwise and seam it on the wrong side, working from both ends toward the center. Leave an opening in the center long enough to bind the waistline of the peplum.

Finish the edges of the peplum with a narrow hem. Insert the peplum into the waistband and seam it in place.

BELTS

Belts can tie, buckle, or button. They are all made with a stiff interlining, which can be a

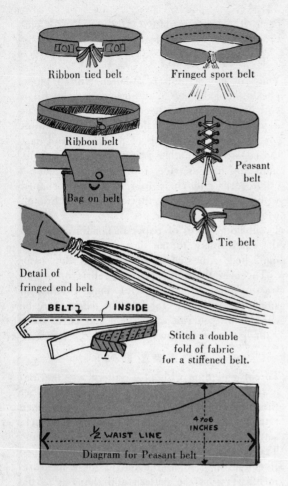

Ribbon tied belt

Fringed sport belt

Ribbon belt

Peasant belt

Bag on belt

Tie belt

Detail of fringed end belt

BELT   INSIDE

Stitch a double fold of fabric for a stiffened belt.

½ WAIST LINE   4 to 6 INCHES

Diagram for Peasant belt

stiff belting bought by the yard, a piece of buckram cut in the correct size, or an old belt you can cover. Old leather belts can be covered to make decorative fabric belts.

Tied Belt: The stiff interlining can be any width desired. Cover it with fabric, cutting the material twice as wide as the interlining, plus ¼ inch on each side for seam allowance, and 3 inches shorter than your waist measure. Fold the fabric on the wrong side and seam the length and one end. Turn it right side out, slip in the interlining, and overcast the other end together. As illustrated, use old bracelets or rings through which to tie the ends; or you can make a fancy end from an old felt hat or leather handbag.

If you have one ring, sew it securely to end of the belt, and to the other end sew a self-fabric

tie made from straight fabric stitched and turned. It should be 10 inches or more long, and any width desired. Slip the tie through the loop and tie it.

If you have two rings, sew one to each end of the belt, and to only one ring sew a double casing of self-fabric.

When you finish the end of a belt with a square, circle, or cut-out design in leather or felt, the belt must first be stitched and then the decorations sewed on. Make the ties of self-fabric and join them securely under each end of the belt.

Fringed Sport Belt: This belt is made from hopsacking or other material which is easily fringed. Cut the fabric long enough to fit your waist plus 10 inches for the fringe. This band should be 2 inches wider than the interlining. Fit the interlining so it is 3 inches shorter than your waist measure. Fold both fabric and interlining in half and mark the center back. Overcast the fabric to the interlining, with the center marks together. The ends to be fringed will extend beyond the interlining. Fringe these ends so the long threads hang free, pulling out the cross threads, until you reach the inner belt; then tie the fringed ends. In a coarse cotton fabric, these ends will not tangle and they make an attractive sport belt.

Ribbon Tie Belt: Fit a stiff interlining belt and close it with hooks and eyes. Cover it with ribbon and fold both ends of the belt in a point. (You can use two different colors of ribbon if you overcast them together.) Overcast the ribbon to the lining, allowing the ends to extend. These ends can be tied in front, or crossed and fastened at the sides of the waistline.

Buckle Belt: You can buy a buckle and sew it to the end of belt, or use a buckled leather belt and cover it with dress fabric. Cut the fabric double plus seam allowances and turn it over the belt, overcasting the edges together. To give a tailored effect, the end of the fabric must be overcast around the point of the belt so it fits smoothly.

Button Belt: Belts are often made in two sections and buttoned together. Begin by fitting an interlining belt and close it with hooks and eyes. Cover this belt with fabric, then try it on and place the buttons on either side. Cut a piece of paper the width of the belt and long enough to extend over the buttons with enough for a buttonhole to be made in each end. Cut fabric twice this size and shape it like the paper pattern. Point each end and make a buttonhole. This piece is now ready to button in place.

Peasant Belt: Cut buckram as shown in the diagram and cover it with lining fabric. Then cut the outside fabric, allowing for seams, and stitch it to the belt. Finish the front with eyelet rings through which ribbon or cord will be laced. When this belt is not interlined, it must be boned to hold it stiff. *Diagram Page* 200.

HANDBAGS

Handbags made of fabric require an interlining of tailor's canvas or buckram. For the softer bags, tailor's canvas is suitable; stiff buckram is necessary for the over-the-shoulder bag. Bag slipcovers can be made of washable or decorative fabrics to fit an old bag, preferably a flat envelope shape. Small bags for the country and the small envelope bag attached to the belt are not interlined when made from felt—perhaps from an old felt hat; but they must be interlined if they are made of fabric.

When you are remaking a bag, remember to save all the leather for trimming bands. An interesting effect is gained by attaching a strip of leather and cutting initials through it so the fabric shows through. You can remodel bags to give more wear by ripping out zippers, changing purses, and other variations.

Handbag Slipcovers: Any envelope bag can be supplied with a slipcover. Examine the shaping on the side of the bag and make a paper pattern of the gusset insert. Cut the pattern in fabric. Measure the bag for your slipcover as follows, allowing ¼-inch seam allowance on all sides: First measure the width from A-B in the diagram; then around the bag from C-D. Cut your fabric in this size and pin back one end for a hem to fit over end D. Fit this end to the top of the bag while it is on the wrong side. Then fit in the gusset and seam it to the sides of the bag cover. Bind the top of the gusset and the unfinished edge of the cover with self-binding or contrasting color texture.

Make slipcovers for bags of linen or any washable fabric.

Button bag.

Cut buckram the length of the zipper. Cover it with an attractive fabric.

Tack this edge to the edge of the bag. For a secure closing, sew to the top edge a loop of trimming cord or a fabric-covered cord, and sew a button to the lower edge so the loop will catch.

Zipper Bag: A zipper bag can be any shape, but it is usually square or oblong. If the fabric is not very heavy, use a buckram interlining. Cut the buckram the exact size and shape of the

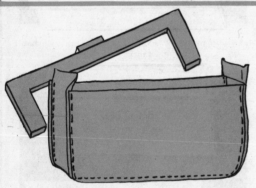

Small evening bags are easy to make.

Cut 3 squares from one handkerchief, fold one through the center for 2 triangles for your pockets. Sew a triangle on each square, piece out remaining fabric for belt.

Stitch seams of bag before adding frame.

bag. Then cut the lining and outside fabric 4½ inches longer and ½ inch wider than the buckram, to allow ¼ inch seam allowance on all sides.

Place the lining over the outside fabric and sew them together on three sides. Turn them to the right side and slip the buckram between, leaving 2 inches free at each end. Turn over a 1-inch fold at each end and baste it in place. You can now attach a change purse or pocket if you wish; use one salvaged from an old bag or buy an inexpensive one. It should be sewed to the lining about 2 inches from one end.

Insert the zipper. Slip the tape edge ⅛ inch under the folded ends of the bag and stitch firmly through the bag fabric. Then sew the sides of the bag together with a firm overcasting

stitch. Be sure to sew the ends of the zipper tapes in firmly, for they will have to stand considerable strain. Attach a smart tassel, ornament, or fabric loop to the metal pull of the zipper.

Evening Bag: Evening bags can be made of velvet, velveteen, lace, and metallic fabrics; or you can use a plain fabric and quilt or bead it. Cut two cardboard disks the size desired for the base, which is usually 4 to 6 inches. Cut lining material to cover both the circles, allowing ¼ inch for seams. Overcast them together. Cut the bag itself in: (1) the outside fabric, (2) the lining material, and (3) the interlining. All three pieces should be long enough to go around the base with 6 inches additional for fullness. Cut lining and interlining the desired depth, at least 6 inches; but the outside fabric should have an additional 3 inches or so to form a double fold for a heading with a casing.

Seam the bag and overcast it to the base on the wrong side. Finish the top with a drawstring run through a casing, or sew tiny metal rings to the outside of the bag and run the drawstring through them. Make the drawstring of ribbon. Velvet ribbon is lovely with a beaded bag.

Bags of this type, finished with spaced metal rings, can be made from velveteen, corded silk, or dress fabrics to wear with print or other daytime dresses.

Frame Handbag: Frames of wood, tortoise shell, or metal are sold in the notion departments of many stores. They are finished with the type of ring or eyelet to which a bag can be attached. Notice the difference between this type of frame and the frame in bags you buy. The latter require a machine for framing.

Make the bag to match or contrast with any coat or dress. The fabric should be heavy enough to hold its shape, and the lining should be

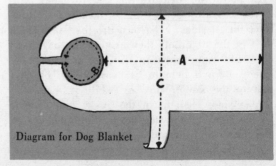

Diagram for Dog Blanket

sturdy. Sateen or heavy rayon crepe are excellent. Cut the bag as in the diagram. To do this, measure your frame and put this measure at the top of the diagram. Now try out a paper pattern to estimate the depth of the bag. Put this measure on the dotted line in the diagram. Cut the bag in fabric in this size. Round the corners and shape the sides as in the diagram. Then cut a straight piece of fabric 2 or 3 inches wide and long enough to go down each side and across the lower edge of the bag. Join this strip to the bag. The edges can be corded.

Make a duplicate of this bag in lining fabric and drop it into the bag; then join bag and lining at each corner. Sew the bag to the rings or eyelets on the frame, overcasting them securely. In some bags the lining is joined after the bag is attached to the frame.

In most bags the lining is slip-stitched to the top of the bag.

DOG BLANKET

To make a simple blanket for your dog shape the fabric as in diagram D. Measure the dog from collar to tail and put the measurement in the center of the diagram, at A. Measure his neck and put this measure at B. Measure around his barrel behind his front legs and put this measure at C. Cut a piece of fabric in these measurements and shape it like the diagram. The edge which meets behind the dog's legs, as well as the one under his chin, must be closed with snap fasteners. For an old dog a rainproof cover of this kind is wise.

Decorative Aprons: Aprons made from prints or plain fabrics joined in gay striped effects or colored poplin or unbleached muslin with an appliqué—all are decorative aprons. Cut the apron like the diagram on this page. Make it 1 inch wider and 1 inch longer for each size over the commercial size 36. This apron can be hemmed or bound, or the edge can be scalloped and finished with rickrack braid. Some are finished with a ruffle. Cut the bib 6 inches wide and as deep as you like, shaped as in the diagram. Plan the shoulder halter and the waistband tie. Two popular types of waistbands

Look in the Ready-Reference Guide at the back for exact page numbers of Detailed Instructions

Cutting diagrams for aprons.

20 INCHES

22" INCHES

6 INCHES

depth

These aprons can be made from directions given in this chapter.

Cutting diagram for slippers.

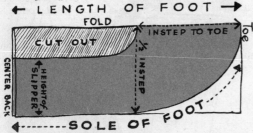

← LENGTH OF FOOT →

FOLD

CUT OUT

INSTEP TO TOE

Toe

CENTER BACK

HEIGHT of SLIPPER

½ INSTEP

------ SOLE OF FOOT ------

To make slippers, draw an outline of the foot
for sole measurement.

are: (1) a straight piece of fabric 3 or 4 inches
wide, folded double to bind the top of the apron
skirt and finished as a single piece of fabric for
the ties; and (2) a double band 3 or 4 inches
wide finished, folded and pinned to the waistline of the apron. This band can be as long as
you like and should be cut double width. Then
cut the ties, as long and as wide as you desire;
shirr the ends and tuck them into the band
before you stitch the band to the apron. These
wide bands are often decorated with rickrack
braid, or embroidery, or it can be made of a
print which is repeated in the skirt of the apron.
To make a prize gift for an older woman, insert
a band of crocheted lace.

The halter in gift aprons should be narrow
and inconspicuous. Make a self-fabric tubing in
the length desired and join it at both ends.

Sewing Aprons: Any woman who sews
will appreciate an apron with pockets to hold
her thimble, scissors, and tape measure, and keep
her sewing clean too. Choose something heavy
and washable in a print, solid color, or white
trimmed with binding. Cut the apron by the diagram on page 203, allowing 4 inches to turn up
for pockets. Finish the waistline with either of
the popular bands. The pockets can be bound
or hemmed.

BEDROOM SLIPPERS

Men's Slippers: Men's slippers can be
made from old felt hats, or from scraps of coating, carpet, or drapery. Use a shoe to make the
pattern, outlining it on a piece of paper. No
seams need be allowed. Cut the top of the
slipper double, by the diagram, fitting it around
the sole. All seams are joined on the right side
and should first be basted. Then bind them with
a strong binding, stitching as close to the edge
as possible. Run a binding flat to cover the front
seam and bind the top edge.

Women's Slippers: Dainty slippers for
Mother can be made from any of the fabrics
mentioned above for men's slippers, or they can
be made with quilted tops made from dress
fabric in plain colors or prints.

Quilt the fabric before you cut out the slipper.
To save work, outline the shape of the slipper
top on the lining; if you don't want a seam in
the center front, join this edge and make your
seam at the center back. (For quilting, see Chapter XLV.) When the quilting is finished, the seam
joining the slipper to the sole should be placed
on the inside before you seam the back.

Children's Slippers: Slippers for children can be made to match their bathrobes. Follow the directions above for men's slippers; but
bathrobe material will not make a suitable sole.
Use felt or scraps from an old coat, or buy a
sole. Slippers for toddlers and tots should be
made of washable material. When the material
is plain, embroider a cat's face on the front of
the slipper (page 198).

CHAPTER XXXI

THE CARE OF CLOTHES

The care of clothing—cleaning, mending, and pressing—is a time-consuming item in any household routine. A systematic plan and a little expert knowledge can substantially reduce the number of hours required for this task. This chapter gives suggestions for time-saving schedules for cleaning and mending, some helpful facts about expert cleaning, and a check list of common spots and how to treat them.

Most homemakers know a great deal more about the care of washable garments than about nonwashable ones. Spots on wools, wool blends, silks, and cottons and rayons are a perpetual trial because most people have one home cleaner and one method of cleaning for everything. Anyone who has had a good dress returned from a cleaner with "persistent spots" knows that clean-cleaning troubles are not confined to the home. Dry cleaning is a problem in chemistry, and the only sound approach to it is to follow expert advice and prepare to act quickly. To do this we must have a "quick cleaning kit" and know how to apply the right cleaner at the first appearance of a spot.

Fully as important as cleaning is the daily care of clothes—brushing, correct hanging, correct pressing, mending ripped seams, replacing loose buttons, and other quick mending.

QUICK CLEANING

Government chemists say that spots should be removed while they are still wet, or as soon afterward as possible; and there would be few stubborn spots to cope with if this practice were followed. Too often a spot is set by the wrong treatment, or a garment is pressed without cleaning, for "just one more wear" before it goes to the cleaner.

The first necessity for immediate removal of spots is to have the equipment handy. If the iron is in the kitchen, the ironing board in the pantry or a closet, one cleaner in the bathroom, one in the kitchen, and another in the laundry—and cleaning pads nowhere to be found—removing a spot becomes a monumental labor. If a place is made on the bedroom floor for an extra iron and ironing board and a complete cleaning kit, every member of the family is more easily encouraged to attend to spots the moment they are discovered.

Spot Removal Kit: You will need two cleaners, an absorbent cleaner and a solvent; also brown paper; a blunt knife; a clothes brush; an assortment of swabs; and a frequent change of pressing pads. Keep all this equipment in a tightly closed box to keep out the dust. Paste the rules for using solvents and abrasives on the lid of the box for ready reference. Always keep the box well supplied with clean pads and swabs.

Absorbent Cleaners: These are cornstarch, chalk, and magnesium. They act like a blotter, absorbing the ingredients of a fresh stain. An absorbent cleaner will not injure any fiber or fabric. To use it, place the garment on an ironing board with the right side up. Spread a layer of it on the wet stain and work it into the stain with a blunt knife, taking care not to injure the fabric. As soon as the powder is grimy, brush it off and apply another layer. Repeat the process patiently until the spot is gone. Check your work in a bright light, then brush away every trace of powder with a piece of clean fabric.

If the spot persists, try leaving a layer of the absorbent on it overnight. To speed the action of the absorbent when the spot has a trace of oil or grease, spread a layer of absorbent, put a piece of brown paper over it, and press with a warm iron. Heat is necessary to dissolve the grease before the absorbent can blot it up.

Solvent Cleaners: These include benzine, turpentine, alcohol, water, and carbon tetrachloride. They dissolve the spot, and it is important to work on the wrong side of the garment so that the spot is eliminated and not soaked through the fabric. Solvents may be used by the pad method, the bowl method, or immersing the whole garment.

Swabs: The swabs used for applying solvent cleaners should be of the same material as the garment if possible. Rub wool with wool, rayon with rayon, cotton with cotton. Swabs must be cleaned after each use.

Pads: Pads are made from old Turkish towels, absorbent cotton, or white blotting paper, and they must be changed frequently to prevent rings.

Press Cloths: At least three press cloths made of unbleached muslin or old sheets should be included in the spot removal kit.

THE CAUSE OF RINGS

A too-generous application of a solvent forms rings. The solvent must evaporate as you work and never be permitted to run. Another cause is that the garment was soiled before the cleaning was started, so a clean spot forms a ring. Solvents often loosen the fabric finish and flood it to the edge of the damp section, thus forming a ring.

PROFESSIONAL CAUTIONS

Stains are hardened by exposure to wear; others grow stubborn with ironing. Protein stains—from meat or milk—are permanently set by hot water. Other stains are set by the alkali soaps used in washing.

At the end of this chapter is a list of stains and how to treat them; here we return to time-saving routines in the care of clothes.

QUICK-STITCH MENDING

A drawer in every bedroom should contain a pincushion with threaded needles so that every member of the family can take a few quick stitches during dressing if he discovers a minor rip in the garment he wants to put on.

Ripped Seams: A small rip should be overcast with a few stitches. Secure the thread with

care and overlap a few of the stitches not ripped. This rip will never trouble you again.

Loose Buttons: Buttons which hang by a thread should be sewed securely on the spot. It takes only a moment and prevents the loss of the button, sometimes a whole row of them.

Ripped Shoulder Straps, Belts, Sashes: They should be caught securely and at once. Attach belts and sashes with a long stitch covered with buttonholing. Shoulder straps should be stitched all around the edge.

Small Rips in Hems and Coat Linings: They can be caught in a few moments and prevent having to sew a long hem or tripping over a loose one.

Rips in Glove Seams: Overcast the seam on the outside.

Runs in Hosiery: Don't overcast a run together, but run the needle in and out of the open space and let one or two threads close the run. In circular or knitted hosiery, be sure to catch both ends of the run and fasten them securely.

PRESSING

Pressing must be distinguished from ironing. In ironing, a hot iron is pressed directly on a fabric to smooth the surface, which is sometimes dry, sometimes damp, sometimes wet. In pressing, the iron is not applied directly to the surface of the fabric. A cloth or paper is put over the fabric, and the iron applied to that. A tailor's iron is heavier than the usual household iron and makes a sharper fold in the edges of the fabric. Ironing is used for lightweight fabrics, particularly cottons; pressing is essential for woolens and worsteds, for heavy cottons and blended fabrics which look like wool. They cannot be ironed.

Dry Pressing: Lightweight dress fabrics of rayon, cotton, and silk are pressed dry. The garment is turned to the wrong side and pressed without a press cloth. Set the iron so it will not scorch, and keep it moving so it does not mark the fabric.

When a stubborn crease persists, wipe the fabric with a damp press cloth and press again.

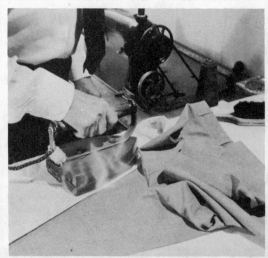

Experts brush the garment inside and outside before pressing. Woolens and worsteds must be steamed.

Wet Pressing: Dress weights of wool or blends of wool must be protected from shine by a press cloth. A damp cloth can be used first, and then replaced with a dry one. Press the garments on the wrong side.

Steam Pressing: All lined garments, or those with double collars or facings, must be steam-pressed. Lined garments are pressed on the right side, using two press cloths. Unbleached muslin is used for lightweight garments, but for heavy coats the press cloth should be canvas or wool. The wetter the press cloth, the better the steam, and these garments require a great deal of steaming. The muslin cloth can be soaked and squeezed out so it is wet but does not drip, but the heavier press cloth must be wet with a sponge dipped in water.

Double thicknesses at the lapels and facings are pressed on both wrong and right sides.

Place a low table beside your ironing board so that the garment will not wrinkle as you work, but can be carefully laid. Put the wet press cloth over the garment and iron it with a hot iron. Keep the iron moving. Press around buttons, not over them. Remove the press cloth and brush the garment vigorously. Use a soft brush for woolens and a hard brush for worsteds. This brushing will eliminate the steam and dry the fabric; it will prevent shine; it will raise the nap; it will prevent sharp marks on the edges of pockets and seams. Then place a dry cloth over the garment and press until it is al-

most dry. A wool or blended fabric should not be pressed dry, because it makes the fabric shine. Hang up the garment while it is still damp and let it dry in the air. The coat-hanger must be as wide as the shoulders of the garment so it will not sag as it dries.

Professionals first press the sleeves, then begin at the underarm on one side of the garment, working toward the front. Then they turn the garment so the pressed side rests carefully on the table beside the board and press across the back toward the other front edge.

Pressing a Sleeve: When you press on a flat surface, fold the sleeve at the underarm seam. If you want a crease on the outside edge of the sleeve, let the iron reach this edge. Most dress sleeves should not have an outside fold, and in this case the sleeve is pressed so that the iron does not reach the outside edge. When all but the edge has been pressed, the sleeve is laid so the center line lies flat in the center, then the center is pressed. This is not difficult to do in a wide sleeve; but a narrow one, fitted at the wrist, should be pressed on a sleeve board.

The rounded shaping of armhole and shoulder in any garment must be protected in pressing. A tailor's cushion, a pressing mitt, or a sleeve board will help. The secret of pressing the armhole joining is to first lay the shoulder flat on the sleeve board and press it with the collar turned out. Never let the iron touch the seam which joins the sleeve to the armhole. When the

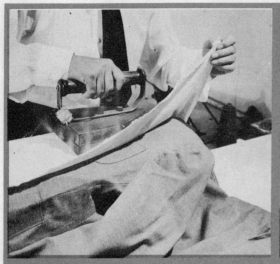
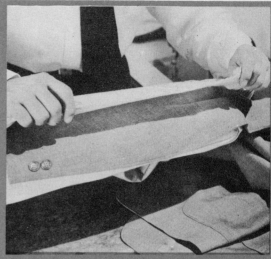

Brush vigorously to raise the nap and prevent marks from iron at edges of pockets.

shoulder has been pressed, place the garment on the sleeve board so that you can press the waist or jacket fabric around the armhole. Do not touch the seam. When this fabric has been pressed, place the top of the sleeve on the broad end of the sleeve board and press the gathers or rounded shaping at the top. The iron comes up to but does not touch the seam. In the making of a garment, this seam joining the sleeve to the armhole is pressed toward the sleeve. To do this, first press the seam firmly; then remove the sharp line by moving the seam back and pressing the sleeve under the seam, removing the press lines from the sleeve.

Removing Shine from Woolens:

Worsteds made from long, tightly twisted brushed wool shine most easily. Woolens made from unbrushed wool in a fuzzy fabric seldom shine. To remove shine from top-quality, fast-color worsteds, wipe the fabric lightly with a solution of vinegar, lay a press cloth over it, and steam it. Lift the press cloth and brush the fabric. If you are not sure of your fabric, test this treatment on the underhem only.

If your fabric will not take the vinegar treatment, use the following method, which can be recommended for all fabrics: Soak a press cloth; it must be wet but not drip. Hold the iron just above the cloth, so it creates steam but does not press the cloth. Move the iron continually, but very slowly, so that the steam penetrates the fabric, over a section of the garment. When that

section has been thoroughly steamed, lift the cloth and brush the fabric. If the shine is not removed, repeat the process. To dry the material, hold the iron close to the dry press cloth so the heat dries the fabric and it seems to have been pressed, even though the iron never touches the fabric.

RULES FOR CLEANING GARMENTS

In dry cleaning, government experts point out, we are using chemistry; and the action of the cleaning fluid upon the spot cannot be predicted unless we know what chemical is in the spot, what chemicals are in the fabric, and what chemical is in the solvent or bleach. The complex problem of removing persistent spots must therefore be broken down in a chart which takes into consideration the age and nature of the stain, and the nature of the fabric.

Colored fabrics, especially prints, present the most troublesome problem. Often the dye is not fast; often the chemical of the spot remover acts on the dye as well as the spot and leaves you with a disheartening white spot. To avoid this, experts always test a colored fabric by trying a little of the spot remover on the hem to be sure it does not take out the color. Do this when the directions say "test for color."

Water is one of the best solvents, and wiping with water will remove many stains; but many fabrics water-mark, so here again it is wise to test the fabric first.

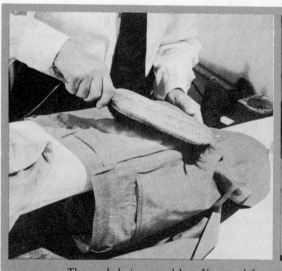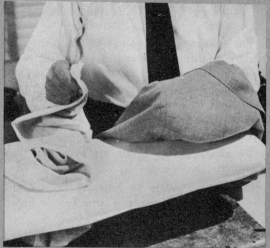

The armhole is pressed last. Use towel for pressing mit and wrap press cloth around iron.

An abundance of clean pads and swabs are the first essential of good cleaning. Soiled swabs and too few swabs are two reasons why homemakers are unsuccessful in removing spots.

Note these fundamental warnings:

1. Is the fabric acetate rayon?—*Don't* use chloroform, ether, or acetone solution.

2. Is the fabric rayon wool or silk?—*Don't* use concentrated or strong acids or alkalis.

3. Is the fabric cotton?—*Don't* use alkalis and hot water solutions too long.

Work Fast: The secret of success is to work fast. Have everything you need ready. Solvent and bleaching chemicals each have a job to do. Apply them carefully as directed. Have a bowl of cold water on your work table, and have a pail and pitcher handy so the water can be continually changed.

METHODS OF CLEANING

Pad Method: Pads are made from white blotting paper or clean pieces of fabric swabs from a fabric like the garment. They must be spotless, and bountiful, as they are changed frequently. Place the spot face down on a pad and apply the cleaning fluid to the back of the fabric with a swab. Be sure that there is not too much moisture on the swab. There must be enough to penetrate the spotted section only, with no surplus to run. Apply it again and again, changing the pad. When the spot is removed wipe the spot dry with a clean swab and blow on it until it is dry.

Bowl Method: You will need two bowls, a medicine dropper—separate ones for acid and alkali solutions—and a swab and several dry pads. Stretch the fabric over a bowl of lukewarm water, holding it over the bowl with an elastic band. With the dropper put a few drops of the cleaning fluid on the spot. When the spot changes color plunge the material into the bowl of water if it is washable; if it is not, steam it over the spout of a teakettle, with a cloth over the spout.

Gasoline Bath: Professional cleaners immerse the garment in a gasoline bath after the spots are removed, to remove rings and freshen the whole garment. Homemakers who have facilities for working outdoors can do this easily. Gasoline is inflammable and should never be used in rooms where there is a fire burning or even a lighted cigarette. All windows must be open. Strain the soiled gasoline through a cloth and reuse it, again and again.

WHAT TO LOOK FOR WHEN YOU BUY

No one—not even professionals in the field—can tell how a fabric will wear just by looking at it or feeling it. Your greatest security in buying all fabrics, including rayons, is to look for a label that gives you the results of standard tests the fabric has passed.

The tests used for "stabilized" fabrics shown in the accompanying charts are based on the following:

C S 59-41   refers to National Bureau of Standards Woven Textile Fabrics Tests

ASTM D231-39   refers to American Society for Testing Materials

AVC   refers to American Viscose Corporation Tests

AATCC   refers to the American Association of Textile Chemists and Colorists

P.Q.D. 38   refers to U. S. Quartermaster Corps

Before shopping for fabrics, check the serviceability standards given in these charts—they are your best prediction of fabric satisfaction.

On the top line of each chart you will find the use to which you will put the fabric. The left-hand column gives the standards for which the fabric is tested; and the column directly under the kind of fabric, shows which tests the fabric should pass for that specific use.

The paragraph below the charts on page 211 explains in detail the actual tests which the fabrics undergo.

TESTS FOR STABILIZED RAYON FABRICS FOR WOMEN'S WEAR

	MINIMUM REQUIREMENTS NO 101 WOMEN'S WOVEN SPORTSWEAR FABRICS			MINIMUM REQUIREMENTS NO. 101A WOMEN'S KNITTED SPORTSWEAR FABRICS			MINIMUM REQUIREMENTS NO. 102 WOMEN'S WOVEN SUITING FABRICS			MINIMUM REQUIRE- MENTS NO. 103 WOMEN'S WOVEN UNIFORM FABRICS		MINIMUM REQUIREMENTS NO 104 WOMEN'S WOVEN COATING FABRICS		
	WASHABLE	HAND WASHABLE	CLEANABLE	WASHABLE	HAND WASHABLE	CLEANABLE	WASHABLE	HAND WASHABLE	CLEANABLE	WASHABLE	CLEANABLE	WASHABLE	HAND WASHABLE	CLEANABLE
Tensile Strength: Dry Wet CS59-41	35 lbs. 20 lbs.	35 lbs. 20 lbs.	35 lbs. 20 lbs.				50 lbs. 25 lbs.	50 lbs. 25 lbs.	50 lbs. 25 lbs.	50 lbs. 25 lbs.	50 lbs. 25 lbs.	35 lbs. 20 lbs.	35 lbs. 20 lbs.	35 lbs. 20 lbs.
*Bursting Strength: Dry Wet ASTM D231-39				50 lbs. 30 lbs.	50 lbs. 30 lbs.	50 lbs. 30 lbs.								
Resistance to Seam Slippage: CS59-41	15 lbs.	15 lbs.	15 lbs.	10 lbs.	10 lbs.	10 lbs.	25 lbs.	25 lbs.	25 lbs.	25 lbs.	25 lbs.	15 lbs.	15 lbs.	15 lbs.
*Dimensional Restorability AVC	2%	2%	2%	2%	2%	2%	2%	2%	2%	2%	2%	2%	2%	2%
Color Fastness: To Laundering Perspiration Dry Cleaning (Wet) Hot Pressing Cracking Sunlight *Atmospheric Fading	Test #3 Test A — Test A Test B Test #3 Test A	Test #1 Test A — Test A Test B Test #3 Test A	— Test A Test A Test A Test B Test #3 Test A	Test #3 Test A — Test A Test B Test #3 Test A	Test #1 Test A — Test A Test B Test #3 Test A	— Test A Test A Test A Test B Test #3 Test A	Tesf #3 Test A — Test A Test B Test #3 Test A	Test #1 Test A — Test A Test B Test #2 Test A	— Test A Test A Test A Test B Test #2 Test A	Test #3 Test A — Test A Test B Test #3 Test A	— Test A Test A Test A Test B Test #2 Test A	Test #3 Test A — Test A Test B Test #3 Test A	Test #1 Test A — Test A Test B Test #3 Test A'	— Test A Test A Test A Test B Test #3 Test A
*Permanence of Finish: Consecutive Tests	3	3	3	3	3	3	3	3	3	3	3	3	3	3

TESTS FOR RAYON DRESS AND LINING FABRICS

	MINIMUM REQUIREMENTS NO. 105 WOMEN'S WOVEN LINING FABRICS			MINIMUM REQUIREMENTS NO. 106 WOMEN'S WOVEN DRESS FABRICS			MINIMUM REQUIREMENTS NO. 107 WOMEN'S WOVEN SHEER DRESS FABRICS		MINIMUM REQUIREMENTS NO. 108 WOMEN'S KNITTED DRESS FABRICS		
	WASHABLE	HAND WASHABLE	CLEANABLE	WASHABLE	HAND WASHABLE	CLEANABLE	HAND WASHABLE	CLEANABLE	WASHABLE	HAND WASHABLE	CLEANABLE
Tensile Strength: Dry — Wet CS59-41	35 lbs. / 20 lbs.	35 lbs. / 20 lbs.	35 lbs. / 20 lbs.	20 lbs. / 10 lbs.	20 lbs. / 10 lbs.	20 lbs. / 10 lbs.	15 lbs. / 10 lbs.	15 lbs. / 10 lbs.			
Bursting Strength: Dry — Wet ASTM D231-39									50 lbs. / 30 lbs.	50 lbs. / 30 lbs.	50 lbs. / 30 lbs.
Resistance to Seam Slippage: CS59-41	15 lbs.	15 lbs.	15 lbs.	15 lbs.	15 lbs.	15 lbs.	8 lbs.	8 lbs.	10 lbs.	10 lbs.	10 lbs.
Dimensional Restorability AVC	2%	2%	2%	2%	2%	2%	2%	2%	2%	2%	2%
Color Fastness: To Laundering	Test #3	Test #1	—	Test #3	Test #1	—	Test #1	—	Test #3	Test #1	—
Perspiration	Test A	Test A	Test A	Test A	Test A	Test A	Test A	Test A	Test A	Test A	Test A
Dry Cleaning (Wet)	Test A	—	Test A	—	—	Test A	—	Test A	—	—	Test A
Hot Pressing	Test A	Test A	Test A	Test A	Test A	Test A	Test A	Test A	Test A	Test A	Test A
Crocking	Test B	Test B	Test B	Test B	Test B	Test B	Test B	Test B	Test B	Test B	Test B
Sunlight	—	—	—	Test #3	Test #1	—	Test #1	—	Test #3	Test #1	—
Atmospheric Fading	Test A	Test A	Test A	Test A	Test A	Test A	Test A	Test A	Test A	Test A	Test A
Permanence of Finish: Consecutive Tests	3	3	3	3	3	3	3	3	3	3	3

TESTS FOR UNDERWEAR AND BATHING SUIT FABRICS

	MINIMUM REQUIREMENTS NO. 109 WOMEN'S WOVEN PAJAMA—NIGHTGOWN—UNDERWEAR FABRICS		MINIMUM REQUIREMENTS NO. 109A WOMEN'S KNITTED PAJAMA—NIGHTGOWN—UNDERWEAR FABRICS		MINIMUM REQUIREMENTS NO. 110 WOMEN'S WOVEN DRESSING GOWN—LOUNGING PAJAMA—NEGLIGEE FABRICS			MINIMUM REQUIREMENTS NO. 110A WOMEN'S KNITTED DRESSING GOWN—LOUNGING PAJAMA—NEGLIGEE FABRICS			MINIMUM REQUIREMENTS NO. 111 WOMEN'S WOVEN BATHING SUIT FABRICS	MINIMUM REQUIREMENTS NO. 111A WOMEN'S KNITTED BATHING SUIT FABRICS (Other than those containing elastic yarns)
	WASHABLE	HAND WASHABLE	WASHABLE	HAND WASHABLE	WASHABLE	HAND WASHABLE	CLEANABLE	WASHABLE	HAND WASHABLE	CLEANABLE	WASHABLE	WASHABLE
Tensile Strength: Dry — Wet CS59-41	20 lbs. / 10 lbs.	20 lbs. / 10 lbs.			20 lbs. / 10 lbs.	20 lbs. / 10 lbs.	20 lbs. / 10 lbs.				— / 40 lbs.	
Bursting Strength: Dry — Wet ASTM D231-39			50 lbs. / 30 lbs.	50 lbs. / 30 lbs.				50 lbs. / 30 lbs.	50 lbs. / 30 lbs.	50 lbs. / 30 lbs.		— / 50 lbs.
Resistance to Seam Slippage: CS59-41	15 lbs.	15 lbs.	10 lbs.	10 lbs.	15 lbs.	15 lbs.	15 lbs.	10 lbs.	10 lbs.	10 lbs.	25 lbs.	25 lbs.
Dimensional Restorability AVC	2%	2%	2%	2%	2%	2%	2%	2%	2%	2%	2%	2%
Color Fastness: To Laundering	Test #3	Test #1	Test #3	Test #1	Test #3	Test #1	—	Test #3	Test #1	—	Test #3	Test #3
Perspiration	Test A	Test A	Test A	Test A	Test A	Test A	Test A	Test A	Test A	Test A	Fresh Water Test A — Salt Water Test A — Chlorinated Test A	Fresh Water Test A — Salt Water Test A — Chlorinated Test A
Dry Cleaning (Wet)	—	—	—	—	—	—	Test A	—	—	Test A	Special Tests	Special Tests
Hot Pressing	Test A	Test A	Test A	Test A	Test A	Test A	Test A	Test A	Test A	Test A		
Crocking	Test B	Test B	Test B	Test B	Test B	Test B	Test B	Test B	Test B	Test B		
Sunlight	Test #1	Test #1	Test #1	Test #1	Test #1	Test #1	—	Test #1	Test #1	—	Test #3	Test #3
Atmospheric Fading	Test A	Test A	Test A	Test A	Test A	Test A	Test A	Test A	Test A	Test A	Test A	Test A
Permanence of Finish: Consecutive Tests	3	3	3	3	3	3	3	3	3	3	3	3

Dimensional Restorability means the ability of a fabric to return to its original size and shape after washing or dry cleaning—by use of normal home handling an l shaping methods. (AVC)

Laundering, Test 3 – Fabric tested in water (strong soap) at 160° F. (Hot). No appreciable loss of color nor staining of other fabrics. CS59-41
Test 1 – Fabric tested in water (mild soap) at 105° F. (Luke Warm). No appreciable loss of color nor staining of other fabrics. CS59-41
Perspiration, Test A – Fabric tested for satisfaction against loss of color or staining through either acid or alkaline perspiration. CS59-41.
Dry Cleaning (Dry) Test A – Fabric tested in solvents without appreciable loss of color. CS59-41

Dry Cleaning (Wet) Test A – Fabric tested in water and mild soap solution at 90° to 100° F. (Cool) without appreciable loss of color or staining of other fabrics. CS59-41

Fresh Water Test A—Salt Water Test A—Chlorinated Water Test A–Passed if fabrics show no appreciable loss of color in tests similar to natural conditions. AATC

Crocking, Test B–(Color Rubbing Off). Tested by fabric-covered mechanical "finger" rubbing fabric. If discoloration on finger cloth results but disappears after scrubbing in mild soap solution, the fabric is passed. CS59-41

Sunlight, Test 3–40 hours in Fadeometer (Sunlight Testing Machine) with no appreciable loss of color. CS59-41
Test 2 – 20 hours in Fadeometer (Sunlight Testing Machine) with no

appreciable loss of color. CS59-41
Test 1 – 10 hours in Fadeometer (Sunlight Testing Machine) with no appreciable loss of color. CS59-41
Atmospheric Fading–Tested against loss of color caused by gases in the air. Passed if no appreciable loss of color is noted after test. AATCC
Permanence of Finish, Consecutive Tests–Passed if fabric shows no appreciable change of finish or texture after either three launderings or three dry cleanings. PQD-38

SPOT CHECK LIST

Kind of Spot	Cleaning Fluid	How to Use It
Cream and coffee Grease, Oil, Lipstick, Fly paper, Chewing gum, Paint	Carbon Tetrachloride	Wipe the stain with a pad moistened with a *little* cleaning fluid.
Butter and butter substitutes	Carbon Tetrachloride Fuller's Earth	With a blunt knife scrape off as much of the butter as possible. Apply the fluid by the pad method. Put the powder on both sides of the fabric and let it stand ½ hour. Brush off. Repeat if necessary.
Grease and oil	Carbon Tetrachloride Warm water and soap	Use the pad method, a very little solvent at a time to keep the grease from spreading. Between applications rub the spot with a clean cloth until thoroughly dry. On delicate fabrics, spread a paste of cleaning fluid mixed with an absorbent powder. Rub it into the spot, let it dry, then brush it off. In washable fabrics, use warm water and soap containing naphtha or kerosene.
Candle wax	Turpentine or lard Blotters and warm iron	Scrape off as much wax as possible. In washable fabrics, rub the spot with turpentine or lard and wash in warm suds. In nonwashable fabrics, place a blotter on both sides of the stain and press with a warm iron. Remove the remaining grease stain with solvent. If any color remains, sponge with denatured alcohol.
Fresh fruit and berries	Oxalic Acid Ammonia Solution Hydrogen Peroxide	White washable cotton and linen: use boiling water or moisten the stain with lemon juice and put it in the sunlight. If a blue-gray stain remains, use a chemical with the bowl method. On silk and wool and colored fabrics, apply hydrogen peroxide with a medicine dropper at 5-minute intervals. Test for color.
Cooked fruit and berries	Oxalic Acid Ammonia Javelle Water Boiling Water	Soap is likely to set this stain. On color-fast materials, when the stain is fresh, pour boiling water from a height. When the stain is old, bleach with javelle water (white cotton or linen only). For other fabrics use alternate treatments of oxalic acid and ammonia (bowl method). Experiment first.
Dye and running color	Hydrogen Peroxide	Ease with which dye is removed depends upon the nature of the dye. Dye stains in white fabrics can often be removed by soaking in warm or cold water for 10 or 12 hours, and then bleaching in the sun. For white wool or silk, soak in hydrogen peroxide solution, made slightly alkaline with a few drops of ammonia. Rinse thoroughly.
Blood	Water Hydrogen Peroxide	Always use cold water first (never soap or warm water). Soak in cold water until the stain is almost gone, then wash with soap and warm water. Delicate fabrics should be sponged with cold or lukewarm water. To remove the last traces, sponge with hydrogen peroxide to which a few drops of ammonia have been added. Heavy material, blankets, mattresses, etc.: make a paste of raw starch and cold water. Apply to the stain and brush off when dry. Repeat.
Egg	Cold Water Carbon Tetrachloride	Cold water first (no hot water). Washable color-fast materials (1) cold water, (2) wash in hot water. Other fabrics: sponge with cold water. Allow stain to dry. Then apply cleaning fluid by the pad method.
Chocolate and cocoa	Carbon Tetrachloride Soap and hot water Javelle Water Wood Alcohol	Washable material: soap and water. On white linen and cotton, when stain remains, use javelle water. For colored material, if dye is fast, soak stained portion in wood alcohol with a few drops of ammonia solution. For nonwashable material, use carbon tetrachloride, pad method.

CHAPTER XXXII

THE FINE ART OF MENDING

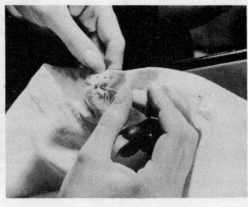

Mending is an inescapable, and in too many case, a time-consuming part of the routine of every household. Skillful mending saves many dollars by prolonging the life of clothing and household linens; and skillful organizing to catch the tear in time saves hours of needless labor. "A stitch in time saves nine" is no idle saying, as many a mother knows; and by systematizing your mending you can make the bottomless mending basket disappear from your home.

TIME-SAVING PLANS

Your own habits and circumstances will determine the exact details of the plan you work out for mending, but whatever it is, "do it now" should be the keynote. One good way is to watch for tears and missing buttons as you iron and make it an iron-clad rule to mend them before the garments or linens are put away. If you send your washing to the laundry, check each item for rips and tears as you check the laundry list, especially sheets and pillow cases.

I know of one mother who cleverly enlists the children in her mending program. In each bureau drawer is a pincushion with threaded needles, and each child has learned to do a little quick mending—catching together the small rip, sewing on the button hanging by a thread.

Look in the Ready-Reference Guide at the back for exact page numbers of Detailed Instructions

APPRAISING YOUR MENDING PROBLEM

There are different kinds of mending appropriate to different cases—quick-stitch mending, tide-over mending, and permanent mending. The last of these can often be decorative mending, in which the mend is concealed by being made to look like part of the trimming. The condition of the garment, of course, will largely determine which kind you use. A well-worn garment, on the last lap of its life, hardly deserves the same careful mending as a perfectly good garment.

Second-Grade Garments: This includes all fabrics which have split or worn thin. Hold the fabric to the light and examine it for slippage and small holes, strained seams, and so forth. Such garments deserve only quick tide-over mending.

Good Outside Garments: When a perfectly good garment has suffered an accident, the problem of mending it needs careful consideration. It should not look mended; so the problem is, can it be repaired with an inconspicuous mend, or must you resort to decorative mending to disguise the spot? If the latter is the case, the nature of the spot to be covered will determine the kind of thing you can do. Is it a tear, a permanent spot, a burn? Has the fabric slipped and worn at the seams? Is the fabric

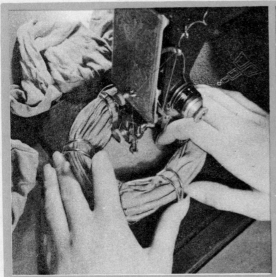

Darning stockings by machine saves hours of time. For small, soft, flat darn use a darning egg and thread drawn from old stocking.

faded? Has the garment shrunk or been out-grown? At this point mending merges into re-modeling or alteration, for which see Chapter XXXIII.

MENDING STOCKINGS

The time spent mending socks and stockings can be cut down by watching for the thinning-out which precedes a hole. This thin fabric is much easier to darn than a hole. An inside heel guard on the shoe saves stockings and is well worth the trouble of having it put in or putting in a ready-made one. If you have an unusually large family to mend for, it will pay you to buy a sock-mending attachment for your sewing ma-chine.

Darning Small Holes: With the stocking right side out, slip a darning egg into place under the hole and draw the stocking tight over the egg. Thread a darning needle with cotton or wool the same shade as the stocking. Begin 1/4 inch above the hole and pass the needle in and out in a weaving motion. The thread line should extend beyond the hole on each side. Draw the thread through—no knot in the end—then run another thread line back the other way, close to the first one. When you pull this second thread, leave a very small loop at the end between the

two lines of stitching. Weave back and forth in this manner until you have passed the hole and gone 1/4 inch on the other side. Turn and do the same thing at right angles to the first set of threads. When you come to the hole, weave under one thread and over the next, and when you come back, alternate—under when the last thread was over, and vice versa. Fill up the hole with close darning in this manner, and when you finish, the darn should lie flat and smooth like part of the stocking. It should not be bulky and thick.

Darning Large Holes: Trim the frayed edges around the hole and cut a piece from a discarded sock to fill it. Catch-stitch the piece in place, then darn back and forth over the catch stitching so there is no seam or bulk at the edge. This is a time-saving way of mending holes, and women who do not like to darn can use it for small holes as well as large ones, or even for thin places.

Mending Runs: Thread the needle with matching mercerized darning thread, or with a thread drawn from a discarded stocking of the same shade. In circular knit constructions, in either sheer hosiery or underwear, you can stop a run permanently if you catch the end loop of the knitting and hold it securely with a thread. Now run the needle in and out of the threads that form the run. Fasten the thread securely.

To mend a stocking run by machine, use matching thread. Fold the garment on the line of the run. Pin this fold to a piece of paper, stretching as you pin. Stitch close to this edge, extending the stitching beyond the run. Tear the paper away and tie the ends of the thread.

Mending Mesh Hose: Mesh knitting does not run, but the hole will grow larger if it is not stopped. Examine the hole carefully and start your mending thread in the looped stitch which pulls easiest. This is the trouble spot. Overcast your thread in and out to hold this loop fast, then overcast all around the hole.

DARNING GARMENT FABRICS

A small tear can often be darned inconspicuously if you use a very fine needle threaded with a thread drawn from the fabric. The hem, a seam edge, or the inside of a pocket are good places to draw out self threads. A short thread is best. First catch the edge of the tear with a basting stitch and then darn. In tears the darning is seldom recrossed; you pass the needle in and out, back and forth across the tear. If there is a corner, cross it twice for strength. On plain fabrics the loops at the end of the darning rows *must be even.* They can be shorter on woven fabrics that do not stretch than on knitted fabrics that do stretch.

If the tear is diagonal or across the grain of the goods, work first across the tear, then work lengthwise of it.

A piece of fine net is often placed under a darn to strengthen the thread without adding bulk.

Darns conspicuously placed can be decorated. For suggestions see Decorative Patching below.

PATCHING

If you have no extra material for a patch, see whether you can cut a piece from the hem or an inside facing. If the garment has faded and the patch is bright and new, wash it first and dry it in the sun. There are four kinds of patches: (1) decorative, (2) hemmed, (3) darned, and (4) pasted.

Decorative Patch: The patch is not cut the size and shape of the hole, but in some decorative shape — diamond, square, heart-shaped, or whatever you wish. Apply it with catch stitch or hem it down on the right side.

Pocket Patch: Making the decorative patch into a pocket can be considered only when the tear is in such a position that the pocket will be right on the garment. Short tears can be made into bound pockets, or patch pockets placed over mended rips. I have seen pockets in flower outlines placed over the darned tears in a child's dress.

Pasted Patch: The new press-on mending tape is fastened with a resin agency and so resists washing. When you use it, you must cut a patch the exact size of the hole and insert it. To do this, straighten the edges of the hole with the patch under it, and cut through both the edges and the patch. Remove the frayed ends and put the mending tape under the hole. Put

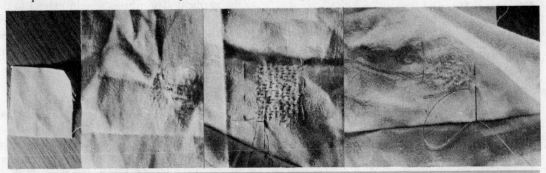

FRENCH DARN
Baste tear face down on paper. Use fine needle with thread drawn from fabric. Smooth thread with needle and darn cross-wise. Begin ½ inch above hole, follow grain of fabric, with running stitch, leaving a little loop of thread at end of each row. When finished pull fabric on bias until threads disappear.

 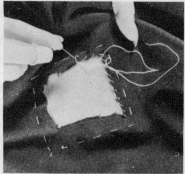 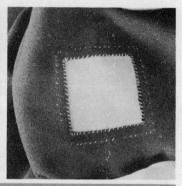

A HEMMED PATCH
Cut patch to more than cover hole. Baste to fabric. Trim hole to square shape beyond torn threads. Press edges of hole and patch so edge lies true and flat. Turn to wrong side and hem.

the patch over the hole on top of the mending tape and press with a hot iron.

These mending tapes are made in an assortment of colors and are sold in small packages. Cut the mending tape a little larger than the hole.

Overcast Patch: Square the hole and snip the corners. Cut your patch ½ inch longer and wider than the hole and join it with a seam. With matching thread, turn this seam and overcast it closely.

Underarm Patch: When a sleeve tears at the underarm, rip the seam a little way so that a square overcast patch can be set in. Snip the seam of the garment above the patch so it will not draw. When a sleeve and underarm are too tight, a band can be set into the seam from the elbow to the waist, or the band can be shorter and tapered into a point at any part of the seam.

Blanket Patch: Cut the patch larger than the hole and square the hole. Pin the patch under the hole and hem the edge of the hole to it, working from the right side. These stitches appear on the wrong side only. Remember—do not turn the edge of the patch, but finish it by catch-stitching the raw edge down. Some people prefer to catch-stitch both edges, and this is preferable in a very heavy blanket.

Patch in Print Fabrics: Whether the garment is a cotton print, shirting, or rayon print, you must match not only the grain of the fabric, as in all patches, but also the design of the print. Examine the pattern of the print you

are using to patch with, and mark with pins the sections which correspond in pattern to the hole in the garment. Allow seams in cutting the patch and place it so that the design matches exactly.

Patches Under Torn-out Buttons: A hole left by a torn-out button or fastening requires a double patch for security. Cut a piece of cotton tape or strong cotton fabric big enough to cover the hole and apply the patch. Then turn to the opposite side and apply a similar patch. Sew the button in place.

Patches Under Torn-out Lingerie Straps: If a shoulder strap tears a hole in the garment or pulls out the finish of the edge, repair it in either of the following ways: (1) If you have fabric left, join a patch and refinish the edge in the shape of the edge of the garment. (2) Cut a band of ribbon 1½ inches long, fold it in half, and bind the edge, then hem the ribbon to the garment. The ribbon should extend to the edge of the garment to replace the fabric torn away, and well below the torn edge to reinforce it. The ribbon can be finished in a bow to cover the mended hole.

FRAYED EDGES

At the first sign of worn or frayed edges on a garment, it will repay you to freshen them. The easiest way to do this is to turn the frayed edge to the right side and brush it; then machine stitch it ½ inch back from the edge. If you have no machine, cut the worn edge—or rip the seam if there is one—and turn both edges so they face.

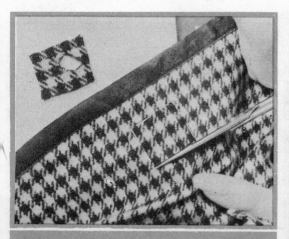

A DARNED PATCH
Cut out tear beyond the damaged threads. Cut duplicate square from hem or facing. Baste paper under hole to prevent stretching. Place patch, matching thread lines, and darn.

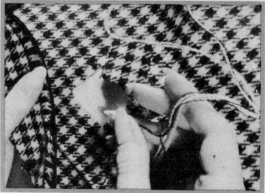

Slip-stitch the two edges together. If this makes the edge too short, consider the possibility of a binding, a band, or a cuff extension. These bands or extensions can be cut from the garment hem or facing.

Turning Men's Shirt Collars and Cuffs: Before ripping off the collar, mark the center of both collar and neckband by folding the neckband in half with edges matching. Use pins to do this marking. Then rip off the collar, reverse it, and replace it in the neckband. Pin it in place and check to make sure that the worn edge of the collar faces the right side of the shirt so it will be inside when you fold the collar. Then you are ready to stitch.

Cuffs are ripped and reversed in the same way as collars.

Split Seams: When the stitching of a seam gives way, it is easy enough to restitch it, on the machine if possible. When the fabric splits at the seam, you can overstitch the seam on the right side. Run the first row of stitching as close to the split edge as possible (do not turn the edge under). Then run several rows of stitching close together, stitching through the seam allowance on the wrong side.

There is a difference between a clean tear at the seam and slipping of the fabric at the seam. Seam slippage must be stayed with a band.

DECORATIVE MENDING
Tears and permanent spots can be covered with appliqué or trimming bands, or, if they come in the right place, turned into a pocket or covered with a pocket.

MENDING GLOVES
Ripped seams in the fingers should be closely overcast with a cotton thread the exact shade of the glove. Do not take the stitch too close to the edge or it will rip out again.

In mesh gloves, try to recreate the mesh. First run a long thread the length of the tear, then join the cross threads securely to this. Make a tie at each cross thread.

In mending gloves do not use knots. Allow extra thread and tie in the ends carefully.

MENDING MACHINE-MADE SWEATERS
Cut a piece from the bottom of the sweater and unravel it to use for darning the hole and over-

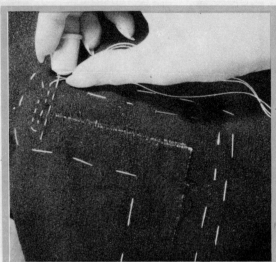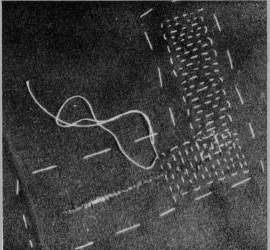

DARNING A CORNER TEAR

Baste fabric to a piece of paper. Darn triangular tears with thread drawn from garment. Begin ½ inch above tear. Use rows of close running stitches. Avoid cross darns at corners.

casting the cut edge of the sweater. If the darn shows, make a few embroidery stitches over or around it in a design. Another possibility is to make allover embroidery on the sweater which will cover the darn. This can be scattered sprays of little flowers in lazy-daisy stitch, or the effect can be achieved with appliqué spots of embroidery or colored felt patches in diamond or heart shapes. If the hole is in the front or side, appliqué a monogram over it.

When a sweater is torn at the elbow, there is little to be done except make a darn or patch. But you can use one of the decorative patches suggested above and place a matching one somewhere on the body. If the sweater is of good wool, cut off the sleeves and make a sleeveless sweater, as described in Chapter XXXIII, or use it as an interlining in a coat or quilted bed jacket. Sometimes you can combine it with a fabric dress. If it is cotton wool, bouclé, or knitted cotton, consign it to your rummage bag for future rag rugs.

You can finish the lower edge by using some of the yarn you raveled out for darning and overcast the cut edge. Stretch the edge as you work and be sure to catch your needle through every row. In a ribbed band, take care to catch every stitch in the back row as well as the front.

Bands to Cover Darns: Sometimes small tears or mothholes are so placed that they can be covered with bands after darning. They should be of sheer rayon crepe or ribbon, applied as directed in the paragraph on Trimming Bands.

REPAIRING GIRDLES

At the first sign of a rip or tear, mend your girdle promptly. Catch the end of each rubber thread and tie it with cotton thread so it will hold. Then darn these threads down into the seam or whatever part of the girdle ripped. Be careful not to put a needle through the rubber threads. If the tear is on a seam, rebind it with tape or a satin ribbon after mending. If the garter rips on a seam, use an overcasting stitch; it holds better and has some give.

MENDING LINEN

Sheets: Put bands of percale (solid color, or gay print) on a torn hem. Small holes can be darned or mended with appliquéd stars or tiny flowers. Large holes must be patched. To overcast a split sheet, join the outside edges and overcast by hand so the seam is flat.

Towels: Torn towels can be cut down to guest size. If the towel is small, appliqué amusing designs for a patch, such as red lips or a small hand. Towels too badly torn for repair can still give service as washcloths or potholders.

CHAPTER XXXIII

RESTYLING--REMODELING--REMAKING

Suggestions for refreshing or remodelling dresses. Worn skirts can be concealed by an attractive apron. Yokes can be added for dress-up, or re-styling.

Dressmakers' tricks of restyling and remodeling can give new life to a worn or outmoded costume—or to one you are merely tired of—or perhaps you want to dress up a garment for a special occasion, or simplify a party dress for everyday wear. Most home sewers think that remodeling always means completely remaking, but frequently some very simple adjustment will give months of wear to a dress which otherwise would have to be discarded. The suggestions in this chapter can be applied to girls' dresses as well as women's.

When you begin to remodel any garment, first check these three things: style, fit, and condition of fabric.

Checking Style: Consider the garment in relation to current fashion. Study the new color combinations and observe the new lines and trimmings. Discover what fabrics are being combined and contrasted, and how contrasts are being used. From the clothes in stores, pattern catalogues, and fashion magazines, you can not only check fashion details, but often get a new idea you can adapt. If you need additional material, first look in your salvage box for something you can use. If that fails you, buy a remnant.

Checking Fitting: When a garment is in fashion but looks wrong on you, examine the fitting. A complete refitting often restores a dress to usefulness. Try on the garment and check the pointers in Chapter XIV on good lines and proportion, as well as the details on how to make alterations.

Checking Fabric: When you are considering remodeling, the condition of the fabric is most important. Naturally, it will not pay you to remodel unless the fabric promises to give additional wear. If the surface is rubbed or faded, can it be dyed or reversed? Are there spots and holes in the fabric? If you decide it will not pay to remodel, cut out whatever material is good and save it for future use in remodeling some other garment.

Minor Adjustments: Such minor adjustments as adding new collars, cuffs, dickies, or belts, and replacing fasteners, button trimmings, and accessories are often enough to give new sparkle to old garments. Chapters XV, XVI and XXX contain detailed instructions and suggestions.

New Yoke

Chiffon blouse recut from skirt of evening dress.

Plastron added to plain dress.

New neck-line cut and ruffle added.

Petticoat ruffle added.

Cummerbund set in waist.

Ruching added.

Dressing up a Plain Dress: When you are tired of a dress, or want to dress it up for a special occasion, an easy way to give it a completely new character is to change the neckline. Insert a yoke of lace or net or a draped color contrast. Chapters XV and XVI will yield other suggestions which may be adaptable for your particular problem.

SKIRTS

Adjusting the Hem: Probably the most frequently needed alteration is adjusting the hem of a skirt. First rip out the hem and press it on the wrong side. If it has a binding in good condition, save it for future use. Try on the garment as you would for a new hemline and mark the new hem. Turn the edge carefully and hem it in place.

Removing a Mark: When a mark shows after lengthening a hem, treat it by one of the following methods, depending upon the fabric. If it is wool, steam the fabric with a wet press cloth and a hot iron; then brush away the steam, using a soft brush on woolens and a stiff one on heavy worsteds. Washing often removes the mark in cottons. In rayons, steam lightly. If the mark still persists, consider covering it with (1) a line of machine stitching. (2) a band of machine stitching, or (3) rows of ribbon or bias trimming.

Lengthening a Hem: When the skirt is too short to turn a new hem at the length you want, consider not only the possibility of a faced hem, but others as well. Can you use a band at the hemline? Stitched bands are decorative, and so are bands of contrast fabric set on with scallops or squared outlines. Ruching or ruffles can be added around the bottom of the skirt and repeated at neck and sleeves.

In many garments, skirt length can be added at the waistline. In pleated skirts, consider the addition of a yokeline, in matching material if possible. One home sewer who worked out a skirt set low on a yoke reports: "It was formerly a double-breasted suit with a pleated skirt, outgrown in length and width. The peplum of the jacket was used for the new skirt yoke, and the jacket opened and finished to form a bolero."

Another waist adjustment is a set-in wide beltline in contrasting fabric. Many young girls will welcome this idea.

For a woman's suit, consider the possibility of using the self-fabric belt for a set-in belt on the skirt. This will add 2 inches or more. To lengthen a ski-suit skirt, select a crepe in matching color and make a blouse and yoke. Open the placket of the skirt and the opposite side seam and let the skirt slip down a little. Join it to the new yoke. The joining must be covered by the jacket when the suit is worn, but the finished effect is right.

Skirt Too Full: When a skirt is too wide through the hipline, fit out the extra fullness at each side seam. Rip the seams and try on the garment, wrong side out, fitting the skirt to your figure. Baste the new seams as soon as you take off the garment. Finish the seam the same way it was originally. In circular skirts, unpressed pleats can be laid in to give a slender effect.

Skirts with gathered front fullness can be changed to a draped style by ripping one seam, near the fullness, and trying on the garment on the right side to refit this seam smoothly. Let the extra material fall in a jabotlike drapery finished with a hand-rolled hem. Possibly there will be enough material in this drapery so you can cut part of it off and continue a small strip from the top of the skirt to the neckline or shoulder, depending upon where the skirt drapery is placed. This gives a slenderizing line to the whole figure.

Adjusting a Skirt Seam: When a skirt seam is taken in to fit a smaller waist or hip, the placket must be ripped off and the seam finished as on a new garment—unless, of course, the adjustment can be made in another seam. Then replace the placket as though in a new garment and sew on the hooks and eyes again. A zipper in a placket must be carefully ripped off and reset. In a buttoned placket, it is sometimes possible to move the buttons and make a deeper lap. But if this cannot be done without hurting the line of the skirt, remove the facing with the buttons and buttonholes and adjust the skirt, then replace the facings neatly so that the edge is like new.

Tight Skirts Stretched in Wear: Bagginess in the front or back of a skirt can be adjusted by raising the skirt at the waistline. Stand in front of a mirror with the skirt on and take a little tuck across the waistline, at center back

Tight basic dress.
Width added by inverted panel, trimming carried out on cuffs.

or center front. When the line of the skirt is straightened and the sag removed, the tuck is deep enough. Rip the waistline and take up this amount of material. Your skirt should hang straight. If it does not, rip the side seams and adjust them too.

Concealing a Worn Spot: When a skirt has a tear or a persistent spot, consider the possibility of turning the skirt so that the bad spot can be covered by a pocket. Make the pocket of self-fabric or contrasting fabric as a decoration. On a soft formal dress, make a pocket of interlaced cording made from self-fabric or bought by the yard and dyed to match. Young people like the idea of a frilly taffeta apron when a simple dress is damaged.

DRESS TOO TIGHT

When the dress is too narrow throughout its entire length, you can set in a panel by slashing the front of the garment from hem to neckline. Adjust it to your figure, pinning a piece of paper into the front to serve as the panel, so that you can decide exactly how wide the panel should be. Keep in mind that no more than 2 or 3 inches in finished width can be allowed in the panel or the side seams will not be placed over your hips.

Types of Panel: Panels can be inserted or overlaid. Overlaid panels are of velveteen,

SOLVING SLEEVE PROBLEMS

New gala sleeves.

New top put on in contrasting color.

New blouse and peplum can be added.

Bands inserted in sleeve torn at elbow.

Yoke and sleeve added to torn dress.

Strip set into narrow sleeve.

velvet, piqué, and other firm fabrics, and they are often buttoned to the dress. They can be straight or shaped. Soft panels of rayon crepe in plain fabrics or prints are gathered or pleated. Other panels are inserted. To do this, face the garment fronts with the contrasting fabric and then cut a plain or print panel wide enough to join the facing 2 or 3 inches back from the edge. A smart

version of this alteration is to use an inverted panel which looks, and is, exactly like an inverted pleat. This makes the finished garment look like a coat dress. The sides of the dress are joined to cover the panel at the waistline with a buckle or some other decorative fastening which will cover the space between the two sides. If the dress has a low neckline, matching collar and cuffs are attractive.

Bolero: When the skirt is good and the waist worn or tight, the skirt can be used as a separate unit and the waist made into a bolero effect. First separate waist and skirt, then turn up the lower edge of the waist to form a becoming line. Stitch this turn in a hem. If the dress has a buttoned front, it may make an attractive bolero. If the front is straight across, put a basting down the center front and cut on this line. This edge can be faced. If you have no self-fabric, make a print blouse and use the same print for the facing .

Worn Buttonholes: Worn buttonholes in a dress can sometimes be concealed by adding a band over the buttoned edge in a simulated fly closing. Ribbon can be used or a band of fabric made into a trimming. Center the band over the buttons and hem one edge of it to the garment.

SLEEVE PROBLEMS

Refurbishing Outmoded Sleeves: *Adding Circular Ruffle*: A ruffle to add to the end of a sleeve can be cut without a pattern. First cut a circle of tissue paper, then shape it into a ruffle and try it on against the sleeve before you cut the fabric. Any lightweight fabric can be used. Make the circle in paper the size of the desired ruffle, and cut a small circular hole in the center, big enough to fit the edge of the sleeve above the elbow. Finish the ruffle with a hand-rolled hem.

Gala Short Sleeves: A smart and simple dress-up addition to a dress is a short sleeve made in the crossed puff illustrated. This kind of short sleeve should be applied only to an easy-fitting armhole. If the armhole is too tight, cut it a little deeper and proceed as follows: (1) Remove the old sleeve and measure the armhole of the dress; then measure the number of inches across the shoulder top of your arm—measure down a few inches on each side, using the shoulder seam as a guide. (2) Cut a straight piece of fabric twice the width of the shoulder-top measurement and as long as the number of inches around the armhole, plus 2 inches. Fold the material after it has been cut to size, and cut off the short ends in a slant from about 2 inches at one end to nothing at the other. (3) Make a hand-rolled hem on the longest side of the fabric. Then take running stitches at each end of the material. Gather these ends so that they are no more than the width of the shoulder-top measurement and fasten the stitches. Place one gathered end on top of the other gathered end and baste them together. (4) You are ready to fit the new sleeve. Pin it in place around the armhole, making sure that the gathered sections are at the top. Try on the garment, and if the sleeve fits, sew the seam as for a regular sleeve.

Sleeves Torn at Armholes: Sleeves torn out of the back or front of a dress can be put back in a broad armhole. Select a pattern with a broad armhole, or a different type of armhole, which may mean recutting the shoulder seam. A piecing for a torn-out sleeve, or one too tight across the back, is an underarm treatment shaped to look like a jacket. In these adjustments it is wise to use a contrasting fabric —it can be the same color and different texture, or a contrasting color, or a print.

Outline the proposed alteration on the dress with basting or a row of pins. This will help you decide what kind of replacement will be most becoming. If you are inserting a piece without a pattern, measure carefully and cut a paper guide, allowing for seams. Baste the new fabric in place before you cut away the old material underneath.

Sleeves Torn at Underarm: First find out why the underarm tore. Did the fabric tear or split? Is the dress too tight? Is the sleeve too narrow to permit movement? Mending will not overcome the difficulty unless you remove the cause. If the sleeve is too narrow, set in a strip 2 inches wide along the entire length. Rip the underarm seam of the sleeve and the blouse; lay the folded end of the dress fabric over the edge of this new strip of material. The insert should be tapered off, wide in the middle and

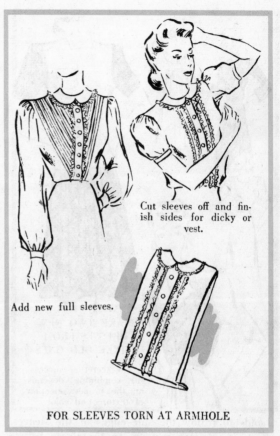

Cut sleeves off and finish sides for dicky or vest.

Add new full sleeves.

FOR SLEEVES TORN AT ARMHOLE

narrow at the ends. When you have no matching material, insert a contrasting band from the neck edge of the shoulder to the end of the sleeve. Open the shoulder seam, slash the sleeve, and set in the new band. This will give you extra inches in the neckline and make the blouse a little longer on each side. The insert must be stitched very evenly so that it looks like a trimming.

Torn Sleeves at Elbow and Underarm: The sleeve can be shortened above the tear and finished with a hem or cuff made from the lower part of the old sleeve. If you want to keep the long sleeve, you can insert a crosswise band to cover the damage. Decide on the width of the band; you may prefer 2 or 3 narrower bands of different colors, and insert it or sew it on top of the sleeve. Use self-fabric, harmonizing texture or contrasting color repeated in the trimming of the dress. Rip the underarm seam of the sleeve, lay it flat, and apply the band or bands. Shape the ends of the

MAKE TWO NEW
DRESSES FROM
THREE OLD ONES

The secret of success-
ful combining depends
on the proper selection
of texture and color.

bands to follow the side edges of the sleeves. Baste it in place and try on the sleeve before you stitch it. If the whole sleeve is shabby, the body of the blouse may make an extra gilet, dicky, or vestee. If you prefer, you can make entirely new sleeves of contrasting or matching material.

Waist Too Tight:
If the waist of a simple dress is too tight, slash the front from neckline to waist, and face the edge back with self-fabric or contrasting material. Extra matching fabric can sometimes be taken from the hem and a false hem added. Dresses with slashed fronts can be used with dickies or gilets, or a smart-looking plastron will completely change the dress.

RECUTTING A GARMENT

Combining Two Garments:
One or more smart new garments can sometimes be made out of several old ones. For instance, a plain woolen dress can be combined with a print, or an old crepe dress with a satin. Two plain fabrics that are opaque and harmonize in tex-

ture can be combined, or velvet or velveteen can be used as a jacket with a wool or crepe dress.

Making Two New Dresses Out of 3 Old Ones:
A home sewer showed me a plaid dress with a badly fitting blouse, worn lower sleeves, and a tight hipline. The skirt was in good condition. She also had an old solid-color dress with worn armholes and sleeves, in which the skirt was too tight and too short. There was also an outgrown wool dress with badly fitting waist.

The solid-color dress was ripped apart and the worn fabric discarded. The good material was pressed flat and measured, and a diagram made of the good pieces. From the skirt a jerkin was cut. Short sleeves were added from the sleeves of the plaid dress. (These plaid sleeves had been ripped apart and the lower part discarded). Smart buttons matching one color of the plaid were added to the jerkin. With the plaid skirt, this made one new dress.

The waist of the wool dress was ripped off the skirt, and a new waist added, made out of the plaid waist. The plaid waist had been ripped and pressed flat, and a new blouse pattern was used.

A major alteration pays only when the fabric is in good condition. First the garment should be cleaned—washed if possible. If it cannot be washed, remove soiled spots as described in Chapter XXXI.

Ripping:
Careful ripping is important. Find a thread in the seam which can be pulled, or clip a thread and pull it out a few stitches at a time until it breaks. Then turn the garment and pull the thread again, and so on until no threads are left in the seams. If you rip with sharp scissors or a razor blade, you may nick the fabric edge. Every piece of the garment must be ripped, and each piece must be pressed. To remove the lines of the old stitching, dampen the edges of the fabric before you press.

Patterns:
Select a pattern to help you in re-cutting all or part of the garment. There are always fashions which adapt themselves to remodeling plans, and frequently you can find one which exactly fits your requirements. Many peo-

ple make a little diagram of the pieces of the garment and put the actual measurements of each piece on the diagram. Such a diagram helps in choosing the pattern, for you can compare the cutting diagrams of the patterns with your diagram of what you have to work with.

Fabrics: In the fashion books illustrating patterns, many garments combine two fabrics. Look for them when you are considering a remake. There may be one which solves your problem. When a little extra fabric is needed, consider new material. Sometimes you will have in the house remnants which match or contrast; sometimes you will have leftover material from some other dress which can be used. If not, consider using another garment and combining the two.

Fabrics which contrast successfully must be considered for texture interest as well as for color and design. In plain fabrics the choice of a contrasting fabric in either a print or contrasting plain color is simple. Don't overlook the possibilities of texture contrasts by using a shiny-surfaced satin with crepe, or velveteen with wool, or a transparent fabric with a cotton print.

Jumper Dresses: Several smart versions of this becoming style are described on page 152. They are easy to make from any kind of dress in which there is enough good fabric. Jumpers can be worn by women and girls of all ages for many different occasions. When made with a long skirt or of a luxurious material, they can be worn with a sheer or metallic blouse, and are suitable for all but the most formal occasions.

How to Cut a Jumper: When the sleeve, underarm, or neck edge of a dress is worn, and the dress is otherwise becoming and in style, cut the armhole in the deep open styling of a jumper. Stand before a mirror and place a row of pins, following the line which seems most becoming. Place another row of pins at the neck edge, outlining a V or an open-front slash. Before you cut, verify these edges. Is the pin line alike on both sides? Is the curve exactly the same on both sides? Are you sure you are not cutting away too much fabric? When all of these questions have been settled, make a basting on the cutting line, placing it far enough outside

Various yoke treatments to rejuvenate old dresses.

the pin line to allow for a seam. Make a row of machine stitching on the cutting line and then cut. The edge can be faced or bound.

Child's Jumper Dress: A heart-shaped jumper dress can be recut for a child of any age from a straight adult skirt. First decide on the finished length of the skirt and add a hem line. This is the length you will use to cut the skirt. Then decide on the width of the skirt. It should be about three times wider than the hip measure. Now cut the skirt according to these measurements. If the dress you are remaking has a gored skirt, use the widest length

JUMPERS RECUT FROM OLD DRESSES

Torn underarm and worn neckline cut away to achieve a drawstring jumper.

Narrow shoulders and outmoded sleeves allow recutting into a fitted jumper style.

Torn underarm.

Child's jumper and diagram for making it.

that approximates these measures and gather in as much fullness as you can. Bind the top of the skirt with a straight band of self-fabric to fit the waist. Cut the dicky according to diagram A. To do this, measure the length for a becoming dicky on the child. Now decide on the number of inches that will be needed for the width of the dicky. Set these measures on the diagram and use them to cut an oblong piece. Fold the piece in half and cut down 2 to 3 inches on the folded edge, shaping it in a curve. When you unfold it, it will be heart-shaped. Bind the edges

and sew it to the waistband of the skirt. Make shoulder straps of self-fabric bands and attach them to the top of the dicky, cross them at the back, and fasten them to the belt.

COTTON GARMENTS

Dresses and Shirts: Good cotton garments with fast color often wear at the underarm and sleeve when the rest of the garment is in good condition. Add a new yoke or sleeve in matching or contrasting colors. If you have a dress which is too tight, insert a band down the front with a tailored finish. If the buttonholes are worn out, cut off this section entirely and put in a new band of fabric and make new buttonholes. If the dress is too short, add a yoke or band to the skirt and use the same fabric to trim the collars and cuffs. When a house dress or a man's shirt cannot be mended and there is enough material, combine the two into something needing little material, such as a slip-on waist, a new apron, or sunsuits and rompers for a child.

Men's and Boys' Shirts: Worn collars should be carefully ripped off and turned over, then sewed back in the original seam. In the case of small-patterned materials or solid colors, new collars and cuffs can be made. Rip the old ones off entirely, press them flat, and use them as patterns for the new ones, which can usually be cut from the tail of the shirt without impairing its usefulness. In a striped shirt it is not possible to do this without destroying the shirt; if new collars and cuffs are added, make them of new material which matches the background color of the shirt. If the shirt is not worth preserving as such, it can be made up into aprons, washable ties, children's smocks, rompers, sunsuits, pajamas, or slips and panties.

Boys' Undershirts: Make an undershirt for the boy of the family from father's old one. You will need a pattern, but you can keep it and enlarge it bit by bit as the child grows. Cut the small shirt from the center of the worn garment where the fabric is still good. Bind the edges with tape, or use a bias binding cut from scraps in your rummage bag.

Look in the Ready-Reference Guide at the back for exact page numbers of Detailed Instructions

RAYON SILK UNDERGARMENTS

Outworn lingerie can often be remade for smaller members of the family. A young girl will gladly remake a fine slip which can be cut down to her size. Let her choose her own pattern and have the fun of making it herself. Silk gowns and slips often have enough good material left to make at least one pair of panties. If the seams are in good condition, use them for the center back and front of the panties. Use an old pair to guide you in cutting them out.

WOOLEN FABRICS

Remaking woolen garments, especially the heavier fabrics used in coats, is an important economy in the family budget. Sweaters and underwear as well as outer clothing can be remade into attractive garments. The first paper pattern, created by Mrs. Butterick in 1862, was a pattern for remaking men's suits into small boys' trousers. Remodeling father's and older brothers' suits is still a useful practice. Although Mrs. Butterick knew nothing about tailored leggings there is no reason why your children shouldn't have fashionable leggings and coat to match, made from a man's tweed suit. Many pattern companies offer patterns to remodel a man's suit into a woman's suit. The skirt is made from the trousers, and the jacket preserves the most important tailoring details of the coat. Ask the salesperson in any pattern department to recommend a suitable one.

Uses for Old Coats: A coat may have fashionable lines even though the fabric is faded. Examine the wrong side. It may be unfaded and the coat can be turned. At least it can be used to make new garments. If you have a skirt which harmonizes with the coat material, make a jacket. Or you may need a coat dress to round out your wardrobe; or a heavy lined skirt, open all the way down the front and fastened with buttons or hooks and eyes to wear with a fur jacket for very cold weather. If the skirt of the old coat is in good condition, cut it off at the waistline, try it on, refit the side seams, and attach belting.

For growing girls, insert waist panels and skirt bands.

Children's suits and pinafores can be recut from old housedresses, aprons and men's shirts.

Tight Shoulders: If the shoulders of an otherwise serviceable coat are too tight, add a yoke of harmonizing fabric to give additional width at the shoulders. Make cuffs to match the yoke. A serviceable type of flat fur is also good for a yoke.

Shortening a Coat Hem: Rip the lining from the facing on the bottom of the coat, then rip both the hem of the lining and the coat hem. Adjust the correct length for the coat, marking it just as you do in a dress. Mark the new place for the facing, then mark the new line for hem and facing by putting pins in the marked line at right angles to it. If you have a lot of material, cut it to 1½ or 2 inches, using a measure. Then shrink out any additional fullness. Pink the raw edges, run a machine stitching close to the edge, and catch-stitch it in place; or bind the hem edge. Finish the lining by pinning it around the bottom of the coat. The hem of the lining should be 1 inch shorter than the coat hem.

Shortening Coat Sleeves: Free the lining from the sleeve fabric and lower the hem. Mark the desired length and check for evenness. Baste the turning, then press it. Trim the hem to 2 inches or less; catch-stitch it in place. Baste the lining to the sleeve about ½ inch to 1 inch from the edge of the sleeve and slip it into place.

Worn Buttonholes: If the buttonholes are worn beyond repair, or if the overlapping edge of the coat is shabby, apply a facing of contrasting fabric or a wide strip of inexpensive flat fur, which can be purchased by the yard. A fur strip should be applied with a felling stitch and can be used all the way down the front. Either use braid loops for the buttons, or take off the buttons and use tailor-bound hooks and eyes, which will not show when the coat is closed. These are large metal fasteners covered with a fine braid which can be purchased at any trimming store.

Worn buttonholes can be rebound with a piece of fabric from the end of the belt or the hem. Undo all the old stitching or binding and proceed as for new buttonholes.

When repair is not possible, you may overcast the opening of the buttonholes so that the garment looks unbroken and put new large buttons—perhaps fur—over each buttonhole. Re-move the buttons from the other side of the coat and replace them with tailor-bound hooks and eyes. Or, if you are not concerned with style, make new buttonholes on the other side and reverse the closing.

Worn Coat Sleeves: A narrow strip of fabric or fur down the entire length of the sleeve and over the shoulder seams to the neckline will disguise a worn spot at the elbow. If a cuff edge or sleeve hem is shabby, it is often possible to rip the edge and bend it back a bit so that no worn edge shows, and slip-stitch it to the lining. When this is not possible, you may be able to salvage material from the skirt hem or pocket to make a false hem or cuff.

Sleeves which are too full can often be taken in at the seams; but if the fullness extends to the shoulder, the sleeve should be taken out and both sleeve and armhole recut. Buy a pattern of the new sleeve you want—but first make sure it can be worked into your coat. If you make a change in the size of the sleeves, it will probably be necessary to use new fabric for this alteration. Either contrasting or harmonizing fabric may be used.

Worn Pocket Edges and Flaps: Take off a worn flap and finish the pocket edges without it, or with a strip of fur placed along the lower edge. If you do this, use fur trimming somewhere else in the garment. If a piece of matching material can be salvaged, the pocket can be rebound.

Collars: Collars can be turned by ripping the seam which holds the collar in place. Reverse the collar, turn it over, and replace it. Baste it before sewing and try it on to see that the collar fits properly around the neck. Or a new collar of contrasting material or fur can be sewn on top of the old one, and in that case the trimming can be extended down the front edge of the coat.

Lengthening a Coat: If it is not possible to let down the hem, a band of fur can be added to the bottom of the coat. Be sure to line this band. A bit of fur should be placed elsewhere on the coat when the band is used—at the edge of the collar, cuffs, buttons, or pockets. If the hem can be let down, rip it out, press the fabric, and mark and turn a new hem like the old one.

Mending Coat Lining: A coat lining usually wears out first under the arms. If you have some scraps of lining material or matching fabric, make underarm shields and put them in. The shields should be inserted so that they extend down into the sleeves as well as under the arm. Match the center seams in the shield and armhole and sew the shield flat to the lining.

The sleeve edge and the neckline are other trouble spots. The best way to mend the sleeve edges is to make a neat patch over the lining. At the neck, where a patch might show, use a harmonizing fabric and make a patch which suggests a yoke.

Worn seams can be covered with harmonizing braid.

Men's and Boys' Clothing: Only minor alterations are possible on men's and boys' clothing. Hems may be lowered to within ¼ inch of their full extent and a small piece of matching lining added to join with the old. Remove the line of the old hem by pressing with a damp cloth and hot iron. A shabby front edge can be concealed by reversing the closing.

Boys' Bathrobes: Bathrobes for boys can be made from worn blankets. Use the child's coat as a guide and follow directions for making a bathrobe in Chapter XXVII.

ALTERING A GARMENT

A knowledge of fitting alterations will come in handy countless times. Some member of your family loses or gains weight, and his clothes have to be altered; or you buy a dress which needs alteration to fit right. The most usual alteration is the hemline, for which you follow the usual directions for lengthening or shortening a hem. Full details on fitting alterations are in Chapter XIV.

Waistline and Hips: When a skirt and waist are too full, take them in at the side seams. Put the dress on with the right side out. Be sure the side seams are adjusted evenly. Pinch the seams in at both sides to gauge the amount you want to take up, beginning at the waistline. Pin this seam from the waist over the hips, taking care not to pull the dress too tightly. After you have pinned it over the hips, look at your

Insert a darned patch for underarm tear.

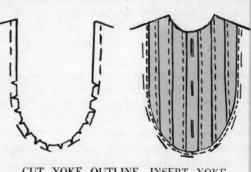

CUT YOKE OUTLINE, INSERT YOKE

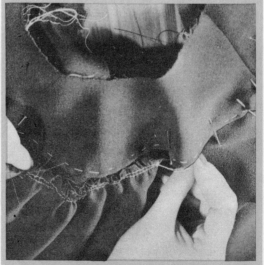

BASTING YOKE INTO DRESS

skirt in a mirror and decide which would look best: (1) to make the skirt narrower all the way down to the hem or to (2) keep the skirt wider at the bottom by tapering the new seam until it comes to a point at or near the lower edge.

Shoulders and Sleeves: First check the shoulder seam. If it seems the right width, check the back, keeping the arms folded to be sure of back action. When a back is too wide, lay a pleat at the neck and stitch it down to a yoke effect, releasing the fullness below the shoulder blades. Check the sleeve. If it is too long, shorten it with the elbow bent. Check the placing of the darts on the sleeve seam. When darts are drawn too low in lengthening a sleeve, an extra dart may be necessary to take care of the elbow activity.

Narrow Shoulders: When sleeves hang over the shoulders, the quickest alteration is a tuck or pleat at the shoulder line. The better alteration is to rip the sleeve out of the armhole and reset it at the right line.

Length of Waist: Sometimes the waist must be shortened. The quick way to do this is to increase the seam at the waistline. Pull up the lower edge of the dress and pin a tuck at the waistline. A better way is to rip the seam and reseam it. When waists are taken up under the arm, the adjustment should be made in a seam that tapers to a point at the armhole so that this is not changed. When the sleeve must be tightened also, taper that seam too so the arm-

hole is not changed. When the armhole must be made smaller, the sleeve must be ripped, the waist fitted, and the sleeve reset.

TAKING OFF AN ALTERED GARMENT

After the alterations have been pinned, take the garment off carefully so that the pins are not lost. Put it on a table and run a basting thread through the seams. Clip the thread from time to time and separate your seam. There should be little particles of thread marking the seam on both sides. Then turn the garment to the wrong side and straighten out the fitting, which means basting the seams straight, ignoring any little irregularities in the pinned line. In necklines, panels, and so forth, fold the garment to make sure both sides are alike. Alterations on the sides need not be made alike, because most figures are not quite the same and the alterations should be different.

Before you stitch the garment, check your alterations. In quick alterations the old stitched seams remain and the new ones are run up beside them; in good alterations the old seams are ripped, the new ones are stitched, and the excess material is cut away.

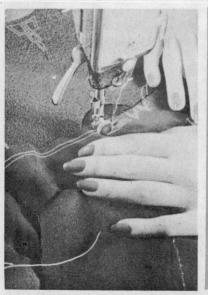

Stitching a joined waistline.

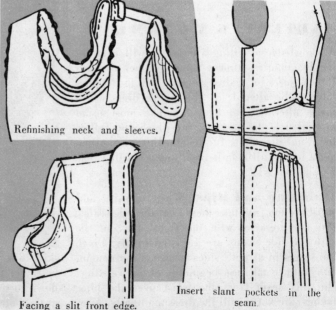

Refinishing neck and sleeves.

Facing a slit front edge.

Insert slant pockets in the seam.

Curtains that no longer fit your new color scheme or windows can be made into a button front jumper. When the center of the cloth becomes worn or if you can't find an attractively flowered border, use an inexpensive table cloth for a summer dirndl.

Make good use of your sewing salvage. The careful placing of large and small scraps makes a gay housedress.

Out of a seersucker twin-bed cover that is no longer in use, you can cut a practical and smart looking house coat.

CHAPTER XXXIV

HOLDING A ROOM TOGETHER

A well-planned room is lovely to enter and livable, because it is held together—made into a unified whole—by the proper use of color in textiles. With a few yards of gay fabrics and a little work, any woman can transform a dreary thrown-together room into a place of cheer and beauty. It is simply a question of planning—not money. When the whole house needs refurnishing, or only one room, or only a few replacements are necessary, it costs nothing to include color and balance in the fabrics you make up.

Good planning does not depend upon the size of the budget. If the budget is ample, a plan can be put into effect immediately; if it is not, the plan can be extended over a period of time, doing a little at a time. This chapter outlines a simple planning program which can be set into the routine for any room in any home. Curtains, hangings, slipcovers, and cushions can be chosen with forethought according to the rules of proportion and harmony. These supplement redecorating and redoing furniture.

Begin by appraising your own problem. This is easier to do just after you have been away for a time. Come into your house and look at it as critically as though you were a stranger. Make a list of everything you would like to change; then make another list of ideas for making the family more comfortable. Review the list carefully, scratching out those items which are obviously beyond reason. The result will be a list of pointed suggestions which describe your need and give you a definite objective.

Make a third list, of the colors which must remain in the room. Note the colors of the wood in the furniture, the upholstery, the rug, the walls, and the woodwork. List all the colors, no matter how many, and whenever possible pin a little swatch to your list which approximates the color. If the rug or upholstery is multicolored, note both the predominating color and the most important contrasting color.

Don't shop for fabrics at once. Do a little window-shopping first. Search for the new ideas in decorating and appraise them in relation to your needs. Put price out of your mind for the minute. When you look at a model room in a store display, note what textile is used and how. Note also how contrasting colors are used. Answer these questions for each display: How often is the print repeated? How often is white or a pale tone introduced? What kind of textile interest or stripe is contrasted to the print? How are trimming touches introduced in slipcovers, bedspreads, curtains, lampshades? What pillow cushions are in the room?

Don't dismiss a model room with the thought, "I can't afford anything like this!" Look at it anyhow and glean ideas from it. Look at the length of the curtains and the fullness in them; look at the type of valance and the curtain headings. There is a great difference in the amount of fullness in curtains you can buy and those you can make at home for the same price. One great decorator advises everyone to buy cheaper fabrics in abundance rather than costly ones.

When you come home list the ideas you gathered together and see how many of them you can use in your room. Perhaps you can rearrange the furniture. You may want to reproportion the windows. You may decide to rearrange the small pieces in new groupings. Forget the things you saw which you can't afford and give your attention both to those which cost nothing and those within your means. At this point your decision should be made about the kind of textile to use in decoration—a print, a geometric design, a stripe, a brocade, a textured fabric, or a crisp cotton.

CHOOSING A PREDOMINATING ROOM COLOR

A successful plan based on the colors already in the room can be developed immediately if you know exactly what you want. If not, develop several plans from which later you can choose the one you like best.

Choose a print, stripe, or textured fabric which is correlated with your rug and upholstery

CARPET COLOR	WALL COLOR	DRAPERY COLOR	DOMINANT UPHOLSTERY COLOR	SECONDARY UPHOLSTERY COLOR
BEIGE TO BROWN	Beige or Ivory	Peach	Brown	Green
	Blue	Rose	Burgundy	Blue
	Green	Gold or Beige	Cedar	Green
	Peach	Green	Cedar	Gold or Beige
	Rose	Turquoise	Burgundy	Beige
BLUE	Beige or Ivory	Rose	Burgundy	Beige
	Blue	Peach	Brown	Beige
	Peach	Beige	Cedar	Blue
	Rose	Blue	Mauve	Beige
	Grey	Rose	Burgundy	Gold or Beige
WINES	Beige or Ivory	Green	Gold	Wine
	Blue	Oyster	Blue	Gold
	Green	Wine	Gold	Green
	Rose	Turquoise	Gold	Beige
	Grey	Rose	Blue	Mauve
GREEN	Beige or Ivory	Green	Cedar	Beige or Gold
	Green	Peach	Cedar	Beige or Gold
	Peach	Beige	Brown	Cedar
	Rose	Green	Mauve	Grey
	Grey	Peach	Green	Gold
PEACH	Beige or Ivory	Green	Brown	Cedar
	Blue	Beige	Cedar	Gold
	Green	Cedar	Green	Beige
	Peach	Beige	Blue	Gold
	Grey	Peach	Green	Brown
ROSE	Beige or Ivory	Mauve	Turquoise	Beige
	Blue	Oyster	Mauve	Blue
	Green	Rose	Mauve	Gold
	Rose	Blue	Burgundy	Oyster
	Grey	Mauve	Turquoise	Oyster
TURQUOISE	Beige or Ivory	Peach	Brown	Beige
	Rose	Beige	Mauve	Blue
	Peach	Turquoise	Cedar	Beige
	Turquoise	Gold	Mauve	Beige
	Grey	Rose	Burgundy	Beige

COLOR CHART
Select the dominant color in your room, check it on the chart for co-ordinating colors.

for each plan. A print or stripe exactly the color of the rug can often be found; sometimes there are several of them from which to choose. Pin a sample of each to a piece of paper and start a color chart. On each color chart pin a plain-textured fabric which matches the color of the predominating design; then to each pin a white

or pale tint matching the background of the prints or stripes.

Next, choose the second most prominent color in each print or stripe and match this in a plain fabric and pin it to the chart. For a large room look for a stripe and a print in the same colorings which can be combined.

Put each chart in a separate pocket of a shoe-bag, and slip into the pockets pictures clipped from magazines in any detail of room decoration or arrangement which interests you. To each pocket add a sample labeled "accent color," a color to be used in the trimmings of curtains, lampshades, slipcovers; and in such accessories as pictures, table mats, pottery for flowers, and ashtrays. If you have no shoebag handy, use en-velopes or paste your samples into a scrapbook.

This kind of color plan helps even for simple rooms—kitchen, children's rooms, playroom, et cetera. This assortment of samples helps you to work out more interesting trimmings and details which give your finished product a more pro-fessional look.

When you have your working color plan com-pleted, the next step is a practical shopping list. Compare prices and replace samples of color fabrics with a fabric within your price range. When you know exactly the type of curtains and slipcovers you want, you can estimate yardages exactly and save money. In deciding on the best styles and types for curtains and slipcovers you must take into consideration the proportions of your room.

Harmonizing Room Proportions:

Good proportions are as important to the success of your plan as good colors. It is wise, then, to analyze the proportions of your room before you decide on the proportions of your draperies and curtains.

Make a list of those things which influence proportion. Begin with the measurements of the room, in feet. Note the ceiling—is it high or low? Set down any irregularities, such as bay window, an alcove, a fireplace. List the doors and draw little plans of the windows without curtains. Make a diagram to show the proportions of the windows in relation to the walls.

Next consider the large pieces of furniture in relation to the room. Can a piano, a bookcase, a secretary, be moved into an alcove? Can the sofa

A great deal can be done with little money, and careful planning. Organdy curtains, striped valances, tie-backs, and a moiré rayon slipcover were made to harmonize with the new color scheme of the room.

and chairs be grouped for conversation or coziness? Can space be made for a game table in a far corner? These are typical questions to apply to a living room, but they illustrate the point of balance between room and furniture, which must be applied to all the rooms in the house. Once you understand defects in the proportions of room and furniture, you can use textiles to disguise them.

Ceilings: The higher the ceiling, the more formal the room; the lower the ceiling, the more cozy and informal the room. High ceilings make

a small room look smaller. To make a high-ceilinged room look less formal, plan tie-back draperies and slipcovers which touch the floor. To make a low-ceilinged room look higher, plan straight-hanging draperies and make slipcovers as short as possible so that the chair legs show.

Windows: Must they be curtained separately or are they so placed that they can be curtained in a group? Think of windows, not as separate items, but in relation to the room as a whole. Remember short tie-back curtains lend a note of informality to the room; long straight ones, amply full, denote comfort and luxury, while tall slender curtains are formal. Many modern rooms use a textile hanging across the whole side of a room. These wall hangings are plain where they cover the side wall and finished with a heading simulating a drapery and valance where they cross the windows. They hang from ceiling to floor. They can be made in plain homespun, textured rayon, chintz, prints, or any fabric which is not transparent. It is an inexpensive way to add new interest to a room.

Long curtains which sweep the floor for 10 or 12 inches add formality to the room. They can be headed with a valance, a valance board, or a French-pleated heading.

When you have considered the relationship between your windows and the room and furniture, you decide upon whether you want long or short, straight or tie-back curtains. Then it is time to decide upon the specific style of your curtains, considering your fabric, the window, and the furnishings.

Room Furnishings: After the window treatment is chosen, consider the other textile furnishings. Slipcovers, bedspreads, dressing-table skirts, and table covers are developed either to repeat the curtain or drapery fabric, or to pick up the contrasting color which breaks the monotony of an all-print room. The style of each furnishing is correlated in type as well as in color. If your room is plain and simple,

In the combination bed-sitting room, candle-wick spreads were combined with a boldly flowered chintz slipcover for an unusual color and textile contrast.

In the lower photograph, crisp embroidered swiss was used for the canopy, curtains, bed and dressing table skirts to create a feminine effect.

confine your desire for frills to such little accessories as lampshades and cushions. In your other room furnishings carry out the tailored or luxury theme. Decide upon the type of slipcovers, curtains, or bedspreads suited to your need—pin a picture of each to the color chart.

Odd Pieces of Furniture: When an odd piece of furniture is out of harmony with the room, consider the following remedies: (1) Can it be cut down? If it is too tall, particularly old tables and chests, it is often possible simply to have it cut down lower. (2) Can it be covered with a slipcover? Old-fashioned wooden chairs can be covered with loose slipcovers and so brought into harmony with any room. Sometimes superfluous fancywork has to be cut off the top of the chair. If the woodwork of the chair is attractive, consider a slipcover which will show it. (3) Can it be painted to match the wall color? This is the remedy for mantelpieces and furniture which cannot be covered. Those the same color as the wall are less conspicuous.

Room Accessories: Like dress accessories, room accessories make or break a well-planned effect. This does not imply that your accessories must be radically changed; but it does often mean eliminating and replacing over a period of time. Note that in store displays the rule seems to be, the more accessories, the higher the cost of the room.

First decide which of the three policies described here are best suited to you. (1) Correlated accessories, each one carrying out an accent color. (2) The little things you love to have around you correlated with the room furnishings. This includes photographs and all types of knicknacks. They can be framed in groups, placed in wall brackets, or made a definite part of the decoration. (3) The trophy type of home, where the color scheme and plan of decoration is built around the trophies. In this case the trophies must be arranged in the room and listed as room furniture when you make your plans for color, type of curtains, and

room furnishings. Children's trophies and fads should be treated this way. If the child collects photographs, put a bulletin board over his desk to save the wall. Put a sectional bookcase in the children's room and let them display their collections proudly.

Accent Color: All trimming details can be developed in accent colors—pipings, edgings on curtains, tie-backs, and so forth. Lampshades and scrap baskets can be correlated with the room by (1) trimming them with bands or bows made from scraps of your material, or (2) by making your lampshades out of your printed fabrics, or (3) covering scrap baskets with leftover pieces, or (4) developing cushions in an accent color.

CO-ORDINATING YOUR COLOR PLAN

You have selected the predominating colors, added contrasting and accent colors, and made notes of the types of curtains and room furnishings best suited to the proportions of your room. You have various assortments of these colors and types collected with your color plan, and now it is time to review them and test them for practicability.

The first step is to lay out the different types so they are grouped together, and all the groups close enough to compare. Imagine yourself living in each of these rooms or color schemes. Which is the kind of background you really like to live in?

When you have finally chosen the scheme you like best, it is time to decide how much you can spend and how you can get the best fabric available for what you can afford. If you go to the store with a definite plan for colors and types, you will not be tempted by a bargain unsuited to your room. You will search out a bargain which suits it ideally, because you know exactly what you want. The time spent in making the plan will repay you many times over when you begin to shop.

Look in the Ready-Reference Guide at the back for exact page numbers of Detailed Instructions

CHAPTER XXXV

FABRICS FOR THE HOME

Home sewers naturally put color and decorative value first in choosing a fabric for the home; but the wise woman expects serviceability as well as beauty in every yard of fabric.

Textile designers supply a group of living-room fabrics, printed, striped, and textured, which permit color harmonies in one room without using too much of any one textile. As you search for ideas, look particularly for textiles which harmonize in a single room and notice how textures of different types complement each other. The correct use of the fabric, as well as the correct use of color, has much to do with the success of your room.

Brocades, bouclés, matelasse, jacquard weaves, chintzes, and satin contribute richness and elegance to rooms in Sheraton, Queen Anne, Hepplewhite, and Chippendale periods.

Modern rooms call for linens, novelty cottons, taffetas, cellophane fabrics, velvet, and such familiar names as scrim, cotton, and unbleached muslin, all too often ignored.

In Early American rooms, homespun effects with self-patterns woven in designs or stripes, combined with quaint patterned chintzes, are very effective.

Fabrics designed for bedrooms feature small prints, ribbon stripes, and designs totally different from those in living-room prints. Both colors and fabrics help to create the kind of bedroom you want. Monastic simplicity carried out in homespun is preferred in many homes. Early American furniture in the bedroom calls for chintz and muslin, and the frilled white curtain is deeply rooted in this tradition. Feminine bedrooms are full of frills made from taffeta or organdy.

Luxurious bedrooms feature satin, chiffon, velvet, and the modern developments in trans-

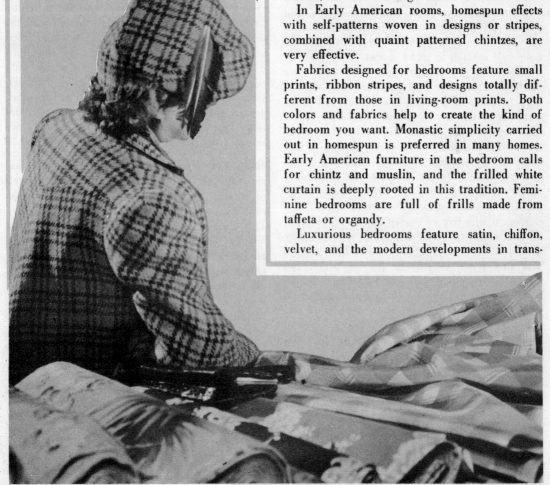

parent rayons, like matelasse or ninon, plain or
banded with ribbon. Modern furniture is ac-
companied by the smooth new rayons with many
colors, or two colors with textured interest, as
well as the plain ninon curtains often used alone.

Gingham, calico, voile, and other novelty cottons are used in the kitchen, nursery, and attic.
Houses built in the Victorian style feature today's
version of the lace curtain. In others the modern
developments of net and lace are made in cotton
and combinations of rayon and cotton. A lasting
luminous effect is gained by using a cotton
warp and a cross thread of rayon in a mesh
curtain.

CONSIDERATIONS IN CHOOSING FABRICS

Serviceability: Curtains and slipcovers can
often be made of the same material, such materials as chintz, cretonne, sateen, velveteen, and
corduroy. When you make this combination, be
sure to pick a fabric which can withstand rubbing well enough to make a seat.

Slipcovers get harder wear and soil more
easily than curtains, and therefore it is well to
keep in mind how much the fabric will show
dirt. Glazed chintz coated with wax, smooth-surface rayons with texture interest, and smooth-
surface fabrics like upholsterers' sateen will not
show soil so quickly. Fabrics with a nap and a
soft weave, such as monk's cloth and homespun,
gather more dust than do drills, denims, mo-
hairs, and other smooth-surface cottons.

Women who live in smoky cities should avoid
the extremes of pale and dark colors; they
should choose clear, intent shades. They should
give preference to smooth fabrics which can
be dusted or wiped and avoid those which demand brushing. They should avoid fringes and
small headings which cannot be dusted.

Budgetary Considerations: If, when
you buy your material, you are cautioned that
the one you selected has to be dry-cleaned, stop
and consider what that will mean to your budget
before you make the final decision. Fortunately
the modern trend in fabrics for the home is
toward washable materials. But ask your questions about washability carefully. A material
colorfast to washing is not always colorfast to
sun. You will find your answer on the label or

the selvage. If the label says "washable," keep
on looking for the comment on sunfastness. Sunfast tests are made for temperate zones. If you
live in the tropics, avoid all colors unless extra
proof of their durability is offered.

When you consider a fabric, decide whether
your household routine and your budget can
take care of it as it should be taken care of. If it
is washable, make sure you have the essentials
for washing it correctly. For instance, some
fabrics have to be stretched every time they are
washed. Have you a stretcher and a place to use
it? Or would you rather substitute a fabric
which can be washed and then ironed? Many
formal overdraperies can be washed; others must
be dry-cleaned. Some can be washed if they
are not lined, but if they are they must be dry-
cleaned.

If your budget forbids the expense of dry
cleaning your draperies, see that the stiffening
or buckram in the valance is as washable as the
draperies; and be sure that any trimming used
on a washable curtain is color-fast and washable.

In analyzing and comparing prices, take into
consideration the fabrics which give extra service, such as a permanent starched finish which
assures that the curtain will always be fresh and
new. Let the developments of modern science
save you work; the additional cost is negligible.

Blended Fabrics: Rayons and wool fabrics are now labeled by law, and the labels tell
of amazing blends. Cotton mixed with rayon,
rayon mixed with wool, rayon mixed with rayon.
The chief reason for these blends is to produce a beautiful style-right effect; the second
reason is to give you that effect at a lower price.
Other ways of producing an effect at low cost
are by using inferior or weaker fibers; by using
less fiber; by using cheap dyes; by stretching
the fabric to give more yardage. Shoppers who
buy what look like bargains without inquiring
for the facts about wearabilty are the ones who
have troubles when their curtains and slipcovers
are washed or cleaned. It is impossible to see
quality in a fabric; you must read the labels on
color and shrinkage.

Coated Fabrics: Many fabrics are finished
with chemicals and coatings which render service—for instance, giving a starchless crispness
to organdy, marquisette, and so on. Because this

chemical penetrates the fibers and is as fast as the dye, it stays through the life of the fabric. Always ask whether the coating on a fabric penetrates, or whether it is just on the surface, as in glazed chintz. The first washing of a glazed chintz removes the coating unless the chintz is labeled washable. When the fabric is finished with a chemical, be sure to keep the label which tells you how to care for it.

Summer Fabrics: For summer months or for life in the tropics, the homemaker should consider linens and cottons for her slipcovers. They look fresh and starched, and they are cool to sit on. Curtains should be functional and shut out the sun. In the tropics, pongee, linen, grass linen, and homespun are used for this purpose. Unbleached muslin can be tailored and arranged to be taken down and sent to the laundry. Transparent fabrics give a cool effect, but they are not actually cool fabrics. Glazed chintzes, cottons, and smooth fabrics are cool when they are selected in cool colors.

Winter Fabrics: Warm fabrics can be elegant or informal. If you change your draperies and slipcovers from summer to winter dress, not only make a change in the color harmony of the room, but also select a fabric which suggests warmth. Napped fabrics, ribbed fabrics, and rough-textured fabrics combine to make a room look warm.

Look in the Ready-Reference Guide at the back for exact page numbers of Detailed Instructions

CHAPTER XXXVI

SLIPCOVERS

Slipcovers were originally designed for protection, but they are now part of the decorating scheme. They can be used to conceal bad proportions and to modernize a piece of furniture. They should contrast with the rug coloring and harmonize with the color of the room. A good plan is to have one or more slipcovers to match the drapes. If the drapes are print, another slipcover should repeat in plain color one of the colors of the print. With white ruffled curtains, striped and flowered slipcovers can be used. In rooms with colorful wallpaper, slipcovers can be striped or made of textured fabrics in solid color.

This chapter gives complete instructions for an easy-to-make slipcover, a professional slipcover with tailored boxing, and an upholstery slipcover which makes the chair look as though it had been upholstered. Covers can be made for any type of chair.

CHOOSING THE FABRIC

Select your fabric not only for its beauty but for its serviceable qualities. Insist upon preshrunk fabrics, and avoid soft weaves which hold dust. The smooth glazed fabrics shed dust and stay clean much longer. In very dusty cities, prints are preferable and strong colors give better wear (see Charts on pages 210 and 211 for wearability of fabrics).

Choose firmly-woven fabrics such as glazed chintz, cretonne, mohair, linen, and the sturdy cotton reps. Plain fabrics cut to best advantage but for allover designs you need allow only ¼ yard more; however in a fabric with motifs or a repeated design which must be centered on the back of the chair and each arm, you will need at least a yard extra for matching the pattern. When your curtains have a large floral figure in the print, consider making the slipcover of plain fabric in one of the colors of the print, then

(Left) Any chair can be slipcovered. The lines of the chair indicate the seam lines of the slipcover.

(Upper left) As you pin the fabric to the shape of the chair clip away the edge leaving ample seams.

This welded type slipcover is the most popular type. The darling of professionals and the aim of all amateurs.

cutting out a floral print design and appliquéing it to the center back of a chair and the cushions of a couch.

The proportions of a slipcover, except for the length of the flounce, are controlled by the measurements of the chair. You are really putting a new skin on the chair. Decide whether you want a loose or a tight fit; decide upon the length, the type of cover, and the trimming details—then see the measurement charts in Chapter XLI for estimating the amount of material you will need.

ORDER OF PROCEDURE

1. Decide on the type of cover you wish to make and list all the style details.
2. Measure the chair and estimate yardage. (See Chapter XLI).
3. Plot your fabric or cut a muslin pattern. Cut fabric or pattern on the chair.
4. Fit the cover to the chair, one piece at a time. Cover back and seat first, then front edge below seat and sides.
5. Pin and fit the long seams.
6. Gather and fit all rounded shaped edges and bands.
7. Set trimmings into seams.
8. Pin all joinings.
9. Prepare the skirt or lower banding.
10. Press the skirt and apply it, or join lower banding.
11. Finish side opening and cover cushions.
12. Press slipcover.

MAKING A SLIPCOVER

Before you cut your fabric, drape it over the chair. Let it lie in front of the chair and pull one end up over the top, across the seat, and down as far as you want the finished cover to go in back. Push the fabric down to the back of the cushion and tuck it into the sides of the chair so you can see the effect. If the design is patterned, center the pattern in both seat cushion and back cover. If it is striped, center the stripe and decide whether you will have the cross sections on the arm running parallel to the back or at right angles.

If the seams are to be welted the fabric must be fitted on the *right side*. If they are double stitched upholstery or plain seams the fabric must be fitted on the *wrong side*.

Drape fabric over back and seat of chair.

Allow generous 3 inch seams to tuck in around chair seat.

Diagram shows the fitting of a chair end.

A curved edge is gathered or darted.

Slipcovers which are frequently removed as you work on the seams, as professionals do, and those made from a tested prefitted pattern, should have the seam lines marked with a colored pencil. Otherwise cut fabric away as you work.

Easy-to-Make Slipcovers: First pin the fabric to the chair around the edges of the back so the pins mark a seam line at the edge, corresponding with the seaming on the chair upholstery. The covering of the back must extend down to the chair seat. Pin it in place. If the cushion is not removable, press the fabric down; if it is removable, take the cushion out. In both cases cut off the fabric at back of the seat. Now cut a piece to fit the seat. Cover the seat of the chair with lining under a removable cushion.

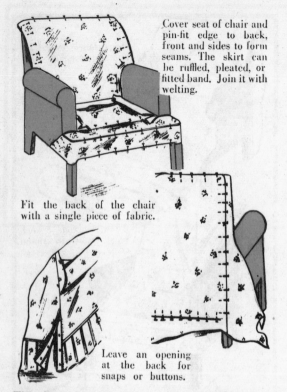

Cover seat of chair and pin-fit edge to back, front and sides to form seams. The skirt can be ruffled, pleated, or fitted band. Join it with welting.

Fit the back of the chair with a single piece of fabric.

Leave an opening at the back for snaps or buttons.

This lining is attached to all the edges which go into the seat. It must be smoothly fitted but not strained. It should be faced across the front edge for 2 or 3 inches of fabric so it does not show when the cushion is in place.

Then analyze the shape of your chair. In some chairs you you can extend a band from the front up the arms, across the arms, up the side of the chair, and across the top. In other chairs the natural seamline is at the far edge of the roll. In these chairs the front is often shaped and must be fitted with a shaped piece. See diagram A and directions and details on page 245. Fit the fabric smoothly over the arms, tucking the ends well down into the sides of the chair. Fit the pieces over the arms and join them to the back section so that you can tuck the fabric well into any section of the chair when the seam is pinned. When the seam falls on a hard surface it must be fitted closely. A curved edge often has to be gathered to fit smoothly.

Consider the best place for the opening—either center back or side back—and decide how you will finish the opening, with snap tape, a zipper, or ties. In bedroom chairs, the slipcover can often be fitted without an opening.

Turn to the rear of the chair. Cut the back section. Pin it in place so that it joins the edge of the front section. Once this seam is pinned, you can cut away the extra fabric on the side of the back section for use in other parts of the chair.

Then fit the fabric across each side of the chair under the arms from the back of the chair to the front. These edges join the back, the end at the roll top of the arms, and the shaped front edge. Often you can cut a strip extending across the front of the chair and across each side, making a boxed effect.

Decide on the length of the skirt, measuring up from the floor and placing a row of pins around the chair. The finished skirt should cover all the upholstery of the chair. Decide on the finished length of the slip cover from the floor and the length of the skirt. Then you are ready to seam your slipcover. Check your seam fitting and prepare to baste seams for stitching or to open them for trimming details such as the welting on page 245. The directions for anchoring a slipcover will be found on page 246. Do not remove the slipcover from the chair until the trimming is inserted and all seams are basted.

Professional Slipcovers: The boxed slipcover with welt seams and a box-pleated skirt is the most popular cover among professional upholsterers.

First he places his fabric on the chair and sets the design, if any, so that the stripe or pattern is centered. Next he decides on the length of the skirt. He begins by shaping the boxing at the front of the chair, pulling the fabric smoothly over the seat, and pinning the apron, or front banding, in place. This work is done on the right side of the fabric, and every seam is folded 3/4 inch so that it can be basted for a welt.

He chalks the line where the seam will be placed, and chalks the outline of the seat and front bands. Then he removes the fabric and places it on the floor. With a yardstick he proves the edges, folding and basting a seam for the welt. He cuts the chair seat, allowing for seams. An allowance must be made at the end of all bands or flaps so they can be given a neat tailored finish when they are joined to the skirt.

Now the upholsterer lays the material he has cut, pinned, and basted on the chair. He meas-

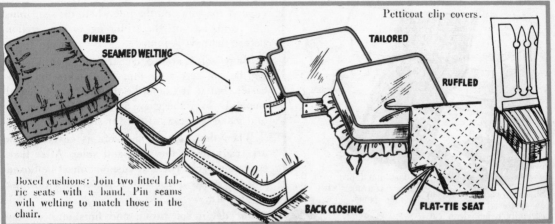

Petticoat clip covers.

PINNED
SEAMED WELTING
TAILORED
RUFFLED
Boxed cushions: Join two fitted fabric seats with a band. Pin seams with welting to match those in the chair.
BACK CLOSING   FLAT-TIE SEAT

ures the inside of the back, from the lowest possible edge where it folds into the chair to the highest point of the back, and chalks the lines. He measures and chalks the width of the back. Then he lays the fabric on the floor again and cuts the back of the chair from his measurements and chalk lines, allowing seams. He turns in the edges and fits the material to the back of the chair, smoothly at all points. Upholsterers always leave generous seam allowances of 3/4 inch.

Next he fits the fabric to the arm of the chair and around the wing section, trimming away the excess material but allowing the material to push into the folds, with 1/4 inch additional for seams. He pulls the fabric around the end of the chair and marks with chalk the edge where he will join the shaped endpiece. Then he pins a piece in place to cover the end and outlines the edge with chalk. This piece is cut, with a duplicate for the other arm, and both are pinned in place; then he trims away the excess material.

He measures, cuts, and pins a small piece for the chair side, and then prepares his skirt, in equal box pleats all around or in spaced pleats. The pleats at the corners require 4 inches. He hems the edge of the skirt and joins it to the band of the cover with a welt seam.

He fits the back in place, leaving an opening to be finished with snap tape; then he removes all parts of the cover from the fabrics and applies the welt to the seams. See page 245. The joining seams that tuck in, however, are not welted; they are stitched. Finally he finishes the box cushion, joining the top and bottom sections with a band and finishing the edges with a welting.

Upholstery Slipcovers: Slipcovers which allow parts of the chair to show should look as much as possible like upholstery. This demands upholsterers' or welt seams and a plain boxed skirt. The boxed skirt can be made with a narrow hem or a fringed edge, or it can be cut long enough to turn over the bottom of the chair. Catch-stitch it in place with a heavy thread in this case, or nail it to the wooden frame of the chair on the underneath side. Slipcovers like this should be fitted just like the upholstery they cover and made with very square corners. The seams should be in the same places as those in the upholstery.

Petticoat Slipcovers: These are for dining-room chairs and wooden armchairs. The seat can be covered with a boxed slipcover. Fit the boxing at the front edge of the chair and fit the seat smoothly. At the back corners cut the fabric around the back of the chair, finishing the corners with snap fasteners or ties.

A petticoat cover can be finished with a ruffle, narrow or wide, pleated or gathered; or it can be finished with a hem, a piping, or a welting; or it can be turned over the bottom of the chair and basted in an upholstered effect. All-wood chairs that have outdated proportions can sometimes be covered loosely so the cover holds good lines. In other chairs the arms and back have to be padded. An unbleached muslin is put over the padding before the slipcover is measured and made.

Look in the Ready-Reference Guide at the back for exact page numbers of Detailed Instructions

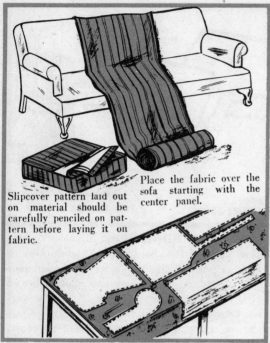

Slipcover pattern laid out on material should be carefully penciled on pattern before laying it on fabric.

Place the fabric over the sofa starting with the center panel.

MAKING A SLIPCOVER PATTERN

Some experts hold that you should always make a pattern of unbleached muslin before you cut a slipcover for a difficult chair. I have made many slipcovers, and I consider a pattern necessary only when you are cutting a very expensive fabric. You then can gain confidence by making a trial cover first, using an inexpensive summer covering.

To make a pattern you follow the directions for either the easy-to-make slipcover or the professional type. When the slipcover is fitted, instead of finishing the seams, mark them carefully with notches and perforations so the pieces can be easily joined. Pencil the seam allowances and press the pattern. Then use it to cut the costly fabric.

SLIPCOVERS FOR SOFAS

The seams of the slipcover will follow the seamlines of the sofa. Work from the top center, covering the top, seat, and band. Then cover the top, seat, and band on each side. When these three sections are fitted into place, join them. The fringe, piping, or welt cord is placed on both edges of the center section, and these are stitched over the side sections. Outline the top edge of the sofa and the line where the seat joins the band, basting the trimming to one section before the next is joined.

Many sofas are so constructed that a band can be run across the top. This makes the work easier, but if it cannot be done, fit the material smoothly over the curve at the top of the sofa and make the seam at the far side of the roll.

When the front of the sofa is covered, you are ready to do the arms and sides. After that, cover the back. The seat cushions must be boxed and the seams finished to correspond with those of the sofa.

For details of fitting and finishing, see the directions for chair slipcovers given earlier in the chapter. You can use either the easy-to-make or the professional routine.

IMPORTANT SLIPCOVER DETAILS

Decide on the details best suited to your type slipcover before you begin to finish it. Allow for seams as you cut the fabric on the chair. For directions for making any seam, see Chapter V. Seams are 1 inch wide until the final fitting, when they are trimmed to $\frac{1}{4}$ of an inch. Professionals prefer a $\frac{3}{4}$ inch finished seam so that the upholsterers' method may be used in applying welting.

Slipcover Seams: The seams in a slipcover can be plain or decorative or both can be used. When both types are used, introduce decorative seams in joinings that show and seam the tucked-in joinings with plain seams.

It is important to decide on the type of seam, as the seam finish dictates whether you fit the chair with the fabric on the right or wrong side.

Right Side Fitting: When you use welted, piped, fringed, or bound seams right-side fitting is necessary.

Wrong Side Fitting: When the seam is finished with an upholsterers' seam or a plain seam, wrong-side fitting is necessary. A slipcover fitted for an upholsterers' seam should be loose enough to allow for the second stitching on the right side. Both these seam treatments are recommended for chintz and other close flowered designs.

FITTING DETAILS

The seams which join the back and arm coverings, and those around the outside edge of the chair, are fitted snugly. The back seams around the cushions are loose. Allow 3 inches on tucked-in seams. Box-spring cushions can be boxed and covered snugly, but down-filled cushions cannot be squeezed. Fit them smoothly and easily. When the slipcover is fitted, check the rounded sections and hold them in with gathers so the seamlines can be joined in a smooth sea. Watch shirred fittings of the arms in front and the rolled sides or the roll in back, or the over-roll of some arms and back constructions in which the plain surface is joined below a deep roll. It is sometimes necessary to introduce darts to fit under heavy overhanging areas.

Shaping Front of Arms: Shaped ends and wings of chairs must be fitted with special attention. To do this place a piece of paper over the shaped edge and outline it with the side edge of a pencil point to get a heavy line. Cut on this pencil line and use it for a pattern in shaping the fabric. Be sure to allow for seams. Baste on the turned edgeline and outline the piece with welting; or, baste the welting to the edge of the fabric while it is on the chair and then add the fitted piece. Be sure the fitted lines fit snugly and are straight and true to the shaping of the chair.

APPLYING WELTING

There are two ways to apply welting successfully: details are illustrated on page 246.

Beginner's Welted Seam: Fit the section of the chair where welted seams will be used. Pin the welting to the seam, taking care to fit the corners accurately. Baste the welting with long stitches. (Do not remove the slipcover from the chair until it is finished.)

Seams are finished with piping, cording, or a fringe. When the front of the slipcover is finished, pin in the cording or piping before you join the seam, taking care to make the corded corners rounded or squared at exactly the same angle. Baste it as you shape it to the chair. Then fit the joining piece over the welting so the cording is sandwiched into the seam. Baste it close to the edge. All bandings should be edged with

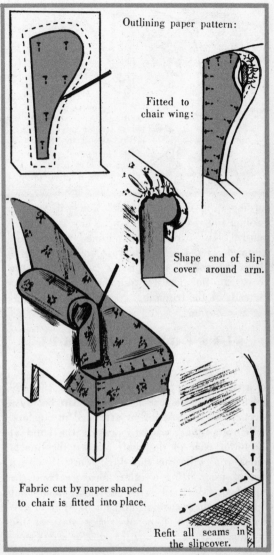

Outlining paper pattern:

Fitted to chair wing:

Shape end of slipcover around arm.

Fabric cut by paper shaped to chair is fitted into place.

Refit all seams in the slipcover.

the piping or cording on both sides before they are attached. When all seams are basted remove the slipcover from the chair and stitch all seams.

Professional's Method: (You remove the slipcover continually). Cut the seams 1½ inches wide where welting is to be used. Fit the slipcover on the right side. When all the seams are fitted, pin them and remove the slipcover. Working on the right side, with the work flat on a table, carefully baste each seam to be corded ½ inch back from the edge. Slip the welting under the seam edge and pin it evenly. Baste the welting close to the edge. You can then choose between stitching the seam on the right side or

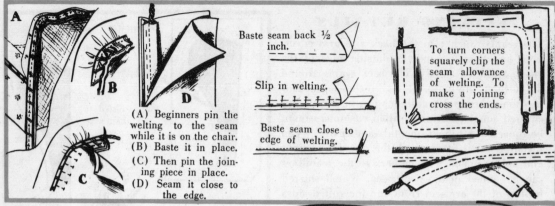

Baste seam back ½ inch.

Slip in welting.

Baste seam close to edge of welting.

To turn corners squarely clip the seam allowance of welting. To make a joining cross the ends.

(A) Beginners pin the welting to the seam while it is on the chair.
(B) Baste it in place.
(C) Then pin the joining piece in place.
(D) Seam it close to the edge.

turning it to the wrong side. You will need a cording foot on your machine. They are not expensive. Be careful that joined seams are trimmed. The straight-line rule holds true here. Often the end of the cord is cut to make the cross seam flat. The drawing shows how to cross the ends of the trimming. Never make this joining at a corner.

SLIPCOVER SKIRTS

Slipcover skirts can be gathered, box-pleated, or a band can be tacked to the bottom like upholstery. If pleats are used, they can be close together, widely spaced, or arranged in clusters.

Before joining a skirt, measure the band at the lower edge of the chair and set the line at which you will join the skirt. Mark it with a row of pins, using a ruler. Measure from the top of the skirt. In some the ruffle shoots out below the chair cushion and no band is in evidence; in others tiers of ruffles start at the cushion.

Full Box-Pleated Skirt: Allow twice the measure of the chair. Hem the lower edge and turn the top in ½ inch. Measure for the pleats, spaced at 2 or 2½ inches. Baste them even, press them, and stitch them down as you stitch the top edge. Baste the welting or trimming to the band at the end of the slipcover, and join the skirt to the lower edge of the band.

Group-Pleated Skirt: Measure around the chair and add to that measure the extra inches needed for the pleats. For example, if you set 6 groups of 5 pleats, multiply the depth of each pleat by total number of pleats and add

Joining a boxpleated skirt.   Joining a gathered skirt.

this amount to the chair measure. Join strips to form this length. Finish top, hem and lay pleats.

Gathered Skirt: Measure the chair and use 1½ times this measure for the gathered flounce. The top of the flounce can be finished over a cord or joined in a welted seam.

Slipcover Closings: Fit the material so carefully that the edges which will be closed are: (1) turned so they meet exactly and (2) finished with a cording or piping or a stitched edge to simulate an upholsterers' seam. Remove the slipcover and lay these edges flat on a table. Baste the narrow snap tape (or zipper) over the unfinished edge of the slipcover and stitch it on both edges with the cording foot. The fabric is turned under and the tape placed over the turned edge. The end of the tape is turned in. Stitch the other edge over the other section of the snap tape.

Anchoring a Slipcover: The lining is stitched to the seam which joins the skirt. Cut the lining the size of the chair with seam allowance and stitch the seams, leaving openings for the legs. Close one edge with snap fasteners or anchor by ties sewed to each corner and tied around the legs of the chair.

CHAPTER XXXVII

BEDSPREADS, COUCH COVERS, AND DRESSING-TABLE SKIRTS

The covering of a bed or couch should harmonize with the furniture and decoration of a room and protect the bedding as well. When twin beds are placed close together, one large cover is often used for both. When they are separated by a small space, the two covers must match; but if they are in different parts of the room, a color or textile contrast can be developed.

Several types of bedspreads are described here so you can choose the one best suited to your room plan and the type of bed. You can also use for beds the suggestions on day beds. Consider the pillows in your choice. Pillows must be comfortable and suited to the individual needs and preferences of each member of the famly. The sketches in this chapter illustrate different types of box pillow arrangements and spread construction that you can make. To estimate yardage for a bedspread or couch cover see Chapter XLI.

CUTTING A BEDSPREAD

Upholstery fabrics are usually 50 inches wide and require no piecing. When narrower fabrics are used, one length is used for the center and the other length split and pieced to each side of the center length. The joining of the pieces is decorated.

Decide whether you want a spread banded around the edge before it turns, banded after it turns, or with a deeper band or ruffle that touches

3. (Left) This room is a study in textile harmony, the coloring of the beds differ yet harmonize with the plaid used on the chair. The same plaid is used for co-ordinating accessories; note lamp-shades, ruffles and tie-backs.
4. (Right) Clear-spaced floral print of curtain and bedspread adds a ruffle of embroidered lawn. It is the color note for a lovely bedroom.

the floor. Decide on the size of the ruffle and band before you start to cut.

Bedspreads are cut as shown in the diagram on page 285. The spread can extend to the top of the mattress at the headboard, or it can be 18 inches longer so that it folds over the pillow, or it can be finished with reversed seams at the end so you can turn it back on top of the pillow. Or you can make a separate straight cover for the pillow.

PLAIN BEDSPREADS

There are four types of plain bedspreads to choose from: (1) an unshaped spread which hangs free on all sides, (2) a spread with boxed seams at the foot, (3) a boxed spread with welt seams, and (4) a spread with decorative bands of contrasting fabric.

Plain Unshaped Bedspread: Unshaped spreads are often made of unbleached muslin, appliquéd, decorated with candlewicking, or finished with a contrasting band of scallops. They can also be made from any cretonne or chintz.

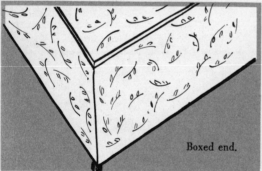

Boxed end.

Plain Bedspread with Boxed End: This spread is boxed only at the foot and can be cut long enough to cover the pillows at the other end. It is particularly suitable for a bed with an open footboard. Turn the spread to the wrong side and join the fabric seams so that the edges of the spread hang straight to the length desired. Box the corner at the footboard. You can also mark the edge line of the mattress if you wish. First stitch a seam along the mattress line, then turn the spread to the right side and stitch the seam again. This seam must be reversed at the top of the spread when it is long enough to turn back and cover the pillows.

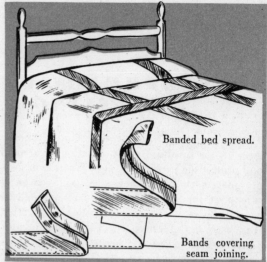

Banded bed spread.

Bands covering seam joining.

Pillow Bolsters: Bolsters are cut in one with the spread or cut separately. They can be finished with a hem, a scalloped facing, a contrasting band, a fringe, or a cording. When the curtains in the bedroom are ruffled or a ruffle is used on the edge of the bedspread, the bolster can be finished with a ruffle.

Plain Spread with Decorative Bands: Sometimes a spread is trimmed with a banding which extends across the pillow bolster and outlines the edge of the mattress. This band can be repeated at the hem of the spread. Bends are pleated, shirred, contrasted, or ruffled. They usually cover a seam joining.

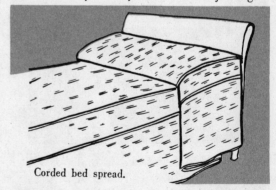

Corded bed spread.

Corded Edges on Bedspreads: The lower edges of the spread can be corded and a double band corded on both sides of the mattress, extending over the pillows. In other corded spreads, the joinings of the seams are finished with a welting.

Corded spreads are made of monk's-cloth, velveteen and other heavy fabrics, and the cording should be heavy. See the Ready Reference Guide for page numbers on directions for covering upholstery cord.

When you join the seams, overlap the seam ¾ inch and pin it smoothly. Make the first basting ½ inch back from the edge and insert the cord in the seam. Then baste the seam close to the cord and stitch it with a cording foot. In heavy material it is wise to rip the basting as you stitch, letting the machine push the material ahead of the foot. This avoids puckering.

To make a rounded corner, tie a pencil to a string so you can draw an edge equal to the side skirt of the spread. Hold the string at the seam and swing the pencil in a true line. Cut your corners on the true curve; turn the edge in and stitch it over a covered cord. This makes a more finished edge than turning the hem over a cord.

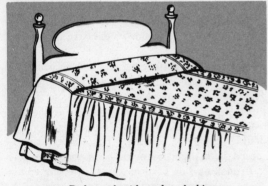

Bedspread with gathered skirt.

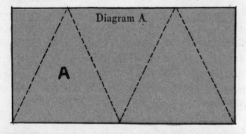

Diagram A

A

BEDSPREADS FOR BEDS WITH FOOTBOARDS

Bedspread with Gathered or Pleated Skirt: Cut a panel for the center of the spread. It should be 90 inches long and wide enough to cover the mattress, including the side bands. Cut these bands and join them to the center strip with piping or welt seams. Mark

off 18 inches at one end for the turn-in at the foot of the bed. Finish these edges with a hem.

Cut the skirt section 26 inches deep, or the size desired. It can be pleated or gathered. Finish the skirt edge in a hem, gather or pleat it, and join it to the side of the spread. The bolster is finished with corresponding bands. The ends can be hemmed or ruffled to match the edge of the spread.

Circular ruffle.

Godet flounce spread.

Tiered ruffle.

Godet Flounce Spread: Cut the spread large enough to cover the top of the mattress. Shape one end so that it tucks in at the footboard. Fit the sides of the spread in a straight boxed line. Divide the side length into even spaces and cut a slash in each space. Insert a godet—a triangular piece of self-fabric—into each slash. Diagram A shows the most economical way to cut a godet. These spreads are finished with a very narrow hem.

Circular Flounce Spreads: This spread requires a great deal of yardage and so is very expensive. To cut a circular flounce, fold the material so that the lengthwise grain parallels the crosswise grain. Put a pin in one corner. Tie a pencil to a string, hold the string at the corner, and draw the circular cutting lines for the flounce across the wider width of the fabric. The radius of the curve depends upon the depth of your ruffle. Hem the edge or bind it with ribbon. Join the circular flounces in seams that are hemstitched when the fabric is transparent. In satin or velvet make welted seams. The edges of the spread are finished with piping or ribbon, and placed above the top edge of the flounce. When elaborate spreads like this are used, the pillows are rolled and covered with a plain fabric.

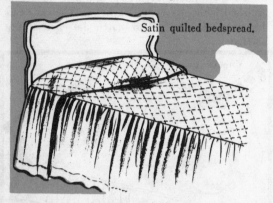

Satin quilted bedspread.

Satin Quilted Bedspreads:

These are often cut in a size to fit the mattress and finished with a circular or gathered self-fabric ruffle which is not quilted, or a transparent rayon.

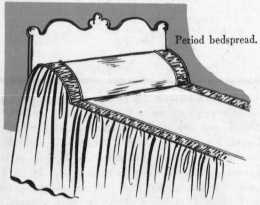

Period bedspread.

Spreads for Period Beds:

When a spread is made of velvet, velveteen, or a rich brocade for a period bed, the fabric covering the mattress is cut long enough to extend over the pillows and be tucked down. In spreads of this type the corded seam outlines the mattress and the pillows, and the gathered skirt is cut long enough at the pillow end so that it can follow the curved line and keep an even line at the floor.

Scalloped Bedspread:

When combinations of chintz and taffeta, or candlewicking and chintz, are used in a bedspread, the gathered or pleated flounce should be mounted on a separate

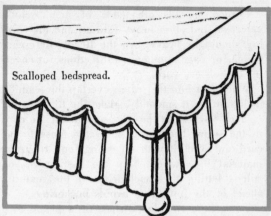

Scalloped bedspread.

lining placed over the bed spring. Then you can make a tailored bedspread with scalloped or fringed edges which extends over the ruffle and looks as though it is joined. This is very practical when one fabric is washable and the other is not. Candlewick spreads can be used with a chintz or organdy ruffle if the spreads are tucked in around the mattress and the ruffle falls below and in back of the wooden sideboard of the bed.

Organdy Bedspreads:

Use embroidered organdy, eyelet, embroidery, or plain organdy. They can have one ruffle, two ruffles, or a ruffle finished with a ruffle. The covering for the mattress can be outlined with ribbon beading or a double organdy ruching. The ruffles can be joined in a piped seam or a gathered heading.

In making this kind of spread, remember that every additional ruffle means extra ironing. Be sure the organdy has a washable finish which requires no starch. You can cover the mattress with the organdy and stitch a ruffle into the seam joining; you can place a double ruffle over the seam joining; or you can use a ribbon beading in the seam joining. (To do this see Ready Reference Guide for page number of detailed instructions.)

A double ruffle is easy to make. Have your fabric hemstitched and run a machine stitching through the center. Cut the edges in a picot. Turn the lower edge of the flounce to the right side and apply the double ruffle on the turned edge, stitching it through the center. The ruffles for the spread over the mattress are done the same way. Fit a plain boxed muslin cover in white or colored sateen over the bed to form a background for all transparent spreads.

Gathered lace skirt over a sateen lining adds a luxurious note to a dressing table.

Spreads for Double Post Beds: Double post beds are often covered with candlewick or quilting. The underflounce and canopies are made of fine muslin or organdy, but some people like linen, silk, or any fabric suitable for a spread. The most popular canopies are gathered on both edges and joined to a ruffle with a heading. The canopy ruffle is usually half the width of the skirt ruffle. Join it just as you would the ruffle of a spread.

DRESSING TABLES

A dressing table can be simple or elaborate, large or small. Decide where you have space in your room for it and plan accordingly. It can be set into a corner, or it can be a table. Dressing tables made of unpainted wood, with drawer space and a bar on either side which opens, are sold in the stores. Sometimes you can use a kitchen table and nail a ruler the length of the table to the top of the center drawer to hold the skirt. A small table or a sewing machine can be transformed into a dressing table, and some women make a frame from old packing boxes. To be really comfortable and serviceable, a dressing table should have drawers or shelves and a washable top, either a sheet of glass, an old mirror, or oilcloth in a delicate color or print.

Dressing-table skirts are usually gathered, but you can make them in ruffled or pleated effects, as tailored or as feminine as you wish. There is no rule to control the dressing table—no matter how tailored the room as a whole, a feminine dressing table is in order. Because the skirt must be removed and washed, it is often applied with snapper tape nailed to the edge of the table.

When you space the material for the skirt, split it so that the section which covers the drawer is made separately. When it is attached, it looks like part of the skirt. When the drawer is pulled out, that section of the skirt comes with it.

Dressing-table skirts can be made of taffeta, organdy, net, chintz, satin, or any sheer cotton fabric used in the decoration of the room. Mount one on a stiffened band or make the heading or shirring with ruffles of very narrow edgings, so that the powder won't accumulate in the edge. For this reason a smooth edge is preferable.

Joining banded skirt to dressing table

Shelves built into corner

Gathered skirt set on a band

Tiered dressing table skirt

Making a Dressing-Table Skirt: First estimate the yardage, measuring from the floor and allowing for a hem. Measure the outside of your table and allow twice this width for making a gathered skirt. For the foundation of tiered skirts, fit the fabric smoothly to the table.

When the hem is finished, gather the skirt or ruffle. Finish it with a 1-inch binding, which can be a contrasting color. When you attach the skirt to the table with thumbtacks, this banding is pulled down over the tacks. You can put a large or small bow in the center of the binding. If the skirt has tiered ruffles, each ruffle can be bound and tied with a bow, or each succeeding ruffle can be attached underneath the previous one.

You can finish the edge of the skirt with a binding and match it in the turned-down binding at the top. You can appliqué little bows to the fabric of the skirt to match this color.

Many dressing-table skirts are finished at the top with a scalloped band. Others are finished with shirred bands emphasized by applied trimming. When your dressing table needs a stiff heading under a shirred band, cut a strip of buckram the desired width and length, and cover it with fabric. Stitch this band to the inside edge of the skirt under the shirring.

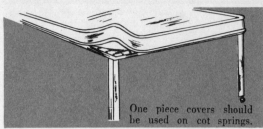

One piece covers should be used on cot springs.

DAY-BED AND COUCH COVERS

One-Piece Covers: Any day-bed, couch, or cot without arms and back can be suitably decorated with a one-piece cover.

Informal Couch Covers: Take a piece of material long enough to cover the couch and touch the floor at both ends. This material should be placed on the couch so that the material not only touches the floor at the ends, but also at the front. If it is not wide enough to extend fully across the couch to the back, seam another piece of cloth to it. If the fabric has a pattern be sure to match the design at the joining. The corners are curved by cutting off the pointed ends which touch the floor. Make a narrow hem on all the edges. This casual cover can hang free on all

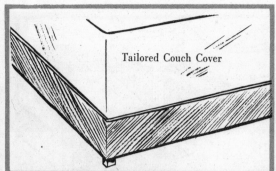

Tailored Couch Cover

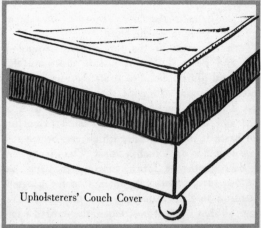

Upholsterers' Couch Cover

sides; but if the day-couch is placed against the wall, the cover will stay neater if it is tucked under the mattress on the wall side.

Tailored Couch Cover: There are two ways of cutting a tailored couch cover: (1) One piece of fabric is cut to fit the top exactly, and a long contrasting band is cut to extend all around the couch on the sides. (2) Two full lengths of fabric can be cut and joined together and fitted at the corners.

For the first type, lay the fabric that fits the top in place, right side down. Begin at one corner and pin the long band of fabric around this top section—it, too, must face away from you. At the corner pin a seam through the band, then continue to pin the strip along the long edge of the couch cover, and so on all around the cover. If you pin carefully and are an expert stitcher, you can stitch these seams without basting. Turn the cover to the right side and stitch the seam close to the seamed edge, making an upholsterers' seam. Then hem the lower edge, and your couch cover is completed.

For type 2, lay the fabric on the couch, wrong side out, and fit all four corners so the cover is smooth but not too tight. To do this, hold the corner points out and pin a seam line straight down the fabric, close to the couch. Stitch these seam lines and hem the cover. You will have a smooth unseamed edge except at the corners.

Upholsterers' Couch Cover: These covers are boxed and tailored, and the seams are finished with a cording or piping. Cut your fabric as directed for type 1 of Tailored Couch Covers above. Before joining the seam, outline the top piece of fabric with a cording by turning the edge over a thick cord and basting it. Be sure the corners are sharp. Lay this piece wrong side out on the top of the couch and pin a long strip of fabric to the corded seam, so that when the seam is stitched the cord will extend around the edge.

Piping is applied the same way, basting it all around the edge of the large center piece so that the seam edge of the piping matches the edge of the cover. Piping is basted to the right side of the fabric. Be sure to turn the corners sharply.

Turn the piece to the wrong side, lay it in place on the top of the couch, and pin the band in place. When the seam is stitched the piping will outline the edge. The lower edge can be hemmed, it can be corded, or the piping color can be continued around the lower edge, or a contrasting band can be stitched to the edge in a faced hem.

Couch cover with pleated edge

Couch Cover with Pleated Edge: This couch cover is cut in three pieces. (1) Cut a large piece of fabric the size of the top of the couch. (2) Cut a band, 1 inch wider than the depth of the mattress and long enough to go all the way around the couch. (3) Cut the pleated extension. It should be wide enough to reach from the band to the floor, allowing for a hem, and twice as long as the band.

Turn the edge of the top section around a cord and baste it. Put it upside down on the couch and pin the band to it all the way around. Stitch this seam—the cord will finish the seamline. Turn the lower edge of the band over a cord and baste it. Hem the pleated extension and baste it in box pleats, which can be spaced close together or 4 inches apart. The pleats can be deep, with the fabric meeting in back, or shallow, turned under 3/4 inch. Join the pleated extension to the corded edge of the band in a seam, so that when it is stitched, the corded edge heads the pleats. Sometimes a cording is run down each corner.

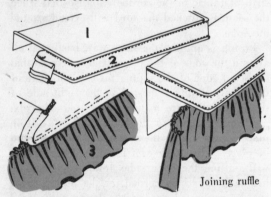

Joining ruffle

Ruffled Couch Cover: A ruffled couch cover is cut in three pieces. (1) Cut a piece large enough to fit the top of the couch. (2) Cut a band as wide as the depth of the mattress or more, and long enough to go around the couch. (3) Cut a ruffle 2½ times as long as the band and as wide as you desire.

Decide upon the finish. You can hem the ruffle and stitch the other seams; you can bind the ruffle and pipe the seams, using a color contrast; you can face the ruffle with a contrasting band and make the top of the couch cover in the same contrasting color.

Put the top piece right side down on the couch. Pin the band in place all around it—first basting the piping if it is used. Stitch the band to the top piece. Finish the lower edge of the ruffle with hem or binding and gather the ruffle at the top edge. Seam the ruffle to the lower edge of the band, spacing the gathers carefully. If the cover is finished with piping, it must be basted to the edge of the band before the ruffle is joined.

Box spring

Two-Piece Couch Covers: This type of cover can be used only on day-beds or couches with box springs.

Upholstered Box Springs: Cut the band which covers the side of the spring 5 inches wider than the width of the spring and long enough to go around all four sides. (Piecings must not be made at the corners.) Turn the springs on end and apply this band with catch stitches on both edges so that it is smooth and secure. If you wish, the edges of the springs can be traced with a cording applied where the band passes over both edges. The cover for the mattress can be made in two ways: Either cut the cover long enough to tuck in at top and bottom —a long tuck so it will not pull out—or fit the cover as directed for Upholstered Mattress Cover and finish the edge to hang over the covered spring. This second method is used when ball fringe and braiding are introduced.

BOXED PILLOWS AND COVERINGS

A boxed pillow covering is sometimes used in a man's room to tuck the pillows into during the day. Boxed pillows are a "must" when you arrange a day-bed or a studio couch.

The Pillow: Cut out two pieces of unbleached muslin of the size of the pillow. Join the two pieces with a 3- or 4-inch band stitched to the edges. Turn this lining to the wrong side and stuff it. When feathers or down are transferred from one pillow to another, overcast the closure and cover with piped or corded seams.

CHAPTER XXXVIII

CURTAIN RODS TO SUIT THE CURTAINS

The use of curtain poles is an important part of the decorator's art. The correct use of curtain poles may make the difference between a well curtained house and one in which the curtains look cheap. Correct curtain poles need not entail expense. In fact, studying the type of window treatment in relation to the curtain pole, and so deciding on the type of window to make, often makes it possible to save money. In this chapter are certain types of curtains which look as though an expensive fixture was used; but close examination will show that the hanging on a costly fixture and the hanging on a simple curtain rod entail a different treatment in the making of the curtain. In other words, you can follow the orthodox method, or you can create the same effect more cheaply. To help you we have arranged pages of detailed illustrations with captions, each explaining the use of the curtain poles. Before making use of this information, you should understand something about the curtain poles which are offered in the stores.

Inexpensive Extension Rods: These rods are sometimes flat, sometimes round, and they are designed to hold light-weight curtains which are not stretched beyond the measure on the inside of the window jamb.

Extension Rods: Many extension rods are especially designed to hold light-weight draperies joined to the outside edge of the window frame. Be sure never to over extend a rod so that it is weak and sags in the center.

Rods Cut to Measure: Both round and flat rods can be cut to the exact measure of your

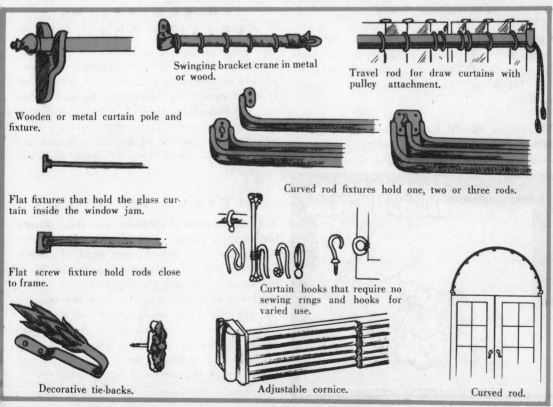

Swinging bracket crane in metal or wood.

Travel rod for draw curtains with pulley attachment.

Wooden or metal curtain pole and fixture.

Flat fixtures that hold the glass curtain inside the window jam.

Curved rod fixtures hold one, two or three rods.

Flat screw fixture hold rods close to frame.

Curtain hooks that require no sewing rings and hooks for varied use.

Decorative tie-backs.

Adjustable cornice.

Curved rod.

windows. It will repay you to buy a sturdy rod. They are not expensive.

Side Brackets: Side brackets are designed to hold one rod or a group of rods. Some of them are screwed inside the window frame, others flat on the outside of the window frame. The side brackets designed to hold a curtain away from the window frame are an important addition to effective window trimming. In the stores you will find them shaped to carry one curtain rod. Two or three curtain rods can be joined so they are hung one behind another, all held in the same bracket.

Costly Rods: Much beautiful art work has been developed in straight rods and in swinging cranes. They are made particularly for curtains without valances and add an important touch to the final decoration of the room. Sometimes these rods are made of wood and are placed on brackets that permit the pole to extend beyond the bracket. This type is particularly good for portières and formal cascade draperies, or those hung on rings. The end of the pole is often finished with an elaborate decoration.

Curved Rods: These rods are especially designed to put over windows in place of a high formal valance. They are particularly good to add height to French doors and casement windows.

Traveler Rods Equipped with Pulleys: Rods equipped with pulleys so that a curtain or drapery may be opened and closed

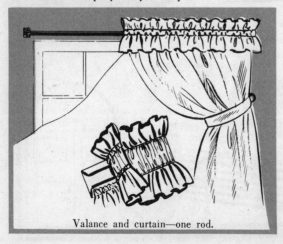
Valance and curtain—one rod.

are made in many types. In the less costly versions, rings finished with an eye to which the curtain can be hooked, are easy to use. Other rods are so elaborate that the rings do not show, but are covered by decoration.

Cornices: Wooden cornices are often used to cover the tops of curtains or to add height to a short window. They can be treated to match the woodwork of the room.

Tie-Backs: Tie-backs made of metal, composition, or glass are offered in the stores in lovely designs. These can be used to hold back simple or elaborate draperies, or you can buy a small hook and ring to join a fabric tie-back.

Rings & Hooks: Your stores also offer upholsterer's pins which can be hooked into a curtain and need no sewing. They also offer hooks and rings which can be sewed to your curtain. Once you know the style of the curtain and the type of pole suited to your need, you will be ready to choose the best type of ring or pin.

CO-ORDINATING CURTAINS AND RODS

The finish at the top of the curtain should be one suitable for the curtain-rod arrangement you plan to use. Below is a check list of the popular types of curtain, explaining the finish required for each rod arrangement. It tells you just what you need for one rod, two rods, or three rods, and explains the use of a valance board and other fixtures which help to make draperies successful.

RUFFLED TIE-BACKS

Valance and Curtain — One Rod: Gather the top edge of the curtain without turning and seam it to a ¾-inch band of curtain material. Make the valance twice the length of the curtain rod and the depth desired. Finish the lower edge with a narrow hem and turn the heading; stitch the heading hem and gather it. Make another row of gathers 1½ inches below. Place this valance over the band at the top of the curtain so that the heading can be stitched to the top of the band and the gathered row of the valance to the lower edge of the band.

**Valance and Crossed Curtains —
Two Rods:** Place one curtain over the other, laying them out carefully on the floor. Turn the top edge of both curtains in a casing extending across both curtains and double in the center. Stitch the casing and hang the curtains on the under-rod. Cut the valance in the desired width, allowing for a heading and a casing. Finish the valance and hang it on the top rod. This makes a permanent cross-line when the curtains are hung.

**Valance and Crossed Curtains —
Three Rods:** In this case the top of each curtain is finished with a separate casing, and the valance with a heading and casing. The valance hangs on the top rod, and one curtain on each of the other two rods. The cross-line of the curtains can be adjusted at the window after the curtains are hung.

Crossed Curtains with a Valance Board: The valance is cut double and finished with a ruffle. Then it is carefully fitted around the valance board and held in place with thumbtacks. The curtains can be hung on one or two rods placed close below the valance board.

PINCH-PLEAT CURTAINS

One Rod: Directions for turning a valance and making French pleats are given on page 268. They can be finished and hung in any of the following ways: Add an applied casing to the back of the curtain to slip over the rod. Finish the curtains with valance pins, which hook over the rod and pin to the curtain. Finish the curtains with rings and make draw curtains, as follows:

Draw Curtains—One Rod: You will need a round rod and small round rings. Sew a ring to the back of each pleat. Secure a cord four times the width of the window, and fixtures which hold the pole to the window frame with a pulley attachment. Slip the cord through the pulley at A, then through the rings, knotting it to the left ring at the center, as at B, and on through the remaining rings at the left. Bring

*Look in the Ready-Reference Guide at the back
for exact page numbers of Detailed Instructions*

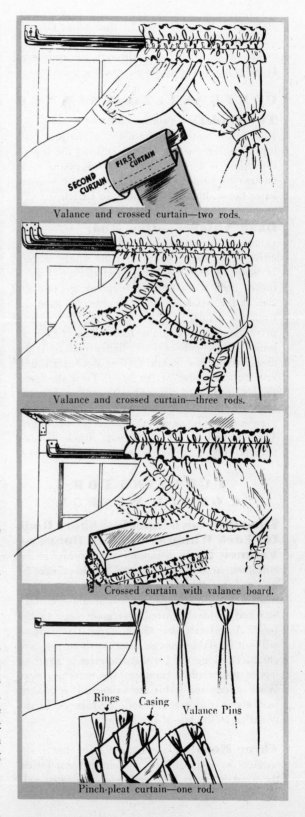

Valance and crossed curtain—two rods.

Valance and crossed curtain—three rods.

Crossed curtain with valance board.

Rings   Casing   Valance Pins

Pinch-pleat curtain—one rod.

it through the pulley at C, then back through the rings, knotting it to the right ring at the center, as at D. Bring it through the pulley at E and put weights at the ends of the cord.

CONTRASTING VALANCE

Two Rods: The valance can be cut 10 inches wide and hemmed, or shaped in a shallow scallop. Turn the top edge so the ruffle at the top of the casing is 3 inches deep and the casing wide enough to go over one rod. Make the valance twice the width of the window in length.

Band Valance—One Rod: A plain valance with contrasting bands gives the tailored effect of a valance board, but the whole curtain is hung on one rod. The band can be 4 or 6 inches deep when finished, depending upon the size of the window. Cut it double. Prepare the trimming bands of the contrasting fabric and press them into straight folds. The curtain is joined to the end of the valance and must be measured in this length. Gather the curtain and sew it to one edge of the band. Turn the band double and hem the opposite edge over the seam. Measure down 2 inches from top edge and place a trimming band, stitching it at both edges. The top casing is for the rod. Stitch another trimming band at the lower edge of the valance.

CURTAINS FOR A GROUP WINDOW

Long Rod for Draperies; Short Rods for Each Window; Valance Board or Valance Rod: Windows in a group can be curtained as one, and spaced windows can be grouped together and curtained as one. Each window should have a rod for a glass curtain attached inside the window frame close to the pane. A rod extended clear across the window will not be stable enough, because these rods are small. The long rod for the draperies is attached ouside the window frame at the extreme edge. When a long rod holds the valance, it is placed just above the drapery rod. A valance board is nailed to the top of the frame.

Three Rods: Place the rods for the glass curtains at each window, attaching them inside the window frame. The gathered or pleated val-

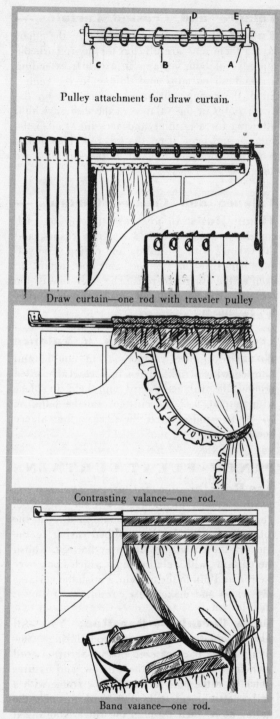

Pulley attachment for draw curtain.

Draw curtain—one rod with traveler pulley

Contrasting valance—one rod.

Band valance—one rod.

ance can extend over the top of the draperies, or the top of the draperies can be finished like the valance and the valance hung on the rod between the draperies.

Place valance board above all windows in the group. Place rod that carries over curtain below valance board. Glass curtains are hung at each window, showing wall space between windows. When 2 or more curtains are used, one must be placed forward of the other so they can all hang freely.

The rods carrying overdraperies and valances are placed at outside of bay windows. To get the effect of one curtain over the entire window space the glass curtain poles are placed end to end even if they must extend beyond window edge.

FORMAL VALANCE

Valance Board and Two Rods: Adjust the valance board on top of the window or nail a board to the front of the window frame. Adjust the rod for the glass curtains inside the window frame as close to the glass as possible; adjust the rod for the drapery on the outside of the window frame as close to the end as possible— or, if you want to make the window look wider, extend it out over the wall. The glass curtains and draperies are finished with casings. The valance is interlined with buckram. Cut a paper pattern of the valance first, and pin it above the curtains so you can decide the right shape and width for the valance. Then cut the duplicate of the pattern in buckram, and the lining, interlining, and valance fabric.

Glass curtain rod hung close to window pane and long rod extending over all windows carries both overdrapery and valance on one rod.

SWINGING CRANES

Doors or windows which swing out can use this Italian type of window treatment particularly well, but it can be used at any window. The cranes can be very simple or very decorative indeed. A swinging bracket is never combined with a valance, but a panel is often used over the window to add height and dignity. The best curtain for this arrangement is a straight floor-length drape with the fullness laid in pleats. Finish the top with pinch or box pleats and put a drapery pin behind each pleat. You can also make a casing and run the swinging crane right through it. See illustration on page 260.

A heavy and transparent fabric can be hung side by side on one rod at the far end of the window. The heavier fabric can be repeated at the outside of the window bay.

Formal valance and drapery.

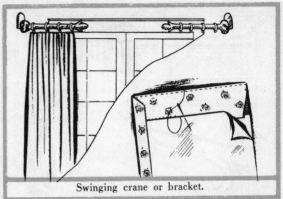

Swinging crane or bracket.

POLE COVERED *with* CORNICE

A drapery extends over the side wall and covers the edges of the glass curtain. The pole can end at the window or extend to an equal distance on the other side.

WINDOW PROPORTIONS
CURTAINS FOR UNUSUAL WINDOWS

The windows of your room can be made to look wider, higher, or narrower, depending on the draperies you plan and the placement of the fixtures to hold them.

The first rule is to hang the rod as high and as wide as the window frame permits. A window can be made to look wider by extending the rod beyond the window frame so the over-drapery extends over the wall and covers only the frame of the window. Use a fixture on the framework that permits the pole to extend out on the wall, or have a board nailed to the wall on each side of the window and set the fixtures for the pole at the end of the wood. From 4 to 8 inches can be added in this way. Swinging fixtures can be hung outside the window frame, and so not shut out the light. Higher windows can be treated in the same way. Have a side

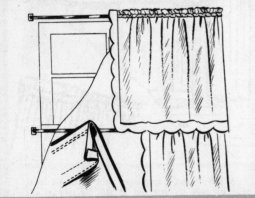

Dutch curtains are hung on separate rods, placed on the window joint of both top and bottom casements.

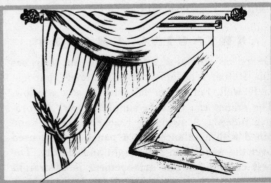

The beauty of soft satin is dramatized on a valance and drapery cut in one piece.

Look in the Ready-Reference Guide at the back for exact page numbers of Detailed Instructions

board and a valance board nailed above the window frame and paint it like the woodwork, or nail a strip of molding where you want the curtain pole and attach the fixture for the pole to the molding. The higher pole adjustments are often wide as well as high and this is a good way to cover the fact that windows are uneven. Ignore the top of the windows and set the curtain poles even, then make the curtains to cover the defect.

Group Windows: When two windows can be treated together, it makes a picture in the room. Make a little diagram of the side of the wall, then cover it with tracing paper and sketch some different types to see which one you like. Windows treated as a group often need the glass curtains hung close so they show a sweeping line instead of a separated one. They can then be framed with the overdrapery at each end, or set in between.

Sometimes a piece of furniture can be placed in the center of the window and covered with a new slipcover that helps the effect. Again, in a small piece of furniture, a mirror or a picture can be moved. Don't forget the possibility of flower boxes or a flower shelf under the window.

In bay, and set-in windows, the window can be brought into the room by extending the treatment across the whole extent. Often the window can be framed as if it were a cut-out. To do this, have a board nailed to the wall and shape valances over buckram to fit the opening.

Narrow Windows: Arrange the curtain poles so they extend beyond the windows and are attached to the wall, making the window look any width you want. Don't use a bracket which turns; use a pole which rests on a bracket attached to the window frame. The inside edge of the drapery which is to extend over the wall must cover the side hem of the glass curtain. In some windows a pole is hung over the wall and does not extend across the window. With this arrangement the whole side wall of the room and both sides of the window can be covered, and the curtains can be floor-length. Glass curtains cover the window, and flower boxes can be put in front of them and hanging flower pots arranged against them.

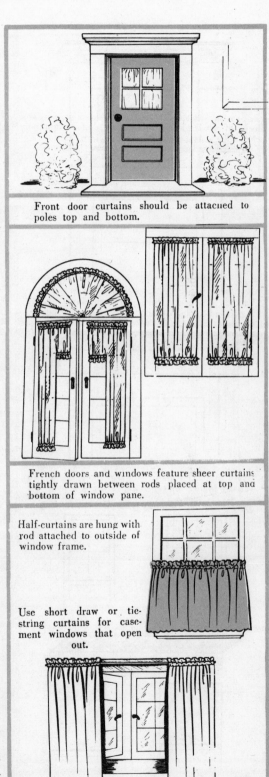

Front door curtains should be attached to poles top and bottom.

French doors and windows feature sheer curtains tightly drawn between rods placed at top and bottom of window pane.

Half-curtains are hung with rod attached to outside of window frame.

Use short draw or tie-string curtains for casement windows that open out.

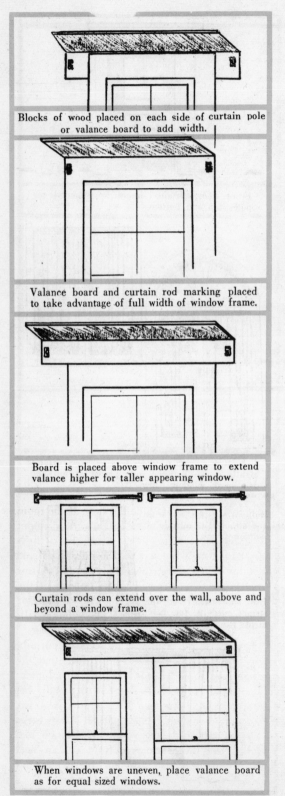

Blocks of wood placed on each side of curtain pole or valance board to add width.

Valance board and curtain rod marking placed to take advantage of full width of window frame.

Board is placed above window frame to extend valance higher for taller appearing window.

Curtain rods can extend over the wall, above and beyond a window frame.

When windows are uneven, place valance board as for equal sized windows.

Short Windows: Place a valance rod above the window frame so that it extends over the wall. Make the curtains long and put a flower box or shelf under the window.

Small Windows: For very small windows, keep the curtains on the outside of the windows, against the wall. Whenever possible, group two windows as one, with a mirror between them. Sometimes a false window is made around a mirror in order to balance a room.

Bay Windows: Outline the window with a floor-length drapery placed on the outside of the bay. Use a gathered or pleated valance. Fit each window in the bay with a glass curtain hung on a rod inside the window frame. If there is a window seat, cover it with a matching or harmonizing fabric. If the outlining drapery is not used, the glass curtains can be hung on the outside of the window frame and feature a gathered heading, French-pleated heading, or a valance. The curtains should be long and touch one another to give a graceful effect.

Swinging Windows: When the window is hinged in the center so that the top swings in and the bottom out, the curtain must be stretched between two rods, one on the top sash and the other on the bottom.

Front Doors: The window in any door should be paneled with lace or finished with a net curtain stretched between two rods placed at each end of the panel. It is a mistake to hang a loosely gathered curtain at a door. If you want to make the door opaque, use semi-transparent rayon stretched between the two rods.

Vestibules: The outside door of the vestbule in a formal city house is not curtained. The front door and any side windows should be curtained alike. In suburban houses with many windows in the vestibule, they can all be curtained like the door or a novelty fabric can be used, depending upon the type of house.

Sun Porches: The windows of a sun porch may be left uncurtained, or uniform glass curtains used. Sometimes draw curtains are arranged to be pulled over the windows when desired. These curtains are usually floor-length and present a formal and colorful note.

CHAPTER XXXIX

HOW TO MAKE CURTAINS

The amount of yardage in the curtains can make all the difference, decorators say, between a really lovely room and a drab, undistinguished one. For this reason it is better to use cheaper fabrics lavishly than expensive ones sparingly. If you make curtains at home, for the same cost you can expect (1) better material, (2) more fullness, and (3) longer wear than in those you buy. When you go to buy fabrics for curtains, look in the dress-fabric department as well as for drapery textiles. Very often you can find a dress fabric which costs less than the drapery fabric and gives the same effect.

Before you make your curtains, you will, of course, have considered carefully the type of window (Chapter XXXVIII), the matter of draperies and valances, and the outlook from the window. If you have a lovely view, you will want to give freedom to the windows which overlook it with transparent tie-backs or draw curtains, or side curtains which fall away from the window. If the outlook is poor, use glass curtains and side draperies that hide the view. If the room needs cheer and sunlight use bright yellow ninon.

Curtains hung close to the glass are ½ inch shorter than the window sill. Those hung outside the window frame can be of any length. A few summer curtains, attached to the outside of the window frame, end in a line with a radiator cover or at the lower end of the window sill. Tie-back curtains must allow for the draping.

The size of the window, the style of curtain, and the width of fabric vary so much that the method used by professionals should be adopted. They decide on the style and test all details before estimating yardage. See Chapter XLI for full instructions on measurements. Most large windows need two full widths of 50-inch material. When the fabric is narrow, full or half lengths must be joined, and don't forget to count this as extra yardage.

The lace glass curtains are finished with a French pleated heading to match those on the side drapery and hung on several poles placed end to end so there is no separation in the sweep of the curtain. Here, the windows join but the same treatment is possible in group windows if mirrors are placed between the windows.

CUTTING CURTAINS

Work on the floor to have space for laying out the work. It is not necessary to spread papers over the floor; vacuum-clean the rug or wipe a wooden floor with a damp rag before you begin. A rug holds transparent fabrics in line so it is easier to cut straight edges and join true seams.

Cutting Straight Edges: Tear curtain fabrics whenever possible. If the fabric does not tear, draw a thread and cut on the thread line. If this is not possible, draw a chalkline on a smooth fabric with a yardstick. Use a yardstick when measuring for length, and a tape measure when working on details. Watch the grains of the fabric in all the cutting, folding, and stitching so the curtain will hang straight.

Remove All Selvages: Very often the selvage is woven more tightly than the rest of the fabric. This will not show up in the new fabric as much as it will after the curtain is washed. It is safer to remove all selvages, because if you don't you may find yourself with a baggy curtain which cannot be ironed smooth.

Press Hem Edges: The side hems are turned first. The hem edge is 1 or 2 inches finished. You can save time in making it by putting an ironing board on the floor and pressing in both the first ¼-inch turn and the second 1-inch turn; then you can pin the hem from the outside edge and stitch it without basting. If the curtain has a ruffle, hem only the wall edge.

Top Curtain Finish or Hem: The top hem is basted so that you can hang the curtain to test its length, width, and the way it drapes. When you have decided upon the correct length, join the ruffle, allowing ½ inch for seams. This hanging test is important in all tie-backs, because a tie-back curtain or drape must be longer than the window length. It is important in straight curtains, too, when the window is uneven, because all straight-hanging hem lines must follow the edge of the woodwork.

The finish at the top of the curtain is a matter of style. If you make a casing, the hem is turned deep enough to let the curtain pole pass easily. If you have a casing with heading, turn the hem deep enough for both casing and heading and stitch it twice, once at the edge and once to mark the top edge of the casing. This leaves a ruffle of double fabric, called a heading, above the casing. It is narrow on glass and kitchen curtains, although wider for others. When the top of the curtain is pleated, the top hem is 3 inches deep or more, depending upon the style and spacing of the pleats. In transparent fabrics all hems are cut double, no matter whether the finish has a casing, heading, or pleats.

Shrinkage Tuck: An allowance for shrinking should be considered in the top of any curtain. In addition to the heading and casing, make a small shrinkage tuck which hangs behind the heading and so does not show. The allowance for shrinking differs with the fabric, but the usual tuck is 2 inches, which permits a 4-inch addition to the length of the curtain in case of need. When a ruffled curtain is turned, set your mark for the heading and casing; but before you turn it, make the shrinkage tuck, which extends the full width of the curtain and should be basted to the outside edge of the ruffle. When the tuck has been basted, turn the edge for the casing and stitch it just above the basted seam. Then stitch the heading casing seams.

Seaming Long Joinings: Smooth the fabric carefully and insert pins without slipping your finger under the fabric. Baste the seam with the fabric still on the floor; pick it up only when you take it to the machine to stitch. Long seams in curtains are joined with an upholsterers' or a flat felled seam.

Pressing Curtains: Many women press curtains on the floor before hanging them. Some lay a blanket on the floor under the curtain, and others use a small ironing board, moving it from spot to spot as needed. This method is used for the final touching up of ruffles, which muss if you iron them on a standing board in the usual way.

RUFFLED WHITE TIE-BACK CURTAINS

America's favorite curtain is the ruffled white tie-back. When they are used for luxury living rooms, they are very ruffled indeed and sweep the floor. They often have a ruffle on all edges

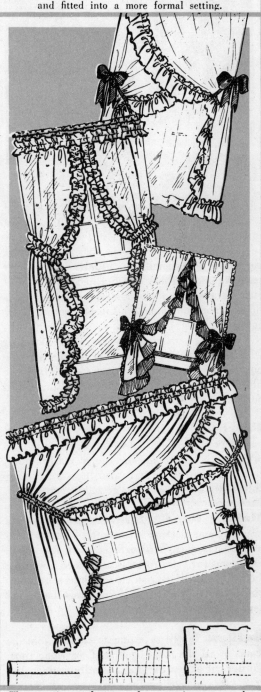

Ruffled curtains can be simple adding only a fresh note of crispness, or they can be frilled and crossed and fitted into a more formal setting.

The turn-in at the top of a curtain governs the formality of the heading. On glass curtains a small heading is usual. In bedrooms the heading is 2 to 3 inches. In living rooms the heading is still wider.

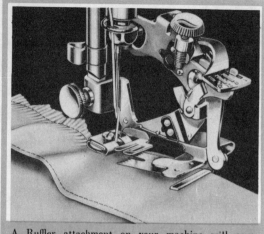

A Ruffler attachment on your machine will save you much time.

and seams and double ruffles in the draped heading. In other living rooms they are crossed, sometimes floor-length but usually short. Some have valances, some are finished with double ruffles across the top, some are headed with a double hem, and some are finished with a heading and casing.

Ruffled tie-back curtains are used alone or with print or checked window shades. In the city a glass curtain is often necessary. Hang the glass curtain close to the window and the ruffled curtain on the outside of the window frame.

Fabrics: The fabrics for ruffled curtains can have a permanent starchless finish. Ask for it in organdy or paper muslin for a really grand ruffled curtain. Ask for it also in lawn, dimity, dotted swiss, dotted scrim, net, and marquisette.

Making the Curtain: Spread the fabric smoothly and measure it carefully. First straighten the edge, then measure and mark the edges. The seams for extra fullness are joined first, then the side hems. If you stitch without basting, use pins lavishly. It will help if you press the turned hem on all the edges.

Ruffles: It will save time to cut and join the seams in all the ruffle lengths at the same time. Fabrics cut across the grain usually require 1¾ or 2 yards of ruffling for each yard of curtain length. For bias ruffles you need only 1½ yards of ruffling for each yard of curtain.

The ruffles should be from 3 to 5 inches wide.

In many fabrics you can tear instead of cutting straight-grain ruffles. Test your fabric to make sure it will tear. Limp fabrics such as marquisette, ninon, and voile should be torn crosswise of the goods, never cut bias. Crisp fabrics like lawn, organdy, and taffeta tear lengthwise, but the ruffles show to better advantage if they are cut on the bias. Use a small French seam for joining the pieces of a straight ruffle. Bias ruffles must be seamed crosswise and the seam pressed flat. Snip off the end of the seam if you hem the ruffle by machine so the machine hemmer will work smoothly and not stop at the bulk of the seam.

Before you gather the ruffle, decide upon the type of joining to the curtain. You can use a heading, overcasting, or a flat fell, or a French fold or an upholsterer's seam. Use the gathering attachment of the machine and set your work in the machine so that the gathers come as close as possible to the edge. If you find that this gathered edge is too short when you come to join it, clip the machine stitching every few inches and stretch out the fabric. Ruffles can be gathered by hand. If you do this, make three rows of gathers and mark them so the spacing is even. Professionals use 3 needles and gather one section at a time.

Joining Ruffle to Curtain: Work on the floor. Lay the edge of the curtain flat and smooth. Lay the ruffle along the edge and full it around the corners. Pin the edges together and baste them.

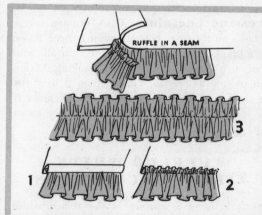

Join the ruffles with (1) a French fold; (2) a small heading or (3) stitch a Double Ruffle to the edge.

French Fold: This joining is used for ruffles when no stitching is to show. Work so the seam is on the wrong side of curtain and ruffle. Place the gathered edge a little back of the curtain edge. Pin and baste the seam, then stitch it. Turn the long edge over the gathered edge and stitch again.

Turning Corners: When you apply a ruffle to a curve or corner, allow twice the length of the curve to make the ruffle lie flat and show equal fullness.

Ruffles Set into Curtains: These ruffles can be seamed in the joining or gathered with a turned edge and applied to the curtain near a marked line.

Double-Ruffle Edge: Cut your ruffle twice the width desired and finish both edges. The center can be finished with machine gathers and the joining stitched through these gathers. To do this, turn the curtain edge up ½ inch on the right side and baste the ruffle over this turn. The ruffle can be gathered by hand if preferred.

Tiered Ruffles: When ruffles are applied in tiers, mark the line where each ruffle is to come. Use pins, a basting thread, a creased line, or a tracing wheel. The ruffle which goes on the edge is joined with a French fold seam. The applied ruffles are basted along each straight line, with the ruffle placed above the line so that when it is basted and stitched it will fall over and conceal the seam.

Small Heading: Turn the top edge of the ruffle over 1 inch before gathering, and gather it ½ to ¾ inch from the edge. Turn the edge of the curtain over ¼ inch on the right side and cover it with the ruffle edge.

Top Finish: A hem at the top, a casing, or a casing and heading finish—whatever the finish, it is stitched when the curtain is finished and extends all the way across the ruffled edge so that the curtain rod will slide the full width from end to end of the curtain.

Ruffled Valance: In informal windows the valance can be from 5 to 10 inches wide, and the ruffle can be placed on the edge or tiered ruffles arranged. Try out the ruffles for the valance to determine (1) the length of the valance, (2) the width of the ruffle, and (3) the spacing of the ruffles. Cut the valance in the length and width desired, allowing for a heading and a casing. Add one or two ruffles to the edge. This valance is set on a separate pole or incorporated in the curtain and extends across the top of the window. When a valance is tacked to a board, cut it double and add a gathered ruffle which should duplicate the type used on the curtain in depth, in fullness, in finish, in type of joining and in heading.

Ruffled Tie-Backs: Tie-backs are an important part of ruffled curtains. They are made of the curtain material and can be developed in many interesting ways. The length depends upon

Tiered ruffles can be joined with a stitching under the ruffle or with a stitching across the gathers on the right side.

Ruffled tie-backs should reflect the ruffle treatment of the curtain. Single Ruffle (1); Double Ruffle (2); All-around Ruffle (3); Triangular Ruffle tie-back (4).

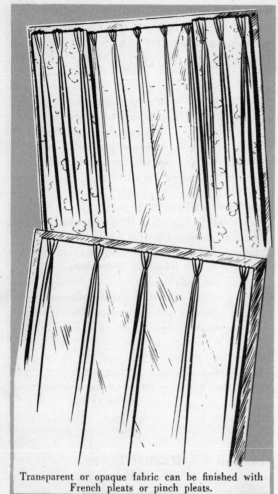

Transparent or opaque fabric can be finished with French pleats or pinch pleats.

PLEAT   PLEAT   PLEAT
1.   2.
3.   4.   5.

French pleat details showing (1) How pleats are marked (2) How pleats are laid and stitched (3) How pleats are folded and caught into three little pleats (4) Side view showing stitching line to hold pleats secure (5) Finished Pleats.

the amount of fullness to be held in. Usually tie-backs are from 14 to 18 inches or longer. The ends are finished with rings or loops which are caught on a hook screwed into the window frame. Most ruffled tie-backs are made on a double band of self-fabric 1 to 2 inches wide. The ruffle should match the ruffle on the curtain in width, finish, and fullness. Attach the ruffle to one or both edges of the tie-backs, or two or more ruffles can be attached to one edge.

Triangle Tie-Backs: Cut a piece of buckram like the arrow in diagram on page 247. It should be 7½ inches across the widest part and about 9 inches long. Try it on the window for size—you may want to make it a little larger or smaller. Cover the buckram with the fabric and attach it to a band of self-fabric 2 inches wide and 9 inches long. Cover the triangle with rows of ruffles and join the tie-back to the window by placing a ring at the point and at the end of the band.

FRENCH-PLEATED CURTAINS

Transparent Rayon Curtains: First decide whether you will finish your curtains with rings, upholstery pins, or an added casing. You will need two lengths of 50-inch transparent material for the average window. If the window is

A simple curtain finished with a French pleated heading and banded in contrasting color.

small, use the dress-weight ninons 40 inches wide. The beauty of these curtains is their simplicity. Cut off the selvage and turn the side hems of the curtains so that they are finished with double hems 1 inch wide. These hems should extend the full length into the tucked section at the top of the curtain.

Stiffening the Hem: Transparent curtains need a stiffening 3 or more inches wide in the heading, of firm crinoline or a light-weight buckram. In measuring the turning necessary for the heading, first decide on the depth of the pleat, then turn the top edge in 2 inches more than this measure. Allow a double turn so the buckram will not show through.

In measuring the length of the buckram, measure in 2 inches from the edge, because top stiffening should not extend into the outside hem of the French-pleated curtain.

Now use the chart which you made when you took your measurements. You can turn the heading at the top of the curtain. First baste the edge of the fabric to the buckram. Turn it twice and stitch the hem or baste it. In some curtains the pleats hold the hem and no hemline shows.

French Pleats: Lay box pleats across the top of your curtain and make a stitched line the length of the pleat on the grain of the fabric. Press the fabric in this pleat into three small folds and stitch across the end of the pleats. With a matching thread make a few stitches across the base of the pleats to hold them on the right side of the material. Work over and over stitches as these hold the pleats.

Finish the back of the curtain with an applied casing basted across the back of the pleats. The casing must be joined securely by hand so that the stitches do not show through on the right side. Or, instead of a casing, use an upholstery pin which is slipped into each group of pleats. The pins hook into the curtain rod. When these curtains are made into draw curtains (see page 257), sew a ring behind each pleat.

Heavier Fabrics: These heavier curtains are used alone, or with Venetian blinds, or with glass curtains in homes, offices, meeting halls, and play rooms. You can make them of any opaque curtain fabric—cretonne, chintz, monk's

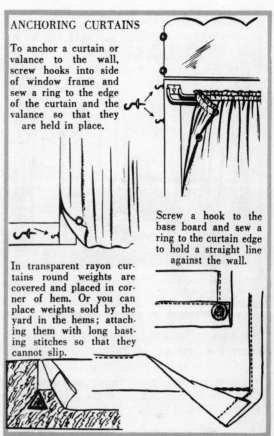

ANCHORING CURTAINS

To anchor a curtain or valance to the wall, screw hooks into side of window frame and sew a ring to the edge of the curtain and the valance so that they are held in place.

Screw a hook to the base board and sew a ring to the curtain edge to hold a straight line against the wall.

In transparent rayon curtains round weights are covered and placed in corner of hem. Or you can place weights sold by the yard in the hems; attaching them with long basting stitches so that they cannot slip.

cloth, linen, or any of the fabrics used for "summer drapes." They can be tied back or straight and should be abundantly full. The top of the curtain is finished with a stiff French-pleated heading which gives the curtain a professional look. Like the transparent curtains, they can be hung on a rod with a casing, on rings, or on upholstery pins. When a curtain is made for a set space, there should be no fullness between the pleats; for a draw curtain the pleats are spaced wider apart to permit fullness between them.

Fabrics which will stand alone, such as glazed chintz or linen, can be pleated without a buckram or crinoline interlining; other fabrics require the stiffening. If you are making washable curtains, remember that buckram and crinoline lose their stiffening with washing, unless you use a kind especially made to be washed. For washable curtains you can also use a washable stiffening with slits cut as eyelets for the curtain pole. This relieves you of the labor of setting in rings.

Estimate your curtain width and the spacing of the pleats and cut the curtain, allowing a

The Venetian blinds are complimented by a frame of chintz finished with a heading. To hang both curtain and valance on one pole see sketch on page 256.

turn-down to form the pleated section 2 inches longer than the pleats. Divide the pleats and mark them as shown in the illustrations on page 268, creasing the fabric firmly at each mark. Pin the box pleats and stitch the length. Divide the box pleat and crease it with your fingers, then stitch across.

When you use a patent washable pleater, buy it wide enough so that the eyelets for the rod can be placed exactly on the pole line of the curtain. Then turn the top of the curtain in and stitch the fabric at both edges of the stiffened band. Make another row of stitching on each side of the eyelets to hold the fabric firm. Next make a row of stitching between the eyelets where the pleat creases. Run the pole through the eyelets and press the pleats into shape. You can group them in clusters of three, held by a small stitch; you can space them evenly in close clusters or space them widely. Hang the pole before you finish the lower edge of the curtain.

EASY VALANCES

Pleated and ruffled valances can be added to casual unlined draperies or used as a heading for ruffled or glass curtains. Cut this kind of valance 14 to 16 inches wide and at least twice the length of the window, measuring around the pole at each end. If you want it really full, add still another length.

Gathered Valance: Turn a 6-inch hem at the top and seam it twice for the casing and the heading. Stitch these lines and hem the lower edge. A flat curtain pole is run through the casing, and you can space the gathers on the pole. This type of valance is sometimes run on the same pole with the side curtains to fill in the space between the draperies. Again, it extends over the top of the draperies in addition to crossing the window. This requires a separate pole for the valance.

Pleated Valance: Turn a 4-inch hem and line it with crinoline or buckram, depending upon the weight of the material. Stitch the hem and finish the edge of the valance as directed for French pleats earlier in this chapter.

GLASS CURTAINS

Curtains hung close to the glass on a rod attached inside the window frame are called glass curtains. They are made of net, marquisette, scrim, or sheer rayon; and they can be used alone or combined with a formal or informal drapery. They are usually neutral in color and hang straight from a casing. They are sill-length and have soft, full gathers, which should never be skimpy. Most glass curtains are finished with a narrow hem.

All glass curtains which can be seen from the street should be uniform. Inside there can be plenty of variation.

Allow twice the width of the window to a pair of curtains. Cut these curtains carefully,

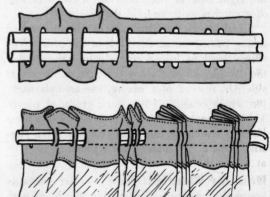

Washable buckram banding with eyelets help you form French pleats without measuring. No rings are needed as the curtain pole is slipped through the eyelets.

spreading them on the floor so they are smooth and the edges straight and true. Turn the top edge in a casing; if you like, make a narrow heading above the casing. Put in a shrinkage tuck. Hang the curtains and measure the hem. When the hem is turned over a second rod at the bottom of the window, the hem must be stretched and pinned to the rod. When your window frames are true and straight you can do this with measurements; if they are crooked or the pole sags, each curtain must be individually fitted.

KITCHEN CURTAINS

A cheerful breakfast nook is an American tradition, and the theme of the breakfast-nook windows should be carried into the kitchen. In older houses, the kitchen-living-room can be modernized or developed traditionally. In other houses the kitchen is simply the kitchen, and the curtains are correlated to the decorative scheme of the room.

Kitchen curtains must be washed frequently, and so they are made of marquisette, scrim, dotted swiss, gingham, chambray, or muslin. They can be gaily colored, white trimmed with color, or all white.

The traditional white tie-backs are standard in kitchen-living-rooms; second choice is a straight-hanging white curtain, simple and plain.

The curtains in dinette windows can hang straight and be finished with a drawstring, or they can be ruffled and tied back. They are usually edged with fringe or trimming stitched all around or at the front, and hemmed.

In other homes the kitchen has a valance and side drapes as well as glass curtains. Oilcloth can be wiped off and kept always clean. Use it for both valance and side curtains, and lay fullness in the side curtains.

When the kitchen curtains are edged with a banding, you can insert bands or face the curtain with a band. These bandings are often scalloped at either the lower edge of the curtain or the top of the hem. They can be banded and scalloped all around or only at the lower edge. They can hang straight or be tied back. The valance is run across a pole on a casing, and it can be cut to allow a small heading.

Glass curtains must be stretched tightly between top and bottom rod. Notice difference between right hand curtain which is hooked and left hand which has yet to be hooked to bottom rod.

A loosely stretched curtain can be tied in the center or it can be separated and tied at each side of the window.

For casement windows that open into the room fasten a rod on each side of the window on the wall so that curtain can be hung beyond the window frame.

To make a curtain with a ruffled edge, stitch the heading and casing seam across the end of the ruffle which edges the curtain.

Double Dutch Curtains: This treatment is attractive for some kitchens which have only one window and is illustrated on page 260. The curtains are finished with a casing and a short heading. They can be banded, bound, or scalloped. A rod is placed at the top of each half of the window sash. Use small glass curtain rods and screw them to the sash frame so they go up and down with the window.

CHAPTER XL

HOW TO MAKE FORMAL DRAPERIES

The modern trend, even in formal rooms, is toward simplicity—in choice of textiles, number of curtains to each window, and construction of the curtains. In selecting window treatments, consider the window as a whole. The style of the overdrapery, its relation to the room, the lines of the window, the color of the walls, and the glass curtains—all these make up the whole.

When you use glass curtains, the textures of the overdrapery fabric and the curtains must be harmonious as well as the color. Make them of net, scrim, lace, or ninon. Some curtains are made of cotton, others of lustrous blends of cotton and rayon. They are always transparent and delicate in color. In dark rooms, yellow can be used to give warmth only when it harmonizes with the window treatment as a whole. Except in very formal treatments, glass curtains are not used with Venetian blinds. The overdrapery should cover the ends of the blinds.

SWEEPING OVERDRAPERIES

Satin, velvet, taffeta, or transparent rayon can be used for a beautiful drapery and valance hung over a pole fastened to the window. Use a fabric 50 inches wide for wide windows, 40 inches for narrower ones. You will need twice the finished length, plus 18 inches. Mark the center of the fabric with a long line of basting and drop the fabric over the pole from the back, draping the center and ends of the valance and drapery in folds. Hold the folds in place with pins. This drapery can be basted or pinned in place. When the valance is securely held, adjust the tie-backs at the sides.

For an added note of luxury, the edges can be faced with a contrasting textile in self-color, and the hem can sweep the floor for 10 or 12 inches.

In draping a curtain, fold it back in pleats so the lower part of the outside edge cascades to the floor. The length of the tie-back and the position of the hooks screwed to the window frame govern this proportion. In formal draperies

Sweeping draperies with a cascade valance can be made at home. The background color of the chintz draperies matches the wall and the color of the tulip design is repeated in the cascade valance.

which slant abruptly, a low-placed short tie-back adds to the formality. In informal rooms, the tie-back is placed higher and the drapery allowed to hang more freely. Test out the sweep of the drapery with your tie-back before you finish the hem.

UNLINED DRAPERY

The easy-to-make unlined drapery can be elegant as well as informal, especially if you add the extra fullness which spells the difference between skimpiness and luxury. Full draperies need not be costly, for you can use joined lengths of plain or print fabrics, or make a striped effect by joining harmonizing tones of sateen in 4-inch stripes. Measure and cut the drapery. See Chapter XLI.

MACHINE-LINED DRAPERIES

Linings were originally used to shut out peeping glances, but today their use is to add body and draping qualities to the fabric. The richness of high-ceilinged rooms with formal windows requires draperies with both lining and interlining.

Many lined overdraperies hang straight and are finished with a formal pleated heading. Others are used for valanced windows.

Lining Fabrics: For most draperies use sateen or muslin in a warm rose tan. Remember the lining must be sunfast. Use white if the background of a printed drapery fabric is tinted. Velvet curtains are lined with satin, and some of the French brochés are lined with taffeta. Taffeta is lined with a contrasting taffeta or with mull.

Making a Lined Drapery: Place the drapery on the floor, right side up. Place the lining on the drapery, right side down (see diagram). The lining must be 3 inches shorter than the hem at the lower edge of the drapery, 5 or more inches shorter than the hem at the top, and 4 inches narrower than the width of the drapery. First arrange the lining along one side of the drapery so that the edges of lining and drapery exactly meet. Pin this edge in place with pins running across the selvage edge. Then move the lining so the opposite edge exactly matches the edge of the drapery fabric and pin these edges together. Stitch the edges on the machine and turn lining and drapery so the seam is inside.

Lay the lined curtain on the floor so the lining is in the center with a 1-inch hem of the drapery fabric on each side. Baste this edge where the lining joins the fabric. Then finish the top of the drapery, sandwiching the stiffening between the

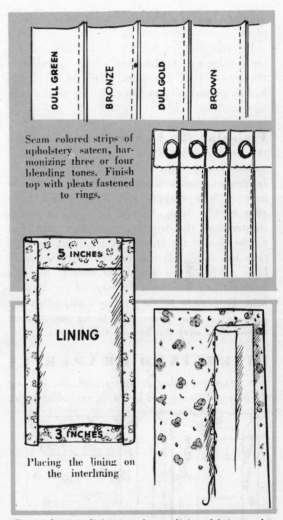

Seam colored strips of upholstery sateen, harmonizing three or four blending tones. Finish top with pleats fastened to rings.

Placing the lining on the interlining

Baste the interlining or heavy lining fabric to the curtain with long tacking stitches that do not show.

hem; described in Stiffening a Top Hem. Baste the hem; turn the edge of the lining in and baste it over the edge of the stiffened hem. Hold this edge in place with slip stitch.

Turn the side hems at the top over the stiffening, cutting a mitered or slanting corner. Slipstitch the mitered edge and the edge of the hem as far as the lining.

Top Finishes: The types of top finish for draperies are these: (1) a turned hem which is sewed to rings, (2) a casing with or without

Look in the Ready-Reference Guide at the back for exact page numbers of Detailed Instructions

heading, and (3) a pleated top in any style of pleat.

Let the drapery hang for two days so the lower edge can be hemmed exactly parallel to the lines of your woodwork. After the fabric has had an opportunity to hang out or stretch, mark this hemline.

Finishing the Lower Hem: First turn the hem and baste the finished edge. Lay it smoothly and draw the lining fabric over it. In this way you can estimate the depth of the hem on both drapery and lining fabric. The edge of the lining should be about 2 inches shorter than the drapery. Baste this edge. Cut off the hem of the drapery so it is 1 inch deeper than the lining. It can be held in place with large catch stitches. Finish the ends of the side hems, turning them over the edge of the drapery hem. Hem them to the end and slip-stitch the open edges which meet. The lining can then be slip-stitched over the hem of the drapery.

INTERLINED DRAPERIES

Few draperies today are interlined, but if your drapery will serve you better in excluding light,

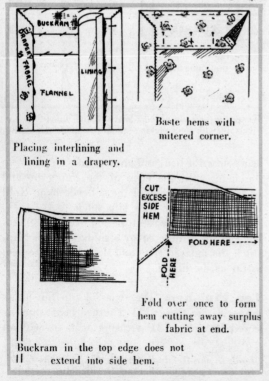

Placing interlining and lining in a drapery.

Baste hems with mitered corner.

CUT EXCESS SIDE HEM

FOLD HERE

FOLD HERE

Fold over once to form hem cutting away surplus fabric at end.

Buckram in the top edge does not extend into side hem.

or if the interlining will add to the richness of the draped line, do not hesitate to use it.

Draperies are interlined with canton flannel, which is much narrower than the usual drapery fabric. The interlining is cut in the exact size of the lining (see diagram, page 273). It is wise to seam the strips of flannel together before cutting, so they can be cut in the correct length and width. These joining seams should be laid flat, one over the other, and stitched on each edge so they will show no mark.

Place the interlining over the drapery fabric so the center of the drapery and the center of the interlining follow the same grain line. Fold the interlining back and tack it to the drapery, following the fold line. The stitches should be spaced far apart, passing long threads from one stitch to the next. When the drapery is very wide, use several rows of tacking to keep it firmly in place. Do not finish the edges of the interlining, but lay drapery and interlining flat and finish the side hems and the top edge of the drapery, following direction for finishing in the section on Points to Remember About Draperies.

When the stiffening band has been basted in place and the hem turned and basted, the side seams of the drapery should be turned so they extend over both stiffening and interlining. Hold them in place with broad catch stitches spaced far apart.

Turn the edges of the lining fabric and stitch them. Then place the lining on the drapery so that it covers the side hems and top hem. At the opposite end it will be much shorter than the drapery fabric. Pin this lining in place on all edges except the lower and slip-stitch it to the drapery.

PORTIERES

Portieres can be used in doorways or as wall panels—to properly proportion an uneven door. Make them of the heavier fabrics and finish the headings with French pleats or rings. It is not necessary to line them unless you wish to, but they must look ample. Do not skimp on the material. The fabric need not be costly. If the heavier fabrics seem high in price, consider velveteen or corduroy.

Finish the top with rings sewed to the edge. They are usually hooked to a ring on a metal

This formal valance shows the correct place of the side drapery. They should be the same width as the side scallops. The floor length glass curtains are made of embroidered net.

swinging bracket or on a wooden pole. Lined portieres can be finished with a double heading and the rings sewed between the headings of drapery and lining. Others are finished with French pleats.

Finishing the Lower Hem: Turn the hem allowance over the interlining and baste it in position. Then catch-stitch this hem to the interlining. The edge of the lining is turned and stitched, then the edge is slip-stitched by hand to the interlining. Be sure to fit the corners of the side hems into mitered smoothness, so the edges of the hem can be slip-stitched together without adding bulk.

POINTS TO REMEMBER ABOUT DRAPERIES

Never try to cut draperies on a small table. Working on the floor, as professional upholsterers do in the homes of customers, insures an accuracy difficult to match any other way.

Side Hems: The side hem of the drapery must be basted first. Cut off all the selvage to make your work easier. Turn the edges 1/4 inch and stitch on the machine. Press the edge, and then it is ready to turn in a hem. It is very important that all hems be turned on the grain of the fabric, and that all seams and hems be pinned and basted in order to avoid the "drawn" seams which so often mark the work of amateurs. Do not baste the side seam at the top and bottom edge of the drapery until the top and bottom hems are adjusted.

When the seams have been basted flat, stitch them and press them. Then you are ready to finish the top.

Stiffening a Top Hem: To make this stiffening, cut a band from 4 to 6 inches deep and as long as the width of the curtain minus the hem allowance. In other words, it should extend to the point where the side hems turn. In a well-made drape the stiffening never extends into the side hems. Lay the top of the drape flat and pin the canvas 1 inch below the top edge. Turn the 1-inch edge over the canvas and baste it. Turn the side hems over the ends of the canvas. Then turn the canvas top down over the curtain to form the top hem. To eliminate bulk, clip away the excess material at the ends of the side hems (see diagram page 274). Turn the side hem over the top hem and stitch in place through the two thicknesses of material and the canvas. The long hem across the top of the drape is usually basted and not stitched; the pleats or other finishes put on later hold it in place.

French Pleats and Box Pleats: For direction in measuring see page 282. For directions in making pleats turn to page 269.

Cartridge Pleats: Finish the drapery before inserting this type of pleat. Be sure to use a stiff buckram. Mark the distances on the top edge so that you provide 4 inches between the pleats and 4 inches for each pleat. Also mark the length of the pleats—usually about 3 to 6 inches long.

To hold this space, catch the top edge of the drapery for the first pleat, beginning about 3 inches from the edge. Catch the other pleats all the way across the top; then lay each pleat and stitch. Before you do this, press the fabric, and be careful not to crease the pleats in stitching. They bulge out from the front of the drapery and are never pressed.

Pipe Organ Pleats: These are like cartridge pleats, but they are filled with padding so they cannot be crushed flat. They are usually placed close together, and they are more appropriate for formal draperies in a modern room where the ceiling is high and no valance is used.

These pleats are usually longer, extending

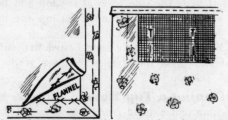

Hem of an interlined drapery catchstitches to interlining. (Right) Buckram in the top edge does not extend into side hem.

about 6 inches into the curtain. You must decide upon the size and length of the pleats before you cut the padding. Cut a buckram piece the length and width of the pleat and fill it with a roll of cotton. Stitch the buckram around the edge of the cotton. When you stitch your pleats, insert a buckram roll in each one.

Finishing the Lower Edge: Window frames are not always true, so it is a good plan to hang your draperies before finishing the lower edge. Let a heavy or stretchy fabric hang for two days before you mark the hemline. If the hemline is not on the grain of the fabric ignore the grain and follow the line of the floor or window sill. If the window is off balance, the drape should be made to look true.

The hem at the lower edge extends the full width of the fabric and is turned up over the side hems. Measure the hem, lay it flat, and trim it off. Turn in the edge 1/4 inch. Slip-stitch this edge to the drapery and slip-stitch up both ends of the hem or miter the corners.

DRAPERY VALANCES

A valance is the decorative strip of fabric stretched across the top of the window. It serves to hide curtain fixtures, to link up two or more windows into one unit, or as a connection between separate draperies. Valances can be French-pleated; they can be draped. They can be made in cascades or on buckram foundations. The buckram valance is sometimes straight, but more often it is shaped—divided into three scallops, one over each drapery and one over the center space. This formal scalloped effect can be arranged in a straight row of scallops; or a scallop can be arranged on either side as a heading for the draperies, and the space in between made into a deeper scallop or a high arch. Sometimes formal draperies have a pleated section set in at either side of the center motif or across the center.

Draped valances can be hung on a curtain pole with brackets which extend a little beyond the window frame. Pleated, ruffled, and scalloped valances can be hung on a rod which extends beyond the rod holding the curtain. Squared formal valances are tacked to a valance board.

When an overdrapery and a glass curtain are used, choose a plain tailored valance or a pleated one, either continuous pleats or spaced groups of pleats. Or, if you prefer, have a wider valance shaped to complement the drapery.

Valances are hung on a straight rod, a curved rod, or a valance board. They are always interlined and often wide. Always allow 4 inches at the end of the valance to turn around the corner of the rod or board so the valance hugs the wall on the sides. This is called "the return."

FORMAL VALANCES

If you want a formal valance, you will need a valance board fitted to your window. Some are shelves which hold the top of the buckram-lined valance away from the curtains; others are boards nailed above the window. Draped valances need not necessarily have a board, but decorators feel that a more flattering draped line is achieved when the drapery is held away from the curtain by a board or rod. Valance boards are usually the exact width of the window frame and 4 inches wide, unless you want an extended board. The valance can be tacked to the top of the board or attached to a buttoned tape tacked to the board. In this case, the valance buttons in place and is easy to remove. The ends of the valance are tacked to the window trim.

Formal Buckram Valance: Choose a shaped straight-line valance. It is always attached with tacks to the valance board. It is lined with heavy buckram and should be interlined with canton flannel as well. Its size and shape are a matter of artistic proportion.

Make a valance out of wrapping paper first and place it over the curtains to try out: (1) the width of the valance, (2) the relation of its shape to the proportions of the drapery, and (3) its relation to the proportions of the room. The corner turn is important. Be sure to allow the 4 inches to meet the wall.

When the size, shape, and proportions of the valance are all decided, use your paper pattern to cut both lining and the buckram with no seam allowance. Cut the outside fabric and the canton flannel interlining by the same pattern, allowing for seams. When the outside fabric has a design, take care to center this design in relation

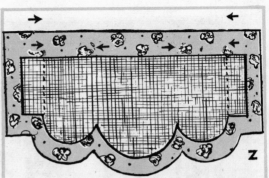

Showing placing of buckram in fabric. The outside arrows point to the window width. The inside arrows show width of side drapery.

Cut the tested valance in fabric taking care to center the design.

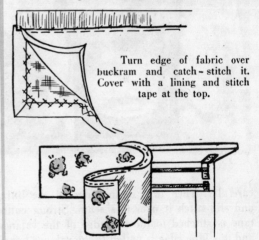

Turn edge of fabric over buckram and catch-stitch it. Cover with a lining and stitch tape at the top.

Tacking valance to valance board.

to both the shaping of the valance and the spotting of the design in the curtains. See illustration Z, which shows a flower motif centered in the valance.

Place the canton flannel interlining over the buckram, and the outside fabric over that. Turn the edges of the interlining and the outside fabric over the buckram and hold them in place with catch stitches. Use a large needle and coarse thread and make big stitches. Miter the corners

Cascade Drapery.

carefully. Then turn in the edge of the lining and slip-stitch it over this seam. Strong cotton tape is stitched to the top edge of the valance, and this tape edge is nailed to the valance board.

Draped Valance on a Pole: This formal valance is one long straight length of a soft fabric like satin, rayon crepe, or taffeta. Use the full 36-inch width. Cut it the length of the window, plus 20 inches. Finish the edges, press the valance, and hang it over the window on a long wooden pole, arranging the soft drapes with pins. This is an easy drapery to take down and keep clean.

Draped Valance with Cascade: Make a paper pattern and set it above your draperies

to test the proportions. To make a cascade with a draped section through the center, cut a pattern in muslin like diagram A. The side cascade turns the corner of the valance board and joins the front drapery 4 inches from the corner.

The Valance: Cut a piece of muslin the length of the valance board and as deep as you want the valance. Fold the muslin in half and measure in 3 inches from the outside edge (X in the Diagram B). From X cut to Y as shown by the dotted line. This line can slant slightly or as much as you wish, depending on the effect you desire.

Then cut a curved line from Y to Z (the center bottom of the valance). Unfold the muslin and divide into three units as shown by numbers 1, 2, 3, on Diagram A. At each of these points make a deep tuck. Pull them so they form a drapery and pin them to the valance board.

The Cascade: Make a muslin pattern before cutting the fabric. Unless your ceilings are very high, the side length of the cascade should be about 30 inches and should measure about 18 inches across the top. In this way a pair of

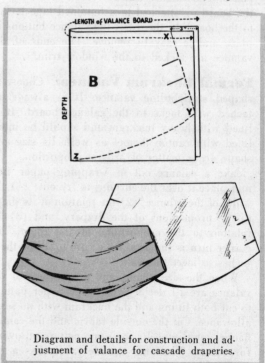

Diagram and details for construction and adjustment of valance for cascade draperies.

cascades can be cut from ½ yard of 40-inch material. Measure down 5 inches from the top edge and 5 inches from the lower edge, and draw a diagonal line (see diagram).

Then pleat the fabric in three large pleats, including all but 4 inches at one end. This 4 inches extends around the corner of the valance board and permits the drapery to hang close to the wall. Baste the pleats across the top and try your cascade at the window. The end should exactly match the end of the drapery section, and the edge should cascade in ripples.

When you have tested the patterns for both drapery and cascade, cut your fabric.

Finishing the Cascade: The edge of the cascade can be hemmed, but it is usually finished with a trimming. Choose a contrasting band of fabric, a band of ribbon, a fringe, a pleated edge, or a ball trimming. Apply the trimming, then press the fabric. Fold the drapery in the pleated lines you have already tested at the window.

Cascades of this kind are often made of contrasting fabric.

For a formal window, combine a cascade valance that is easy to make with a pleated side drapery and gathered glass curtains.

TIE-BACKS
FOR DRAPERIES

Fabric Tie-Backs: The tie-backs for draperies can be cut straight or in a curved shape. Use the fabric of the drapery or a contrasting fabric, and make the tie-back plain or pleated. The tie-back for a heavy drapery should be interlined with buckram. For a plain tie-back, cut the buckram and bind the edge to prevent it from cutting the fabric. Then lay canton flannel over the buckram and cover it smoothly with the fabric. For a straight tie-back, cut the fabric double, seam it, and turn it to the right side. If you like, it can be pleated. Shape the ends in a curve.

Whatever kind of tie-back you make, finish the ends with rings which slip over a hook in the woodwork. Place the hook carefully and try the effect with the curtain draped at different angles, so you can find the draping line which best suits your draperies and your room.

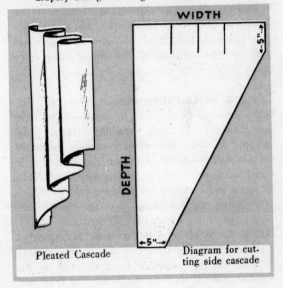

Pleated Cascade   Diagram for cutting side cascade

Cord Tie-Backs: When you make tie-backs of cording, buy them in white and have them dyed to match your draperies. Use a double cord which is knotted. It can hang in tassels or be weighted with covered balls.

Look in the Ready-Reference Guide at the back for exact page numbers of Detailed Instructions

CHAPTER XLI

MEASUREMENTS FOR HOME SEWING

This chapter outlines the detailed steps to compute the yardage for curtains, slipcovers, bedspreads, and dressing-table skirts. Before you use them you must have decided what type of curtain or cover you will make, and you should have a list of all the details necessary, including types of ruffles or pleats, cording, valances, and kinds of seams and hems.

ESTIMATING YARDAGE FOR CURTAINS

Use these directions for measuring for glass curtains, one-curtain draperies, group-window curtains, draperies, and valances.

Window Measurements: Measure *all* the windows. They may look alike, but sometimes you will find that not all of them have been set true, or the settling of the house may have thrown one out as much as 2 inches.

Length of Curtain Rod: For glass curtains, measure from jamb to jamb—A to B in the diagram. For an outside curtain pole, measure between the extreme outside edges of the woodwork—C to D in the diagram. For a wider window treatment, set the widening blocks in place and measure for pole or valance which extends beyond the frame.

Basic Length of Curtain or Drapery: To find a working basis for the finished length of your curtain, measure from the rod to the window sill (E to F in diagram), or from the rod to the floor (G to H). Which measurement you use, depends upon whether you are making sill-length or floor-length curtains. Once you have this basic or finished curtain measurement, you can add to or subtract from it as needed—for instance, you may want the drapery to sweep over the floor from 10 to 12 inches, or fall an inch above the floor, or at radiator height. The rod should be hung and the length measurement

Look in the Ready-Reference Guide at the back for exact page numbers of Detailed Instructions

verified before a curtain is cut. Always measure from the bottom of the rod.

Number of Curtains: Make a list of everything you will need—right overdrapery, left overdrapery, right glass curtain, left glass curtain, ruffle, valance, tie-back, trimming—everything down to the last detail. With this list before you, make another, this time of the exact allowances for turns and hems at top, bottom, and sides, plus shrinkage allowances.

Allowance for Lower Hem: The first turn in any hem should be $\frac{1}{4}$ inch. This means, for example, that the allowance for a hem 2 inches deep is $2\frac{1}{4}$ inches. The hem at the lower edge of glass curtains may be from 1 to 3 inches deep; in formal draperies, from $2\frac{1}{2}$ to $3\frac{1}{2}$ inches. A double hem is used in transparent fabrics, so in this case you must allow twice the measurement of the hem.

Allowance for Casing and Heading: The allowance for casing and heading at the top should be added to the lower-hem measurement. The casing should be deep enough to allow the rod to slide easily. A 4-inch allowance (plus $\frac{1}{4}$ inch for the first turn) makes a 1-inch casing and a $2\frac{1}{2}$-inch heading. Yours should be at least that. In pleated curtains the top hem is twice the width of the stiffening bands.

Shrinkage Allowance: To the total length so far, add shrinkage of 1 inch to the yard for rayon fabrics, 2 inches to the yard for cottons. If the material is preshrunk, no shrinkage allowance is necessary.

Example of Computing Length: Here is an example of how to find the necessary length of fabric for a curtain. The curtain in this case is a glass curtain 69 inches from rod to sill.

Finished length ....69 in.

Lower-hem allowance (1¾-inch
   hem plus ¼ inch for turn) .... 2 in.
Casing and heading allowance
   (4-inch plus ¼ inch for turn)........ 4¼ in.
Shrinkage allowance (1 inch per
   yard) .... 2 in.
      Cutting length ....77¼ in.

If this curtain were made of transparent material, another 2 inches for the double hem would make a total cutting length of 79¼ inches.

Make a diagram showing the length measurements you will use in your curtain.

Width Measurements:
The width of the curtain depends upon the fullness desired. Make the allowance for side hems and estimate fullness as described below.

Allowance for Side Hems:
The side hem is measured without selvages but with ¼ inch for the first turn. On some curtains both side hems have the same allowance; on others they are different, because (1) the hem at the center of the window is wider for emphasis, (2) a ruffle is joined (allow ¾ inch for joining a ruffle) or (3) the pole or valance board curves, and an allowance for the return to the wall must be added to the outside hem. The same size hem is repeated in a valance or ruffle

Estimating Fullness:
To estimate fullness, either for gathers or for pleats, you can follow popular rules. Allow the finished width of the curtain as it will hang on the pole and double this figure; or take the same measurement and add one-half to it. The fuller the curtain, the better the finished effect. For the average window, two 50-inch widths of fabric are skimpy; three 50-inch widths is the best rule. Transparent fabrics must be fuller than stiff ones.

In making your estimate for gathered or

Compare the skimpy width of the curtains at right with the luxurious effect gained by use of fuller width as shown above. (Left) Diagram shows basic window measurements.

pleated curtains, you can use the professional method of carefully working out a plan and adjusting the width of the fabric by adding a piece to make it wide enough to carry out the sweeping effect of the plan—or, like most home sewers, decide to use the set yardage of the fabric and adjust it as best you can to your window.

ESTIMATING YARDAGE FOR RUFFLES

The measurement for ruffles on curtains, slipcover skirts, bedspreads, and dressing-table skirts is based on the measurement of the edge to which the ruffle will be attached. In furniture, measure all around the chair, sofa, or bed, or across one part.

Take the exact measurement of the edge. To add fullness, depending upon the effect you wish, allow double this measure or add one-half to it for the cutting length of the ruffle.

For example, if the edge measures 48 inches, the cutting length of your ruffle would be either 96 inches or 72 inches, depending upon how much fullness you wanted.

Next, set down the width of your fabric—36, 40, or 50 inches—and also the depth of the ruffle, including hem allowance at top and bottom. Divide the cutting length of the ruffle by the fabric width; the answer gives the number of widths of fabric you need to join for ruffles. Multiply this figure by the depth of the ruffle (including hems); the answer gives you the total yardage for one length of ruffle. Multiply this by the number of curtains, and you have the total yardage needed for all the ruffles.

Ruffles for curtains can be from 3 to 5 inches deep; the depth of ruffles for slipcovers and bedspreads is the length from the joining to the floor. The hem is from ½ to 1 inch.

ESTIMATING PLEATS

The following instructions for estimating pleats in curtains, draperies and valances can also be applied to pleated skirts for slipcovers, bedspreads or dressing-tables.

Set down the finished width the curtain will occupy on the pole when hung. Add to this the width of the finished hem, plus the additional measurement required for turning the corner when the curtain is hung on a curved rod or a valance board.

Next, estimate the amount of extra fullness you will use. Divide this extra fullness by the number of pleats you will use; the answer gives the size of each pleat. Always use an odd number of pleats—five or seven, say—never six or eight. Bear in mind that the size of the pleats should be related to the depth of the stiffening band or skirt. The deeper the band, the wider each pleat should be. In simple curtains with a 3-inch stiffening band, use a French pleat 2½ or 3 inches wide, spaced 2 to 2½ inches apart. If the band is 5 inches deep, the pleat should be 4 inches wide.

Box Pleats: For box pleats the space between the pleats should be the same as the width of the pleats. Allow 2½ to 3 inches.

Cartridge Pleats: The pleats should be 2 to 2½ inches wide, and spaced 3 to 3½ inches apart.

Pipe Organ Pleats: These longer and larger versions of cartridge pleats require a deeper stiffening band. The pleats are 6 to 9 inches, with a 5-inch spacing. This space must always be smooth and equal. Remember that in curtains which will be hung on pulleys, the space must be. wide enough to let the folded fullness fall into place between each pleat.

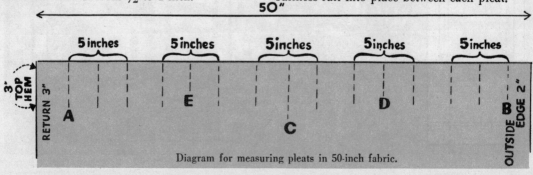

Diagram for measuring pleats in 50-inch fabric.

Making a Diagram: The next step is to make an accurate diagram representing the width of one curtain. At the ends, note the amount you will need for the center hem, including the outside return only if the pole is far from the wall. At these two points put marks indicating a pleat. At the exact center between these two pleats, place a third one; then fill in the space between the central pleats and each side one.

Example of Estimating Pleats: In the case of a curtain with a finished width of 45 inches; estimate pleats as follows: (See diagram on page 281).

To the 45 inches, add 3 inches for the return and 2 inches for a hem. This makes 50 inches. Allowing one-half the measure for extra fullness, you have a width of 75 inches. Suppose that you have decided upon five pleats: 5 into 25 (the measure of the excess fullness) gives you 5 inches as the width for each pleat.

The next step is a diagram representing a 50-inch width. On the left side 3 inches for the return is marked off at A; on the right side, 2 inches for the hem is marked off at B. At A and B a pleat is marked; then midway between A and B (half of 45 inches) a center pleat is marked at C. That leaves two pleats still to place. The first goes midway between A and C, at D; the other midway between C and B, at E.

ESTIMATING YARDAGE FOR VALANCES

Gathered or Pleated Valance: The yardage for gathered or pleated valances should be estimated when you figure the extra fullness for the curtain ruffles and other details. The valance is measured the same way, and it will help if you make a separate chart for the valance, setting down the details for the hems.

Straight Valance: It does not matter whether a plain straight valance is shaped on buckram or cut double and hung on a pole. Take the measurements carefully, allowing 3 extra inches of length and 3 extra inches of width. At the same time measure for the crinoline or buckram, if it is to be used.

ESTIMATING YARDAGE FOR TIE-BACKS

The yardage for tie-backs, and any ruffles or stiffening used with them, should be noted when you estimate your curtain yardage. In some widths of fabric, they can be cut from the waste ends from other pieces; other times it will be necessary to buy extra for the tie-backs.

BUYING CURTAIN POLES

In ordering curtain poles, explain that the length you order is the final length, not the length to which the pole is cut. This means that the fixture which holds the pole is included in the length, and the pole is cut long enough to fit the fixtures, so that the total length of pole and fixtures equals your measure. Making this fact clear at the outset will save disappoint-

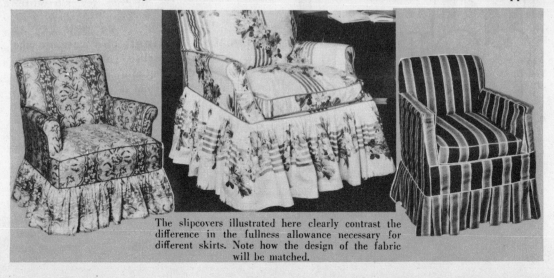

The slipcovers illustrated here clearly contrast the difference in the fullness allowance necessary for different skirts. Note how the design of the fabric will be matched.

ments in measuring for curtain poles. Be sure also to say that you have used a yardstick.

ESTIMATING YARDAGE FOR SLIPCOVERS

Determining the yardage necessary to cover a certain type of chair in a certain width of fabric is very difficult unless you use an accurate measuring chart. The rule is to take the length measures so that you know how much yardage is required to go over the chair, from the floor in front to the floor in back. When the fabric is wide and the chair small, you can often cover the sides of the chair or cut ruffles or pleats out of the excess fabric from this one length. When the fabric is narrow or the chair large, you must buy twice or three times the length.

Make a list of all the details you will use in your slipcover—including the style of skirt and the trimming. When welting is used in the seams, you must estimate the yardage both of the cord and of the bias strips of self-fabric which will cover the cord.

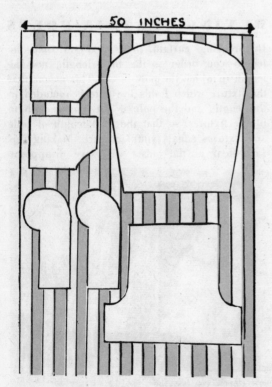

50 INCHES

Remove the cushion from the chair seat when you take your measurements. The estimate for yardage is made the same way, whether you cover a small chair or a large sofa.

Length Measurements: The total of the following measurements is the length of the fabric yardage: (1) front from floor to chair seat; (2) front across chair seat, plus 3 inches; (3) front back from chair seat to top, including width of top; (4) back from top to floor.

Width Measurements: The width measurements are: (5) width across front of chair; (6) width across seat, plus 3 inches; (7) width across back of seat; (8) width across front back of chair; (9) height of arm inside, plus 3 inches; (10) width of arm outside; (11) width of arm inside; (12) length of arm outside to floor; (13) bands around chair.

Consider the longest width measure in relation to the width of the fabric and find out whether the sides can be covered from the extra width of one length of fabric, or whether you must buy an extra length.

Type of Fabric: If the fabric is plain, your final estimate will be the amount you buy; if it is striped, you will need a little extra for centering and matching stripes. Allow at least a yard for this in covering an overstuffed chair. When the fabric has a large floral design which must be centered, see whether you can use the side yardage from these pieces for ruffles or a pleated skirt, or for the bias covering of the welting.

Estimating Welting: First measure the seams which will be welted. This gives the yardage for the cording, but allow ½ yard extra for joinings if the cord is not in one piece. To estimate the amount of fabric needed to cover the cord, figure as follows: From ¾ yard of material, bias strips 1½ inches wide can be cut—from 36-inch material 25 yards, from 50-inch material 34 yards.

ESTIMATING YARDAGE FOR SEAT CUSHIONS

Measure the top of the cushion at the widest (14) and narrowest width (15) ; measure the

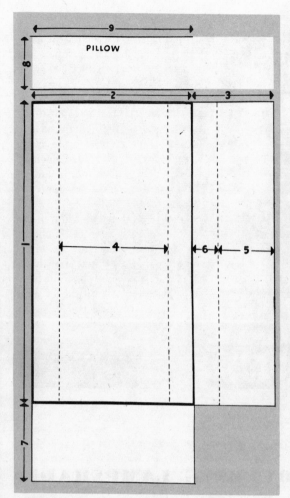

Diagram for taking basic measurements on bedspreads.

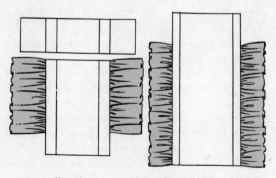

Two ways to space bands and ruffles.

length (16) of the cushion. Then (17) measure the cushion all around and (18) its depth. Allow 2-inch seams all around.

Then decide whether the bottom of the cushion

and the seat of the chair will be covered with the fabric of the slipcover or with an inexpensive lining fabric.

ESTIMATING YARDAGE FOR BEDSPREADS

Decide upon the style of spread and make a list of your needs for that style, listing the side pieces separately so you know where a band or ruffle comes, how wide each will be, and how much you will need for hems and joinings. Decide upon the treatment of the top—whether one piece of fabric will cover the whole top or a strip through the center—see Chapter XXXVII.

Measurements for Bedspreads: (1) Length of bed from headboard to footboard; (2) width of bed from edge to edge; (3) length from top of mattress to floor; (4) width of fabric; (5) length of ruffle from floor to heading; (6) length of band above ruffle; (7) width of tuck-in at foot; (8) length of pillow cover; (9) width of pillow cover.

Count the complete length, including width of pillow cover and tuck-in at the footboard (line X), for the fabric length. To estimate how many lengths of fabric, check the width measures with the width of your fabric. Add hem measurements and all measurements for ruffles or pleated skirts.

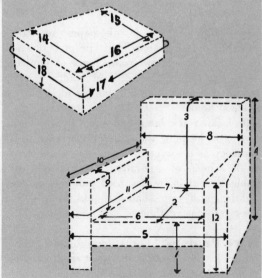

Diagram for taking basic measurements of slipcovers.

CHAPTER XLII

COVERING AND RE-COVERING LAMPSHADES

Lampshades are made of paper or fabric stretched over a frame. The type of frame will to a large extent limit your choice of covering, so an analysis of the kinds of frames is given before the descriptions of lampshades you can make at home.

In making new lampshades and in re-covering old ones, keep in mind the importance of its efficiency as a source of light as well as its part in the scheme of decoration. Electric light companies are giving widespread publicity to good lighting, and your shades should comply with these recommendations.

Wire Frames: For a lampshade made of fabric, a wire frame is the most secure foundation. There are several qualities of wire frame,

Look in the Ready-Reference Guide at the back for exact page numbers of Detailed Instructions

and the strength of the frame should be considered. When you are planning to stretch a plain fabric over the frame, it should be a strong one. A weaker frame is permissible for a gathered covering; and skirt coverings can be put on any kind of frame.

Wire frames come in all sizes and shapes, and the unskilled eye finds it difficult to measure the proportions of an uncovered frame. For this reason many people find it more satisfactory to buy a frame covered with a cheap fabric and replace it with the desired fabric. If you are planning to recover an old shade and the frame seems to be out of shape or out of proportion, you can have it reshaped for less than the cost of a new one. Good wire frames are expensive.

Parchment Frames: Many old frames are parchment, and they can be used for the lining of a fabric shade even if the shade is torn on one side; or it can be used as the foundation for a skirt covering. Old parchment shades which use only two metal rings which are separated can be restored only by using a stiff new paper shade.

PAPER LAMPSHADES

Paper shades can be smoothly fitted or pleated. Use any heavy wrapping paper or wallpaper— all types of paper can be shellacked on both sides; use coated paper, which means the surface is coated with a quick-drying enamel; or use old maps.

Smooth Shades: To make a pattern for a smooth paper shade, put a large newspaper on the floor and paint the edges of the frame with white or a color. While the paint is *still wet,* roll the frame across the newspaper (if the shade is not round, turn it evenly). The wet paint will leave the marks of a perfect pattern on the paper.

Cut out this pattern as soon as the paint dries, leaving enough extra at the edge for a joining. Cut your map or shellacked paper by this pattern and join the ends with paper fasteners. With coarse thread overcast the shade to the frame at top and bottom. Cover the overcasting with braid which sews on, or *passe partout,* which pastes.

Pleated Shades: Pleated paper shades are usually cut circular before they are pleated, and it is very important to test both the shape and the size of the pleat before you start to work on the shade. Cut a piece of newspaper and shape it to your frame, making the pleats the size desired. Pin this paper pattern to the frame between each pleat. When you have finished, remove the paper and use it for a pattern.

Shellacked and lacquered paper must be carefully creased *before* the shellac or lacquer is applied. The top can be overcast to the top of the frame, between each pleat. This is easier than punching holes through which a cord is run. Fasten the joining with paper fasteners.

FABRIC LAMPSHADES

Taffeta Shades: Shades made of taffeta can be gathered or stretched tight on a frame. The rayon taffeta used for lampshades is sheer

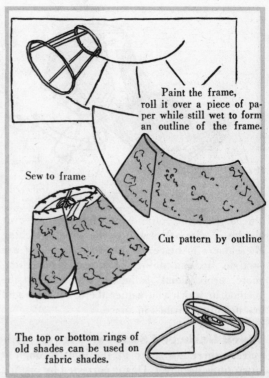

Paint the frame, roll it over a piece of paper while still wet to form an outline of the frame.

Sew to frame

Cut pattern by outline

The top or bottom rings of old shades can be used on fabric shades.

and comes in a wide assortment of lovely colors. The beige rose tones give good light. If your color scheme requires a still wider assortment of colors, you can also use dress-weight taffeta.

Before you make the shade, decide whether all edges will be finished with a double fold of self-fabric, a decorative ribbon or braid, or a ruffle. Assemble everything you will need for the trimming before you start to work. All wire frames must be wound with seam binding or a bias of self-fabric before they are covered.

Some gathered shades made of dress-weight taffeta are unlined, others are lined; a stretched shade is always lined. Select the color of the lining carefully. No matter what the color of the outside fabric, the lining usually gives a rose-colored glow. Look at the lining fabric over a light when you test its color.

Unlined Gathered Shade: Cut the fabric the width of the frame, allowing 2 inches for seam allowance. It should be 1½ times the length of the largest circumference of the frame. Turn in the top edge and gather it. Space the gathers carefully around the top of the frame, pinning them to the binding. Then overcast the gathers to the top of the frame with strong

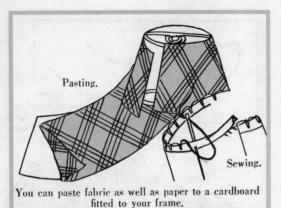

Pasting.

Sewing.

You can paste fabric as well as paper to a cardboard fitted to your frame.

thread. Pull the lower edge of the fabric over the lower wire and sew it to the wire, stretching the gathers in place as you do so, so they are straight up and down. This makes a tighter, more professional gathered frame than the method in which you gather the lower edge and try to hold it firmly in place.

Lined Gathered Shades: When the fabric is very sheer, the glare of the light through it often ruins the effect. This is corrected by making a lining of the sheer rayon taffeta used for lampshades. Cut the lining the size of the largest circumference of the frame, with seam allowances, and 3 inches wider than the depth of the frame. Seam the joining; turn in the top edge and gather it. Space these gathers at the top of the frame. The lining is placed on the inside of the frame with the seams facing out. When the top edge has been securely sewed to the frame, pull the lower edge over the wire at the bottom of the frame and overcast it securely to the frame. Cut away the extra fabric, not too close.

Then cut the outside gathered section as directed above for Unlined Gathered Shade and apply it. When you stretch the lower edge, proceed as though the lining were not there; this edge is overcast over the lining.

Finishing Edges for Shades: The top edge of a gathered shade can be bound with a decorative ribbon. It must bind the inside as well as the outside, so that anyone looking down on the shade sees a finished edge on both sides. Many shades are finished at the lower edge with scalloped-edge, French or straight ribbon.

Shades can also be finished at top and bottom with tailored folds of self-fabric. Cut a true bias

twice the width of the finished fold. Stitch and turn it. Apply the fold so that the seam is slipstitched to the top of the frame, and the fold extends a little above the frame. The lower edge can be finished with the same kind of fold, or a wide fold can extend below the frame—to cover the light or the base of an ugly fixture. In some lamps this type of fold is headed with a narrow ribbon; in others with a trimming braid.

Stretched Shade: This kind of shade is not hard to make if you work with a true bias. Before you cut the material, stretch it around

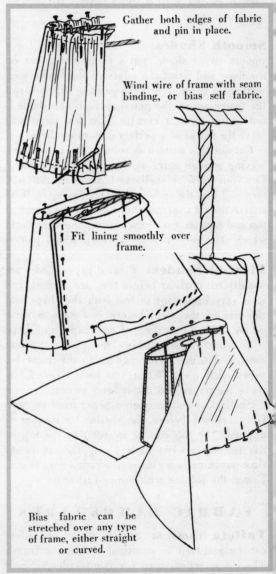

Gather both edges of fabric and pin in place.

Wind wire of frame with seam binding, or bias self fabric.

Fit lining smoothly over frame.

Bias fabric can be stretched over any type of frame, either straight or curved.

the lamp so that: (1) the ends securely meet, (2) the fabric really stretches, and (3) the lower edge is securely covered. Trim the material away only a little, then start to pin the fabric around the lower edge of the frame. Before you overcast it in place, press the pinned end against you and pull the fabric over the top edge of the frame, placing pins in the edge as you work. When the fabric is stretched smoothly in all but two or three places, turn the frame again and continue to stretch the fabric at the lower edge, replacing pins as necessary. You often have to loosen a pin at the opposite edge and pull the fabric into a different position to remove a stubborn wrinkle. When the cover looks smooth, join the ends by slip-stitching them together with matching thread and small stitches. With strong thread and big stitches, overcast the fabric to the frame, pulling it as you release each pin.

A stretched shade must be lined. In very costly shades the lining fabric is stretched first and then the top covering. In less expensive ones, only the covering is stretched. The lining is then cut on a true bias and overcast to the lower edge, then stretched to the top of the frame, fitting out all the wrinkles possible. This latter way is

Petticoat ruffles can be made for any shade. Join them to the frame with snap fasteners.

successful only in a straight frame. When the frame slopes, both lining and covering must be stretched. The edges of a stretched frame are finished as described in Finishing Edges for Shades.

Heavier Fabric Shades: To make lampshades of the same material as the curtains or other room furnishings, you can use a wire frame and make a stretched shade as described here, or you can use the top and lower band of an old shade, by first using your old shade as a pattern to cut cardboard and then pasting the fabric to the edges of the cardboard.

The edges of the shade can be finished with ball fringe or a folded bias strip. Overcast them in place with soft yarn which will not tear the cardboard.

Petticoat Lampshades: A petticoat shade can be used to cover an old shade, or a new wire frame, for a bedroom lamp. If the frame is wire, with no lining, you can make an unlined shade of glazed chintz, cretonne, sateen, or taffeta. If you want a transparent shade of dotted swiss, organdy, or a sheer rayon, you must either make a lined shade or use the old shade for lining. Test the shade with a light. If the bulb glares through, you need a lining. If the shade gives a pleasant light in the test, you can make the petticoat effect.

Cut the ruffle three times as long as the largest circumference of the shade and 5 inches deeper than the shade. Finish one edge with a hem or binding and turn in the other edge 3 inches for a heading. Pleat or gather the fabric and join the ends. Set this petticoat on the shade and adjust the gathers or pleats so that the top is finished with the heading. This joining can be finished with a ribbon bow, or a plain band of ribbon or trimming can be placed below the heading as a finish.

CHAPTER XLIII

CAMPS, RECREATION AND CHILDREN'S ROOMS

Camps, ranches, and play rooms are only a few of the rooms which must "take it" and still be gay and comfortable. The seashore home, the gypsy life and short stays in furnished apartments present the same kind of problem. This chapter is given over to suggestions for the decoration of these less formal rooms which include rooms for children of all ages. In all of them, remember that fabrics must be strong.

CAMPS AND RANCHES

The frontier home has a character all its own, and camps must be practical first and decorative afterward. The same type of decoration described here is appropriate to children's play rooms, adult game rooms, and any home with craft furnishings, what is usually known as Mission furniture or its cooler counterpart in reed or rattan.

I have memories of huge stone fireplaces and the rugged comfort of ranches and camps stretch-ing from Maine to California. The fabrics which add color and comfort to these interesting interiors differ. The casual types use fabrics which blend with unfinished walls of stone, bark, or plain board; in more formal types of ranches—with plastered or adobe walls. The most suitable fabrics for these interiors are colorful homespuns, often the homecraft of the locality. The Indian country, the Spanish country, the North and the deep South—each has its own characteristic homecraft. Novelty fabrics of this kind are made in the simplest type of straight-hanging curtain with a hem and casing.

In casual interiors coverings of couches and sofas or the tie-on cushions for chairs in heavier and darker fabrics are made without boxing and are often trimmed with fringe. When the ranch is more formal, the same homespuns are tailored and fitted in beautifully boxed couch and bed covers. Cushions are plentiful and planned for use, not for decoration, unless the fabric itself makes a decorative note. People in these communities like comfort without frills, and they insist upon fabrics which can stand wear.

More homes of this type should use drawstring attachments and long simple draperies which can be drawn. This kind of curtain can be pushed aside from the window with a view. These draw curtains are easy to make because the solid fabrics suitable to these interiors need no lining. They should be finished with box pleats, but the heading should be interlined with stiffening as directed for French pleats. See Ready Reference Guide for page number.

SEASHORE HOMES

Cotton and linen are the best fabrics to withstand dampness, especially if they are treated with wax finishes which repel moisture. This is a big step in the conquest of mildew, and modern science has developed textiles costing very little which are treated to repel water. All fabrics in the oilcloth class are adaptable, and the new trend toward using oilcloth for curtains in kitchens, dinettes, bedrooms, and the living rooms of camps and cottages will help keep these rooms gay. These print fabrics, which look tailored and decorative, can be cleaned by wiping with a damp cloth.

For slipcovers use hard-finish denim and drill in dark or gay colors. In wealthy homes this kind of slipcover is joined with a narrow fringe, red or white often set into navy blue; and the effect is lovely. It will pay you to make boxed cushions for couches and sofas to make them comfortable. Remember that soft cushions merely add a note of luxury; they do not support a relaxed body seeking comfort; for that you need boxed cushions.

Porch and outdoor furnishings and the beach cushions can be made of drill or smooth-surface heavy fabrics, or from plain glazed chintz. You can also make them of lightweight oilcloth or from old canvas awnings painted.

Stitching Oilcloth: When you stitch oilcloth, open the tension of your machine as wide as possible. Use a large needle and do not worry if it grows blunt; it will still carry the thread. Stitch all seams on the right side, because you cannot turn stiff fabric seams. Bind them if you do not like the effect of a cut edge. Coated

fabrics do not ravel, and so need none of the protections against raveling. When you would like to use a binding for decoration, hold it over the edges and make one stitching hold both sides of the binding as well as both edges. If you have no machine, overcast the edges by hand, using a large needle threaded with a heavy thread, or a twisted embroidery thread, or wool yarn. The stitches should be at least ½ inch deep, spaced ¼ inch apart, and they should be even.

Oilcloth Curtains: Curtains made of oilcloth are cut like any others, but without hem allowances. Use pinking shears if you like. Be sure to allow ample width for pleats or fullness. Lay the fullness in box pleats across the top and overcast this edge. Then stitch a piece of fabric across the top in a double binding. This will form a casing through which to slip the curtain rod.

Oilcloth Valances: These are used with oilcloth curtains, and they are also decorative with fabric curtains. Cut them in the required width and finish the edge with scallops shaped with a saucer. Mark the scalloped outline on the

A little-used bedroom is converted to double duty as a sewing room. Instead of a desk, use a drop leaf table that can be opened for cutting.

can bind this edge if you like, but most oilcloth valances are self-finished. When the valance is straight cut it with a pinking shears. To join the valance to the curtain place the edge below the cornice board of the window, with the valance extending up; and on the wrong side of the curtain edge place a row of tacks or thumbtacks to hold the valance to the window frame. This line must extend straight across the cornice to give a proper finish. When the valance drops, it covers this joining and should be wide enough to cover the top of the curtain. If the window has no cornice board, the top of the curtain can be faced with fabric to form a casing for the curtain pole.

Compressed Textiles: This is a new development of science. Compressed textiles are decorative and inexpensive. They look like chintz in color and design; but they are not woven fabrics coated with a wax finish; they are made of pressed cellulose. They do not wash, but they can be wiped off with a damp cloth. The smooth surface repels dirt. These textiles can be cut and sewed like oilcloth, and the edges are finished the same way. They are especially recommended for play rooms, children's camps, and boarding-school and college rooms. They have their use, too, for transitory decorations in furnished rooms. They are not suitable for couch or bed covers, but they make decorative curtains and wall panels. They can be used for boxed cushions also; and as substitutes for chair tidies they can lend gaiety to a drab piece of furniture.

TRANSITORY HOMES

Women who have to live for a time in hotels or furnished rooms are often disturbed by their unhomelike surroundings. They want to freshen the place up with as little expense and labor as possible. If the migration is a long one, slipcovers and curtains of inexpensive fabric can be made quickly, and they will work wonders with a drab room. If you travel and change your home frequently, take with you a plain cover, not boxed, which can be thrown over any bed or couch. A washable cotton spread can be sent to the laundry wherever you are. Plan pillow covers to match, made for a standard bed pillow. Add to this, two lengths of matching or contrasting fabric for side drapes, and take a bureau and a table cover which you like. This little kit is easily packed and adapted to any room.

PLAY ROOMS AND GAME ROOMS

Play rooms for children and game rooms for adults must be gay, simple, and tidy. They will never function smoothly unless all the paraphernalia of play have a place. The first consideration, therefore, in making a room in the attic or the cellar function as the fun spot in the house, is a large closet and proper shelves. After you have attended to places to put things is time enough to think of color. The walls and floor are the largest color areas, and they should be considered first. Paint is easy to apply, and any homemaker can paint this kind of room. When a rug is not available, paint the floor as well as the walls, and use a washable paint for both.

Next consider the furniture. Build a new table or use several old ones. An old dining-room table will make a good game table. Be sure there is at least one day-bed or couch in the room, and sometimes two or three. If you want to convert an old bed, have a carpenter attach feet to the springs or cut down the headboard and footboard. Add folding chairs, straight chairs and comfortable chairs. Be sure there is a radio and several lamps, and that the room has ample working space for the hobby of every member of the family. One end of an adult game room can be given over to a carpenter's workbench, amateur photographer's equipment, a sewing corner, or a shop for the budding electrical engineer or a screen for home movies. Bring into this room all the trophies and diplomas— all the treasures so dear and so undecorative in other rooms.

Slipcovers and curtains should be boxed and simple. If there are not enough bed cushions to make up the assortment necessary to comfort, stuff some boxed cushions with excelsior or shaved paper. It is important to stuff the cushion lining until it is solid and squared. Then you can put a padding of cotton over the edges and cover it like any boxed cushion.

The fabrics used in playrooms and nurseries must be able to stand wear, be washable, and

The striped novelty cotton rep used for curtains and bunk covers of this room, add to a ship-shape appearance.

need no ironing. Use homespuns, denims, rep, and the heavier cotton weaves which repel dirt. Use oilcloth, linen, or glazed chintz at the windows.

CHILDREN'S ROOMS

Mothers everywhere are learning more about child psychology. They know now that the child who has a place all his own, which he knows is his own, can be more easily taught consideration for others.

Infants' Nurseries: Every mother has a vision of a lovely frilly bassinette and a beautiful nursery for her baby, and there is no reason why that dream picture cannot be realized in proportion to the space and income of any home. If there is a room available for a nursery, by all means decorate it. Otherwise find some spare part of the house which can be turned into baby's corner, and there assemble all the things you need for his care. This will save you many steps in a day.

There should be a small chest of drawers and a small closet close to the bathinette. After you have arranged everything needed, think of the decoration. Frilly white curtains which tie back with ribbon fit into the scheme; and if there is no bassinette to decorate with frilly white ruffles, you can pad and line an ordinary clothes basket. To do this, fit a small hair mattress exactly into the basket, then smooth pink or blue sateen across the sides of the basket, pinning it to the top edge and gathering it to fit the lower edge. Cut a piece of paper the exact size of the bottom of the basket and use it as a pattern for cutting the fabric, allowing seams. Seam this piece to the fabric on the sides of the basket at the lower edge. Then cut a strip of sateen as wide as the outside of the basket and long enough to extend around it. Seam this strip to the top edge of the lining, leaving an opening for the handle of the basket. Finish the lower edge of the outside covering with a narrow hem and run a cord or string through it. In this way you can pull the lower edge to fit the basket and hold tight. The mattress will hold the inside covering in place. This cover can easily be removed and washed. Then make an outer cover of white, shaping and joining it like the inside one. It should be full and gathered. Cut a ruffle twice as wide as the basket edge and deep enough to allow a hem and a heading. Gather the ruffle and join it to the top edge of the lining. You can trim this cover with bows of ribbon, and wind the handles of the basket with ribbon to match.

Tots' Nurseries: Provide a small washable rug, a little larger than the play pen. The rest of the room can be covered with oilcloth. Be sure there are low shelves within reach of a toddling child. If you stencil decorations on the wall or have panels or pictures, be sure to place them low. Even a baby's eye is attracted to bright decoration when it is low enough for him to see. Be sure the room has a comfortable chair for mother. It should be covered with a slip-cover which will add color interest to the room and be easily laundered too. The child's crib can be in this room and a day-bed as well, with a matching cover that is boxed so it does not trip up unsteady little feet. Clear the room of everything unnecessary and everything a child might trip over. Provide low, steady furniture he can hang onto, such as a day-bed or couch. As the child grows, you can add small furniture; but while he is learning to walk, substantial furniture which will steady his footsteps is an asset.

Rooms for School Children: Besides the bed, the two most essential pieces of furniture are a desk or table for homework, equipped with a functional, not decorative, lamp, and low shelves for toys. Psychologists say that a feeling for having "everything in its place" can be cultivated very early by providing a place for the child's own things, and making sure this place is low enough to be handy. Bedspreads, slipcovers, and curtains should be made of washable fabrics which resist wear. Colorful homespuns make covers which need no ironing, and washable fabrics which do need ironing are no more decorative. Oilcloth curtains give gaiety and cleanliness, and reduce work. Somewhere on the wall should be a bulletin board to display the changing hobbies of the child. It is a mistake to decorate the room of a child at this stage, because his interests change so frequently. It is better to use maps and bulletin boards, which can be kept up to date.

Boys will appreciate circus-tent awning effects instead of ruffles in the curtains. A boy usually has at least one hobby, perhaps several; and each hobby should be given room, for both equipment and display. Have nothing superfluous in a boy's room, and it will be easier to establish practical rules for neatness.

It is wise to follow the same principle of simplicity in a girl's room during the tomboy period. When the girl begins to take an interest in decoration and expresses a desire to "pretty up" her room, make this a mother-and-daughter program. Exchange ideas with her, but insofar as possible follow out hers. This will help her to develop her own talent and to learn the difference between practical and impractical ideas. I know of one eleven-year-old girl who wanted frilly bedspreads and curtains in her room. There was no one to do the extra ironing, so her mother gave her her wish on the understanding that she would iron the ruffles herself. The child took pride in doing the ironing herself and continually changed sets of tie-backs for the curtains. She matched these trimming notes in petticoat lampshades for her room, and as she grew older she learned to make saucy sofa cushions which tied into these decorative effects.

Mothers with good taste must be patient with the fads of school and high-school daughters. They are always gay, but often crude. Nevertheless, the child should be allowed to express herself freely in her own room. It is only natural that she should continually be wanting to change everything. That is part of growth. In many homes the girls are given a small allowance for this on condition that they make up their ideas themselves. It is amazing how quickly they get to work, once the small budget is established.

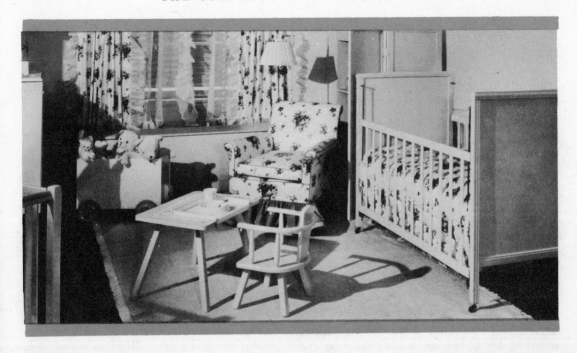

The ideas must be simple and easy to make, or they will not be finished. Let the child stencil and do all the things she learns in school.

Rooms for Adolescents: Many children in this age group yearn to express their artistic talents. Expect them to be modernists. These youthful ideas need not be welcomed into the family living room or adult bedrooms; but the youth can and should express his own ideas, as far as practicable, in his own room, and he might also be permitted to use them in the family play room.

When sisters share a room and disagree on decoration, face the situation squarely. One mother divided the room in half and assigned one half to each girl. The girls were asked to outline their ideas on decoration, and a time was set to compare them. When the girls presented their plans, each with samples of textiles, it developed that they agreed on the types of construction of curtains, bedspread, and slipcovers; but they had unalterable color preferences. These colors were selected so that they harmonized, and by rearranging the furniture a little, each girl could develop her own color scheme and still have the room as a whole harmonious.

When the ideas of youth excede the family budget and a room cannot be papered, consider using decorative panels. The drapery fabric can be used for a wall panel anywhere in the room. A panel can form the background behind the headboard of the bed or a group of pictures; panels can extend the theme of the drapery across one whole side of a room. They can be placed all around the room at the height of the window sill. To attach a panel to the wall, first nail a piece of plywood to the wall and then tack the fabric to the plywood. Cover the edges with molding.

If a child wants to paste paper over his furniture to form panel effects, do not be alarmed. The wood will not be spoiled by this pasting—it will only have to be refinished when the panel is no longer used. Adolescents love to paint furniture, and this, too, is not as destructive as it sounds. One mother let her son paint his mahogany bureau. Three years later the same son came to appreciate the mahogany furniture in the rest of the house, and his bureau disturbed him. Then his mother let him remove the paint and refinish the wood, and he did an excellent job of it. Imaginative children are not really destructive, they are simply avid to express themselves; and one of a mother's greatest interests is to watch this talent develop.

CHAPTER XLIV

OLD CURTAINS FOR NEW WINDOWS

Old curtains and drapes which do not fit the windows of new homes are familiar problems for many. Suggestions for lengthening curtains are given in this chapter, classified as to types of curtain—straight curtains, ruffled tie-backs, and formal draperies and valances. In every case first try the curtain at your window and analyze your need.

LENGTHENING CURTAINS

Straight Curtains: When the possibilities of letting out tucks, letting down the hem, the casing, and the heading are exhausted, we must resort to facings and bandings. In this case the textile interest of the added band is as important as its color. Some kind of false hem which will make the curtain look like new can be found for any straight curtain. Once you have selected a fabric in matching or contrasting color which complements your curtain in texture interest, the trimming band or false hem can be shaped to conform with simplicity or formality of line.

Curtains with French-Pleated Tops: Rich curtains with French-pleated tops can use an added band of lightweight velvet, satin, or velveteen in matching color. It should be lined and joined with a cording. It will make the curtains look like new.

Cotton Curtains: Cotton curtains for bedrooms and informal rooms can be lengthened with a trimming band in self-color or contrasting color. The top of the trimming band is usually scalloped, and when it's well done the curtain looks like new. All-white dotted swiss curtains with colored dotted swiss bands joined with matching rickrack are very effective.

Lengthening with Ruffles: When curtains are narrow as well as short, they can often be adjusted by adding a ruffle. Decide exactly how wide the ruffle should be and what fabric suitable for ruffles would harmonize with your curtain material and your room. Contrasting ruffles like those used on new curtains should be

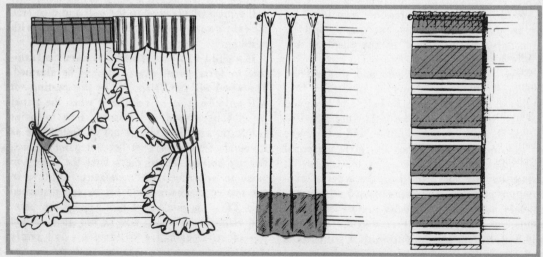

(Left) When you patch curtains or draperies plan a valance wide enough to cover the added lines and make a tie-back to match. (Center) When a transparent ninon or net curtain is too short, band it with a contrasting fabric in matching color. (Right) Banded curtains made from sewing salvage.

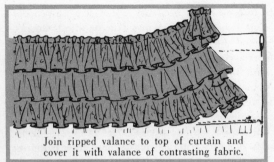

Join ripped valance to top of curtain and cover it with valance of contrasting fabric.

the basis for rejuvenating curtains. The possibilities include: (1) a ruffle of the same material in a contrasting color, (2) a chintz ruffle on a white curtain, (3) a white organdy ruffle on a chintz curtain; (4) plain-colored chintz ruffles on transparent rayons.

Ruffled Curtains: When you can match the fabric, add a straight band to the end of the curtain and finish it with a ruffle exactly the fullness and finish of the ruffle already on the curtain. When it is not possible to match the fabric, consider the possibilty of a contrasting band that looks like a valance.

Another way of lengthening, if the curtain has a ruffled valance, is to use the valance to lengthen the curtain at the top, then replace it with a valance in a contrasting fabric and color. Cut the original valance in half. Rip the heading and casing at the top of the curtain. Sew the end of the curtain to the old valance under the ruffle and use its casing for the top of the curtain.

Formal Draperies: In the case of formal draperies which need lengthening, the first thought should be, "Is the fabric worth remaking?" A beautiful rich fabric can be remade at very little expense; but a shoddy or worn fabric is not worth the time and money. It would be better to spend the money for new draperies in a cheaper fabric.

The trimming band which lengthens a drapery of napped fabric, such as velours or velvet, should be a matching satin or brocade. If you cannot find the right color, consider buying white and dyeing it. This is not very expensive, and if your local community does not offer such service, you can send your draperies to a city cleaner who specializes in dyeing to match.

For a drapery in brocade or a rich ribbed fabric in one or several colors, the trimming band can be velvet or velveteen.

Both drapery and lining must be lengthened, and the joining should be corded. Duplicate on the trimming band the finish of the drapery. If there is no valance you can piece the top of the drapery and add a contrasting valance to cover the piecing.

BANDED CURTAINS FROM SEWING SALVAGE

Gay striped curtains are made from leftover materials or the good pieces of worn sheets. The

When curtains are too short and too narrow use them as a panel inset into a similar texture.

A small window between windows can be treated as a picture frame and decorations placed inside of it.

plan for this kind of curtain depends upon the fabric available. Sometimes the stripes run lengthwise, sometimes crosswise. When they run crosswise, follow any of the following three plans:

1. Use a long strip of sheet or fabric for the top of the curtain and band the lower edge of the curtain.

2. Cut all your odd pieces into the curtain width and arrange them in a decorative effect. Stitch the pieces to a long strip of sheeting. Often the sheeting is tucked between the colored and print stripes.

3. Join the colored and print stripes and seam them, with strips of sheeting run between them. This band can extend the full length of the curtain or end wherever the material gives out.

A good plan is to cut duplicates for the other side of the curtain whenever bands are cut, and if there are more curtains in the room, cut all the duplicates of each band so the effect will be uniform.

PAINTED WINDOW SHADES

Shades: Window shades can now be repainted to look like new at small cost. Get a waterproof paint especially designed for painting canvas. Spread the shade smoothly on the cellar or attic floor and paint it with a brush, just as you would paint anything in the house. A glazed coating is formed, which does not crack off when the shade is rolled. You will find, too, that the paint waterproofs the shade.

If the shade has a torn hem or is missing its stick or needs a patch, make these repairs before you paint. The new mending tape is the best way to patch a shade. You can buy paint in the usual tan shades or work out a decorative color in your home by choosing a colored shade.

Faded Sofa Cushions: Cushions used on the porch, in boats, or at the beach can be painted with waterproof paint if the fabric is the right kind. Before you paint the cushions, try it on a sample piece of fabric.

Sofa cushions indoors are continually having to be freshened up when the room is changed or redecorated. Consider the tie between the decorative scheme and the cushions. Ruffles to match those on the curtains can be added to the cushions.

TIGHTENING SAGGING SPRINGS

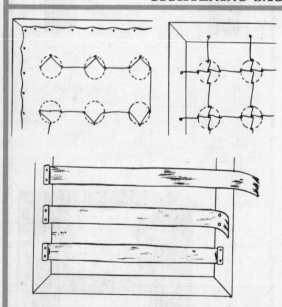

Turn chair bottom-side up and remove all webbing. Adjust sagging springs. Retie with upholsterers' twine. Tie to adjoining springs from front to back and side to side at both top and bottom.

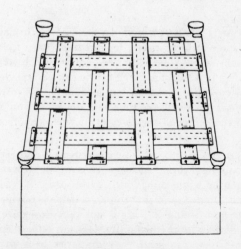

Fold webbing at ends and tack to chair with double row of tacks. Do not tack in old holes. Use three or more rows of webbing and tighten with block of wood.

Interweave cross webbing and fasten to springs with upholsterers' twine.

CHAPTER XLV

QUILTING SPREADS AND ACCESSORIES

American quilting follows the traditional English method, in which a layer of padding is placed between two fabrics and all three are held together by tiny stitchery in close or open designs that form puffs of fabric. The Italian method does not use padding until the double lines of the design holding the fabric and lining together are completed. Then a heavy padding yarn is run between the two layers of the design. Both types are found in antique quilts, which are works of art; and the value of these fine quilts lies in the close, fine handwork. Modern quilting is often done by machine, which is of course much faster. Some quilters make the background by machine and work the design by hand.

CHOOSING THE DESIGN

If you want to use a traditional design, look in your library for books showing old quilts in the Early American tradition, as well as historical English designs. There are also books on Italian quilting back as far as the Renaissance. The English quilts were designed for warmth, the Italian for luxury. In modern quilting you will find both warm quilts and light summer ones, as well as a wide assortment of luxury designs for bedrooms, table covers, and small accessories for the house and some dresses. Most modern quilting uses the padding between the two fabrics, but it is not unusual to find Italian cords introduced into the design and worked out to emphasize the center motif or the edge.

A good deal of modern quilting is made with straight rows of stitching spaced in squares, or in lattice, trellis, or sunburst effects, omitting the decorative motif. In machine quilting, straight lines are highly desirable. The pressure foot or a cording foot can be used for straight lines or for curved designs made in continuous lines.

CHOOSING THE FABRICS

Outside Fabric: The choice of the outside fabric is a question of appearance—that is, which will best give the effect you are striving for in your design. All fabrics can be quilted.

Cottons make lovely quilts. Many exhibits show quilts of white sheeting or unbleached muslins in full bed size. In others, color is introduced in the stitching or in the joining of contrasting fabrics. The large squares blocked out in cream, tan, or yellow are more modern than patchwork, but both kinds have a place in home decoration. Chintz, calico, and other printed fabrics are effective too. Luxury quilts of satin, taffeta, velvet, velveteen, and sateen are best suited to some homes; in others, chiffon, china silk, and transparent cottons are used for luxury details. Dress accessories feature heavier fabrics like velvet or velveteen as well as dress-weight rayon crepes.

Lining: Quilt linings are made of sheeting or velveteen. The lining for Italian quilting is cheesecloth, and is often covered with a china silk, chiffon, or other transparent cover.

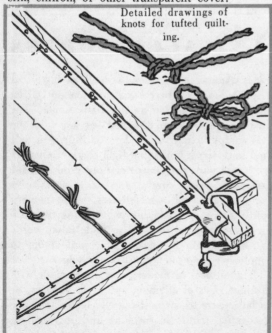

Detailed drawings of knots for tufted quilting.

Pin any quilt to the muslin, tack it to the quilting frames and then set the clamps that stretch the work so they are firm and will hold.

Padding: The interlining, or padding in the English tradition, is usually three layers of cotton batting spread smoothly over the lining. An old blanket or muslin sheet may also be used. In wool-growing communities, teased wool is often used in both quilts and tufted spreads. For Italian quilting a soft double yarn is generally used.

Thread and Needles: Quilting is usually done with fine matching thread, using as fine a thread and needle as possible. There are times, however, when a blunt embroidery needle is preferred. Sometimes a colored thread or a heavy thread is used to emphasize a contrast in the design; sometimes the whole spread is quilted in a contrasting color. Decide on the effect desired and secure enough buttonhole-twist cotton, twisted embroidery floss, or sewing cotton or silk, to finish the work. Be sure the thread is as sunfast as the fabric.

Chalk, Pins, Basting Thread: Secure also a box of long pins, some chalk for tracing the design, and basting thread for tacking.

Quilting Frame: For bed quilts or large covers a quilting frame is essential. Small articles can be quilted with or without an embroidery frame. You can buy a quilting frame or make one at home. If you buy one, be sure of these things: (1) The clamps are adjustable. (2) The muslin to which you pin the quilt is firm and will wear. (3) The frame can be adjusted for a narrow width as well as wide. (4) The folding crossbar that holds the frame is strong and set at the correct height. Don't be afraid of the size of the frame. Most experienced quilters who work alone roll the quilt on one side bar of the frame and set the working section in a narrow strip which fits easily into the room.

Small Articles: In quilting small pieces for dress or home accessories—book cover, table cover, beret, muff, or coat—never cut out the article before you quilt it. Instead, outline the design, do the quilting, and when it is completed finish the edge in the size required. Often you will find that the quilting has shrunk the outline you originally had, and the edge you first marked must be extended. Make this adjust-

QUILTING DESIGNS YOU CAN TRACE

Motifs from traditional designs that can be used singly or
joined in continuous bands.

ment by developing an edge or extending the design.

ORDER OF PROCEDURE IN QUILTING

Decide upon the fabric and design before you start. Then proceed as follows:

1. Trace the design on the fabric or lining.
2. Lay the fabric, lining and padding in place.
3. Tack the fabric in place.
4. Set the quilt in the frame.
5. Work the pattern.
6. Finish the edge.

Tracing the Design: Trace the design on the *outside fabric* if you are going to work it in backstitch; or if decorative stitches are introduced; or if you are doing Italian quilting on an opaque fabric. Trace the design on the back of lining if you are going to work in outline stitch. Trace the design on the front of the lining to show through transparent fabrics for Italian quilting.

On white or plain-colored fabrics, trace the design on the wrong side with an indelible pencil that will not rub off, or use carbon paper. On printed fabrics, use a colored chalk which will show up. On the outside fabric, trace the design lightly, then outline it at once with thread; or you can prick the design with a tracing wheel. You can also prick a design in paper with a tracing wheel and rub chalk hard over the paper on which the design has been pricked, then outline the design immediately with thread.

Laying Out the Fabrics: The lining is laid on a table or on the floor. It must be spread out to its full length and width. When the design is on the lining, be sure the design faces down so you can see it when you work. Over the lining spread the padding. When it is narrow, match the edges so they really meet or overlap a little. Lining and padding are not sewed together—the tacking holds them in place. Be sure the padding lies smooth and is even. Lay the outside fabric on top of the padding. It must be the exact size. If the edges are to be scalloped later, they must not be cut at this point. If the fabric for the cover has to be pieced, it must be seamed and stitched before the cover is placed on the padding. Pin the edges all around and prepare to

set them in the frame. When no frame is used, the edges are pinned and basted.

Tacking a Quilt: To prevent the fabric, lining and interlining from slipping as they work, experienced quilters tack them together with basting thread, beginning at the center. Take these stitches around and around the center, then up and down, then across, until you are sure the fabrics cannot slip. This tacking is sometimes done by machine, using an open stitch and following the background.

Setting the Quilt in the Frame: Large pieces of English and Italian quilting are set in a frame, and the threads can be worked in while the work is still on the frame. Small pieces require no frame. Lay the frame over the quilt as it lies on the floor and pin the edges of the quilt to the muslin at the edge of the frame. Screw the clamps in the frame.

Working the Pattern: In English quilting follow the design with small even stitches, made by pushing the needle straight through the design to the other side and bringing it back. Outline stitch is worked on the wrong side and backstitch is worked on the right side. You can also introduce couching, French knots, or chain stitch to emphasize some section of the design. These decorative stitches are worked on the outside fabric only, and the background stitches hold the layers of the quilt in place.

Finishing the Edge: Turn the edges of lining and outside fabric so they face each other. The edge can be stitched, slip-stitched, or finished with piping or cording. When the edge is planned, consider the edge decoration as well as its finish. On pillows and decorative bedspreads, the edge is often scalloped, and sometimes the scallops are bound. The quilting at the edge can follow a scalloped outline or a straight banded effect. Stitching several rows, equally spaced, and running a soft cord through them makes a lovely edge.

On a quilted sofa cushion, the edge is usually finished with a cording, and all the seams are corded. This edge can be quilted with a raised cord run through in the traditional fashion, or a cable cord about the size of the quilted outline can be placed in the edge as you turn it.

When a garment is quilted, it must be cut out and lined after the quilting is finished.

Italian Quilting: Full directions are given on page 74.

Machine-Made Quilts: Machine quilting can be done with great speed. The quilt fabric, padding and lining are prepared exactly as for any English quilting. Stamp the design on the wrong side of the fabric. Loosen the tension of the machine. The work goes faster if you use a quilting attachment which marks the rows. When you do this, the quilt must be tacked more closely to prevent slipping, and the tension must be opened wide. The best designs for a machine-made quilt have continuous lines which do not turn abruptly.

Many home sewers use machine quilting as a background for hand quilting. Others use it to tack the quilt. To do this, you stitch the design all over with a very loose tension in self-matching thread. You can then cover these lines and additional ones with hand quilting.

TUFTED QUILTS

Tufted quilts are easy and quick to make. People who live in wood-raising districts can use teased wool; those who live on farms can save down from plucked chickens; and those in cities can use cotton batting interlinings or an old blanket.

Make the cover of gay cotton, or a lovely colored sateen, rayon taffeta, or a luxury rayon fabric. The lining is usually sateen.

Cut the quilt fabric a little larger than the finished size of the quilt. Should you use wool or feathers, first enclose them in a cover the size of the finished quilt. Lay the three fabrics out smoothly. Before inserting the work in the quilting frame, tie strings to the frame, running both ways, in a squared or lattice effect. This string design will make the work faster and easier by showing where to spot each tie in the quilt. Pin the quilt to the muslin at the edge of the frame and stretch it. Using a double thread, pass a needle up and down through all the fabrics from one side to the other, bringing the needle out a short distance away from its original insertions. Tie the knot double before you clip the ends, and be sure not to clip them too close. The knot illustrated will help you to make your design exact. The thread for tying can be yarn or embroidery thread, or some quilts are tied with fine ribbon.

When you take the quilt out of the frame, turn the edges all around with a hot iron so the edges of the seam face each other. Baste the edges carefully and stitch as close to the outside edge as possible.

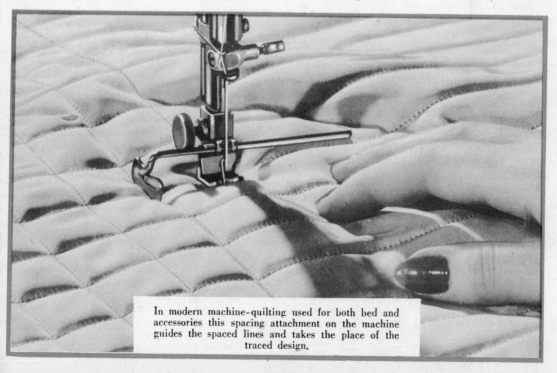

In modern machine-quilting used for both bed and accessories this spacing attachment on the machine guides the spaced lines and takes the place of the traced design.

READY REFERENCE GUIDE